I0605060

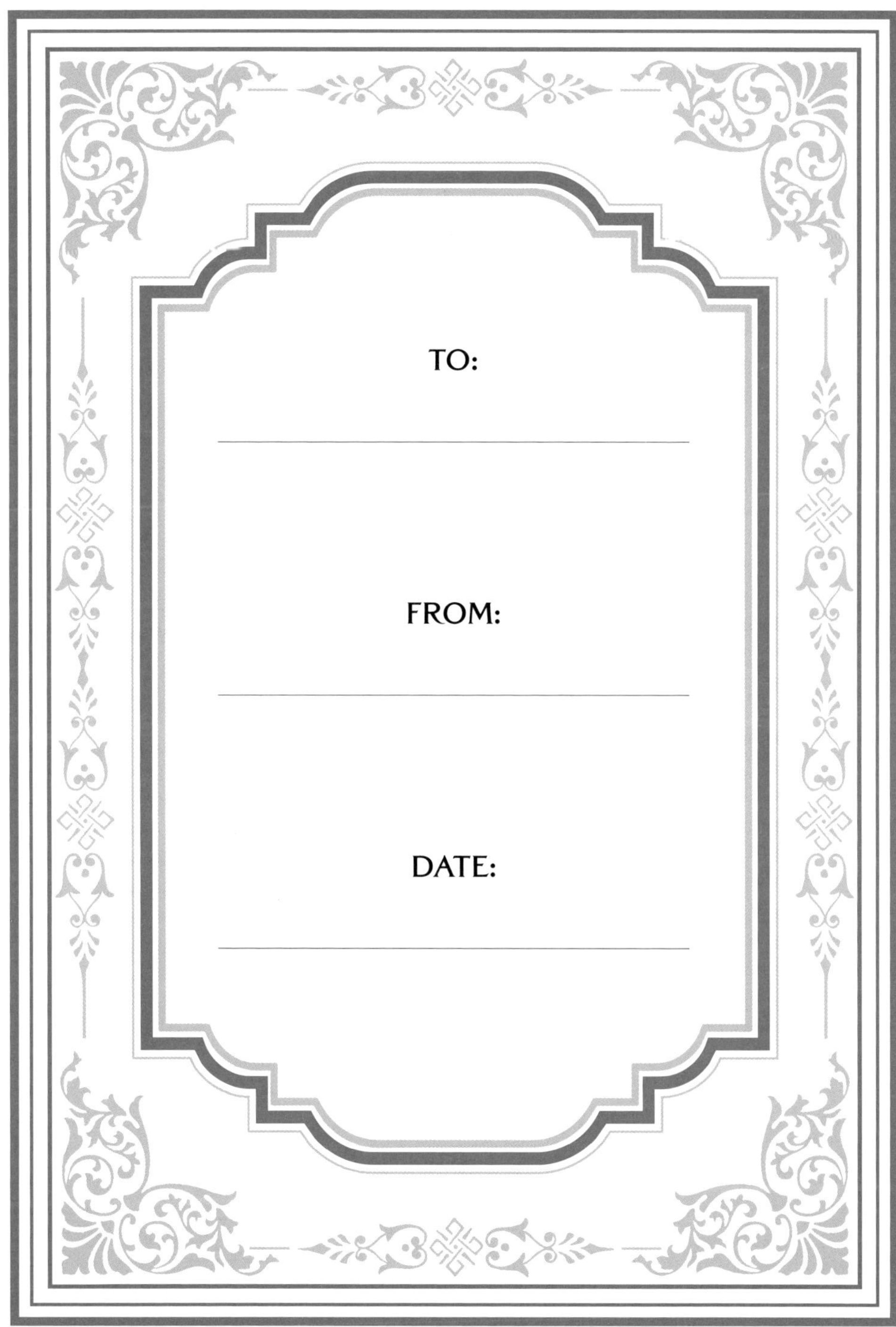
TO:
FROM:
DATE:

Visit Christian Art Gifts, Inc., at www.christianartgifts.com.

365 Days through the Bible: A Devotional Journey from Genesis to Revelation

Previously published by Tyndale House Publishers under the title *The Best of the Bible*.
Copyright © 2008.

Published by Christian Art Gifts, Inc., Bloomingdale, IL, USA under license from Tyndale House Publishers.

First edition 2025.

Designed by Christian Art Gifts, Inc. Content developed by The Barton-Veerman Company.

Cover and interior images used under license from Shutterstock.com.

Most Christian Art titles may be purchased at bulk discounts by churches, nonprofits, and corporations. For more information, please email SpecialMarkets@cagifts.com.

ISBN 978-1-63952-890-5

Printed in China.

30 29 28 27 26 25
12 11 10 9 8 7 6 5 4 3

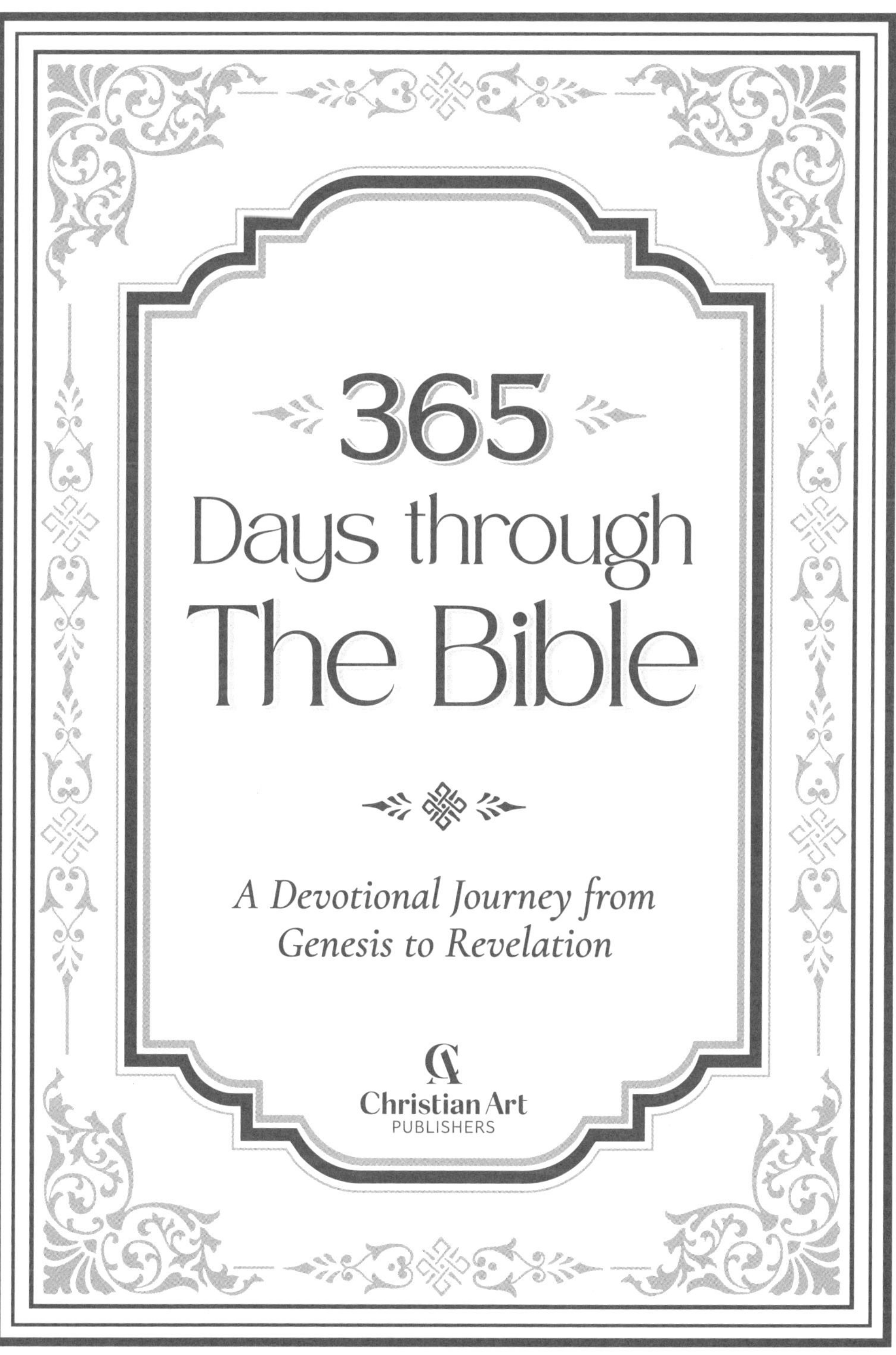

365 Days through The Bible

A Devotional Journey from Genesis to Revelation

Christian Art
PUBLISHERS

Introduction

Many plans are available to help you read through the Bible, but this one's different. Instead of reading every verse of the Bible, the approach taken here is designed to help you get a flavor of the whole Bible by reading selections from it throughout the year. You will journey through the Bible with 365 passages that have been chosen because they're the most read, the most quoted, and are considered key to understanding the Bible's message.

In addition to the Bible text, each day's reading has a question designed to help you interact with the story and the characters. These questions ask how you react to situations, people, yourself, and God. A thought is offered each day as well, to help you apply the lessons to your life.

Enjoy the time you spend in God's Word. May he grant you understanding and bless you throughout the year.

All Scripture is inspired
by God and is useful to teach us
what is true and to make us
realize what is wrong in our lives.
It corrects us when we are wrong
and teaches us to do what is right.

2 Timothy 3:16

January

JANUARY 1

How It All Started

GENESIS 1:1–2:2

In the beginning God created the heavens and the earth. [2]The earth was formless and empty, and darkness covered the deep waters. And the Spirit of God was hovering over the surface of the waters.

[3]Then God said, "Let there be light," and there was light. [4]And God saw that the light was good. Then he separated the light from the darkness. [5]God called the light "day" and the darkness "night."

And evening passed and morning came, marking the first day. . . .

[24]Then God said, "Let the earth produce every sort of animal, each producing offspring of the same kind—livestock, small animals that scurry along the ground, and wild animals." And that is what happened. [25]God made all sorts of wild animals, livestock, and small animals, each able to produce offspring of the same kind. And God saw that it was good.

[26]Then God said, "Let us make human beings in our image, to be like us. They will reign over the fish in the sea, the birds in the sky, the livestock, all the wild animals on the earth, and the small animals that scurry along the ground."

[27]So God created human beings in his own image.
In the image of God he created them;
male and female he created them.

[28]Then God blessed them and said, "Be fruitful and multiply. Fill the earth and govern it. Reign over the fish in the sea, the birds in the sky, and all the animals that scurry along the ground."

[29]Then God said, "Look! I have given you every seed-bearing plant throughout the earth and all the fruit trees for your food. [30]And I have given every green plant as food for all the wild animals, the birds in the sky, and the small animals that scurry along the ground—everything that has life." And that is what happened.

[31]Then God looked over all he had made, and he saw that it was very good!

And evening passed and morning came, marking the sixth day.

[2:1]So the creation of the heavens and the earth and everything in them was completed. [2]On the seventh day God had finished his work of creation, so he rested from all his work.

Why do human beings have value and worth? The phrase "Let us make human beings in our image" does not mean that God created us exactly like himself, especially in a physical sense. Instead, we are reflections of God's glory. Our worth is not defined by possessions, achievements, physical attractiveness, or popularity. Self-worth is knowing that God created us in his likeness. Downgrading ourselves is criticizing what God has made. Knowing that you are a person of infinite worth gives you the freedom to love God, know him personally, and make valuable contributions to those around you.

Adam and Eve

JANUARY 2

GENESIS 2:15-17; 3:1-23

[15]The LORD God placed the man in the Garden of Eden to tend and watch over it. [16]But the
LORD God warned him, "You may freely eat the fruit of every tree in the garden—[17]except
the tree of the knowledge of good and evil. If you eat its fruit, you are sure to die."

[3:1]The serpent was the shrewdest of all the wild animals the LORD God had made. One day
he asked the woman, "Did God really say you must not eat the fruit from any of the trees
in the garden?"

[2]"Of course we may eat fruit from the trees in the garden," the woman replied. [3]"It's only
the fruit from the tree in the middle of the garden that we are not allowed to eat. God said,
'You must not eat it or even touch it; if you do, you will die.'"

[4]"You won't die!" the serpent replied to the woman. [5]"God knows that your eyes will be
opened as soon as you eat it, and you will be like God, knowing both good and evil."

[6]The woman was convinced. She saw that the tree was beautiful and its fruit looked delicious, and she wanted the wisdom it would give her. So she took some of the fruit and ate it.
Then she gave some to her husband, who was with her, and he ate it, too. [7]At that moment
their eyes were opened, and they suddenly felt shame at their nakedness. So they sewed fig
leaves together to cover themselves.

[8]When the cool evening breezes were blowing, the man and his wife heard the LORD God
walking about in the garden. So they hid from the LORD God among the trees. [9]Then the
LORD God called to the man, "Where are you?"

[10]He replied, "I heard you walking in the garden, so I hid. I was afraid because I was
naked."

[11]"Who told you that you were naked?" the LORD God asked. "Have you eaten from the
tree whose fruit I commanded you not to eat?"

[12]The man replied, "It was the woman you gave me who gave me the fruit, and I ate it." . . .

[22]Then the LORD God said, "Look, the human beings have become like us, knowing both
good and evil. What if they reach out, take fruit from the tree of life, and eat it? Then they
will live forever!" [23]So the LORD God banished them from the Garden of Eden, and he sent
Adam out to cultivate the ground from which he had been made.

In what ways are you like those first humans? Adam and Eve got what they wanted: an intimate knowledge of both good and evil. But they got it by doing what was wrong, and the results were disastrous. Many people think that freedom means doing anything they want. God says true freedom comes from obedience and knowing what not to do and then doing what is right. The restrictions he gives us are for our good, helping us to avoid evil. Don't listen to Satan's temptations. Don't think you have to experience evil to learn more about life.

JANUARY 3

Cain and Abel

GENESIS 4:1-16

Now Adam had sexual relations with his wife, Eve, and she became pregnant. When she gave birth to Cain, she said, "With the LORD's help, I have produced a man!" 2Later she gave birth to his brother and named him Abel.

When they grew up, Abel became a shepherd, while Cain cultivated the ground. 3When it was time for the harvest, Cain presented some of his crops as a gift to the LORD. 4Abel also brought a gift—the best portions of the firstborn lambs from his flock. The LORD accepted Abel and his gift, 5but he did not accept Cain and his gift. This made Cain very angry, and he looked dejected.

6"Why are you so angry?" the LORD asked Cain. "Why do you look so dejected? 7You will be accepted if you do what is right. But if you refuse to do what is right, then watch out! Sin is crouching at the door, eager to control you. But you must subdue it and be its master."

8One day Cain suggested to his brother, "Let's go out into the fields." And while they were in the field, Cain attacked his brother, Abel, and killed him.

9Afterward the LORD asked Cain, "Where is your brother? Where is Abel?"

"I don't know," Cain responded. "Am I my brother's guardian?"

10But the LORD said, "What have you done? Listen! Your brother's blood cries out to me from the ground! 11Now you are cursed and banished from the ground, which has swallowed your brother's blood. 12No longer will the ground yield good crops for you, no matter how hard you work! From now on you will be a homeless wanderer on the earth."

13Cain replied to the LORD, "My punishment is too great for me to bear! 14You have banished me from the land and from your presence; you have made me a homeless wanderer. Anyone who finds me will kill me!"

15The LORD replied, "No, for I will give a sevenfold punishment to anyone who kills you." Then the LORD put a mark on Cain to warn anyone who might try to kill him. 16So Cain left the LORD's presence and settled in the land of Nod, east of Eden.

How do you handle anger? How do you react when someone suggests that you have done something wrong? Do you move to correct the mistake? Or do you deny that you need to correct it? After Cain's offering was rejected, God gave him the chance to right his wrong and try again. God even encouraged him to do this! But Cain refused, and the rest of his life is a startling example of what happens to those who refuse to admit their mistakes. The next time someone suggests you have done something wrong, take an honest look at yourself and choose God's way instead of Cain's.

Noah Builds a Boat

JANUARY 4

GENESIS 6:9-22

9This is the account of Noah and his family. Noah was a righteous man, the only blameless
person living on earth at the time, and he walked in close fellowship with God. 10Noah was
the father of three sons: Shem, Ham, and Japheth.

11Now God saw that the earth had become corrupt and was filled with violence. 12God
observed all this corruption in the world, for everyone on earth was corrupt. 13So God said
to Noah, "I have decided to destroy all living creatures, for they have filled the earth with
violence. Yes, I will wipe them all out along with the earth!

14"Build a large boat from cypress wood and waterproof it with tar, inside and out. Then
construct decks and stalls throughout its interior. 15Make the boat 450 feet long, 75 feet wide,
and 45 feet high. 16Leave an 18-inch opening below the roof all the way around the boat.
Put the door on the side, and build three decks inside the boat—lower, middle, and upper.

17"Look! I am about to cover the earth with a flood that will destroy every living thing that
breathes. Everything on earth will die. 18But I will confirm my covenant with you. So enter
the boat—you and your wife and your sons and their wives. 19Bring a pair of every kind of
animal—a male and a female—into the boat with you to keep them alive during the flood.
20Pairs of every kind of bird, and every kind of animal, and every kind of small animal that
scurries along the ground, will come to you to be kept alive. 21And be sure to take on board
enough food for your family and for all the animals."

22So Noah did everything exactly as God had commanded him.

What is the most difficult act that God has asked you to do? Although Noah lived among evil people, he tried to do what pleased God by conducting his affairs according to God's will. For a lifetime he walked step-by-step in faith, a living example to his generation. Like Noah, we live in a world filled with evil. Are we influencing others, or are we being influenced? Either the world is becoming more like us, or we are becoming more like it.

JANUARY 5

All Aboard!

GENESIS 7:1-24

When everything was ready, the LORD said to Noah, "Go into the boat with all your family, for among all the people of the earth, I can see that you alone are righteous. [2]Take with you seven pairs—male and female—of each animal I have approved for eating and for sacrifice, and take one pair of each of the others. [3]Also take seven pairs of every kind of bird. There must be a male and a female in each pair to ensure that all life will survive on the earth after the flood. [4]Seven days from now I will make the rains pour down on the earth. And it will rain for forty days and forty nights, until I have wiped from the earth all the living things I have created."

[5]So Noah did everything as the LORD commanded him.

[6]Noah was 600 years old when the flood covered the earth. [7]He went on board the boat to escape the flood—he and his wife and his sons and their wives. [8]With them were all the various kinds of animals—those approved for eating and for sacrifice and those that were not—along with all the birds and the small animals that scurry along the ground. [9]They entered the boat in pairs, male and female, just as God had commanded Noah. [10]After seven days, the waters of the flood came and covered the earth.

[11]When Noah was 600 years old, on the seventeenth day of the second month, all the underground waters erupted from the earth, and the rain fell in mighty torrents from the sky. [12]The rain continued to fall for forty days and forty nights.

[13]That very day Noah had gone into the boat with his wife and his sons—Shem, Ham, and Japheth—and their wives. [14]With them in the boat were pairs of every kind of animal—domestic and wild, large and small—along with birds of every kind. [15]Two by two they came into the boat, representing every living thing that breathes. [16]A male and female of each kind entered, just as God had commanded Noah. Then the LORD closed the door behind them.

[17]For forty days the floodwaters grew deeper, covering the ground and lifting the boat high above the earth. [18]As the waters rose higher and higher above the ground, the boat floated safely on the surface. . . . [23]God wiped out every living thing on the earth—people, livestock, small animals that scurry along the ground, and the birds of the sky. All were destroyed. The only people who survived were Noah and those with him in the boat. [24]And the floodwaters covered the earth for 150 days.

If you were alive at this time and were invited to get on the boat, would you have accepted? Many have wondered how this animal kingdom roundup happened. In reality, Noah and God's creation were doing just as God had commanded. God took care of the details of gathering the animals while Noah did his part by building the boat. Often we do just the opposite of Noah. We worry about details in our lives over which we have no control while neglecting specific areas (such as attitudes, relationships, responsibilities) that are under our control. Like Noah, concentrate on what God has given you to do, and leave the rest to him.

A Long Wait

GENESIS 8:1-22

But God remembered Noah and all the wild animals and livestock with him in the boat. He sent a wind to blow across the earth, and the floodwaters began to recede. [2]The underground waters stopped flowing, and the torrential rains from the sky were stopped. [3]So the floodwaters gradually receded from the earth. After 150 days, [4]exactly five months from the time the flood began, the boat came to rest on the mountains of Ararat. [5]Two and a half months later, as the waters continued to go down, other mountain peaks became visible.

[6]After another forty days, Noah opened the window he had made in the boat [7]and released a raven. The bird flew back and forth until the floodwaters on the earth had dried up. [8]He also released a dove to see if the water had receded and it could find dry ground. [9]But the dove could find no place to land because the water still covered the ground. So it returned to the boat, and Noah held out his hand and drew the dove back inside. [10]After waiting another seven days, Noah released the dove again. [11]This time the dove returned to him in the evening with a fresh olive leaf in its beak. Then Noah knew that the floodwaters were almost gone. [12]He waited another seven days and then released the dove again. This time it did not come back.

[13]Noah was now 601 years old. On the first day of the new year, ten and a half months after the flood began, the floodwaters had almost dried up from the earth. Noah lifted back the covering of the boat and saw that the surface of the ground was drying. [14]Two more months went by, and at last the earth was dry!

[15]Then God said to Noah, [16]"Leave the boat, all of you—you and your wife, and your sons and their wives. [17]Release all the animals—the birds, the livestock, and the small animals that scurry along the ground—so they can be fruitful and multiply throughout the earth."

[18]So Noah, his wife, and his sons and their wives left the boat. [19]And all of the large and small animals and birds came out of the boat, pair by pair.

[20]Then Noah built an altar to the LORD, and there he sacrificed as burnt offerings the animals and birds that had been approved for that purpose. [21]And the LORD was pleased with the aroma of the sacrifice and said to himself, "I will never again curse the ground because of the human race, even though everything they think or imagine is bent toward evil from childhood. I will never again destroy all living things. [22]As long as the earth remains, there will be planting and harvest, cold and heat, summer and winter, day and night."

How would you have spent your time on the boat? Occasionally Noah would send a bird out to test the earth and see if it was dry. But Noah didn't get out of the boat until God told him to. He was waiting for God's timing. God knew that even though the water was gone, the earth was not dry enough for Noah and his family to venture out. What patience Noah showed, especially after spending an entire year inside his boat! We, like Noah, must trust God to give us patience during those difficult times when we must wait.

JANUARY 7

Rules and Rainbows

GENESIS 9:1-17

Then God blessed Noah and his sons and told them, "Be fruitful and multiply. Fill the earth. 2All the animals of the earth, all the birds of the sky, all the small animals that scurry along the ground, and all the fish in the sea will look on you with fear and terror. I have placed them in your power. 3I have given them to you for food, just as I have given you grain and vegetables. 4But you must never eat any meat that still has the lifeblood in it.

5"And I will require the blood of anyone who takes another person's life. If a wild animal kills a person, it must die. And anyone who murders a fellow human must die. 6If anyone takes a human life, that person's life will also be taken by human hands. For God made human beings in his own image. 7Now be fruitful and multiply, and repopulate the earth."

8Then God told Noah and his sons, 9"I hereby confirm my covenant with you and your descendants, 10and with all the animals that were on the boat with you—the birds, the livestock, and all the wild animals—every living creature on earth. 11Yes, I am confirming my covenant with you. Never again will floodwaters kill all living creatures; never again will a flood destroy the earth."

12Then God said, "I am giving you a sign of my covenant with you and with all living creatures, for all generations to come. 13I have placed my rainbow in the clouds. It is the sign of my covenant with you and with all the earth. 14When I send clouds over the earth, the rainbow will appear in the clouds, 15and I will remember my covenant with you and with all living creatures. Never again will the floodwaters destroy all life. 16When I see the rainbow in the clouds, I will remember the eternal covenant between God and every living creature on earth." 17Then God said to Noah, "Yes, this rainbow is the sign of the covenant I am confirming with all the creatures on earth."

What could you do the next time you see a rainbow in order to help you remember God's faithfulness? Noah stepped out of the boat onto an earth devoid of human life. But God gave him a reassuring promise. This covenant had two parts: (1) Never again will a flood do such destruction. (2) A rainbow will be visible when it rains as a sign to all that God will keep his promises. The earth's order is still preserved, and rainbows still remind us of God's faithfulness to his Word.

The Tower of Babel

GENESIS 11:1-9

At one time all the people of the world spoke the same language and used the same words. [2]As
the people migrated to the east, they found a plain in the land of Babylonia and settled there.
[3]They began saying to each other, "Let's make bricks and harden them with fire." (In
this region bricks were used instead of stone, and tar was used for mortar.) [4]Then they said,
"Come, let's build a great city for ourselves with a tower that reaches into the sky. This will
make us famous and keep us from being scattered all over the world."
[5]But the LORD came down to look at the city and the tower the people were building.
[6]"Look!" he said. "The people are united, and they all speak the same language. After this,
nothing they set out to do will be impossible for them! [7]Come, let's go down and confuse the
people with different languages. Then they won't be able to understand each other."
[8]In that way, the LORD scattered them all over the world, and they stopped building the
city. [9]That is why the city was called Babel, because that is where the LORD confused the
people with different languages. In this way he scattered them all over the world.

Whom do you trust more than God? The tower of Babel was a great human achievement, a wonder of the world. But it was a monument to the people themselves rather than to God. We often build monuments to ourselves (expensive clothes, big house, fancy car, important job) to call attention to our achievements. These may not be wrong in themselves, but when we use them to give us identity and self-worth, they take God's place in our life. We are free to develop in many areas, but we are not free to think we have replaced God. What "monuments" are in your life?

JANUARY 9 God's Promises to Abraham

GENESIS 12:1-9; 17:1-8

The LORD had said to Abram, "Leave your native country, your relatives, and your father's
family, and go to the land that I will show you. 2I will make you into a great nation. I will
bless you and make you famous, and you will be a blessing to others. 3I will bless those who
bless you and curse those who treat you with contempt. All the families on earth will be
blessed through you."
4So Abram departed as the LORD had instructed, and Lot went with him. Abram was
seventy-five years old when he left Haran. 5He took his wife, Sarai, his nephew Lot, and all
his wealth—his livestock and all the people he had taken into his household at Haran—and
headed for the land of Canaan. . . .
7Then the LORD appeared to Abram and said, "I will give this land to your descendants."
And Abram built an altar there and dedicated it to the LORD, who had appeared to him. 8After
that, Abram traveled south and set up camp in the hill country, with Bethel to the west and
Ai to the east. There he built another altar and dedicated it to the LORD, and he worshiped
the LORD. 9Then Abram continued traveling south by stages toward the Negev.

17:1When Abram was ninety-nine years old, the LORD appeared to him and said, "I am El-
Shaddai—'God Almighty.' Serve me faithfully and live a blameless life. 2I will make a covenant with you, by which I will guarantee to give you countless descendants."
3At this, Abram fell face down on the ground. Then God said to him, 4"This is my covenant with you: I will make you the father of a multitude of nations! 5What's more, I am
changing your name. It will no longer be Abram. Instead, you will be called Abraham, for
you will be the father of many nations. 6I will make you extremely fruitful. Your descendants
will become many nations, and kings will be among them!
7"I will confirm my covenant with you and your descendants after you, from generation
to generation. This is the everlasting covenant: I will always be your God and the God of
your descendants after you. 8And I will give the entire land of Canaan, where you now live
as a foreigner, to you and your descendants. It will be their possession forever, and I will be
their God."

How does knowing God affect the way you make decisions? God promised to bless Abram and make him great, but there was one condition: Abram had to do what God wanted him to do. This meant leaving his home and friends and traveling to a new land where God promised to build a great nation from Abram's family. Abram obeyed, leaving his home for God's promise of even greater blessings in the future. God may be trying to lead you to a place of greater service and usefulness for him. Don't let the comfort and security of your present position cause you to miss God's plan for you.

Unusual Visitors

JANUARY 10

GENESIS 18:1-15

The LORD appeared again to Abraham near the oak grove belonging to Mamre. One day
Abraham was sitting at the entrance to his tent during the hottest part of the day. 2He looked
up and noticed three men standing nearby. When he saw them, he ran to meet them and
welcomed them, bowing low to the ground.

3"My lord," he said, "if it pleases you, stop here for a while. 4Rest in the shade of this tree
while water is brought to wash your feet. 5And since you've honored your servant with this
visit, let me prepare some food to refresh you before you continue on your journey."

"All right," they said. "Do as you have said."

6So Abraham ran back to the tent and said to Sarah, "Hurry! Get three large measures of
your best flour, knead it into dough, and bake some bread." 7Then Abraham ran out to the
herd and chose a tender calf and gave it to his servant, who quickly prepared it. 8When the
food was ready, Abraham took some yogurt and milk and the roasted meat, and he served it
to the men. As they ate, Abraham waited on them in the shade of the trees.

9"Where is Sarah, your wife?" the visitors asked.

"She's inside the tent," Abraham replied.

10Then one of them said, "I will return to you about this time next year, and your wife,
Sarah, will have a son!"

Sarah was listening to this conversation from the tent. 11Abraham and Sarah were both
very old by this time, and Sarah was long past the age of having children. 12So she laughed
silently to herself and said, "How could a worn-out woman like me enjoy such pleasure,
especially when my master—my husband—is also so old?"

13Then the LORD said to Abraham, "Why did Sarah laugh? Why did she say, 'Can an old
woman like me have a baby?' 14Is anything too hard for the LORD? I will return about this
time next year, and Sarah will have a son."

15Sarah was afraid, so she denied it, saying, "I didn't laugh."

But the LORD said, "No, you did laugh."

What is your basic attitude toward strangers? Abraham was eager to show hospitality to these three visitors, as was Lot (Genesis 19:2). In Abraham's day, a person's reputation was largely connected to his hospitality—the sharing of home and food. Even strangers were to be treated as highly honored guests. Meeting another's need for food or shelter was and still is one of the most immediate and practical ways to obey God. It is also a time-honored relationship builder. Hebrews 13:2 suggests that we, like Abraham, might actually entertain angels. This thought should be on our mind the next time we have the opportunity to meet a stranger's needs.

JANUARY 11

Sodom and Gomorrah

GENESIS 19:1-26

That evening the two angels came to the entrance of the city of Sodom. Lot was sitting there,
and when he saw them, he stood up to meet them. Then he welcomed them and bowed with
his face to the ground. 2“My lords,” he said, “come to my home to wash your feet, and be my
guests for the night. You may then get up early in the morning and be on your way again.”
“Oh no,” they replied. “We’ll just spend the night out here in the city square.”
3But Lot insisted, so at last they went home with him. Lot prepared a feast for them,
complete with fresh bread made without yeast, and they ate. 4But before they retired for the
night, all the men of Sodom, young and old, came from all over the city and surrounded the
house. 5They shouted to Lot, “Where are the men who came to spend the night with you?
Bring them out to us so we can have sex with them!” . . .
12Meanwhile, the angels questioned Lot. “Do you have any other relatives here in the
city?” they asked. “Get them out of this place—your sons-in-law, sons, daughters, or anyone
else. 13For we are about to destroy this city completely. The outcry against this place is so great
it has reached the Lord, and he has sent us to destroy it.”
14So Lot rushed out to tell his daughters’ fiancés, “Quick, get out of the city! The Lord
is about to destroy it.” But the young men thought he was only joking.
15At dawn the next morning the angels became insistent. “Hurry,” they said to Lot. “Take
your wife and your two daughters who are here. Get out right now, or you will be swept away
in the destruction of the city!”
16When Lot still hesitated, the angels seized his hand and the hands of his wife and two
daughters and rushed them to safety outside the city, for the Lord was merciful. 17When
they were safely out of the city, one of the angels ordered, “Run for your lives! And don’t look
back or stop anywhere in the valley! Escape to the mountains, or you will be swept away!” . . .
24Then the Lord rained down fire and burning sulfur from the sky on Sodom and
Gomorrah. 25He utterly destroyed them, along with the other cities and villages of the plain,
wiping out all the people and every bit of vegetation. 26But Lot’s wife looked back as she was
following behind him, and she turned into a pillar of salt.

How does God feel about sin? Lot’s wife turned back to look at the smoldering city of Sodom. Clinging to the past, she was unwilling to turn completely from sin. Are you looking back longingly at sin while trying to move forward with God? You can’t make progress with God as long as you are holding on to pieces of your old life. Jesus said it this way in Matthew 6:24: “No one can serve two masters.”

Hagar and Ishmael

GENESIS 21:8-21

8 When Isaac grew up and was about to be weaned, Abraham prepared a huge feast to celebrate the occasion. 9 But Sarah saw Ishmael—the son of Abraham and her Egyptian servant
Hagar—making fun of her son, Isaac. 10 So she turned to Abraham and demanded, "Get rid
of that slave woman and her son. He is not going to share the inheritance with my son, Isaac.
I won't have it!"

11 This upset Abraham very much because Ishmael was his son. 12 But God told Abraham,
"Do not be upset over the boy and your servant. Do whatever Sarah tells you, for Isaac is the
son through whom your descendants will be counted. 13 But I will also make a nation of the
descendants of Hagar's son because he is your son, too."

14 So Abraham got up early the next morning, prepared food and a container of water, and
strapped them on Hagar's shoulders. Then he sent her away with their son, and she wandered
aimlessly in the wilderness of Beersheba.

15 When the water was gone, she put the boy in the shade of a bush. 16 Then she went and
sat down by herself about a hundred yards away. "I don't want to watch the boy die," she
said, as she burst into tears.

17 But God heard the boy crying, and the angel of God called to Hagar from heaven,
"Hagar, what's wrong? Do not be afraid! God has heard the boy crying as he lies there. 18 Go
to him and comfort him, for I will make a great nation from his descendants."

19 Then God opened Hagar's eyes, and she saw a well full of water. She quickly filled her
water container and gave the boy a drink.

20 And God was with the boy as he grew up in the wilderness. He became a skillful archer,
21 and he settled in the wilderness of Paran. His mother arranged for him to marry a woman
from the land of Egypt.

How does God deal with the messes in your life? What happened to Ishmael, and who are his descendants? Ishmael became ruler of a large tribe or nation. The Ishmaelites were nomads living in the wilderness of Sinai and Paran, south of Israel. One of Ishmael's daughters married Esau, Ishmael's nephew (Genesis 28:9). While people sometimes make mistakes, God always keeps his promises and always cares for his children. God was with Ishmael as he grew up (Genesis 21:20), and he is with you, too.

JANUARY 13 Abraham's Painful Decision

GENESIS 22:1-14

Some time later, God tested Abraham's faith. "Abraham!" God called.

"Yes," he replied. "Here I am."

2"Take your son, your only son—yes, Isaac, whom you love so much—and go to the land of Moriah. Go and sacrifice him as a burnt offering on one of the mountains, which I will show you."

3The next morning Abraham got up early. He saddled his donkey and took two of his servants with him, along with his son, Isaac. Then he chopped wood for a fire for a burnt offering and set out for the place God had told him about. 4On the third day of their journey, Abraham looked up and saw the place in the distance. 5"Stay here with the donkey," Abraham told the servants. "The boy and I will travel a little farther. We will worship there, and then we will come right back."

6So Abraham placed the wood for the burnt offering on Isaac's shoulders, while he himself carried the fire and the knife. As the two of them walked on together, 7Isaac turned to Abraham and said, "Father?"

"Yes, my son?" Abraham replied.

"We have the fire and the wood," the boy said, "but where is the sheep for the burnt offering?"

8"God will provide a sheep for the burnt offering, my son," Abraham answered. And they both walked on together.

9When they arrived at the place where God had told him to go, Abraham built an altar and arranged the wood on it. Then he tied his son, Isaac, and laid him on the altar on top of the wood. 10And Abraham picked up the knife to kill his son as a sacrifice. 11At that moment the angel of the Lord called to him from heaven, "Abraham! Abraham!"

"Yes," Abraham replied. "Here I am!"

12"Don't lay a hand on the boy!" the angel said. "Do not hurt him in any way, for now I know that you truly fear God. You have not withheld from me even your son, your only son."

13Then Abraham looked up and saw a ram caught by its horns in a thicket. So he took the ram and sacrificed it as a burnt offering in place of his son. 14Abraham named the place Yahweh-Yireh (which means "the Lord will provide"). To this day, people still use that name as a proverb: "On the mountain of the Lord it will be provided."

What do you have trouble giving up to God? Why did God ask Abraham to perform human sacrifice? Heathen nations practiced human sacrifice, but God condemned this as a terrible sin (Leviticus 20:1-5). God did not want Isaac to die, but he wanted Abraham to prove that he loved God more than he loved his promised and long-awaited son. God was testing Abraham. The purpose of testing is to strengthen our character and deepen our commitment to God and his perfect timing. Through this difficult experience, Abraham strengthened his commitment to obey God. He also learned about God's ability to provide.

Eliezer Gets It Done

JANUARY 14

GENESIS 24:1-27

Abraham was now a very old man, and the Lord had blessed him in every way. 2One day
Abraham said to his oldest servant, the man in charge of his household, "Take an oath by
putting your hand under my thigh. 3Swear by the LORD, the God of heaven and earth, that
you will not allow my son to marry one of these local Canaanite women. 4Go instead to my
homeland, to my relatives, and find a wife there for my son Isaac." . . .

9So the servant took an oath by putting his hand under the thigh of his master, Abraham.
He swore to follow Abraham's instructions. 10Then he loaded ten of Abraham's camels with
all kinds of expensive gifts from his master, and he traveled to distant Aram-naharaim. There
he went to the town where Abraham's brother Nahor had settled. 11He made the camels
kneel beside a well just outside the town. It was evening, and the women were coming out
to draw water.

12"O LORD, God of my master, Abraham," he prayed. "Please give me success today, and
show unfailing love to my master, Abraham. 13See, I am standing here beside this spring, and
the young women of the town are coming out to draw water. 14This is my request. I will ask
one of them, 'Please give me a drink from your jug.' If she says, 'Yes, have a drink, and I will
water your camels, too!'—let her be the one you have selected as Isaac's wife. This is how I
will know that you have shown unfailing love to my master."

15Before he had finished praying, he saw a young woman named Rebekah coming out
with her water jug on her shoulder. She was the daughter of Bethuel, who was the son of
Abraham's brother Nahor and his wife, Milcah. 16Rebekah was very beautiful and old enough
to be married, but she was still a virgin. She went down to the spring, filled her jug, and
came up again. 17Running over to her, the servant said, "Please give me a little drink of water
from your jug."

18"Yes, my lord," she answered, "have a drink." And she quickly lowered her jug from her
shoulder and gave him a drink. 19When she had given him a drink, she said, "I'll draw water
for your camels, too, until they have had enough to drink." 20So she quickly emptied her
jug into the watering trough and ran back to the well to draw water for all his camels. . . .

26The man bowed low and worshiped the LORD. 27"Praise the LORD, the God of my master, Abraham," he said. "The LORD has shown unfailing love and faithfulness to my master,
for he has led me straight to my master's relatives."

How do you approach difficult tasks? Was it right for Abraham's servant Eliezer to ask God for such a specific sign? The sign he requested was only slightly out of the ordinary. The hospitality of the day required women at the well to offer water to weary travelers but not to their animals. Eliezer was simply asking God to show him a woman with an attitude of service—someone who would go beyond the expected. An offer to water his camels would indicate that kind of attitude. Eliezer did not ask for a woman with looks or wealth. He knew the importance of having the right heart, and he asked God to help him with his task.

JANUARY 15

Jacob and Esau

GENESIS 25:19-34

19 This is the account of the family of Isaac, the son of Abraham. 20 When Isaac was forty years old, he married Rebekah, the daughter of Bethuel the Aramean from Paddan-aram and the sister of Laban the Aramean.

21 Isaac pleaded with the LORD on behalf of his wife, because she was unable to have children. The LORD answered Isaac's prayer, and Rebekah became pregnant with twins. 22 But the two children struggled with each other in her womb. So she went to ask the LORD about it. "Why is this happening to me?" she asked.

23 And the LORD told her, "The sons in your womb will become two nations. From the very beginning, the two nations will be rivals. One nation will be stronger than the other; and your older son will serve your younger son."

24 And when the time came to give birth, Rebekah discovered that she did indeed have twins! 25 The first one was very red at birth and covered with thick hair like a fur coat. So they named him Esau. 26 Then the other twin was born with his hand grasping Esau's heel. So they named him Jacob. Isaac was sixty years old when the twins were born.

27 As the boys grew up, Esau became a skillful hunter. He was an outdoorsman, but Jacob had a quiet temperament, preferring to stay at home. 28 Isaac loved Esau because he enjoyed eating the wild game Esau brought home, but Rebekah loved Jacob.

29 One day when Jacob was cooking some stew, Esau arrived home from the wilderness exhausted and hungry. 30 Esau said to Jacob, "I'm starved! Give me some of that red stew!" (This is how Esau got his other name, Edom, which means "red.")

31 "All right," Jacob replied, "but trade me your rights as the firstborn son."

32 "Look, I'm dying of starvation!" said Esau. "What good is my birthright to me now?"

33 But Jacob said, "First you must swear that your birthright is mine." So Esau swore an oath, thereby selling all his rights as the firstborn to his brother, Jacob.

34 Then Jacob gave Esau some bread and lentil stew. Esau ate the meal, then got up and left. He showed contempt for his rights as the firstborn.

Do you seek instant gratification without considering the long-term consequences? Esau traded the lasting benefits of his birthright for the immediate pleasure of food. He acted on impulse, satisfying his immediate desires without pausing to consider the long-range consequences of what he was about to do. We can fall into the same trap. When we see something we want, our first impulse is to get it. At first we feel intensely satisfied and sometimes even powerful because we have obtained what we set out to get. But immediate pleasure often causes us to lose sight of the future. We can avoid making Esau's mistake by comparing the short-term satisfaction with its long-range consequences before we act.

Jacob Tricks His Father

JANUARY 16

GENESIS 27:1-19

One day when Isaac was old and turning blind, he called for Esau, his older son, and said, "My son."

"Yes, Father?" Esau replied.

2"I am an old man now," Isaac said, "and I don't know when I may die. 3Take your bow
and a quiver full of arrows, and go out into the open country to hunt some wild game for
me. 4Prepare my favorite dish, and bring it here for me to eat. Then I will pronounce the
blessing that belongs to you, my firstborn son, before I die."

5But Rebekah overheard what Isaac had said to his son Esau. So when Esau left to hunt
for the wild game, 6she said to her son Jacob, "Listen. I overheard your father say to Esau,
7'Bring me some wild game and prepare me a delicious meal. Then I will bless you in the
LORD's presence before I die.' 8Now, my son, listen to me. Do exactly as I tell you. 9Go out to
the flocks, and bring me two fine young goats. I'll use them to prepare your father's favorite
dish. 10Then take the food to your father so he can eat it and bless you before he dies."

11"But look," Jacob replied to Rebekah, "my brother, Esau, is a hairy man, and my skin
is smooth. 12What if my father touches me? He'll see that I'm trying to trick him, and then
he'll curse me instead of blessing me."

13But his mother replied, "Then let the curse fall on me, my son! Just do what I tell you.
Go out and get the goats for me!"

14So Jacob went out and got the young goats for his mother. Rebekah took them and
prepared a delicious meal, just the way Isaac liked it. 15Then she took Esau's favorite clothes,
which were there in the house, and gave them to her younger son, Jacob. 16She covered his
arms and the smooth part of his neck with the skin of the young goats. 17Then she gave Jacob
the delicious meal, including freshly baked bread.

18So Jacob took the food to his father. "My father?" he said.

"Yes, my son," Isaac answered. "Who are you—Esau or Jacob?"

19Jacob replied, "It's Esau, your firstborn son. I've done as you told me. Here is the wild
game. Now sit up and eat it so you can give me your blessing."

How honestly have you treated your parents? How we react to a moral dilemma often exposes our real motives. Frequently we are more worried about getting caught than about doing what is right. Jacob did not seem concerned about the deceitfulness of his mother's plan; instead, he was afraid of getting in trouble while carrying it out. If you are worried about getting caught, you are probably in a position that is less than honest. Let your fear of getting caught be a warning to do right. Jacob paid a huge price for carrying out this dishonest plan.

JANUARY 17

Jacob Meets God

GENESIS 28:10-22

10 Meanwhile, Jacob left Beersheba and traveled toward Haran. 11 At sundown he arrived at a good place to set up camp and stopped there for the night. Jacob found a stone to rest his head against and lay down to sleep. 12 As he slept, he dreamed of a stairway that reached from the earth up to heaven. And he saw the angels of God going up and down the stairway.

13 At the top of the stairway stood the LORD, and he said, "I am the LORD, the God of your grandfather Abraham, and the God of your father, Isaac. The ground you are lying on belongs to you. I am giving it to you and your descendants. 14 Your descendants will be as numerous as the dust of the earth! They will spread out in all directions—to the west and the east, to the north and the south. And all the families of the earth will be blessed through you and your descendants. 15 What's more, I am with you, and I will protect you wherever you go. One day I will bring you back to this land. I will not leave you until I have finished giving you everything I have promised you."

16 Then Jacob awoke from his sleep and said, "Surely the LORD is in this place, and I wasn't even aware of it!" 17 But he was also afraid and said, "What an awesome place this is! It is none other than the house of God, the very gateway to heaven!"

18 The next morning Jacob got up very early. He took the stone he had rested his head against, and he set it upright as a memorial pillar. Then he poured olive oil over it. 19 He named that place Bethel (which means "house of God"), although it was previously called Luz.

20 Then Jacob made this vow: "If God will indeed be with me and protect me on this journey, and if he will provide me with food and clothing, 21 and if I return safely to my father's home, then the LORD will certainly be my God. 22 And this memorial pillar I have set up will become a place for worshiping God, and I will present to God a tenth of everything he gives me."

In what places in your life has God been the most real? God's covenant promise to Abraham and Isaac was offered to Jacob as well. But it was not enough to be Abraham's grandson; Jacob had to establish his own personal relationship with God. God has no grandchildren; each of us must have a personal relationship with him. It is not enough to hear wonderful stories about Christians in your family. You need to become part of the story yourself (see Galatians 3:6-7).

Jacob's Marriages

JANUARY 18

GENESIS 29:14-30

14 Laban exclaimed, "You really are my own flesh and blood!"

After Jacob had stayed with Laban for about a month, 15 Laban said to him, "You shouldn't
work for me without pay just because we are relatives. Tell me how much your wages should
be."

16 Now Laban had two daughters. The older daughter was named Leah, and the younger
one was Rachel. 17 There was no sparkle in Leah's eyes, but Rachel had a beautiful figure and
a lovely face. 18 Since Jacob was in love with Rachel, he told her father, "I'll work for you for
seven years if you'll give me Rachel, your younger daughter, as my wife."

19 "Agreed!" Laban replied. "I'd rather give her to you than to anyone else. Stay and work
with me." 20 So Jacob worked seven years to pay for Rachel. But his love for her was so strong
that it seemed to him but a few days.

21 Finally, the time came for him to marry her. "I have fulfilled my agreement," Jacob said
to Laban. "Now give me my wife so I can sleep with her."

22 So Laban invited everyone in the neighborhood and prepared a wedding feast. 23 But
that night, when it was dark, Laban took Leah to Jacob, and he slept with her. 24 (Laban had
given Leah a servant, Zilpah, to be her maid.)

25 But when Jacob woke up in the morning—it was Leah! "What have you done to me?"
Jacob raged at Laban. "I worked seven years for Rachel! Why have you tricked me?"

26 "It's not our custom here to marry off a younger daughter ahead of the firstborn," Laban
replied. 27 "But wait until the bridal week is over; then we'll give you Rachel, too—provided
you promise to work another seven years for me."

28 So Jacob agreed to work seven more years. A week after Jacob had married Leah, Laban
gave him Rachel, too. 29 (Laban gave Rachel a servant, Bilhah, to be her maid.) 30 So Jacob
slept with Rachel, too, and he loved her much more than Leah. He then stayed and worked
for Laban the additional seven years.

What are the qualities that make up the way you love others? People often wonder if waiting a long time for something they want is worth it. Jacob waited seven years to marry Rachel. After being tricked, he agreed to work seven more years for her! Our most important goals and desires are worth working and waiting for. Movies and television have created the illusion that people have to wait only about an hour to solve their problems or get what they want. Don't be trapped into thinking the same is true in real life. Patience is hardest when we need it the most, but it is the key to achieving our goals.

JANUARY 19

Jacob Meets Esau Again

GENESIS 32:3-28; 33:1-4

3Then Jacob sent messengers ahead to his brother, Esau, who was living in the region of Seir in the land of Edom. . . .

6After delivering the message, the messengers returned to Jacob and reported, "We met your brother, Esau, and he is already on his way to meet you—with an army of 400 men!" 7Jacob was terrified at the news. He divided his household, along with the flocks and herds and camels, into two groups. 8He thought, "If Esau meets one group and attacks it, perhaps the other group can escape."

9Then Jacob prayed, "O God of my grandfather Abraham, and God of my father, Isaac—O Lord, you told me, 'Return to your own land and to your relatives.' And you promised me, 'I will treat you kindly.' 10I am not worthy of all the unfailing love and faithfulness you have shown to me, your servant. When I left home and crossed the Jordan River, I owned nothing except a walking stick. Now my household fills two large camps! 11O Lord, please rescue me from the hand of my brother, Esau. I am afraid that he is coming to attack me, along with my wives and children. 12But you promised me, 'I will surely treat you kindly, and I will multiply your descendants until they become as numerous as the sands along the seashore—too many to count.'" . . .

22During the night Jacob got up and took his two wives, his two servant wives, and his eleven sons and crossed the Jabbok River with them. 23After taking them to the other side, he sent over all his possessions.

24This left Jacob all alone in the camp, and a man came and wrestled with him until the dawn began to break. 25When the man saw that he would not win the match, he touched Jacob's hip and wrenched it out of its socket. 26Then the man said, "Let me go, for the dawn is breaking!"

But Jacob said, "I will not let you go unless you bless me."

27"What is your name?" the man asked.

He replied, "Jacob."

28"Your name will no longer be Jacob," the man told him. "From now on you will be called Israel, because you have fought with God and with men and have won."

33:1Then Jacob looked up and saw Esau coming with his 400 men. . . . 4Then Esau ran to meet him and embraced him, threw his arms around his neck, and kissed him. And they both wept.

What happens inside you when you try to avoid a problem? It is refreshing to see Esau's change of heart. The bitterness over losing his birthright and blessing (Genesis 25:29-34) seems to be gone. Instead, Esau is content with what he has. Life can deal us some bad situations, but we don't have to remain bitter. We can remove bitterness from our lives by honestly expressing our feelings to God, forgiving those who have wronged us, and being content with what we have.

Joseph's Dreams

JANUARY 20

GENESIS 37:3-28

3Jacob loved Joseph more than any of his other children because Joseph had been born to him
in his old age. So one day Jacob had a special gift made for Joseph—a beautiful robe. 4But
his brothers hated Joseph because their father loved him more than the rest of them. They
couldn't say a kind word to him.

5One night Joseph had a dream, and when he told his brothers about it, they hated him
more than ever. 6"Listen to this dream," he said. 7"We were out in the field, tying up bundles
of grain. Suddenly my bundle stood up, and your bundles all gathered around and bowed
low before mine!"

8His brothers responded, "So you think you will be our king, do you? Do you actually
think you will reign over us?" And they hated him all the more because of his dreams and
the way he talked about them. . . .

12Soon after this, Joseph's brothers went to pasture their father's flocks at Shechem. 13When
they had been gone for some time, Jacob said to Joseph, "Your brothers are pasturing the
sheep at Shechem. Get ready, and I will send you to them." . . .

18When Joseph's brothers saw him coming, they recognized him in the distance. As he
approached, they made plans to kill him. 19"Here comes the dreamer!" they said. 20"Come on,
let's kill him and throw him into one of these cisterns. We can tell our father, 'A wild animal
has eaten him.' Then we'll see what becomes of his dreams!" . . .

23So when Joseph arrived, his brothers ripped off the beautiful robe he was wearing.
24Then they grabbed him and threw him into the cistern. Now the cistern was empty; there
was no water in it. 25Then, just as they were sitting down to eat, they looked up and saw a
caravan of camels in the distance coming toward them. It was a group of Ishmaelite traders
taking a load of gum, balm, and aromatic resin from Gilead down to Egypt.

26Judah said to his brothers, "What will we gain by killing our brother? We'd have to cover
up the crime. 27Instead of hurting him, let's sell him to those Ishmaelite traders. After all, he is
our brother—our own flesh and blood!" And his brothers agreed. 28So when the Ishmaelites,
who were Midianite traders, came by, Joseph's brothers pulled him out of the cistern and sold
him to them for twenty pieces of silver. And the traders took him to Egypt.

How are disagreements settled in your family? Could jealousy ever make you feel like killing someone? Before saying, "Of course not," look at what happened in this story. Ten men were willing to kill their younger brother over a cloak and a few reported dreams. Their deep-seated jealousy had grown into ugly rage, blinding them completely to what was right. Jealousy can be hard to recognize because our reasons for it seem to make sense. But left unchecked, jealousy grows quickly and leads to serious sins. The longer you cultivate jealous feelings, the harder it is to uproot them. The time to deal with jealousy is when you notice yourself keeping score of what others own or have accomplished.

JANUARY 21

Joseph in Trouble

GENESIS 39:1-21

When Joseph was taken to Egypt by the Ishmaelite traders, he was purchased by Potiphar, an Egyptian officer. Potiphar was captain of the guard for Pharaoh, the king of Egypt.

2The LORD was with Joseph, so he succeeded in everything he did as he served in the home of his Egyptian master. 3Potiphar noticed this and realized that the LORD was with Joseph, giving him success in everything he did. 4This pleased Potiphar, so he soon made Joseph his personal attendant. He put him in charge of his entire household and everything he owned. . . . 6So Potiphar gave Joseph complete administrative responsibility over everything he owned. With Joseph there, he didn't worry about a thing—except what kind of food to eat!

Joseph was a very handsome and well-built young man, 7and Potiphar's wife soon began to look at him lustfully. "Come and sleep with me," she demanded.

8But Joseph refused. "Look," he told her, "my master trusts me with everything in his entire household. 9No one here has more authority than I do. He has held back nothing from me except you, because you are his wife. How could I do such a wicked thing? It would be a great sin against God."

10She kept putting pressure on Joseph day after day, but he refused to sleep with her, and he kept out of her way as much as possible. 11One day, however, no one else was around when he went in to do his work. 12She came and grabbed him by his cloak, demanding, "Come on, sleep with me!" Joseph tore himself away, but he left his cloak in her hand as he ran from the house.

13When she saw that she was holding his cloak and he had fled, 14she called out to her servants. Soon all the men came running. "Look!" she said. "My husband has brought this Hebrew slave here to make fools of us! He came into my room to rape me, but I screamed. 15When he heard me scream, he ran outside and got away, but he left his cloak behind with me."

16She kept the cloak with her until her husband came home. 17Then she told him her story. "That Hebrew slave you've brought into our house tried to come in and fool around with me," she said. 18"But when I screamed, he ran outside, leaving his cloak with me!"

19Potiphar was furious when he heard his wife's story about how Joseph had treated her. 20So he took Joseph and threw him into the prison where the king's prisoners were held, and there he remained. 21But the LORD was with Joseph.

What is your main reason for resisting sin? Potiphar's wife failed to seduce Joseph, who resisted this temptation by saying it would be a sin against God. Joseph didn't say, "I'd be hurting you," or "I'd be sinning against Potiphar," or "I'd be sinning against myself." Under pressure, such excuses are easily rationalized away. Remember that sexual sin is not just between two consenting adults. It is an act of disobedience to God.

Dreams in Prison

GENESIS 40:1-23

JANUARY 22

Some time later, Pharaoh's chief cup-bearer and chief baker offended their royal master.
2Pharaoh became angry with these two officials, 3and he put them in the prison where Joseph
was . . .

5While they were in prison, Pharaoh's cup-bearer and baker each had a dream one night,
and each dream had its own meaning. 6When Joseph saw them the next morning, he noticed
that they both looked upset. 7"Why do you look so worried today?" he asked them.

8And they replied, "We both had dreams last night, but no one can tell us what they
mean."

"Interpreting dreams is God's business," Joseph replied. "Go ahead and tell me your dreams."

9So the chief cup-bearer told Joseph his dream first. "In my dream," he said, "I saw a
grapevine in front of me. 10The vine had three branches that began to bud and blossom, and
soon it produced clusters of ripe grapes. 11I was holding Pharaoh's wine cup in my hand,
so I took a cluster of grapes and squeezed the juice into the cup. Then I placed the cup in
Pharaoh's hand."

12"This is what the dream means," Joseph said. "The three branches represent three days.
13Within three days Pharaoh will lift you up and restore you to your position as his chief cup-
bearer. 14And please remember me and do me a favor when things go well for you. Mention
me to Pharaoh, so he might let me out of this place. 15For I was kidnapped from my homeland, the land of the Hebrews, and now I'm here in prison, but I did nothing to deserve it."

16When the chief baker saw that Joseph had given the first dream such a positive interpretation, he said to Joseph, "I had a dream, too. In my dream there were three baskets of white
pastries stacked on my head. 17The top basket contained all kinds of pastries for Pharaoh, but
the birds came and ate them from the basket on my head."

18"This is what the dream means," Joseph told him. "The three baskets also represent
three days. 19Three days from now Pharaoh will lift you up and impale your body on a pole.
Then birds will come and peck away at your flesh."

20Pharaoh's birthday came three days later . . . 21He then restored the chief cup-bearer
to his former position, so he could again hand Pharaoh his cup. 22But Pharaoh impaled the
chief baker, just as Joseph had predicted when he interpreted his dream. 23Pharaoh's chief
cup-bearer, however, forgot all about Joseph, never giving him another thought.

When God gives you an opportunity to use your gifts, do you use them to glorify yourself or to glorify him? When the subject of dreams came up, Joseph focused everyone's attention on God. Rather than using the situation to make himself look good, he turned it into a powerful witness for the Lord. One secret of effective witnessing is to recognize opportunities to relate God to the other person's experience. When the opportunity arises, we need the courage to speak, as Joseph did.

JANUARY 23

Dreams in the Palace

GENESIS 41:1-27

Two full years later, Pharaoh dreamed that he was standing on the bank of the Nile River.
2In his dream he saw seven fat, healthy cows come up out of the river and begin grazing in
the marsh grass. 3Then he saw seven more cows come up behind them from the Nile, but
these were scrawny and thin. These cows stood beside the fat cows on the riverbank. 4Then
the scrawny, thin cows ate the seven healthy, fat cows! At this point in the dream, Pharaoh
woke up.

5But he fell asleep again and had a second dream. This time he saw seven heads of grain,
plump and beautiful, growing on a single stalk. 6Then seven more heads of grain appeared,
but these were shriveled and withered by the east wind. 7And these thin heads swallowed
up the seven plump, well-formed heads! Then Pharaoh woke up again and realized it was a
dream.

8The next morning Pharaoh was very disturbed by the dreams. So he called for all the
magicians and wise men of Egypt. When Pharaoh told them his dreams, not one of them
could tell him what they meant.

9Finally, the king's chief cup-bearer spoke up. "Today I have been reminded of my failure,"
he told Pharaoh. 10"Some time ago, you were angry with the chief baker and me, and you
imprisoned us in the palace of the captain of the guard. 11One night the chief baker and I
each had a dream, and each dream had its own meaning. 12There was a young Hebrew man
with us in the prison who was a slave of the captain of the guard. We told him our dreams,
and he told us what each of our dreams meant. . . .

15Then Pharaoh said to Joseph, "I had a dream last night, and no one here can tell me
what it means. But I have heard that when you hear about a dream you can interpret it."

16"It is beyond my power to do this," Joseph replied. "But God can tell you what it means
and set you at ease." . . .

25Joseph responded, "Both of Pharaoh's dreams mean the same thing. God is telling
Pharaoh in advance what he is about to do. 26The seven healthy cows and the seven healthy
heads of grain both represent seven years of prosperity. 27The seven thin, scrawny cows that
came up later and the seven thin heads of grain, withered by the east wind, represent seven
years of famine."

What do you do when presented with unexpected opportunities to do something for God? Our most important opportunities may come when we least expect them. Joseph was brought hastily from the dungeon and pushed before Pharaoh. Did he have time to prepare? Yes and no. He had no warning that he would be suddenly pulled from prison and questioned by the king. Yet Joseph was ready for almost anything because of his right relationship with God. It was not Joseph's knowledge of dreams that helped him interpret their meaning. It was his knowledge of God. Be ready for opportunities by getting to know God better. Then you will be ready to take on almost anything that comes your way.

Joseph in Charge

GENESIS 41:37-57

[37]Joseph's suggestions were well received by Pharaoh and his officials. [38]So Pharaoh asked his
officials, "Can we find anyone else like this man so obviously filled with the spirit of God?"
[39]Then Pharaoh said to Joseph, "Since God has revealed the meaning of the dreams to you,
clearly no one else is as intelligent or wise as you are. [40]You will be in charge of my court,
and all my people will take orders from you. Only I, sitting on my throne, will have a rank
higher than yours."

[41]Pharaoh said to Joseph, "I hereby put you in charge of the entire land of Egypt." [42]Then
Pharaoh removed his signet ring from his hand and placed it on Joseph's finger. He dressed
him in fine linen clothing and hung a gold chain around his neck. [43]Then he had Joseph ride
in the chariot reserved for his second-in-command. And wherever Joseph went, the command
was shouted, "Kneel down!" So Pharaoh put Joseph in charge of all Egypt. [44]And Pharaoh
said to him, "I am Pharaoh, but no one will lift a hand or foot in the entire land of Egypt
without your approval."

[45]Then Pharaoh gave Joseph a new Egyptian name, Zaphenath-paneah. He also gave
him a wife, whose name was Asenath. She was the daughter of Potiphera, the priest of On.
So Joseph took charge of the entire land of Egypt. [46]He was thirty years old when he began
serving in the court of Pharaoh, the king of Egypt. And when Joseph left Pharaoh's presence,
he inspected the entire land of Egypt.

[47]As predicted, for seven years the land produced bumper crops. [48]During those years,
Joseph gathered all the crops grown in Egypt and stored the grain from the surrounding
fields in the cities. . . .

[53]At last the seven years of bumper crops throughout the land of Egypt came to an end.
[54]Then the seven years of famine began, just as Joseph had predicted. The famine also struck
all the surrounding countries, but throughout Egypt there was plenty of food. [55]Eventually,
however, the famine spread throughout the land of Egypt as well. And when the people cried
out to Pharaoh for food, he told them, "Go to Joseph, and do whatever he tells you." [56]So
with severe famine everywhere, Joseph opened up the storehouses and distributed grain to
the Egyptians, for the famine was severe throughout the land of Egypt. [57]And people from all
around came to Egypt to buy grain from Joseph because the famine was severe throughout
the world.

How well do you handle big responsibilities? Joseph rose quickly to the top, from prison walls to Pharaoh's palace. His training for this important position involved being first a slave and then a prisoner. In each situation he learned the importance of serving God and others. Whatever your situation, no matter how undesirable, consider it part of your training program for serving God.

JANUARY 25

Joseph's Brothers Arrive

GENESIS 42:1-21

When Jacob heard that grain was available in Egypt, he said to his sons, "Why are you standing around looking at one another? 2I have heard there is grain in Egypt. Go down there, and buy enough grain to keep us alive. Otherwise we'll die."

3So Joseph's ten older brothers went down to Egypt to buy grain. 4But Jacob wouldn't let Joseph's younger brother, Benjamin, go with them, for fear some harm might come to him. 5So Jacob's sons arrived in Egypt along with others to buy food, for the famine was in Canaan as well.

6Since Joseph was governor of all Egypt and in charge of selling grain to all the people, it was to him that his brothers came. When they arrived, they bowed before him with their faces to the ground. 7Joseph recognized his brothers instantly, but he pretended to be a stranger and spoke harshly to them. "Where are you from?" he demanded.

"From the land of Canaan," they replied. "We have come to buy food."

8Although Joseph recognized his brothers, they didn't recognize him. 9And he remembered the dreams he'd had about them many years before. He said to them, "You are spies! You have come to see how vulnerable our land has become."

10"No, my lord!" they exclaimed. "Your servants have simply come to buy food. 11We are all brothers—members of the same family. We are honest men, sir! We are not spies!"

12"Yes, you are!" Joseph insisted. "You have come to see how vulnerable our land has become."

13"Sir," they said, "there are actually twelve of us. We, your servants, are all brothers, sons of a man living in the land of Canaan. Our youngest brother is back there with our father right now, and one of our brothers is no longer with us." . . .

17So Joseph put them all in prison for three days. 18On the third day Joseph said to them, "I am a God-fearing man. If you do as I say, you will live. 19If you really are honest men, choose one of your brothers to remain in prison. The rest of you may go home with grain for your starving families. 20But you must bring your youngest brother back to me. This will prove that you are telling the truth, and you will not die." To this they agreed.

21Speaking among themselves, they said, "Clearly we are being punished because of what we did to Joseph long ago. We saw his anguish when he pleaded for his life, but we wouldn't listen. That's why we're in this trouble."

What would you do with a chance for revenge? Joseph remembered his dreams about his brothers bowing down to him (Genesis 37:6-9). Those dreams were coming true! As a young boy, Joseph was boastful about his dreams. As a man, he no longer flaunted his superior status. He did not feel the need to say "I told you so." It was not yet time to reveal his identity, so he kept quiet. Sometimes it is best to remain quiet, even when we would like to have the last word.

Judah Makes a Promise

JANUARY 26

GENESIS 43:1-34

But the famine continued to ravage the land of Canaan. 2When the grain they had brought
from Egypt was almost gone, Jacob said to his sons, "Go back and buy us a little more food."
3But Judah said, "The man was serious when he warned us, 'You won't see my face again
unless your brother is with you.' 4If you send Benjamin with us, we will go down and buy
more food. 5But if you don't let Benjamin go, we won't go either. Remember, the man said,
'You won't see my face again unless your brother is with you.'" . . .
8Judah said to his father, "Send the boy with me, and we will be on our way. Otherwise
we will all die of starvation—and not only we, but you and our little ones. 9I personally
guarantee his safety. You may hold me responsible if I don't bring him back to you. Then
let me bear the blame forever. 10If we hadn't wasted all this time, we could have gone and
returned twice by now." . . .
16When Joseph saw Benjamin with them, he said to the manager of his household, "These
men will eat with me this noon. Take them inside the palace. Then go slaughter an animal,
and prepare a big feast." 17So the man did as Joseph told him and took them into Joseph's
palace. . . .
26When Joseph came home, they gave him the gifts they had brought him, then bowed
low to the ground before him. 27After greeting them, he asked, "How is your father, the old
man you spoke about? Is he still alive?"
28"Yes," they replied. "Our father, your servant, is alive and well." And they bowed low
again.
29Then Joseph looked at his brother Benjamin, the son of his own mother. "Is this your
youngest brother, the one you told me about?" Joseph asked. "May God be gracious to you,
my son." 30Then Joseph hurried from the room because he was overcome with emotion for
his brother. . . . 31After washing his face, he came back out, keeping himself under control.
Then he ordered, "Bring out the food!"
32The waiters served Joseph at his own table, and his brothers were served at a separate
table. The Egyptians who ate with Joseph sat at their own table, because Egyptians despise
Hebrews and refuse to eat with them. 33Joseph told each of his brothers where to sit, and to
their amazement, he seated them according to age, from oldest to youngest. 34And Joseph
filled their plates with food from his own table, giving Benjamin five times as much as he
gave the others. So they feasted and drank freely with him.

How seriously do you take your responsibilities? Judah accepted full responsibility for Benjamin's safety. He did not know what that might mean for him, but he was determined to carry it out. Accepting and fulfilling responsibilities is difficult, but it builds character and confidence, earns others' respect, and motivates us to complete our work. When you have been given an assignment to complete or a responsibility to fulfill, commit yourself to seeing it through.

JANUARY 27

Finding a Lost Son

GENESIS 45:1-18

Joseph could stand it no longer. There were many people in the room, and he said to his attendants, “Out, all of you!” So he was alone with his brothers when he told them who he was. . . .

3“I am Joseph!” he said to his brothers. “Is my father still alive?” But his brothers were speechless! They were stunned to realize that Joseph was standing there in front of them. 4“Please, come closer,” he said to them. So they came closer. And he said again, “I am Joseph, your brother, whom you sold into slavery in Egypt. 5But don’t be upset, and don’t be angry with yourselves for selling me to this place. It was God who sent me here ahead of you to preserve your lives. 6This famine that has ravaged the land for two years will last five more years, and there will be neither plowing nor harvesting. 7God has sent me ahead of you to keep you and your families alive and to preserve many survivors. 8So it was God who sent me here, not you! And he is the one who made me an adviser to Pharaoh—the manager of his entire palace and the governor of all Egypt.

9“Now hurry back to my father and tell him, ‘This is what your son Joseph says: God has made me master over all the land of Egypt. So come down to me immediately! 10You can live in the region of Goshen, where you can be near me with all your children and grandchildren, your flocks and herds, and everything you own. 11I will take care of you there, for there are still five years of famine ahead of us. Otherwise you, your household, and all your animals will starve.’”

12Then Joseph added, “Look! You can see for yourselves, and so can my brother Benjamin, that I really am Joseph! 13Go tell my father of my honored position here in Egypt. Describe for him everything you have seen, and then bring my father here quickly.” 14Weeping with joy, he embraced Benjamin, and Benjamin did the same. 15Then Joseph kissed each of his brothers and wept over them, and after that they began talking freely with him.

16The news soon reached Pharaoh’s palace: “Joseph’s brothers have arrived!” Pharaoh and his officials were all delighted to hear this.

17Pharaoh said to Joseph, “Tell your brothers, ‘This is what you must do: Load your pack animals, and hurry back to the land of Canaan. 18Then get your father and all of your families, and return here to me. I will give you the very best land in Egypt, and you will eat from the best that the land produces.’”

When did you last let your family know that you appreciate them? Although Joseph’s brothers had wanted to get rid of him, God used even their evil actions to fulfill his ultimate plan. He sent Joseph ahead to preserve their lives, save Egypt, and prepare the way for the beginning of the nation of Israel. God is in control. His plans are not dictated by human actions. When others intend evil toward you, remember that they are only God’s tools. As Joseph said to his brothers, “You intended to harm me, but God intended it all for good. He brought me to this position so I could save the lives of many people” (Genesis 50:20).

Moses Is Born

EXODUS 1:8-16; 2:1-10

8Eventually, a new king came to power in Egypt who knew nothing about Joseph or what he had done. 9He said to his people, "Look, the people of Israel now outnumber us and are stronger than we are. 10We must make a plan to keep them from growing even more. If we don't, and if war breaks out, they will join our enemies and fight against us. Then they will escape from the country."

11So the Egyptians made the Israelites their slaves. . . . 12But the more the Egyptians oppressed them, the more the Israelites multiplied and spread, and the more alarmed the Egyptians became. . . .

15Then Pharaoh, the king of Egypt, gave this order to the Hebrew midwives, Shiphrah and Puah: 16"When you help the Hebrew women as they give birth, watch as they deliver. If the baby is a boy, kill him; if it is a girl, let her live."

2:1About this time, a man and woman from the tribe of Levi got married. 2The woman became pregnant and gave birth to a son. She saw that he was a special baby and kept him hidden for three months. 3But when she could no longer hide him, she got a basket made of papyrus reeds and waterproofed it with tar and pitch. She put the baby in the basket and laid it among the reeds along the bank of the Nile River. 4The baby's sister then stood at a distance, watching to see what would happen to him.

5Soon Pharaoh's daughter came down to bathe in the river, and her attendants walked along the riverbank. When the princess saw the basket among the reeds, she sent her maid to get it for her. 6When the princess opened it, she saw the baby. The little boy was crying, and she felt sorry for him. "This must be one of the Hebrew children," she said.

7Then the baby's sister approached the princess. "Should I go and find one of the Hebrew women to nurse the baby for you?" she asked.

8"Yes, do!" the princess replied. So the girl went and called the baby's mother.

9"Take this baby and nurse him for me," the princess told the baby's mother. "I will pay you for your help." So the woman took her baby home and nursed him.

10Later, when the boy was older, his mother brought him back to Pharaoh's daughter, who adopted him as her own son. The princess named him Moses, for she explained, "I lifted him out of the water."

How have you appreciated the gift of life? Moses' mother knew how wrong it would be to destroy her child. But there was little she could do to change Pharaoh's new law. Her only alternative was to hide the child and later place him in a tiny reed basket on the river. God used her courageous act to place her son, the Hebrew of his choice, in the house of Pharaoh. Do you sometimes feel surrounded by evil and frustrated by how little you can do about it? When faced with evil, look for ways to act against it. Then trust God to use your effort, however small it seems, in his war against evil.

JANUARY 29

Moses on the Run

EXODUS 2:11-25

[11]Many years later, when Moses had grown up, he went out to visit his own people, the Hebrews, and he saw how hard they were forced to work. During his visit, he saw an Egyptian beating one of his fellow Hebrews. [12]After looking in all directions to make sure no one was watching, Moses killed the Egyptian and hid the body in the sand.

[13]The next day, when Moses went out to visit his people again, he saw two Hebrew men fighting. "Why are you beating up your friend?" Moses said to the one who had started the fight.

[14]The man replied, "Who appointed you to be our prince and judge? Are you going to kill me as you killed that Egyptian yesterday?"

Then Moses was afraid, thinking, "Everyone knows what I did." [15]And sure enough, Pharaoh heard what had happened, and he tried to kill Moses. But Moses fled from Pharaoh and went to live in the land of Midian.

When Moses arrived in Midian, he sat down beside a well. [16]Now the priest of Midian had seven daughters who came as usual to draw water and fill the water troughs for their father's flocks. [17]But some other shepherds came and chased them away. So Moses jumped up and rescued the girls from the shepherds. Then he drew water for their flocks.

[18]When the girls returned to Reuel, their father, he asked, "Why are you back so soon today?"

[19]"An Egyptian rescued us from the shepherds," they answered. "And then he drew water for us and watered our flocks."

[20]"Then where is he?" their father asked. "Why did you leave him there? Invite him to come and eat with us."

[21]Moses accepted the invitation, and he settled there with him. In time, Reuel gave Moses his daughter Zipporah to be his wife. [22]Later she gave birth to a son, and Moses named him Gershom, for he explained, "I have been a foreigner in a foreign land."

[23]Years passed, and the king of Egypt died. But the Israelites continued to groan under their burden of slavery. They cried out for help, and their cry rose up to God. [24]God heard their groaning, and he remembered his covenant promise to Abraham, Isaac, and Jacob. [25]He looked down on the people of Israel and knew it was time to act.

When was the last time you found yourself running from God? Moses tried to make sure no one was watching before he killed the Egyptian. But as it turned out, someone did see him, and Moses had to flee the country. Sometimes we mistakenly think we can get away with doing wrong if no one sees or catches us. Sooner or later, however, doing wrong will catch up with us as it did with Moses. Even if we are not caught in this life, we will still have to face God's evaluation of our actions.

God's Burning Bush

EXODUS 3:1-14

One day Moses was tending the flock of his father-in-law, Jethro, the priest of Midian. He led
the flock far into the wilderness and came to Sinai, the mountain of God. 2There the angel
of the LORD appeared to him in a blazing fire from the middle of a bush. Moses stared in
amazement. Though the bush was engulfed in flames, it didn't burn up. 3"This is amazing,"
Moses said to himself. "Why isn't that bush burning up? I must go see it."

4When the LORD saw Moses coming to take a closer look, God called to him from the
middle of the bush, "Moses! Moses!"

"Here I am!" Moses replied.

5"Do not come any closer," the LORD warned. "Take off your sandals, for you are standing on holy ground. 6I am the God of your father—the God of Abraham, the God of Isaac,
and the God of Jacob." When Moses heard this, he covered his face because he was afraid
to look at God.

7Then the LORD told him, "I have certainly seen the oppression of my people in Egypt. I
have heard their cries of distress because of their harsh slave drivers. Yes, I am aware of their
suffering. 8So I have come down to rescue them from the power of the Egyptians and lead
them out of Egypt into their own fertile and spacious land. It is a land flowing with milk and
honey—the land where the Canaanites, Hittites, Amorites, Perizzites, Hivites, and Jebusites
now live. 9Look! The cry of the people of Israel has reached me, and I have seen how harshly
the Egyptians abuse them. 10Now go, for I am sending you to Pharaoh. You must lead my
people Israel out of Egypt."

11But Moses protested to God, "Who am I to appear before Pharaoh? Who am I to lead
the people of Israel out of Egypt?"

12God answered, "I will be with you. And this is your sign that I am the one who has
sent you: When you have brought the people out of Egypt, you will worship God at this
very mountain."

13But Moses protested, "If I go to the people of Israel and tell them, 'The God of your
ancestors has sent me to you,' they will ask me, 'What is his name?' Then what should I tell
them?"

14God replied to Moses, "I AM WHO I AM. Say this to the people of Israel: I AM has sent
me to you."

In what ways has God made himself known to you? God spoke to Moses from an unexpected source: a burning bush. When Moses saw it, he went to investigate. God often uses unexpected sources when communicating with us, too. Be willing to investigate. Whether he uses people, thoughts, or experiences, be ready for God's surprises. He may have guidance for you that can come when you are ready to listen to a "burning bush."

JANUARY 31

Moses Isn't Sure

EXODUS 4:1-15

But Moses protested again, "What if they won't believe me or listen to me? What if they say,
'The LORD never appeared to you'?"
2 Then the LORD asked him, "What is that in your hand?"
"A shepherd's staff," Moses replied.
3 "Throw it down on the ground," the LORD told him. So Moses threw down the staff,
and it turned into a snake! Moses jumped back.
4 Then the LORD told him, "Reach out and grab its tail." So Moses reached out and
grabbed it, and it turned back into a shepherd's staff in his hand.
5 "Perform this sign," the LORD told him. "Then they will believe that the LORD, the God
of their ancestors—the God of Abraham, the God of Isaac, and the God of Jacob—really
has appeared to you."
6 Then the LORD said to Moses, "Now put your hand inside your cloak." So Moses put
his hand inside his cloak, and when he took it out again, his hand was white as snow with
a severe skin disease. 7 "Now put your hand back into your cloak," the LORD said. So Moses
put his hand back in, and when he took it out again, it was as healthy as the rest of his body.
8 The LORD said to Moses, "If they do not believe you and are not convinced by the first
miraculous sign, they will be convinced by the second sign. 9 And if they don't believe you or
listen to you even after these two signs, then take some water from the Nile River and pour
it out on the dry ground. When you do, the water from the Nile will turn to blood on the
ground."
10 But Moses pleaded with the LORD, "O Lord, I'm not very good with words. I never
have been, and I'm not now, even though you have spoken to me. I get tongue-tied, and my
words get tangled."
11 Then the LORD asked Moses, "Who makes a person's mouth? Who decides whether
people speak or do not speak, hear or do not hear, see or do not see? Is it not I, the LORD?
12 Now go! I will be with you as you speak, and I will instruct you in what to say."
13 But Moses again pleaded, "Lord, please! Send anyone else."
14 Then the LORD became angry with Moses. "All right," he said. "What about your
brother, Aaron the Levite? I know he speaks well. And look! He is on his way to meet you
now. He will be delighted to see you. 15 Talk to him, and put the words in his mouth. I will
be with both of you as you speak, and I will instruct you both in what to do."

How willing are you to do what God wants you to do? Moses pleaded with God to let him out of his mission. After all, he was not a good speaker. But God looked at Moses' problem quite differently. All Moses needed was some help, and who better than God to help him say and do the right things? God made Moses' mouth and would give him the words to say. It is easy for us to focus on our weaknesses. But if God asks us to do something, he will help us get the job done. He will provide words, strength, courage, and ability where needed.

February

FEBRUARY 1

Resistance and Persistence

EXODUS 5:1-23

After this presentation to Israel's leaders, Moses and Aaron went and spoke to Pharaoh. They told him, "This is what the LORD, the God of Israel, says: Let my people go so they may hold a festival in my honor in the wilderness."

2"Is that so?" retorted Pharaoh. "And who is the LORD? Why should I listen to him and let Israel go? I don't know the LORD, and I will not let Israel go."

3But Aaron and Moses persisted. "The God of the Hebrews has met with us," they declared. "So let us take a three-day journey into the wilderness so we can offer sacrifices to the LORD our God. If we don't, he will kill us with a plague or with the sword."

4Pharaoh replied, "Moses and Aaron, why are you distracting the people from their tasks? Get back to work! 5Look, there are many of your people in the land, and you are stopping them from their work."

6That same day Pharaoh sent this order to the Egyptian slave drivers and the Israelite foremen: 7"Do not supply any more straw for making bricks. Make the people get it themselves! 8But still require them to make the same number of bricks as before. Don't reduce the quota. They are lazy. That's why they are crying out, 'Let us go and offer sacrifices to our God.' 9Load them down with more work. Make them sweat! That will teach them to listen to lies!" . . .

15So the Israelite foremen went to Pharaoh and pleaded with him. "Please don't treat your servants like this," they begged. . . .

17But Pharaoh shouted, "You're just lazy! Lazy! That's why you're saying, 'Let us go and offer sacrifices to the LORD.' 18Now get back to work! No straw will be given to you, but you must still produce the full quota of bricks."

19The Israelite foremen could see that they were in serious trouble when they were told, "You must not reduce the number of bricks you make each day." 20As they left Pharaoh's court, they confronted Moses and Aaron, who were waiting outside for them. 21The foremen said to them, "May the LORD judge and punish you for making us stink before Pharaoh and his officials. You have put a sword into their hands, an excuse to kill us!"

22Then Moses went back to the LORD and protested, "Why have you brought all this trouble on your own people, Lord? Why did you send me? 23Ever since I came to Pharaoh as your spokesman, he has been even more brutal to your people. And you have done nothing to rescue them!"

What have people said when you've tried to obey God? Pharaoh would not listen to Moses and Aaron because he did not know or respect God. People who do not know God may not listen to his Word or his messengers. Like Moses and Aaron, we need to persist. When others reject you or your faith, don't be surprised or discouraged. Continue to tell them about God, trusting him to open minds and soften stubborn hearts.

Refusal and Rejection

EXODUS 6:1-13

Then the LORD told Moses, "Now you will see what I will do to Pharaoh. When he feels the
force of my strong hand, he will let the people go. In fact, he will force them to leave his land!"
2And God said to Moses, "I am Yahweh—'the LORD.' 3I appeared to Abraham, to Isaac,
and to Jacob as El-Shaddai—'God Almighty'—but I did not reveal my name, Yahweh, to
them. 4And I reaffirmed my covenant with them. Under its terms, I promised to give them
the land of Canaan, where they were living as foreigners. 5You can be sure that I have heard
the groans of the people of Israel, who are now slaves to the Egyptians. And I am well aware
of my covenant with them.
6"Therefore, say to the people of Israel: 'I am the LORD. I will free you from your oppression and will rescue you from your slavery in Egypt. I will redeem you with a powerful arm
and great acts of judgment. 7I will claim you as my own people, and I will be your God.
Then you will know that I am the LORD your God who has freed you from your oppression
in Egypt. 8I will bring you into the land I swore to give to Abraham, Isaac, and Jacob. I will
give it to you as your very own possession. I am the LORD!'"
9So Moses told the people of Israel what the LORD had said, but they refused to listen
anymore. They had become too discouraged by the brutality of their slavery.
10Then the LORD said to Moses, 11"Go back to Pharaoh, the king of Egypt, and tell him
to let the people of Israel leave his country."
12"But LORD!" Moses objected. "My own people won't listen to me anymore. How can I
expect Pharaoh to listen? I'm such a clumsy speaker!"
13But the LORD spoke to Moses and Aaron and gave them orders for the Israelites and for
Pharaoh, the king of Egypt. The LORD commanded Moses and Aaron to lead the people of
Israel out of Egypt.

What would it cost you to do what God wants? Small problems need only small answers. But when we face great problems, God has an opportunity to exercise his great power. As the Hebrews' troubles grew steadily worse, God planned to intervene with his mighty power and perform great miracles to deliver them. How big are your problems? Big problems put you in a perfect position to watch God give big answers.

FEBRUARY 3

A Stubborn Ruler

EXODUS 7:1-13

Then the LORD said to Moses, "Pay close attention to this. I will make you seem like God to Pharaoh, and your brother, Aaron, will be your prophet. 2Tell Aaron everything I command you, and Aaron must command Pharaoh to let the people of Israel leave his country. 3But I will make Pharaoh's heart stubborn so I can multiply my miraculous signs and wonders in the land of Egypt. 4Even then Pharaoh will refuse to listen to you. So I will bring down my fist on Egypt. Then I will rescue my forces—my people, the Israelites—from the land of Egypt with great acts of judgment. 5When I raise my powerful hand and bring out the Israelites, the Egyptians will know that I am the LORD."

6So Moses and Aaron did just as the LORD had commanded them. 7Moses was eighty years old, and Aaron was eighty-three when they made their demands to Pharaoh.

8Then the LORD said to Moses and Aaron, 9"Pharaoh will demand, 'Show me a miracle.' When he does this, say to Aaron, 'Take your staff and throw it down in front of Pharaoh, and it will become a serpent.'"

10So Moses and Aaron went to Pharaoh and did what the LORD had commanded them. Aaron threw down his staff before Pharaoh and his officials, and it became a serpent! 11Then Pharaoh called in his own wise men and sorcerers, and these Egyptian magicians did the same thing with their magic. 12They threw down their staffs, which also became serpents! But then Aaron's staff swallowed up their staffs. 13Pharaoh's heart, however, remained hard. He still refused to listen, just as the LORD had predicted.

How does stubbornness affect your relationship with God? After repeated warnings, Pharaoh still refused to obey God. He hardened his heart every time there was a break in the plagues. His stubborn disobedience brought suffering upon himself and his entire country. While persistence is good, stubbornness is usually self-centered. Stubbornness toward God is always disobedience. Avoid disobedience, because the consequences may spill onto others.

First Three Plagues

FEBRUARY 4

EXODUS 7:14-20; 8:1-19

14Then the LORD said to Moses, "Pharaoh's heart is stubborn, and he still refuses to let the
people go. 15So go to Pharaoh in the morning as he goes down to the river. Stand on the
bank of the Nile and meet him there. Be sure to take along the staff that turned into a snake.
16Then announce to him, 'The LORD, the God of the Hebrews, has sent me to tell you, "Let
my people go, so they can worship me in the wilderness." Until now, you have refused to
listen to him. 17So this is what the LORD says: "I will show you that I am the LORD." Look! I
will strike the water of the Nile with this staff in my hand, and the river will turn to blood.
18The fish in it will die, and the river will stink. The Egyptians will not be able to drink any
water from the Nile.'" . . .

20So Moses and Aaron did just as the LORD commanded them. As Pharaoh and all of his
officials watched, Aaron raised his staff and struck the water of the Nile. Suddenly, the whole
river turned to blood!

8:1Then the LORD said to Moses, "Go back to Pharaoh and announce to him, 'This is what
the LORD says: Let my people go, so they can worship me. 2If you refuse to let them go, I
will send a plague of frogs across your entire land. 3The Nile River will swarm with frogs.
They will come up out of the river and into your palace, even into your bedroom and onto
your bed! They will enter the houses of your officials and your people. They will even jump
into your ovens and your kneading bowls. 4Frogs will jump on you, your people, and all
your officials.'" . . .

16So the LORD said to Moses, "Tell Aaron, 'Raise your staff and strike the ground. The
dust will turn into swarms of gnats throughout the land of Egypt.'" 17So Moses and Aaron did
just as the LORD had commanded them. When Aaron raised his hand and struck the ground
with his staff, gnats infested the entire land, covering the Egyptians and their animals. All
the dust in the land of Egypt turned into gnats. 18Pharaoh's magicians tried to do the same
thing with their secret arts, but this time they failed. And the gnats covered everyone, people
and animals alike.

19"This is the finger of God!" the magicians exclaimed to Pharaoh. But Pharaoh's heart
remained hard. He wouldn't listen to them, just as the LORD had predicted.

How can you know what to believe? Pharaoh's magicians could duplicate the first few of Moses' miracles through trickery, but finally they had to acknowledge that the plague of gnats was "the finger of God." Although miracles can help us to believe, it is dangerous to rely on them alone. Satan can imitate some parts of God's work and lead people astray. Pharaoh focused on the miracle rather than the message. We can avoid this error by letting the Word of God be the basis of our faith. No miracle from God would endorse any message that is contrary to the teachings of his Word.

An Attempt at a Bargain

EXODUS 8:20-32

[20]Then the LORD told Moses, "Get up early in the morning and stand in Pharaoh's way as he goes down to the river. Say to him, 'This is what the LORD says: Let my people go, so they can worship me. [21]If you refuse, then I will send swarms of flies on you, your officials, your people, and all the houses. The Egyptian homes will be filled with flies, and the ground will be covered with them. [22]But this time I will spare the region of Goshen, where my people live. No flies will be found there. Then you will know that I am the LORD and that I am present even in the heart of your land. [23]I will make a clear distinction between my people and your people. This miraculous sign will happen tomorrow.'"

[24]And the LORD did just as he had said. A thick swarm of flies filled Pharaoh's palace and the houses of his officials. The whole land of Egypt was thrown into chaos by the flies.

[25]Pharaoh called for Moses and Aaron. "All right! Go ahead and offer sacrifices to your God," he said. "But do it here in this land."

[26]But Moses replied, "That wouldn't be right. The Egyptians detest the sacrifices that we offer to the LORD our God. Look, if we offer our sacrifices here where the Egyptians can see us, they will stone us. [27]We must take a three-day trip into the wilderness to offer sacrifices to the LORD our God, just as he has commanded us."

[28]"All right, go ahead," Pharaoh replied. "I will let you go into the wilderness to offer sacrifices to the LORD your God. But don't go too far away. Now hurry and pray for me."

[29]Moses answered, "As soon as I leave you, I will pray to the LORD, and tomorrow the swarms of flies will disappear from you and your officials and all your people. But I am warning you, Pharaoh, don't lie to us again and refuse to let the people go to sacrifice to the LORD."

[30]So Moses left Pharaoh's palace and pleaded with the LORD to remove all the flies. [31]And the LORD did as Moses asked and caused the swarms of flies to disappear from Pharaoh, his officials, and his people. Not a single fly remained. [32]But Pharaoh again became stubborn and refused to let the people go.

When do you try to bargain with God? Pharaoh wanted a compromise. He would allow the Hebrews to sacrifice, but only if they would do it nearby. God's requirement, however, was firm: The Hebrews had to leave Egypt. Sometimes people urge believers to compromise and give only partial obedience to God's commands. But commitment and obedience to God cannot be negotiated. When it comes to obeying God, halfway measures won't do.

Three More Plagues

FEBRUARY 6

EXODUS 9:1-26

"Go back to Pharaoh," the LORD commanded Moses. "Tell him, 'This is what the LORD, the God of the Hebrews, says: Let my people go, so they can worship me. 2If you continue to hold them and refuse to let them go, 3the hand of the LORD will strike all your livestock—your horses, donkeys, camels, cattle, sheep, and goats—with a deadly plague. 4But the LORD will again make a distinction between the livestock of the Israelites and that of the Egyptians. Not a single one of Israel's animals will die! 5The LORD has already set the time for the plague to begin. He has declared that he will strike the land tomorrow.'"

6And the LORD did just as he had said. The next morning all the livestock of the Egyptians died, but the Israelites didn't lose a single animal. 7Pharaoh sent his officials to investigate, and they discovered that the Israelites had not lost a single animal! But even so, Pharaoh's heart remained stubborn, and he still refused to let the people go.

8Then the LORD said to Moses and Aaron, "Take handfuls of soot from a brick kiln, and have Moses toss it into the air while Pharaoh watches. 9The ashes will spread like fine dust over the whole land of Egypt, causing festering boils to break out on people and animals throughout the land."

10So they took soot from a brick kiln and went and stood before Pharaoh. As Pharaoh watched, Moses threw the soot into the air, and boils broke out on people and animals alike. 11Even the magicians were unable to stand before Moses, because the boils had broken out on them and all the Egyptians. 12But the LORD hardened Pharaoh's heart, and just as the LORD had predicted to Moses, Pharaoh refused to listen. . . .

22Then the LORD said to Moses, "Lift your hand toward the sky so hail may fall on the people, the livestock, and all the plants throughout the land of Egypt."

23So Moses lifted his staff toward the sky, and the LORD sent thunder and hail, and lightning flashed toward the earth. The LORD sent a tremendous hailstorm against all the land of Egypt. 24Never in all the history of Egypt had there been a storm like that, with such devastating hail and continuous lightning. 25It left all of Egypt in ruins. The hail struck down everything in the open field—people, animals, and plants alike. Even the trees were destroyed. 26The only place without hail was the region of Goshen, where the people of Israel lived.

How does God get your attention? God gave Pharaoh many opportunities to heed Moses' warnings. But finally God seemed to say, "All right, Pharaoh, have it your way," and Pharaoh's heart became permanently hardened. Did God intentionally harden Pharaoh's heart and overrule his free will? No, he simply confirmed that Pharaoh freely chose a life of resisting God. Similarly, after a lifetime of resisting God, some people may find it impossible to turn to him. Don't wait to turn to God. Do it now while you still have the chance. If you continually ignore God's voice, eventually you will be unable to hear it at all.

Two More Plagues

EXODUS 10:1-23

Then the LORD said to Moses, "Return to Pharaoh and make your demands again. I have made him and his officials stubborn so I can display my miraculous signs among them. [2]I've also done it so you can tell your children and grandchildren about how I made a mockery of the Egyptians and about the signs I displayed among them—and so you will know that I am the LORD."

[3]So Moses and Aaron went to Pharaoh and said, "This is what the LORD, the God of the Hebrews, says: How long will you refuse to submit to me? Let my people go, so they can worship me. [4]If you refuse, watch out! For tomorrow I will bring a swarm of locusts on your country. . . ." [13]So Moses raised his staff over Egypt, and the LORD caused an east wind to blow over the land all that day and through the night. When morning arrived, the east wind had brought the locusts. [14]And the locusts swarmed over the whole land of Egypt, settling in dense swarms from one end of the country to the other. It was the worst locust plague in Egyptian history, and there has never been another one like it. [15]For the locusts covered the whole country and darkened the land. They devoured every plant in the fields and all the fruit on the trees that had survived the hailstorm. Not a single leaf was left on the trees and plants throughout the land of Egypt.

[16]Pharaoh quickly summoned Moses and Aaron. "I have sinned against the LORD your God and against you," he confessed. [17]"Forgive my sin, just this once, and plead with the LORD your God to take away this death from me."

[18]So Moses left Pharaoh's court and pleaded with the LORD. [19]The LORD responded by shifting the wind, and the strong west wind blew the locusts into the Red Sea. Not a single locust remained in all the land of Egypt. [20]But the LORD hardened Pharaoh's heart again, so he refused to let the people go.

[21]Then the LORD said to Moses, "Lift your hand toward heaven, and the land of Egypt will be covered with a darkness so thick you can feel it." [22]So Moses lifted his hand to the sky, and a deep darkness covered the entire land of Egypt for three days. [23]During all that time the people could not see each other, and no one moved. But there was light as usual where the people of Israel lived.

What stories do you have to tell? God told Moses that his miraculous experiences with Pharaoh should be retold to his descendants. What stories Moses had to tell! Living out one of the greatest dramas in biblical history, he witnessed events few people would ever see. It is important to tell others about God's work in our past and to help them see what he is doing right now. What are the turning points in your life when God intervened? What is God doing for you now? Your stories may well form the foundations for others' belief in God.

The Ultimate Plague

EXODUS 11:1-7; 12:29-36

Then the LORD said to Moses, "I will strike Pharaoh and the land of Egypt with one more
blow. After that, Pharaoh will let you leave this country. In fact, he will be so eager to get rid
of you that he will force you all to leave. 2Tell all the Israelite men and women to ask their
Egyptian neighbors for articles of silver and gold." 3(Now the LORD had caused the Egyptians
to look favorably on the people of Israel. And Moses was considered a very great man in the
land of Egypt, respected by Pharaoh's officials and the Egyptian people alike.)

4Moses had announced to Pharaoh, "This is what the LORD says: At midnight tonight I
will pass through the heart of Egypt. 5All the firstborn sons will die in every family in Egypt,
from the oldest son of Pharaoh, who sits on his throne, to the oldest son of his lowliest servant
girl who grinds the flour. Even the firstborn of all the livestock will die. 6Then a loud wail
will rise throughout the land of Egypt, a wail like no one has heard before or will ever hear
again. 7But among the Israelites it will be so peaceful that not even a dog will bark. Then
you will know that the LORD makes a distinction between the Egyptians and the Israelites."

12:29And that night at midnight, the LORD struck down all the firstborn sons in the land of
Egypt, from the firstborn son of Pharaoh, who sat on his throne, to the firstborn son of the
prisoner in the dungeon. Even the firstborn of their livestock were killed. 30Pharaoh and all
his officials and all the people of Egypt woke up during the night, and loud wailing was heard
throughout the land of Egypt. There was not a single house where someone had not died.

31Pharaoh sent for Moses and Aaron during the night. "Get out!" he ordered. "Leave
my people—and take the rest of the Israelites with you! Go and worship the LORD as you
have requested. 32Take your flocks and herds, as you said, and be gone. Go, but bless me as
you leave." 33All the Egyptians urged the people of Israel to get out of the land as quickly as
possible, for they thought, "We will all die!"

34The Israelites took their bread dough before yeast was added. They wrapped their
kneading boards in their cloaks and carried them on their shoulders. 35And the people of Israel
did as Moses had instructed; they asked the Egyptians for clothing and articles of silver and
gold. 36The LORD caused the Egyptians to look favorably on the Israelites, and they gave the
Israelites whatever they asked for. So they stripped the Egyptians of their wealth!

What does it mean to fear God in your life? You may wonder how Pharaoh could be so foolish as to see God's miraculous power and still not listen to Moses. But Pharaoh had his mind made up long before the plagues began. He couldn't believe that someone was greater than he. Finally, it took the greatest of all calamities, the loss of his son, to force him to recognize God's authority. But even then he wanted God to leave, not to rule his country. We must not wait for great calamities to drive us to God, but we must open our hearts and minds to his direction now.

FEBRUARY 9

A Narrow Escape

EXODUS 14:1-31

Then the LORD gave these instructions to Moses: 2“Order the Israelites to turn back and
camp by Pi-hahiroth between Migdol and the sea. Camp there along the shore, across from
Baal-zephon. 3Then Pharaoh will think, ‘The Israelites are confused. They are trapped in the
wilderness!’ 4And once again I will harden Pharaoh’s heart, and he will chase after you. I have
planned this in order to display my glory through Pharaoh and his whole army. After this
the Egyptians will know that I am the LORD!” . . .

10As Pharaoh approached, the people of Israel looked up and panicked when they saw
the Egyptians overtaking them. They cried out to the LORD, 11and they said to Moses, “Why
did you bring us out here to die in the wilderness? Weren’t there enough graves for us in
Egypt? What have you done to us? Why did you make us leave Egypt? 12Didn’t we tell you
this would happen while we were still in Egypt? We said, ‘Leave us alone! Let us be slaves to
the Egyptians. It’s better to be a slave in Egypt than a corpse in the wilderness!’”

13But Moses told the people, “Don’t be afraid. Just stand still and watch the LORD rescue
you today. The Egyptians you see today will never be seen again. 14The LORD himself will
fight for you. Just stay calm.” . . .

21Then Moses raised his hand over the sea, and the LORD opened up a path through the
water with a strong east wind. The wind blew all that night, turning the seabed into dry land.
22So the people of Israel walked through the middle of the sea on dry ground, with walls of
water on each side! . . .

26When all the Israelites had reached the other side, the LORD said to Moses, “Raise
your hand over the sea again. Then the waters will rush back and cover the Egyptians and
their chariots and charioteers.” 27So as the sun began to rise, Moses raised his hand over the
sea, and the water rushed back into its usual place. The Egyptians tried to escape, but the
LORD swept them into the sea. 28Then the waters returned and covered all the chariots and
charioteers—the entire army of Pharaoh. . . .

29But the people of Israel had walked through the middle of the sea on dry ground, as
the water stood up like a wall on both sides. 30That is how the LORD rescued Israel from the
hand of the Egyptians that day. And the Israelites saw the bodies of the Egyptians washed
up on the seashore. 31When the people of Israel saw the mighty power that the LORD had
unleashed against the Egyptians, they were filled with awe before him. They put their faith
in the LORD and in his servant Moses.

When have you experienced God’s protection? The people were hostile and despairing, but Moses encouraged them to watch the wonderful way God would rescue them. Moses had a positive attitude! When it looked as if they were trapped, Moses called upon God to intervene. We may not be chased by an army, but we may still feel trapped. Instead of giving in to despair, we should adopt Moses’ attitude to “watch” and see what God will do.

God Provides Water

FEBRUARY 10

EXODUS 15:22-26; 17:1-7

[22]Then Moses led the people of Israel away from the Red Sea, and they moved out into the desert of Shur. They traveled in this desert for three days without finding any water. [23]When they came to the oasis of Marah, the water was too bitter to drink. So they called the place Marah (which means "bitter").

[24]Then the people complained and turned against Moses. "What are we going to drink?" they demanded. [25]So Moses cried out to the LORD for help, and the LORD showed him a piece of wood. Moses threw it into the water, and this made the water good to drink.

It was there at Marah that the LORD set before them the following decree as a standard to test their faithfulness to him. [26]He said, "If you will listen carefully to the voice of the LORD your God and do what is right in his sight, obeying his commands and keeping all his decrees, then I will not make you suffer any of the diseases I sent on the Egyptians; for I am the LORD who heals you."

[17:1]At the LORD's command, the whole community of Israel left the wilderness of Sin and moved from place to place. Eventually they camped at Rephidim, but there was no water there for the people to drink. [2]So once more the people complained against Moses. "Give us water to drink!" they demanded.

"Quiet!" Moses replied. "Why are you complaining against me? And why are you testing the LORD?"

[3]But tormented by thirst, they continued to argue with Moses. "Why did you bring us out of Egypt? Are you trying to kill us, our children, and our livestock with thirst?"

[4]Then Moses cried out to the LORD, "What should I do with these people? They are ready to stone me!"

[5]The LORD said to Moses, "Walk out in front of the people. Take your staff, the one you used when you struck the water of the Nile, and call some of the elders of Israel to join you. [6]I will stand before you on the rock at Mount Sinai. Strike the rock, and water will come gushing out. Then the people will be able to drink." So Moses struck the rock as he was told, and water gushed out as the elders looked on.

[7]Moses named the place Massah (which means "test") and Meribah (which means "arguing") because the people of Israel argued with Moses and tested the LORD by saying, "Is the LORD here with us or not?"

What do you complain to God about? Again the people complained about their problem instead of praying. Some problems can be solved by careful thought or by good counsel, but other problems can be solved only by prayer. We should make a determined effort to pray when we feel like complaining, because complaining only adds to our worries and stress. Prayer quiets our thoughts and emotions, and prepares us to listen.

FEBRUARY 11

God's Unusual Food Supply

EXODUS 16:1-31

Then the whole community of Israel set out from Elim and journeyed into the wilderness of Sin, between Elim and Mount Sinai. They arrived there on the fifteenth day of the second month, one month after leaving the land of Egypt. 2There, too, the whole community of Israel complained about Moses and Aaron.

3"If only the LORD had killed us back in Egypt," they moaned. "There we sat around pots filled with meat and ate all the bread we wanted. But now you have brought us into this wilderness to starve us all to death."

4Then the LORD said to Moses, "Look, I'm going to rain down food from heaven for you. . . ."

6So Moses and Aaron said to all the people of Israel, "By evening you will realize it was the LORD who brought you out of the land of Egypt. . . ."

9Then Moses said to Aaron, "Announce this to the entire community of Israel: 'Present yourselves before the LORD, for he has heard your complaining.'" 10And as Aaron spoke to the whole community of Israel, they looked out toward the wilderness. There they could see the awesome glory of the LORD in the cloud.

11Then the LORD said to Moses, 12"I have heard the Israelites' complaints. Now tell them, 'In the evening you will have meat to eat, and in the morning you will have all the bread you want. Then you will know that I am the LORD your God.'"

13That evening vast numbers of quail flew in and covered the camp. And the next morning the area around the camp was wet with dew. 14When the dew evaporated, a flaky substance as fine as frost blanketed the ground. 15The Israelites were puzzled when they saw it. "What is it?" they asked each other. They had no idea what it was.

And Moses told them, "It is the food the LORD has given you to eat. 16These are the LORD's instructions: Each household should gather as much as it needs. Pick up two quarts for each person in your tent." . . .

31The Israelites called the food manna. It was white like coriander seed, and it tasted like honey wafers.

What specific gift did you last thank God for? As the Israelites encountered danger, shortages, and inconvenience, they complained bitterly and longed to be back in Egypt. But God provided for their needs. Difficult circumstances often lead to stress, and complaining is a natural response. The Israelites didn't really want to be back in Egypt; they just wanted life to get a little easier. In the pressure of the moment, they could not focus on the cause of their stress (in this case, lack of trust in God); they could only think about the quickest way of escape. When pressure comes your way, resist the temptation to make a quick escape. Instead, focus on God's power and wisdom to help you deal with the cause of your stress.

Helpful Advice

FEBRUARY 12

EXODUS 18:1-27

Moses' father-in-law, Jethro, the priest of Midian, heard about everything God had done for Moses and his people, the Israelites. He heard especially about how the LORD had rescued them from Egypt. . . .

5Jethro, Moses' father-in-law, now came to visit Moses in the wilderness. . . .

13The next day, Moses took his seat to hear the people's disputes against each other. They waited before him from morning till evening.

14When Moses' father-in-law saw all that Moses was doing for the people, he asked, "What are you really accomplishing here? Why are you trying to do all this alone while everyone stands around you from morning till evening?"

15Moses replied, "Because the people come to me to get a ruling from God. 16When a dispute arises, they come to me, and I am the one who settles the case between the quarreling parties. I inform the people of God's decrees and give them his instructions."

17"This is not good!" Moses' father-in-law exclaimed. 18"You're going to wear yourself out—and the people, too. This job is too heavy a burden for you to handle all by yourself. 19Now listen to me, and let me give you a word of advice, and may God be with you. You should continue to be the people's representative before God, bringing their disputes to him. 20Teach them God's decrees, and give them his instructions. Show them how to conduct their lives. 21But select from all the people some capable, honest men who fear God and hate bribes. Appoint them as leaders over groups of one thousand, one hundred, fifty, and ten. 22They should always be available to solve the people's common disputes, but have them bring the major cases to you. Let the leaders decide the smaller matters themselves. They will help you carry the load, making the task easier for you. 23If you follow this advice, and if God commands you to do so, then you will be able to endure the pressures, and all these people will go home in peace."

24Moses listened to his father-in-law's advice and followed his suggestions. 25He chose capable men from all over Israel and appointed them as leaders over the people. He put them in charge of groups of one thousand, one hundred, fifty, and ten. 26These men were always available to solve the people's common disputes. They brought the major cases to Moses, but they took care of the smaller matters themselves.

27Soon after this, Moses said good-bye to his father-in-law, who returned to his own land.

Who are the dependable advisers in your life? Moses was spending so much time and energy hearing the Hebrews' complaints that he could not get to other important work. Jethro suggested that Moses delegate most of the work to others and focus his efforts on jobs only he could do. People in positions of responsibility sometimes feel they are the only ones who can do necessary tasks, but others are capable of handling part of the load. Proper delegation can multiply your effectiveness while giving others a chance to grow.

FEBRUARY 13

An Appointment with God

EXODUS 19:1-20

Exactly two months after the Israelites left Egypt, they arrived in the wilderness of Sinai. . . .

[3]Then Moses climbed the mountain to appear before God. The LORD called to him from the mountain and said, "Give these instructions to the family of Jacob; announce it to the descendants of Israel: [4]'You have seen what I did to the Egyptians. You know how I carried you on eagles' wings and brought you to myself. [5]Now if you will obey me and keep my covenant, you will be my own special treasure from among all the peoples on earth; for all the earth belongs to me. [6]And you will be my kingdom of priests, my holy nation.' This is the message you must give to the people of Israel."

[7]So Moses returned from the mountain and called together the elders of the people and told them everything the LORD had commanded him. [8]And all the people responded together, "We will do everything the LORD has commanded." So Moses brought the people's answer back to the LORD. . . .

[10]Then the LORD told Moses, "Go down and prepare the people for my arrival. Consecrate them today and tomorrow, and have them wash their clothing. [11]Be sure they are ready on the third day, for on that day the LORD will come down on Mount Sinai as all the people watch. . . ."

[14]So Moses went down to the people. He consecrated them for worship, and they washed their clothes. [15]He told them, "Get ready for the third day, and until then abstain from having sexual intercourse."

[16]On the morning of the third day, thunder roared and lightning flashed, and a dense cloud came down on the mountain. There was a long, loud blast from a ram's horn, and all the people trembled. [17]Moses led them out from the camp to meet with God, and they stood at the foot of the mountain. [18]All of Mount Sinai was covered with smoke because the LORD had descended on it in the form of fire. The smoke billowed into the sky like smoke from a brick kiln, and the whole mountain shook violently. [19]As the blast of the ram's horn grew louder and louder, Moses spoke, and God thundered his reply. [20]The LORD came down on the top of Mount Sinai and called Moses to the top of the mountain. So Moses climbed the mountain.

How would you prepare to meet with God? In Genesis 15 and 17, God made a covenant with Abraham, promising to make his descendants into a great nation. Here that promise was being realized as God restated his agreement with the Israelite nation, the descendants of Abraham. God promised to bless and care for them. The people promised to obey him. The covenant was thus sealed. But the good intentions of the people quickly wore off. Have you made a commitment to God? How are you holding up your end of the bargain?

The Ten Commandments

FEBRUARY 14

EXODUS 20:1-17

Then God gave the people all these instructions:

[2]"I am the LORD your God, who rescued you from the land of Egypt, the place of your slavery.
[3]"You must not have any other god but me.
[4]"You must not make for yourself an idol of any kind or an image of anything in the heavens
or on the earth or in the sea. [5]You must not bow down to them or worship them, for I,
the LORD your God, am a jealous God who will not tolerate your affection for any other
gods. I lay the sins of the parents upon their children; the entire family is affected—even
children in the third and fourth generations of those who reject me. [6]But I lavish unfailing
love for a thousand generations on those who love me and obey my commands.
[7]"You must not misuse the name of the LORD your God. The LORD will not let you go
unpunished if you misuse his name.
[8]"Remember to observe the Sabbath day by keeping it holy. [9]You have six days each week
for your ordinary work, [10]but the seventh day is a Sabbath day of rest dedicated to the
LORD your God. On that day no one in your household may do any work. This includes
you, your sons and daughters, your male and female servants, your livestock, and any
foreigners living among you. [11]For in six days the LORD made the heavens, the earth, the
sea, and everything in them; but on the seventh day he rested. That is why the LORD
blessed the Sabbath day and set it apart as holy.
[12]"Honor your father and mother. Then you will live a long, full life in the land the LORD
your God is giving you.
[13]"You must not murder.
[14]"You must not commit adultery.
[15]"You must not steal.
[16]"You must not testify falsely against your neighbor.
[17]"You must not covet your neighbor's house. You must not covet your neighbor's wife, male
or female servant, ox or donkey, or anything else that belongs to your neighbor."

How often do you think about God's standards? The command to "honor your father and mother" has a clear promise attached. To live in peace for generations in the Promised Land, the Israelites would need to respect authority and build strong families. But what does it mean to "honor" your parents? Partly, it means speaking well of them and politely to them. It also means acting in a way that shows them courtesy and respect (but not to obey them if this means disobedience to God). It means following their teaching and example of putting God first. Parents have a special place in God's sight. Even those who find it difficult to get along with their parents are still commanded to honor them.

FEBRUARY 15

The Golden Calf

EXODUS 32:1-20

When the people saw how long it was taking Moses to come back down the mountain, they
gathered around Aaron. “Come on,” they said, “make us some gods who can lead us. We don’t
know what happened to this fellow Moses, who brought us here from the land of Egypt.”
2So Aaron said, “Take the gold rings from the ears of your wives and sons and daughters,
and bring them to me.”
3All the people took the gold rings from their ears and brought them to Aaron. 4Then
Aaron took the gold, melted it down, and molded it into the shape of a calf. When the
people saw it, they exclaimed, “O Israel, these are the gods who brought you out of the land
of Egypt!”
5Aaron saw how excited the people were, so he built an altar in front of the calf. Then he
announced, “Tomorrow will be a festival to the Lord!”
6The people got up early the next morning to sacrifice burnt offerings and peace offerings.
After this, they celebrated with feasting and drinking, and they indulged in pagan revelry.
7The Lord told Moses, “Quick! Go down the mountain! Your people whom you brought
from the land of Egypt have corrupted themselves. 8How quickly they have turned away from
the way I commanded them to live! They have melted down gold and made a calf, and they
have bowed down and sacrificed to it. They are saying, ‘These are your gods, O Israel, who
brought you out of the land of Egypt.’” . . .
15Then Moses turned and went down the mountain. He held in his hands the two stone
tablets inscribed with the terms of the covenant. They were inscribed on both sides, front
and back. 16These tablets were God’s work; the words on them were written by God himself.
17When Joshua heard the boisterous noise of the people shouting below them, he
exclaimed to Moses, “It sounds like war in the camp!”
18But Moses replied, “No, it’s not a shout of victory nor the wailing of defeat. I hear the
sound of a celebration.”
19When they came near the camp, Moses saw the calf and the dancing, and he burned
with anger. He threw the stone tablets to the ground, smashing them at the foot of the
mountain. 20He took the calf they had made and burned it. Then he ground it into powder,
threw it into the water, and forced the people to drink it.

What distracts you from obeying God? Even though Israel had seen the invisible God in action, they still wanted the familiar gods they could see. How much like them we are! Our great temptation is still to shape God to our liking, to make him convenient to obey or ignore. God responds in great anger when his mercy is trampled on. The gods we create blind us to the love that the living God wants to shower on us. God cannot work in us when we elevate anyone or anything above him. What idols are in your life?

Instructions about God's Tabernacle

EXODUS 40:1-34

Then the LORD said to Moses, 2"Set up the Tabernacle on the first day of the new year. 3Place
the Ark of the Covenant inside, and install the inner curtain to enclose the Ark within the
Most Holy Place. 4Then bring in the table, and arrange the utensils on it. And bring in the
lampstand, and set up the lamps.

5"Place the gold incense altar in front of the Ark of the Covenant. Then hang the curtain
at the entrance of the Tabernacle. 6Place the altar of burnt offering in front of the Tabernacle
entrance. 7Set the washbasin between the Tabernacle and the altar, and fill it with water.
8Then set up the courtyard around the outside of the tent, and hang the curtain for the
courtyard entrance.

9"Take the anointing oil and anoint the Tabernacle and all its furnishings to consecrate
them and make them holy. 10Anoint the altar of burnt offering and its utensils to consecrate
them. Then the altar will become absolutely holy. 11Next anoint the washbasin and its stand
to consecrate them.

12"Present Aaron and his sons at the entrance of the Tabernacle, and wash them with
water. 13Dress Aaron with the sacred garments and anoint him, consecrating him to serve me
as a priest. 14Then present his sons and dress them in their tunics. 15Anoint them as you did
their father, so they may also serve me as priests. With their anointing, Aaron's descendants
are set apart for the priesthood forever, from generation to generation."

16Moses proceeded to do everything just as the LORD had commanded him. 17So the
Tabernacle was set up on the first day of the first month of the second year. 18Moses erected
the Tabernacle by setting down its bases, inserting the frames, attaching the crossbars, and
setting up the posts. 19Then he spread the coverings over the Tabernacle framework and put
on the protective layers, just as the LORD had commanded him.

20He took the stone tablets inscribed with the terms of the covenant and placed them
inside the Ark. Then he attached the carrying poles to the Ark, and he set the Ark's cover—
the place of atonement—on top of it. 21Then he brought the Ark of the Covenant into the
Tabernacle and hung the inner curtain to shield it from view, just as the LORD had commanded him. . . .

34Then the cloud covered the Tabernacle, and the glory of the LORD filled the Tabernacle.

When are you most aware of God's presence in your life? God told Moses how to build the Tabernacle, and Moses obeyed immediately. God allows people to participate with him in carrying out his will. Your task is not just to sit and watch God work but to give your best effort when work needs to be done.

FEBRUARY 17

Moses under Fire

NUMBERS 12:1-15

While they were at Hazeroth, Miriam and Aaron criticized Moses because he had married a
Cushite woman. 2They said, "Has the LORD spoken only through Moses? Hasn't he spoken
through us, too?" But the LORD heard them. 3(Now Moses was very humble—more humble
than any other person on earth.)

4So immediately the LORD called to Moses, Aaron, and Miriam and said, "Go out to the
Tabernacle, all three of you!" So the three of them went to the Tabernacle. 5Then the LORD
descended in the pillar of cloud and stood at the entrance of the Tabernacle. "Aaron and
Miriam!" he called, and they stepped forward. 6And the LORD said to them, "Now listen to
what I say:

"If there were prophets among you,
  I, the LORD, would reveal myself in visions.
  I would speak to them in dreams.
7But not with my servant Moses.
  Of all my house, he is the one I trust.
8I speak to him face to face,
  clearly, and not in riddles!
  He sees the LORD as he is.
So why were you not afraid
  to criticize my servant Moses?"

9The LORD was very angry with them, and he departed. 10As the cloud moved from above
the Tabernacle, there stood Miriam, her skin as white as snow from leprosy. When Aaron saw
what had happened to her, 11he cried out to Moses, "Oh, my master! Please don't punish us
for this sin we have so foolishly committed. 12Don't let her be like a stillborn baby, already
decayed at birth."

13So Moses cried out to the LORD, "O God, I beg you, please heal her!"

14But the LORD said to Moses, "If her father had done nothing more than spit in her face,
wouldn't she be defiled for seven days? So keep her outside the camp for seven days, and after
that she may be accepted back."

15So Miriam was kept outside the camp for seven days, and the people waited until she
was brought back before they traveled again.

What do you do when you find yourself feeling jealous of someone? People often argue over minor disagreements, leaving the real issue untouched. Miriam and Aaron were jealous of Moses' position and influence. Since they could not find fault with the way Moses was leading the people, they chose to criticize his wife. When you are in a disagreement, stop and ask yourself if you are arguing over the real issue or if you have introduced a smoke screen by attacking someone's character. If you are unjustly criticized, remember that your critics may be afraid to face the real problem. Don't take this type of criticism personally. Ask God to help you identify the real issue and deal with it.

Spying on the Promised Land

FEBRUARY 18

NUMBERS 13:1–14:4

The LORD now said to Moses, 2“Send out men to explore the land of Canaan, the land I am giving to the Israelites. Send one leader from each of the twelve ancestral tribes.” . . .

25After exploring the land for forty days, the men returned 26to Moses, Aaron, and the whole community of Israel at Kadesh in the wilderness of Paran. They reported to the whole community what they had seen and showed them the fruit they had taken from the land. 27This was their report to Moses: “We entered the land you sent us to explore, and it is indeed a bountiful country—a land flowing with milk and honey. Here is the kind of fruit it produces. 28But the people living there are powerful, and their towns are large and fortified. We even saw giants there, the descendants of Anak! 29The Amalekites live in the Negev, and the Hittites, Jebusites, and Amorites live in the hill country. The Canaanites live along the coast of the Mediterranean Sea and along the Jordan Valley.”

30But Caleb tried to quiet the people as they stood before Moses. “Let’s go at once to take the land,” he said. “We can certainly conquer it!”

31But the other men who had explored the land with him disagreed. “We can’t go up against them! They are stronger than we are!” 32So they spread this bad report about the land among the Israelites: “The land we traveled through and explored will devour anyone who goes to live there. All the people we saw were huge. 33We even saw giants there, the descendants of Anak. Next to them we felt like grasshoppers, and that’s what they thought, too!”

14:1Then the whole community began weeping aloud, and they cried all night. 2Their voices rose in a great chorus of protest against Moses and Aaron. “If only we had died in Egypt, or even here in the wilderness!” they complained. 3“Why is the LORD taking us to this country only to have us die in battle? Our wives and our little ones will be carried off as plunder! Wouldn’t it be better for us to return to Egypt?” 4Then they plotted among themselves, “Let’s choose a new leader and go back to Egypt!”

How does knowing God change how you think about the word *impossible*? The Israelites didn’t trust God—they believed victory was impossible. In their self-doubt, their decision made sense. But they failed to realize that God doesn’t operate from a human perspective. A promise from God is a sure thing, no matter how unlikely it seems. Caleb stood for the truth he knew about God. God had said very plainly that he would help the people conquer the Promised Land. But the other spies forgot what they knew about God and made their decision on the basis of what they knew of themselves. Are you willing to stand against the pressure of popular opinion to do what God’s Word says?

FEBRUARY 19

A Majority That Was Wrong

NUMBERS 14:6-45

[6]Two of the men who had explored the land, Joshua son of Nun and Caleb son of Jephunneh, tore their clothing. [7]They said to all the people of Israel, "The land we traveled through and explored is a wonderful land! [8]And if the LORD is pleased with us, he will bring us safely into that land and give it to us. It is a rich land flowing with milk and honey. [9]Do not rebel against the LORD, and don't be afraid of the people of the land. . . ."

[10]But the whole community began to talk about stoning Joshua and Caleb. Then the glorious presence of the LORD appeared to all the Israelites at the Tabernacle. [11]And the LORD said to Moses, "How long will these people treat me with contempt? Will they never believe me, even after all the miraculous signs I have done among them? [12]I will disown them and destroy them with a plague. Then I will make you into a nation greater and mightier than they are!"

[13]But Moses objected. . . .

[17]"Please, Lord, prove that your power is as great as you have claimed. For you said, [18]'The LORD is slow to anger and filled with unfailing love, forgiving every kind of sin and rebellion. . . . [19]In keeping with your magnificent, unfailing love, please pardon the sins of this people, just as you have forgiven them ever since they left Egypt."

[20]Then the LORD said, "I will pardon them as you have requested. [21]But as surely as I live, and as surely as the earth is filled with the LORD's glory, [22]not one of these people will ever enter that land. . . ."

[39]When Moses reported the LORD's words to all the Israelites, the people were filled with grief. [40]Then they got up early the next morning and went to the top of the range of hills. "Let's go," they said. "We realize that we have sinned, but now we are ready to enter the land the LORD has promised us."

[41]But Moses said, "Why are you now disobeying the LORD's orders to return to the wilderness? It won't work. [42]Do not go up into the land now. You will only be crushed by your enemies because the LORD is not with you. [43]When you face the Amalekites and Canaanites in battle, you will be slaughtered. The LORD will abandon you because you have abandoned the LORD."

[44]But the people defiantly pushed ahead toward the hill country, even though neither Moses nor the Ark of the LORD's Covenant left the camp. [45]Then the Amalekites and the Canaanites who lived in those hills came down and attacked them and chased them back as far as Hormah.

How often are your decisions based on peer pressure? When the Israelites realized their foolish mistake, they were suddenly ready to return to God. But God didn't confuse their admission of guilt with true repentance, because he knew their hearts. Sure enough, they soon went their own way again. Sometimes good actions or intentions come too late. We must not only act rightly but also act at the right time. The kind of obedience God wants is complete and instant.

The Bronze Snake

FEBRUARY 20

NUMBERS 21:4-9

4 Then the people of Israel set out from Mount Hor, taking the road to the Red Sea to go
around the land of Edom. But the people grew impatient with the long journey, 5 and they
began to speak against God and Moses. "Why have you brought us out of Egypt to die here
in the wilderness?" they complained. "There is nothing to eat here and nothing to drink.
And we hate this horrible manna!"

6 So the LORD sent poisonous snakes among the people, and many were bitten and died.
7 Then the people came to Moses and cried out, "We have sinned by speaking against the
LORD and against you. Pray that the LORD will take away the snakes." So Moses prayed for
the people.

8 Then the LORD told him, "Make a replica of a poisonous snake and attach it to a pole.
All who are bitten will live if they simply look at it!" 9 So Moses made a snake out of bronze
and attached it to a pole. Then anyone who was bitten by a snake could look at the bronze
snake and be healed!

What can you do to avoid repeating mistakes? When the bronze snake was hung on the pole, the Israelites didn't know the fuller meaning Jesus Christ would bring to this event (see John 3:14-15). Jesus explained that just as the Israelites were rescued from death by looking at the snake on the pole, all believers today can be rescued from eternal death by looking to Jesus on the cross. It was not the snake that healed the people but their belief that God could heal them, which was demonstrated by their obedience to God's instructions. In the same way, we should continue to look to Christ (see Hebrews 12:2).

FEBRUARY 21

Balaam and His Donkey

NUMBERS 22:4-34

4Balak, king of Moab, 5sent messengers to call Balaam son of Beor, who was living in his native land of Pethor near the Euphrates River. His message said:

> "Look, a vast horde of people has arrived from Egypt. They cover the face of the earth and are threatening me. 6Please come and curse these people for me because they are too powerful for me. Then perhaps I will be able to conquer them and drive them from the land. I know that blessings fall on any people you bless, and curses fall on people you curse."

7Balak's messengers, who were elders of Moab and Midian, set out with money to pay Balaam to place a curse upon Israel. . . .

22But God was angry that Balaam was going, so he sent the angel of the Lord to stand in the road to block his way. As Balaam and two servants were riding along, 23Balaam's donkey saw the angel of the Lord standing in the road with a drawn sword in his hand. The donkey bolted off the road into a field, but Balaam beat it and turned it back onto the road. 24Then the angel of the Lord stood at a place where the road narrowed between two vineyard walls. 25When the donkey saw the angel of the Lord, it tried to squeeze by and crushed Balaam's foot against the wall. So Balaam beat the donkey again. 26Then the angel of the Lord moved farther down the road and stood in a place too narrow for the donkey to get by at all. 27This time when the donkey saw the angel, it lay down under Balaam. In a fit of rage Balaam beat the animal again with his staff.

28Then the Lord gave the donkey the ability to speak. "What have I done to you that deserves your beating me three times?" it asked Balaam. . . .

31Then the Lord opened Balaam's eyes, and he saw the angel of the Lord standing in the roadway with a drawn sword in his hand. Balaam bowed his head and fell face down on the ground before him.

32"Why did you beat your donkey those three times?" the angel of the Lord demanded. "Look, I have come to block your way because you are stubbornly resisting me. 33Three times the donkey saw me and shied away; otherwise, I would certainly have killed you by now and spared the donkey."

34Then Balaam confessed to the angel of the Lord, "I have sinned. I didn't realize you were standing in the road to block my way. I will return home if you are against my going."

What happens when you do what you know you shouldn't do? God let Balaam go with Balak's messengers, but he was angry about Balaam's greedy attitude. Balaam claimed that he would not go against God just for money, but his resolve was slipping. The wealth offered by the king blinded him; he could not see how God was trying to stop him. We may know what God wants us to do, but we can be blinded by desires. We can avoid Balaam's mistake by looking past the allure of fame or fortune to the long-range benefits of following God.

Moses Reviews God's Actions

DEUTERONOMY 29:2-29

2 Moses summoned all the Israelites and said to them, "You have seen with your own eyes everything the LORD did in the land of Egypt to Pharaoh and to all his servants and to his whole country—3 all the great tests of strength, the miraculous signs, and the amazing wonders. 4 But to this day the LORD has not given you minds that understand, nor eyes that see, nor ears that hear! 5 For forty years I led you through the wilderness, yet your clothes and sandals did not wear out. 6 You ate no bread and drank no wine or other alcoholic drink, but he provided for you so you would know that he is the LORD your God. . . .

9 "Therefore, obey the terms of this covenant so that you will prosper in everything you do. . . .

19 "Those who hear the warnings of this curse should not congratulate themselves, thinking, 'I am safe, even though I am following the desires of my own stubborn heart.' This would lead to utter ruin! 20 The LORD will never pardon such people. Instead his anger and jealousy will burn against them. All the curses written in this book will come down on them, and the LORD will erase their names from under heaven. 21 The LORD will separate them from all the tribes of Israel, to pour out on them all the curses of the covenant recorded in this Book of Instruction.

22 "Then the generations to come, both your own descendants and the foreigners who come from distant lands, will see the devastation of the land and the diseases the LORD inflicts on it. 23 They will exclaim, 'The whole land is devastated by sulfur and salt. It is a wasteland with nothing planted and nothing growing, not even a blade of grass. It is like the cities of Sodom and Gomorrah, Admah and Zeboiim, which the LORD destroyed in his intense anger.'

24 "And all the surrounding nations will ask, 'Why has the LORD done this to this land? Why was he so angry?'

25 "And the answer will be, 'This happened because the people of the land abandoned the covenant that the LORD, the God of their ancestors, made with them when he brought them out of the land of Egypt. 26 Instead, they turned away to serve and worship gods they had not known before, gods that were not from the LORD. . . .

29 "The LORD our God has secrets known to no one. We are not accountable for them, but we and our children are accountable forever for all that he has revealed to us, so that we may obey all the terms of these instructions."

What is the best way to prosper in life? For the Israelites, their first step was to keep their part of the covenant (verse 9). At Mount Sinai forty years earlier, God and Israel had made a covenant (Exodus 20). Its purpose can be summed up in two sentences: God promised to bless the Israelites by making them the nation through whom the rest of the world could know him. In return, the Israelites promised to love and obey God in order to receive physical and spiritual blessings. Today, God's people should do no less; we must love and obey God.

FEBRUARY 23

God Gives a Choice

DEUTERONOMY 30:1-20

"In the future, when you experience all these blessings and curses I have listed for you, and when you are living among the nations to which the LORD your God has exiled you, take to heart all these instructions. 2If at that time you and your children return to the LORD your God, and if you obey with all your heart and all your soul all the commands I have given you today, 3then the LORD your God will restore your fortunes. He will have mercy on you and gather you back from all the nations where he has scattered you. . . .

9"The LORD your God will then make you successful in everything you do. He will give you many children and numerous livestock, and he will cause your fields to produce abundant harvests, for the LORD will again delight in being good to you as he was to your ancestors. 10The LORD your God will delight in you if you obey his voice and keep the commands and decrees written in this Book of Instruction, and if you turn to the LORD your God with all your heart and soul.

11"This command I am giving you today is not too difficult for you, and it is not beyond your reach. 12It is not kept in heaven, so distant that you must ask, 'Who will go up to heaven and bring it down so we can hear it and obey?' 13It is not kept beyond the sea, so far away that you must ask, 'Who will cross the sea to bring it to us so we can hear it and obey?' 14No, the message is very close at hand; it is on your lips and in your heart so that you can obey it.

15"Now listen! Today I am giving you a choice between life and death, between prosperity and disaster. 16For I command you this day to love the LORD your God and to keep his commands, decrees, and regulations by walking in his ways. If you do this, you will live and multiply, and the LORD your God will bless you and the land you are about to enter and occupy.

17"But if your heart turns away and you refuse to listen, and if you are drawn away to serve and worship other gods, 18then I warn you now that you will certainly be destroyed. You will not live a long, good life in the land you are crossing the Jordan to occupy.

19"Today I have given you the choice between life and death, between blessings and curses. Now I call on heaven and earth to witness the choice you make. Oh, that you would choose life, so that you and your descendants might live! 20You can make this choice by loving the LORD your God, obeying him, and committing yourself firmly to him. This is the key to your life. And if you love and obey the LORD, you will live long in the land the LORD swore to give your ancestors Abraham, Isaac, and Jacob."

How do you show that you love God? Moses challenged Israel to show their love for God by choosing to obey him and thereby continue to experience his blessings. God doesn't force his will on anyone. He lets us decide whether to follow him or reject him. This decision, however, is a life-or-death matter. God wants us to realize this, for he would like us all to choose life. Daily, in each new situation, we must decide again.

Moses Appoints Joshua

FEBRUARY 24

DEUTERONOMY 31:1-8

When Moses had finished giving these instructions to all the people of Israel, 2he said, "I am
now 120 years old, and I am no longer able to lead you. The LORD has told me, 'You will not
cross the Jordan River.' 3But the LORD your God himself will cross over ahead of you. He will
destroy the nations living there, and you will take possession of their land. Joshua will lead
you across the river, just as the LORD promised.

4"The LORD will destroy the nations living in the land, just as he destroyed Sihon and Og,
the kings of the Amorites. 5The LORD will hand over to you the people who live there, and
you must deal with them as I have commanded you. 6So be strong and courageous! Do not
be afraid and do not panic before them. For the LORD your God will personally go ahead of
you. He will neither fail you nor abandon you."

7Then Moses called for Joshua, and as all Israel watched, he said to him, "Be strong and
courageous! For you will lead these people into the land that the LORD swore to their ancestors he would give them. You are the one who will divide it among them as their grants of
land. 8Do not be afraid or discouraged, for the LORD will personally go ahead of you. He will
be with you; he will neither fail you nor abandon you."

If you were Joshua, who would be "Moses" in your life? Joshua had been Moses' assistant for many years and had learned much from him (Joshua 1:1). One of his key qualifications was his faith. Joshua had been appointed to take over the leadership of Israel and guide the people into the Promised Land, since Moses could not enter the land due to his disobedience (Numbers 20:12). Indeed, this was a frightening task with three million people to care for, settle disputes for, and lead into battle. Finding courage would be Joshua's greatest test. He was strong and courageous because he knew God was with him and because he had faith that God would do all he had promised to Israel.

FEBRUARY 25

The Death of Moses

DEUTERONOMY 34:1-12

Then Moses went up to Mount Nebo from the plains of Moab and climbed Pisgah Peak, which is across from Jericho. And the LORD showed him the whole land, from Gilead as far as Dan; 2all the land of Naphtali; the land of Ephraim and Manasseh; all the land of Judah, extending to the Mediterranean Sea; 3the Negev; the Jordan Valley with Jericho—the city of palms—as far as Zoar. 4Then the LORD said to Moses, "This is the land I promised on oath to Abraham, Isaac, and Jacob when I said, 'I will give it to your descendants.' I have now allowed you to see it with your own eyes, but you will not enter the land."

5So Moses, the servant of the LORD, died there in the land of Moab, just as the LORD had said. 6The LORD buried him in a valley near Beth-peor in Moab, but to this day no one knows the exact place. 7Moses was 120 years old when he died, yet his eyesight was clear, and he was as strong as ever. 8The people of Israel mourned for Moses on the plains of Moab for thirty days, until the customary period of mourning was over.

9Now Joshua son of Nun was full of the spirit of wisdom, for Moses had laid his hands on him. So the people of Israel obeyed him, doing just as the LORD had commanded Moses.

10There has never been another prophet in Israel like Moses, whom the LORD knew face to face. 11The LORD sent him to perform all the miraculous signs and wonders in the land of Egypt against Pharaoh, and all his servants, and his entire land. 12With mighty power, Moses performed terrifying acts in the sight of all Israel.

How would you most like to be remembered? Moses, the man who did not want to be sent to Egypt because his words "get tangled" (Exodus 4:10), delivered the three addresses to Israel that make up the book of Deuteronomy. God gave him the power to develop from a stuttering shepherd into a national leader and powerful orator. His courage, humility, and wisdom molded the Hebrew slaves into a nation. But Moses was one person who did not let success go to his head. In the end, God was still Moses' best friend. His love, respect, and awe for God had grown daily throughout his life. Moses knew that it was not any greatness in himself that made him successful; it was the greatness of the all-powerful God in whom he trusted. Allow God to lead and guide you, to be your friend, and, like Moses, you will live a life of honor, integrity, courage, humility, and wisdom.

Be Strong and Courageous

FEBRUARY 26

JOSHUA 1:1-18

After the death of Moses the LORD's servant, the LORD spoke to Joshua son of Nun, Moses' assistant. He said, 2"Moses my servant is dead. Therefore, the time has come for you to lead these people, the Israelites, across the Jordan River into the land I am giving them. 3I promise you what I promised Moses: 'Wherever you set foot, you will be on land I have given you—4from the Negev wilderness in the south to the Lebanon mountains in the north, from the Euphrates River in the east to the Mediterranean Sea in the west, including all the land of the Hittites.' 5No one will be able to stand against you as long as you live. For I will be with you as I was with Moses. I will not fail you or abandon you.

6"Be strong and courageous, for you are the one who will lead these people to possess all the land I swore to their ancestors I would give them. 7Be strong and very courageous. Be careful to obey all the instructions Moses gave you. Do not deviate from them, turning either to the right or to the left. Then you will be successful in everything you do. 8Study this Book of Instruction continually. Meditate on it day and night so you will be sure to obey everything written in it. Only then will you prosper and succeed in all you do. 9This is my command—be strong and courageous! Do not be afraid or discouraged. For the LORD your God is with you wherever you go."

10Joshua then commanded the officers of Israel, 11"Go through the camp and tell the people to get their provisions ready. In three days you will cross the Jordan River and take possession of the land the LORD your God is giving you." . . .

16They answered Joshua, "We will do whatever you command us, and we will go wherever you send us. 17We will obey you just as we obeyed Moses. And may the LORD your God be with you as he was with Moses. 18Anyone who rebels against your orders and does not obey your words and everything you command will be put to death. So be strong and courageous!"

Which of these qualities would you most need to be like Joshua? Many people think success is based on power, influential personal contacts, and a relentless drive to get ahead. But the strategy for success that God taught Joshua goes against such criteria. He told Joshua that to succeed he must (1) be strong and brave because the task ahead would not be easy, (2) obey God's law, and (3) read and study God's Word daily. To be successful, follow God's words to Joshua. You may not succeed by the world's standards, but you will be a success in God's eyes, and his opinion lasts forever.

FEBRUARY 27

Spies Visit Jericho

JOSHUA 2:1-18

Then Joshua secretly sent out two spies from the Israelite camp at Acacia Grove. He instructed them, “Scout out the land on the other side of the Jordan River, especially around Jericho.” So the two men set out and came to the house of a prostitute named Rahab and stayed there that night.

2But someone told the king of Jericho, “Some Israelites have come here tonight to spy out the land.” 3So the king of Jericho sent orders to Rahab: “Bring out the men who have come into your house, for they have come here to spy out the whole land.”

4Rahab had hidden the two men, but she replied, “Yes, the men were here earlier, but I didn’t know where they were from. 5They left the town at dusk, as the gates were about to close. I don’t know where they went. If you hurry, you can probably catch up with them.” 6(Actually, she had taken them up to the roof and hidden them beneath bundles of flax she had laid out.) 7So the king’s men went looking for the spies along the road leading to the shallow crossings of the Jordan River. And as soon as the king’s men had left, the gate of Jericho was shut.

8Before the spies went to sleep that night, Rahab went up on the roof to talk with them. 9“I know the LORD has given you this land,” she told them. “We are all afraid of you. Everyone in the land is living in terror. . . .

12“Now swear to me by the LORD that you will be kind to me and my family since I have helped you. Give me some guarantee that 13when Jericho is conquered, you will let me live, along with my father and mother, my brothers and sisters, and all their families.”

14“We offer our own lives as a guarantee for your safety,” the men agreed. “If you don’t betray us, we will keep our promise and be kind to you when the LORD gives us the land.”

15Then, since Rahab’s house was built into the town wall, she let them down by a rope through the window. 16“Escape to the hill country,” she told them. “Hide there for three days from the men searching for you. Then, when they have returned, you can go on your way.”

17Before they left, the men told her, “We will be bound by the oath we have taken only if you follow these instructions. 18When we come into the land, you must leave this scarlet rope hanging from the window through which you let us down.”

What people has God used in your life unexpectedly? Why would the spies stop at the house of Rahab the prostitute? (1) It was a good place to gather information and have no questions asked in return. (2) Rahab’s house was in an ideal location for a quick escape because it was built into the city wall. (3) God directed the spies to Rahab’s house because he knew her heart was open to him and that she would be instrumental in the Israelite victory over Jericho. God often uses people with simple faith to accomplish his great purposes, no matter what kind of past they have or how insignificant they seem to be.

The Invasion of Canaan

FEBRUARY 28

JOSHUA 3:1-17

Early the next morning Joshua and all the Israelites left Acacia Grove and arrived at the banks of the Jordan River, where they camped before crossing. . . .

[5]Then Joshua told the people, "Purify yourselves, for tomorrow the LORD will do great wonders among you."

[6]In the morning Joshua said to the priests, "Lift up the Ark of the Covenant and lead the people across the river." And so they started out and went ahead of the people.

[7]The LORD told Joshua, "Today I will begin to make you a great leader in the eyes of all the Israelites. They will know that I am with you, just as I was with Moses. [8]Give this command to the priests who carry the Ark of the Covenant: 'When you reach the banks of the Jordan River, take a few steps into the river and stop there.'"

[9]So Joshua told the Israelites, "Come and listen to what the LORD your God says. [10]Today you will know that the living God is among you. He will surely drive out the Canaanites, Hittites, Hivites, Perizzites, Girgashites, Amorites, and Jebusites ahead of you. [11]Look, the Ark of the Covenant, which belongs to the Lord of the whole earth, will lead you across the Jordan River! [12]Now choose twelve men from the tribes of Israel, one from each tribe. [13]The priests will carry the Ark of the LORD, the Lord of all the earth. As soon as their feet touch the water, the flow of water will be cut off upstream, and the river will stand up like a wall."

[14]So the people left their camp to cross the Jordan, and the priests who were carrying the Ark of the Covenant went ahead of them. [15]It was the harvest season, and the Jordan was overflowing its banks. But as soon as the feet of the priests who were carrying the Ark touched the water at the river's edge, [16]the water above that point began backing up a great distance away at a town called Adam, which is near Zarethan. And the water below that point flowed on to the Dead Sea until the riverbed was dry. Then all the people crossed over near the town of Jericho.

[17]Meanwhile, the priests who were carrying the Ark of the LORD's Covenant stood on dry ground in the middle of the riverbed as the people passed by. They waited there until the whole nation of Israel had crossed the Jordan on dry ground.

How would you illustrate God's guidance in your life? Just before crossing over into the Promised Land, Joshua gathered the people to hear the words of the Lord. Their excitement was high. No doubt they wanted to rush on, but Joshua made them stop and listen. We live in a fast-paced age where we feel we have to rush just to keep up. It is easy to get caught up in our daily tasks, becoming too busy for what God says is most important—listening to his words. Take time to focus on what God wants from you during all your activities. Knowing what God has said before you rush into your day may help you avoid foolish mistakes.

March

MARCH 1

The Battle of Jericho

JOSHUA 5:13–6:19

13When Joshua was near the town of Jericho, he looked up and saw a man standing in front
of him with sword in hand. Joshua went up to him and demanded, "Are you friend or foe?"
14"Neither one," he replied. "I am the commander of the LORD's army."
At this, Joshua fell with his face to the ground in reverence. "I am at your command,"
Joshua said. "What do you want your servant to do?"
15The commander of the LORD's army replied, "Take off your sandals, for the place where
you are standing is holy." And Joshua did as he was told.

6:1Now the gates of Jericho were tightly shut because the people were afraid of the Israelites.
No one was allowed to go out or in. 2But the LORD said to Joshua, "I have given you Jericho,
its king, and all its strong warriors. 3You and your fighting men should march around the
town once a day for six days. 4Seven priests will walk ahead of the Ark, each carrying a ram's
horn. On the seventh day you are to march around the town seven times, with the priests
blowing the horns. 5When you hear the priests give one long blast on the rams' horns, have
all the people shout as loud as they can. Then the walls of the town will collapse, and the
people can charge straight into the town."
6So Joshua called together the priests and said, "Take up the Ark of the LORD's Covenant,
and assign seven priests to walk in front of it, each carrying a ram's horn." 7Then he gave
orders to the people: "March around the town, and the armed men will lead the way in front
of the Ark of the LORD." . . .
15On the seventh day the Israelites got up at dawn and marched around the town as
they had done before. But this time they went around the town seven times. 16The seventh
time around, as the priests sounded the long blast on their horns, Joshua commanded the
people, "Shout! For the LORD has given you the town! 17Jericho and everything in it must be
completely destroyed as an offering to the LORD. Only Rahab the prostitute and the others
in her house will be spared, for she protected our spies.
18"Do not take any of the things set apart for destruction, or you yourselves will be completely destroyed, and you will bring trouble on the camp of Israel. 19Everything made from
silver, gold, bronze, or iron is sacred to the LORD and must be brought into his treasury."

How serious are you about allowing God to use you? It must have seemed strange to the Israelites that instead of going to battle, they were going to march around the city for a week! But this was God's plan, and the Israelites had a guaranteed victory if they would follow it. As strange as the plan sounded, it worked. God may require you to do things that don't make sense at first. Even as you follow him, you may wonder how things can possibly work out. Like the Israelites, take one day at a time and follow step-by-step. You may not see the logic of God's plan until after you have obeyed.

Ultimate Consequences

MARCH 2

JOSHUA 7:1-13

But Israel violated the instructions about the things set apart for the LORD. A man named
Achan had stolen some of these dedicated things, so the LORD was very angry with the
Israelites. Achan was the son of Carmi, a descendant of Zimri son of Zerah, of the tribe of
Judah.
2Joshua sent some of his men from Jericho to spy out the town of Ai, east of Bethel, near
Beth-aven. 3When they returned, they told Joshua, "There's no need for all of us to go up
there; it won't take more than two or three thousand men to attack Ai. Since there are so few
of them, don't make all our people struggle to go up there."
4So approximately 3,000 warriors were sent, but they were soundly defeated. The men
of Ai 5chased the Israelites from the town gate as far as the quarries, and they killed about
thirty-six who were retreating down the slope. The Israelites were paralyzed with fear at this
turn of events, and their courage melted away.
6Joshua and the elders of Israel tore their clothing in dismay, threw dust on their heads,
and bowed face down to the ground before the Ark of the LORD until evening. 7Then Joshua
cried out, "Oh, Sovereign LORD, why did you bring us across the Jordan River if you are going
to let the Amorites kill us? If only we had been content to stay on the other side! 8Lord, what
can I say now that Israel has fled from its enemies? 9For when the Canaanites and all the other
people living in the land hear about it, they will surround us and wipe our name off the face
of the earth. And then what will happen to the honor of your great name?"
10But the LORD said to Joshua, "Get up! Why are you lying on your face like this? 11Israel
has sinned and broken my covenant! They have stolen some of the things that I commanded
must be set apart for me. And they have not only stolen them but have lied about it and
hidden the things among their own belongings. 12That is why the Israelites are running from
their enemies in defeat. For now Israel itself has been set apart for destruction. I will not
remain with you any longer unless you destroy the things among you that were set apart for
destruction.
13"Get up! Command the people to purify themselves in preparation for tomorrow. For
this is what the LORD, the God of Israel, says: Hidden among you, O Israel, are things set
apart for the LORD. You will never defeat your enemies until you remove these things from
among you."

What strongly negative or positive consequences have you experienced? When Joshua first went against Ai, he did not consult God but relied on the strength of his army to defeat the small city. Only after Israel was defeated did they turn to God and ask, "What happened?" Too often we rely on our own skills and strength, especially when the task before us seems easy. We go to God only when the obstacles seem too great. However, only God knows what lies ahead. Consulting him, even when we are on a winning streak, may save us from grave mistakes. God may want us to learn lessons, remove pride, or consult others.

MARCH 3

The Sun Stands Still

JOSHUA 10:1-13

Adoni-zedek, king of Jerusalem, heard that Joshua had captured and completely destroyed Ai and killed its king, just as he had destroyed the town of Jericho and killed its king. He also learned that the Gibeonites had made peace with Israel and were now their allies. 2He and his people became very afraid when they heard all this because Gibeon was a large town—as large as the royal cities and larger than Ai. And the Gibeonite men were strong warriors.

3So King Adoni-zedek of Jerusalem sent messengers to several other kings: Hoham of Hebron, Piram of Jarmuth, Japhia of Lachish, and Debir of Eglon. 4"Come and help me destroy Gibeon," he urged them, "for they have made peace with Joshua and the people of Israel." 5So these five Amorite kings combined their armies for a united attack. They moved all their troops into place and attacked Gibeon.

6The men of Gibeon quickly sent messengers to Joshua at his camp in Gilgal. "Don't abandon your servants now!" they pleaded. "Come at once! Save us! Help us! For all the Amorite kings who live in the hill country have joined forces to attack us."

7So Joshua and his entire army, including his best warriors, left Gilgal and set out for Gibeon. 8"Do not be afraid of them," the Lord said to Joshua, "for I have given you victory over them. Not a single one of them will be able to stand up to you."

9Joshua traveled all night from Gilgal and took the Amorite armies by surprise. 10The Lord threw them into a panic, and the Israelites slaughtered great numbers of them at Gibeon. Then the Israelites chased the enemy along the road to Beth-horon, killing them all along the way to Azekah and Makkedah. 11As the Amorites retreated down the road from Beth-horon, the Lord destroyed them with a terrible hailstorm from heaven that continued until they reached Azekah. The hail killed more of the enemy than the Israelites killed with the sword.

12On the day the Lord gave the Israelites victory over the Amorites, Joshua prayed to the Lord in front of all the people of Israel. He said,

"Let the sun stand still over Gibeon,
    and the moon over the valley of Aijalon."

13So the sun stood still and the moon stayed in place until the nation of Israel had defeated its enemies.

How do you know God is powerful? How did the sun stand still? Of course, in relation to the earth the sun always stands still, but the wording should not cause us to doubt the miracle. After all, we are not confused when someone tells us the sun rises or sets. The point is that the day was prolonged, not that God used a particular method to prolong it. Regardless of God's chosen method, the Bible is clear that the day was prolonged by a miracle, and God's intervention turned the tide of battle for his people. Do not be afraid to ask God for what might seem impossible. If it is in his will, he has the power to do it.

Joshua Warns the Leaders

MARCH 4

JOSHUA 23:1-16

Joshua, who was now very old, [2]called together all the elders, leaders, judges, and officers of Israel. He said to them, “I am now a very old man. [3]You have seen everything the LORD your God has done for you during my lifetime. The LORD your God has fought for you against your enemies. [4]I have allotted to you as your homeland all the land of the nations yet unconquered, as well as the land of those we have already conquered—from the Jordan River to the Mediterranean Sea in the west. . . .

[6]“So be very careful to follow everything Moses wrote in the Book of Instruction. Do not deviate from it, turning either to the right or to the left. [7]Make sure you do not associate with the other people still remaining in the land. Do not even mention the names of their gods, much less swear by them or serve them or worship them. [8]Rather, cling tightly to the LORD your God as you have done until now.

[9]“For the LORD has driven out great and powerful nations for you, and no one has yet been able to defeat you. [10]Each one of you will put to flight a thousand of the enemy, for the LORD your God fights for you, just as he has promised. [11]So be very careful to love the LORD your God.

[12]“But if you turn away from him and cling to the customs of the survivors of these nations remaining among you, and if you intermarry with them, [13]then know for certain that the LORD your God will no longer drive them out of your land. Instead, they will be a snare and a trap to you, a whip for your backs and thorny brambles in your eyes, and you will vanish from this good land the LORD your God has given you.

[14]“Soon I will die, going the way of everything on earth. Deep in your hearts you know that every promise of the LORD your God has come true. Not a single one has failed! [15]But as surely as the LORD your God has given you the good things he promised, he will also bring disaster on you if you disobey him. He will completely destroy you from this good land he has given you. [16]If you break the covenant of the LORD your God by worshiping and serving other gods, his anger will burn against you, and you will quickly vanish from the good land he has given you.”

Which of Joshua’s warnings do you most need to obey? Joshua knew the nation’s weak spots. Before dying, he called the people together and gave commands to help them where they were most likely to slip: (1) Follow all that is written in the book of the laws of Moses without turning aside. (2) Don’t associate with the heathen nations or worship their gods. (3) Don’t intermarry with the heathen nations. These temptations were right in their backyard. Our associations and relationships can be temptations to us as well. It’s wise to identify our weak spots before we break down. Then we can develop strategies to overcome these temptations instead of being overcome by them.

MARCH 5

Joshua's Last Words

JOSHUA 24:2-31

2Joshua said to the people, "This is what the LORD, the God of Israel, says: . . .

13"I gave you land you had not worked on, and I gave you towns you did not build—the towns where you are now living. I gave you vineyards and olive groves for food, though you did not plant them.

14"So fear the LORD and serve him wholeheartedly. Put away forever the idols your ancestors worshiped when they lived beyond the Euphrates River and in Egypt. Serve the LORD alone. 15But if you refuse to serve the LORD, then choose today whom you will serve. Would you prefer the gods your ancestors served beyond the Euphrates? Or will it be the gods of the Amorites in whose land you now live? But as for me and my family, we will serve the LORD."

16The people replied, "We would never abandon the LORD and serve other gods. 17For the LORD our God is the one who rescued us and our ancestors from slavery in the land of Egypt. He performed mighty miracles before our very eyes. As we traveled through the wilderness among our enemies, he preserved us. 18It was the LORD who drove out the Amorites and the other nations living here in the land. So we, too, will serve the LORD, for he alone is our God."

19Then Joshua warned the people, "You are not able to serve the LORD, for he is a holy and jealous God. He will not forgive your rebellion and your sins. 20If you abandon the LORD and serve other gods, he will turn against you and destroy you, even though he has been so good to you."

21But the people answered Joshua, "No, we will serve the LORD!"

22"You are a witness to your own decision," Joshua said. "You have chosen to serve the LORD."

"Yes," they replied, "we are witnesses to what we have said."

23"All right then," Joshua said, "destroy the idols among you, and turn your hearts to the LORD, the God of Israel."

24The people said to Joshua, "We will serve the LORD our God. We will obey him alone."

25So Joshua made a covenant with the people that day at Shechem, committing them to follow the decrees and regulations of the LORD. . . .

31The people of Israel served the LORD throughout the lifetime of Joshua and of the elders who outlived him—those who had personally experienced all that the LORD had done for Israel.

How can you get hope from history? The people had to decide whether they would obey the Lord, who had proven his trustworthiness, or obey the local gods, which were only man-made idols. It's easy to slip into a quiet rebellion—going about life in your own way. But the time comes when you have to choose who or what will control you. The choice is yours. Will it be God, your own limited personality, or another imperfect substitute? Once you have chosen to be controlled by God's Spirit, reaffirm your choice every day.

Judge Deborah

MARCH 6

JUDGES 4:4-16

4Deborah, the wife of Lappidoth, was a prophet who was judging Israel at that time. 5She
would sit under the Palm of Deborah, between Ramah and Bethel in the hill country of
Ephraim, and the Israelites would go to her for judgment. 6One day she sent for Barak son
of Abinoam, who lived in Kedesh in the land of Naphtali. She said to him, "This is what the
LORD, the God of Israel, commands you: Call out 10,000 warriors from the tribes of Naphtali
and Zebulun at Mount Tabor. 7And I will call out Sisera, commander of Jabin's army, along
with his chariots and warriors, to the Kishon River. There I will give you victory over him."
8Barak told her, "I will go, but only if you go with me."
9"Very well," she replied, "I will go with you. But you will receive no honor in this venture, for the LORD's victory over Sisera will be at the hands of a woman." So Deborah went
with Barak to Kedesh. 10At Kedesh, Barak called together the tribes of Zebulun and Naphtali,
and 10,000 warriors went up with him. Deborah also went with him.
11Now Heber the Kenite, a descendant of Moses' brother-in-law Hobab, had moved
away from the other members of his tribe and pitched his tent by the oak of Zaanannim
near Kedesh.
12When Sisera was told that Barak son of Abinoam had gone up to Mount Tabor,
13he called for all 900 of his iron chariots and all of his warriors, and they marched from
Harosheth-haggoyim to the Kishon River.
14Then Deborah said to Barak, "Get ready! This is the day the LORD will give you victory
over Sisera, for the LORD is marching ahead of you." So Barak led his 10,000 warriors down
the slopes of Mount Tabor into battle. 15When Barak attacked, the LORD threw Sisera and
all his chariots and warriors into a panic. Sisera leaped down from his chariot and escaped
on foot. 16Then Barak chased the chariots and the enemy army all the way to Harosheth-
haggoyim, killing all of Sisera's warriors. Not a single one was left alive.

How do people know that you care about them? How did Deborah command such respect? She was responsible for leading the people into battle, but more than that, she influenced them to live for God. Her personality drew people together and commanded the respect of even Barak, a military general. She was also a prophet, whose main role was to encourage the people to obey God. If you are a leader among your friends, don't forget about the spiritual condition of those being led. A true leader is concerned about people, not just success.

MARCH 7

Gideon Becomes a Judge

JUDGES 6:1-40

The Israelites did evil in the LORD's sight. So the LORD handed them over to the Midianites
for seven years. 2The Midianites were so cruel that the Israelites made hiding places for themselves in the mountains, caves, and strongholds. . . .

11Then the angel of the LORD came and sat beneath the great tree at Ophrah, which
belonged to Joash of the clan of Abiezer. Gideon son of Joash was threshing wheat at the bottom of a winepress to hide the grain from the Midianites. 12The angel of the LORD appeared
to him and said, "Mighty hero, the LORD is with you!"

13"Sir," Gideon replied, "if the LORD is with us, why has all this happened to us? And
where are all the miracles our ancestors told us about? Didn't they say, 'The LORD brought us
up out of Egypt'? But now the LORD has abandoned us and handed us over to the Midianites."

14Then the LORD turned to him and said, "Go with the strength you have, and rescue
Israel from the Midianites. I am sending you!"

15"But Lord," Gideon replied, "how can I rescue Israel? My clan is the weakest in the
whole tribe of Manasseh, and I am the least in my entire family!"

16The LORD said to him, "I will be with you. And you will destroy the Midianites as if
you were fighting against one man." . . .

36Then Gideon said to God, "If you are truly going to use me to rescue Israel as you
promised, 37prove it to me in this way. I will put a wool fleece on the threshing floor tonight.
If the fleece is wet with dew in the morning but the ground is dry, then I will know that
you are going to help me rescue Israel as you promised." 38And that is just what happened.
When Gideon got up early the next morning, he squeezed the fleece and wrung out a whole
bowlful of water.

39Then Gideon said to God, "Please don't be angry with me, but let me make one more
request. Let me use the fleece for one more test. This time let the fleece remain dry while the
ground around it is wet with dew." 40So that night God did as Gideon asked. The fleece was
dry in the morning, but the ground was covered with dew.

What examples of obedience can be found in your life? Gideon questioned God about the problems he and his nation faced and about God's apparent lack of help. What he didn't acknowledge was the fact that the people had brought calamity upon themselves when they decided to disobey and neglect God. How easy it is to overlook personal accountability and blame our problems on God and others. Unfortunately, this does not solve our problems. When problems come, the first place to look is within. Our first action should be confession to God of sins that may have created our problems.

Gideon's Outnumbered Army

MARCH 8

JUDGES 7:1-14

So Jerub-baal (that is, Gideon) and his army got up early and went as far as the spring of Harod. The armies of Midian were camped north of them in the valley near the hill of Moreh. [2]The LORD said to Gideon, "You have too many warriors with you. If I let all of you fight the Midianites, the Israelites will boast to me that they saved themselves by their own strength. [3]Therefore, tell the people, 'Whoever is timid or afraid may leave this mountain and go home.'" So 22,000 of them went home, leaving only 10,000 who were willing to fight.

[4]But the LORD told Gideon, "There are still too many! Bring them down to the spring, and I will test them to determine who will go with you and who will not." [5]When Gideon took his warriors down to the water, the LORD told him, "Divide the men into two groups. In one group put all those who cup water in their hands and lap it up with their tongues like dogs. In the other group put all those who kneel down and drink with their mouths in the stream." [6]Only 300 of the men drank from their hands. All the others got down on their knees and drank with their mouths in the stream.

[7]The LORD told Gideon, "With these 300 men I will rescue you and give you victory over the Midianites. Send all the others home." [8]So Gideon collected the provisions and rams' horns of the other warriors and sent them home. But he kept the 300 men with him.

The Midianite camp was in the valley just below Gideon. [9]That night the LORD said, "Get up! Go down into the Midianite camp, for I have given you victory over them! [10]But if you are afraid to attack, go down to the camp with your servant Purah. [11]Listen to what the Midianites are saying, and you will be greatly encouraged. Then you will be eager to attack."

So Gideon took Purah and went down to the edge of the enemy camp. [12]The armies of Midian, Amalek, and the people of the east had settled in the valley like a swarm of locusts. Their camels were like grains of sand on the seashore—too many to count! [13]Gideon crept up just as a man was telling his companion about a dream. The man said, "I had this dream, and in my dream a loaf of barley bread came tumbling down into the Midianite camp. It hit a tent, turned it over, and knocked it flat!"

[14]His companion answered, "Your dream can mean only one thing—God has given Gideon son of Joash, the Israelite, victory over Midian and all its allies!"

In what area of your life do you need to trust God more? Facing overwhelming odds, Gideon was afraid. God understood his fear, but he didn't excuse Gideon from his task. Instead he allowed Gideon to slip into the enemy camp and overhear a conversation that would give him courage. Are you facing a battle? God can give you the strength you need for any situation. And don't be startled by the way he helps you. Like Gideon, you must listen to God and be ready to take the first step. Only after you begin to obey God will you find the courage to move ahead.

MARCH 9

Gideon and the Midianites

JUDGES 7:15-25

[15]When Gideon heard the dream and its interpretation, he bowed in worship before the
Lord. Then he returned to the Israelite camp and shouted, "Get up! For the Lord has given
you victory over the Midianite hordes!" [16]He divided the 300 men into three groups and gave
each man a ram's horn and a clay jar with a torch in it.

[17]Then he said to them, "Keep your eyes on me. When I come to the edge of the camp,
do just as I do. [18]As soon as I and those with me blow the rams' horns, blow your horns, too,
all around the entire camp, and shout, 'For the Lord and for Gideon!'"

[19]It was just after midnight, after the changing of the guard, when Gideon and the
100 men with him reached the edge of the Midianite camp. Suddenly, they blew the rams'
horns and broke their clay jars. [20]Then all three groups blew their horns and broke their jars.
They held the blazing torches in their left hands and the horns in their right hands, and they
all shouted, "A sword for the Lord and for Gideon!"

[21]Each man stood at his position around the camp and watched as all the Midianites
rushed around in a panic, shouting as they ran to escape. [22]When the 300 Israelites blew their
rams' horns, the Lord caused the warriors in the camp to fight against each other with their
swords. Those who were not killed fled to places as far away as Beth-shittah near Zererah and
to the border of Abel-meholah near Tabbath.

[23]Then Gideon sent for the warriors of Naphtali, Asher, and Manasseh, who joined in
chasing the army of Midian. [24]Gideon also sent messengers throughout the hill country of
Ephraim, saying, "Come down to attack the Midianites. Cut them off at the shallow crossings
of the Jordan River at Beth-barah."

So all the men of Ephraim did as they were told. [25]They captured Oreb and Zeeb, the
two Midianite commanders, killing Oreb at the rock of Oreb, and Zeeb at the winepress of
Zeeb. And they continued to chase the Midianites. Afterward the Israelites brought the heads
of Oreb and Zeeb to Gideon, who was by the Jordan River.

What can you do when the odds are stacked against you? Gideon's warriors simply watched as the army of Midian fell into panic, confusion, and disordered retreat. Not one man had to draw a sword to defeat the enemy. Gideon's small army could never have brought about such a victory in its own strength. God wanted to demonstrate to Israel that victory depends not on strength or numbers but on obedience and commitment to him. When you face an uphill battle with overwhelming odds stacked against you, remember Gideon and his three hundred men. You and God are unbeatable.

The Birth of Samson

MARCH 10

JUDGES 13:1-24

Again the Israelites did evil in the LORD's sight, so the LORD handed them over to the Philistines, who oppressed them for forty years.

2In those days a man named Manoah from the tribe of Dan lived in the town of Zorah. His wife was unable to become pregnant, and they had no children. 3The angel of the LORD appeared to Manoah's wife and said, "Even though you have been unable to have children, you will soon become pregnant and give birth to a son. 4So be careful; you must not drink wine or any other alcoholic drink nor eat any forbidden food. 5You will become pregnant and give birth to a son, and his hair must never be cut. For he will be dedicated to God as a Nazirite from birth. He will begin to rescue Israel from the Philistines."

6The woman ran and told her husband, "A man of God appeared to me! He looked like one of God's angels, terrifying to see. I didn't ask where he was from, and he didn't tell me his name. 7But he told me, 'You will become pregnant and give birth to a son. You must not drink wine or any other alcoholic drink nor eat any forbidden food. For your son will be dedicated to God as a Nazirite from the moment of his birth until the day of his death.' "

8Then Manoah prayed to the LORD, saying, "Lord, please let the man of God come back to us again and give us more instructions about this son who is to be born."

9God answered Manoah's prayer, and the angel of God appeared once again to his wife as she was sitting in the field. But her husband, Manoah, was not with her. 10So she quickly ran and told her husband, "The man who appeared to me the other day is here again!"

11Manoah ran back with his wife and asked, "Are you the man who spoke to my wife the other day?"

"Yes," he replied, "I am."

12So Manoah asked him, "When your words come true, what kind of rules should govern the boy's life and work?"

13The angel of the LORD replied, "Be sure your wife follows the instructions I gave her. 14She must not eat grapes or raisins, drink wine or any other alcoholic drink, or eat any forbidden food." . . .

24When her son was born, she named him Samson. And the LORD blessed him as he grew up.

In which part of your life do you need more discipline? Samson's tribe, Dan, continued to wander in their inherited land (Judges 18:1), which was yet unconquered (Joshua 19:47-48). God promised that Samson would become a deliverer and would "begin to rescue Israel from the Philistines." As with Samson, this preparation often begins long before adulthood. God uses a variety of means to develop and prepare us: hereditary traits, environmental influences, and personal experiences. Be sensitive to the Holy Spirit's leading and the tasks God has prepared for you. Your past may be more useful to you than you imagine.

MARCH 11

Samson Chooses a Bride

JUDGES 14:1-11

One day when Samson was in Timnah, one of the Philistine women caught his eye. [2]When he returned home, he told his father and mother, "A young Philistine woman in Timnah caught my eye. I want to marry her. Get her for me."

[3]His father and mother objected. "Isn't there even one woman in our tribe or among all the Israelites you could marry?" they asked. "Why must you go to the pagan Philistines to find a wife?"

But Samson told his father, "Get her for me! She looks good to me." [4]His father and mother didn't realize the LORD was at work in this, creating an opportunity to work against the Philistines, who ruled over Israel at that time.

[5]As Samson and his parents were going down to Timnah, a young lion suddenly attacked Samson near the vineyards of Timnah. [6]At that moment the Spirit of the LORD came powerfully upon him, and he ripped the lion's jaws apart with his bare hands. He did it as easily as if it were a young goat. But he didn't tell his father or mother about it. [7]When Samson arrived in Timnah, he talked with the woman and was very pleased with her.

[8]Later, when he returned to Timnah for the wedding, he turned off the path to look at the carcass of the lion. And he found that a swarm of bees had made some honey in the carcass. [9]He scooped some of the honey into his hands and ate it along the way. He also gave some to his father and mother, and they ate it. But he didn't tell them he had taken the honey from the carcass of the lion.

[10]As his father was making final arrangements for the marriage, Samson threw a party at Timnah, as was the custom for elite young men. [11]When the bride's parents saw him, they selected thirty young men from the town to be his companions.

How carefully do you consider the wisdom of your parents? Samson's parents objected to his marrying the Philistine woman for several reasons: (1) It was against God's law (Exodus 34:15-17; Deuteronomy 7:1-4). A stark example of what happened when the Israelites married their heathen neighbors can be found in Judges 3:5-8. (2) The Philistines were Israel's greatest enemies. Marriage to a hated Philistine would be a disgrace to Samson's family. But Samson's father gave in to Samson's demand and allowed the marriage, even though he had the right to refuse his son. Perhaps his father knew Samson wouldn't listen anyway. Your parents know you better than anyone. Be careful to listen to their advice as you make decisions for your life.

Samson's Riddle

MARCH 12

JUDGES 14:12-20

[12]Samson said to them, "Let me tell you a riddle. If you solve my riddle during these seven days of the celebration, I will give you thirty fine linen robes and thirty sets of festive clothing. [13]But if you can't solve it, then you must give me thirty fine linen robes and thirty sets of festive clothing."

"All right," they agreed, "let's hear your riddle."

[14]So he said:

"Out of the one who eats came something to eat;
out of the strong came something sweet."

Three days later they were still trying to figure it out. [15]On the fourth day they said to Samson's wife, "Entice your husband to explain the riddle for us, or we will burn down your father's house with you in it. Did you invite us to this party just to make us poor?"

[16]So Samson's wife came to him in tears and said, "You don't love me; you hate me! You have given my people a riddle, but you haven't told me the answer."

"I haven't even given the answer to my father or mother," he replied. "Why should I tell you?" [17]So she cried whenever she was with him and kept it up for the rest of the celebration. At last, on the seventh day he told her the answer because she was tormenting him with her nagging. Then she explained the riddle to the young men.

[18]So before sunset of the seventh day, the men of the town came to Samson with their answer:

"What is sweeter than honey?
What is stronger than a lion?"

Samson replied, "If you hadn't plowed with my heifer, you wouldn't have solved my riddle!"

[19]Then the Spirit of the Lord came powerfully upon him. He went down to the town of Ashkelon, killed thirty men, took their belongings, and gave their clothing to the men who had solved his riddle. But Samson was furious about what had happened, and he went back home to live with his father and mother. [20]So his wife was given in marriage to the man who had been Samson's best man at the wedding.

How do you use the gifts God has given you? Samson impulsively used the special gift God gave him for selfish purposes. God had given him great strength and he used it to kill thirty men. God gives his followers gifts (special skills and abilities). The apostle Paul states that these gifts are to be used "to do [God's] work and build up the church, the body of Christ" (Ephesians 4:12). To use your abilities for selfish purposes is to rob the church and fellow believers of strength. As you use the gifts God has given you, be sure you are helping others, not just yourself.

MARCH 13

Samson and Delilah

JUDGES 16:4-18

[4]Some time later Samson fell in love with a woman named Delilah, who lived in the valley
of Sorek. [5]The rulers of the Philistines went to her and said, "Entice Samson to tell you what makes him so strong and how he can be overpowered and tied up securely. Then each of us will give you 1,100 pieces of silver."

[6]So Delilah said to Samson, "Please tell me what makes you so strong and what it would take to tie you up securely."

[7]Samson replied, "If I were tied up with seven new bowstrings that have not yet been dried, I would become as weak as anyone else."

[8]So the Philistine rulers brought Delilah seven new bowstrings, and she tied Samson
up with them. [9]She had hidden some men in one of the inner rooms of her house, and she cried out, "Samson! The Philistines have come to capture you!" But Samson snapped the bowstrings as a piece of string snaps when it is burned by a fire. So the secret of his strength was not discovered. . . .

[13]Then Delilah said, "You've been making fun of me and telling me lies! Now tell me how you can be tied up securely."

Samson replied, "If you were to weave the seven braids of my hair into the fabric on your loom and tighten it with the loom shuttle, I would become as weak as anyone else."

So while he slept, Delilah wove the seven braids of his hair into the fabric. [14]Then she
tightened it with the loom shuttle. Again she cried out, "Samson! The Philistines have come to capture you!" But Samson woke up, pulled back the loom shuttle, and yanked his hair away from the loom and the fabric.

[15]Then Delilah pouted, "How can you tell me, 'I love you,' when you don't share your secrets with me? You've made fun of me three times now, and you still haven't told me what
makes you so strong!" [16]She tormented him with her nagging day after day until he was sick
to death of it.

[17]Finally, Samson shared his secret with her. "My hair has never been cut," he confessed, "for I was dedicated to God as a Nazirite from birth. If my head were shaved, my strength would leave me, and I would become as weak as anyone else."

[18]Delilah realized he had finally told her the truth, so she sent for the Philistine rulers. "Come back one more time," she said, "for he has finally told me his secret."

In what situations do you find yourself flirting with disaster? Although he could strangle a lion, Samson could not smother his burning lust and see Delilah for who she really was. How can you keep your desires from deceiving you? (1) You must decide what kind of a person you will love before passion takes over. Determine whether a person's character and faith in God are as desirable as his or her physical appearance. (2) Since most of the time you spend with your spouse will not involve sex, your companion's personality, temperament, and commitment to solve problems must be as gratifying as his or her kisses. (3) Be patient. Wait for time to reveal what is beneath the pleasant appearance and attentive touch.

Samson's Death

MARCH 14

JUDGES 16:22-31

22 But before long, his hair began to grow back.

23 The Philistine rulers held a great festival, offering sacrifices and praising their god, Dagon. They said, "Our god has given us victory over our enemy Samson!"

24 When the people saw him, they praised their god, saying, "Our god has delivered our enemy to us! The one who killed so many of us is now in our power!"

25 Half drunk by now, the people demanded, "Bring out Samson so he can amuse us!" So he was brought from the prison to amuse them, and they had him stand between the pillars supporting the roof.

26 Samson said to the young servant who was leading him by the hand, "Place my hands against the pillars that hold up the temple. I want to rest against them." 27 Now the temple was completely filled with people. All the Philistine rulers were there, and there were about 3,000 men and women on the roof who were watching as Samson amused them.

28 Then Samson prayed to the Lord, "Sovereign Lord, remember me again. O God, please strengthen me just one more time. With one blow let me pay back the Philistines for the loss of my two eyes." 29 Then Samson put his hands on the two center pillars that held up the temple. Pushing against them with both hands, 30 he prayed, "Let me die with the Philistines." And the temple crashed down on the Philistine rulers and all the people. So he killed more people when he died than he had during his entire lifetime.

31 Later his brothers and other relatives went down to get his body. They took him back home and buried him between Zorah and Eshtaol, where his father, Manoah, was buried. Samson had judged Israel for twenty years.

How well do you understand God's patience? In spite of Samson's past, God still answered his prayer and destroyed the heathen temple and worshipers. God still loved him. He was willing to hear Samson's prayer of confession and repentance and use him this final time. Sin in our life keeps us from feeling like praying. But perfect moral behavior is not a condition for prayer. Don't let guilt over your sin keep you apart from God. No matter how long you have been away from God, he is ready to hear from you and restore you to a right relationship. Every situation can be salvaged if you are willing to turn again to him. If God could still work in Samson's situation, he can certainly make something worthwhile out of yours.

MARCH 15

Ruth and Naomi

RUTH 1:1-21

In the days when the judges ruled in Israel, a severe famine came upon the land. So a man
from Bethlehem in Judah left his home and went to live in the country of Moab, taking his
wife and two sons with him. 2The man's name was Elimelech, and his wife was Naomi. Their
two sons were Mahlon and Kilion. They were Ephrathites from Bethlehem in the land of
Judah. And when they reached Moab, they settled there.

3Then Elimelech died, and Naomi was left with her two sons. 4The two sons married
Moabite women. One married a woman named Orpah, and the other a woman named Ruth.
But about ten years later, 5both Mahlon and Kilion died. This left Naomi alone, without her
two sons or her husband.

6Then Naomi heard in Moab that the LORD had blessed his people in Judah by giving
them good crops again. So Naomi and her daughters-in-law got ready to leave Moab to return
to her homeland. 7With her two daughters-in-law she set out from the place where she had
been living, and they took the road that would lead them back to Judah.

8But on the way, Naomi said to her two daughters-in-law, "Go back to your mothers'
homes. And may the LORD reward you for your kindness to your husbands and to me. 9May
the LORD bless you with the security of another marriage." Then she kissed them good-bye,
and they all broke down and wept. . . .

16But Ruth replied, "Don't ask me to leave you and turn back. Wherever you go, I will go;
wherever you live, I will live. Your people will be my people, and your God will be my God.
17Wherever you die, I will die, and there I will be buried. May the LORD punish me severely
if I allow anything but death to separate us!" 18When Naomi saw that Ruth was determined
to go with her, she said nothing more.

19So the two of them continued on their journey. When they came to Bethlehem, the
entire town was excited by their arrival. "Is it really Naomi?" the women asked.

20"Don't call me Naomi," she responded. "Instead, call me Mara, for the Almighty has
made life very bitter for me. 21I went away full, but the LORD has brought me home empty.
Why call me Naomi when the LORD has caused me to suffer and the Almighty has sent such
tragedy upon me?"

How do difficulties affect your friendships? Naomi had experienced severe hardships. She had left Israel married and secure; she returned widowed and poor. Naomi changed her name to express her bitterness and pain. Naomi was not rejecting God by openly expressing her feelings. However, she seems to have lost sight of the tremendous resources she had in her relationship with Ruth and with God. When you face bitter times, God welcomes your honest prayers, but be careful not to overlook the love, strength, and resources that he provides in relationships. And don't allow bitterness and disappointment to blind you to positive opportunities.

Ruth Meets Boaz

MARCH 16

RUTH 2:1-12

Now there was a wealthy and influential man in Bethlehem named Boaz, who was a relative
of Naomi's husband, Elimelech.

2One day Ruth the Moabite said to Naomi, "Let me go out into the harvest fields to pick
up the stalks of grain left behind by anyone who is kind enough to let me do it."

Naomi replied, "All right, my daughter, go ahead." 3So Ruth went out to gather grain
behind the harvesters. And as it happened, she found herself working in a field that belonged
to Boaz, the relative of her father-in-law, Elimelech.

4While she was there, Boaz arrived from Bethlehem and greeted the harvesters. "The
Lord be with you!" he said.

"The Lord bless you!" the harvesters replied.

5Then Boaz asked his foreman, "Who is that young woman over there? Who does she
belong to?"

6And the foreman replied, "She is the young woman from Moab who came back with
Naomi. 7She asked me this morning if she could gather grain behind the harvesters. She has
been hard at work ever since, except for a few minutes' rest in the shelter."

8Boaz went over and said to Ruth, "Listen, my daughter. Stay right here with us when
you gather grain; don't go to any other fields. Stay right behind the young women working
in my field. 9See which part of the field they are harvesting, and then follow them. I have
warned the young men not to treat you roughly. And when you are thirsty, help yourself to
the water they have drawn from the well."

10Ruth fell at his feet and thanked him warmly. "What have I done to deserve such kindness?" she asked. "I am only a foreigner."

11"Yes, I know," Boaz replied. "But I also know about everything you have done for your
mother-in-law since the death of your husband. I have heard how you left your father and
mother and your own land to live here among complete strangers. 12May the Lord, the God
of Israel, under whose wings you have come to take refuge, reward you fully for what you
have done."

When have you found your reputation to be an advantage? Foreigners were not always warmly welcomed in Israel, but Boaz gladly welcomed Ruth because she had gained a reputation for showing kindness and generosity to others. Boaz was so impressed with Ruth that he let her follow directly behind his reapers in order to pick up the best grain that was dropped. Ruth's past actions were a report card by which others judged her. Her good reputation was her most valuable asset. It came as a result of her hard work, her strong moral character, and her sensitivity, kindness, and loyalty to Naomi. A good reputation is built upon godly character and kindness. What kind of reputation are you building?

MARCH 17

Ruth Finds a Husband

RUTH 3:1-15

One day Naomi said to Ruth, "My daughter, it's time that I found a permanent home for you, so that you will be provided for. 2Boaz is a close relative of ours, and he's been very kind by letting you gather grain with his young women. Tonight he will be winnowing barley at the threshing floor. 3Now do as I tell you—take a bath and put on perfume and dress in your nicest clothes. Then go to the threshing floor, but don't let Boaz see you until he has finished eating and drinking. 4Be sure to notice where he lies down; then go and uncover his feet and lie down there. He will tell you what to do."

5"I will do everything you say," Ruth replied. 6So she went down to the threshing floor that night and followed the instructions of her mother-in-law.

7After Boaz had finished eating and drinking and was in good spirits, he lay down at the far end of the pile of grain and went to sleep. Then Ruth came quietly, uncovered his feet, and lay down. 8Around midnight Boaz suddenly woke up and turned over. He was surprised to find a woman lying at his feet! 9"Who are you?" he asked.

"I am your servant Ruth," she replied. "Spread the corner of your covering over me, for you are my family redeemer."

10"The Lord bless you, my daughter!" Boaz exclaimed. "You are showing even more family loyalty now than you did before, for you have not gone after a younger man, whether rich or poor. 11Now don't worry about a thing, my daughter. I will do what is necessary, for everyone in town knows you are a virtuous woman. 12But while it's true that I am one of your family redeemers, there is another man who is more closely related to you than I am. 13Stay here tonight, and in the morning I will talk to him. If he is willing to redeem you, very well. Let him marry you. But if he is not willing, then as surely as the Lord lives, I will redeem you myself! Now lie down here until morning."

14So Ruth lay at Boaz's feet until the morning, but she got up before it was light enough for people to recognize each other. For Boaz had said, "No one must know that a woman was here at the threshing floor." 15Then Boaz said to her, "Bring your cloak and spread it out." He measured six scoops of barley into the cloak and placed it on her back. Then he returned to the town.

What unexpected methods has God used in your life? As a foreigner, Ruth may have thought that Naomi's advice was odd. But Ruth followed her advice because she knew Naomi was kind, trustworthy, and had integrity. Each of us knows a parent, older friend, or relative who is always looking out for our best interests. The experience and knowledge of such a person can be invaluable. Imagine what Ruth's life would have been like had she ignored her mother-in-law. Take care to listen to the advice of trusted people. It may change your life.

A Happy Ending

RUTH 4:1-17

Boaz went to the town gate and took a seat there. Just then the family redeemer he had men-
tioned came by, so Boaz called out to him, "Come over here and sit down, friend. I want to
talk to you." So they sat down together. [2]Then Boaz called ten leaders from the town and
asked them to sit as witnesses. [3]And Boaz said to the family redeemer, "You know Naomi,
who came back from Moab. She is selling the land that belonged to our relative Elimelech.
[4]I thought I should speak to you about it so that you can redeem it if you wish. . . ."

The man replied, "All right, I'll redeem it."

[5]Then Boaz told him, "Of course, your purchase of the land from Naomi also requires
that you marry Ruth, the Moabite widow. That way she can have children who will carry on
her husband's name and keep the land in the family."

[6]"Then I can't redeem it," the family redeemer replied, "because this might endanger my
own estate. You redeem the land; I cannot do it."

[7]Now in those days it was the custom in Israel for anyone transferring a right of purchase
to remove his sandal and hand it to the other party. This publicly validated the transaction.
[8]So the other family redeemer drew off his sandal as he said to Boaz, "You buy the land."

[9]Then Boaz said to the elders and to the crowd standing around, "You are witnesses that
today I have bought from Naomi all the property of Elimelech, Kilion, and Mahlon. [10]And
with the land I have acquired Ruth, the Moabite widow of Mahlon, to be my wife. This way
she can have a son to carry on the family name of her dead husband and to inherit the family
property here in his hometown. You are all witnesses today." . . .

[13]So Boaz took Ruth into his home, and she became his wife. When he slept with her,
the LORD enabled her to become pregnant, and she gave birth to a son. [14]Then the women
of the town said to Naomi, "Praise the LORD, who has now provided a redeemer for your
family! May this child be famous in Israel. [15]May he restore your youth and care for you in
your old age. For he is the son of your daughter-in-law who loves you and has been better
to you than seven sons!"

[16]Naomi took the baby and cuddled him to her breast. And she cared for him as if he were
her own. [17]The neighbor women said, "Now at last Naomi has a son again!" And they named
him Obed. He became the father of Jesse and the grandfather of David.

What future reasons could there be for obeying God today? God brought great blessings out of Naomi's tragedy, even greater blessings than "seven sons" (indicating the great blessing of an abundance of heirs). Throughout her tough times, Naomi continued to trust God. And God, in his time, blessed her greatly. Even in our sorrow and calamity, God can bring great blessings. Be like Naomi, and don't turn your back on God when tragedy strikes. Don't ask, "How can God allow this to happen to me?" Instead, trust him. He will be with you even in the hard times.

MARCH 19

Hannah's Serious Prayer

1 SAMUEL 1:1-28

There was a man named Elkanah . . . [2]Elkanah had two wives, Hannah and Peninnah. Peninnah had children, but Hannah did not. . . .

[9]Once after a sacrificial meal at Shiloh, Hannah got up and went to pray. Eli the priest was sitting at his customary place beside the entrance of the Tabernacle. [10]Hannah was in deep anguish, crying bitterly as she prayed to the LORD. [11]And she made this vow: "O LORD of Heaven's Armies, if you will look upon my sorrow and answer my prayer and give me a son, then I will give him back to you. He will be yours for his entire lifetime, and as a sign that he has been dedicated to the LORD, his hair will never be cut."

[12]As she was praying to the LORD, Eli watched her. [13]Seeing her lips moving but hearing no sound, he thought she had been drinking. [14]"Must you come here drunk?" he demanded. "Throw away your wine!"

[15]"Oh no, sir!" she replied. "I haven't been drinking wine or anything stronger. But I am very discouraged, and I was pouring out my heart to the LORD. [16]Don't think I am a wicked woman! For I have been praying out of great anguish and sorrow."

[17]"In that case," Eli said, "go in peace! May the God of Israel grant the request you have asked of him."

[18]"Oh, thank you, sir!" she exclaimed. Then she went back and began to eat again, and she was no longer sad.

[19]The entire family got up early the next morning and went to worship the LORD once more. Then they returned home to Ramah. When Elkanah slept with Hannah, the LORD remembered her plea, [20]and in due time she gave birth to a son. She named him Samuel, for she said, "I asked the LORD for him." . . .

[24]When the child was weaned, Hannah took him to the Tabernacle in Shiloh. They brought along a three-year-old bull for the sacrifice and a basket of flour and some wine. [25]After sacrificing the bull, they brought the boy to Eli. [26]"Sir, do you remember me?" Hannah asked. "I am the very woman who stood here several years ago praying to the LORD. [27]I asked the LORD to give me this boy, and he has granted my request. [28]Now I am giving him to the LORD, and he will belong to the LORD his whole life." And they worshiped the LORD there.

What promises have you made to God lately that you have kept? Be careful what you promise in prayer because God may take you up on it. Hannah so desperately wanted a child that she was willing to strike a bargain with God. God took her up on her promise, and, to Hannah's credit, she did her part, even though it was painful. Although we are not in a position to barter with God, he may choose to answer a prayer that has an attached promise. When you pray, ask yourself, Will I follow through on any promises I make to God if he grants my request? God keeps his promises, and he expects you to keep yours.

God Calls Samuel

MARCH 20

1 SAMUEL 3:1-21

Meanwhile, the boy Samuel served the Lord by assisting Eli. Now in those days messages from the Lord were very rare, and visions were quite uncommon.

[2]One night Eli, who was almost blind by now, had gone to bed. [3]The lamp of God had not yet gone out, and Samuel was sleeping in the Tabernacle near the Ark of God. [4]Suddenly the Lord called out, "Samuel!"

"Yes?" Samuel replied. "What is it?" [5]He got up and ran to Eli. "Here I am. Did you call me?"

"I didn't call you," Eli replied. "Go back to bed." So he did.

[6]Then the Lord called out again, "Samuel!"

Again Samuel got up and went to Eli. "Here I am. Did you call me?"

"I didn't call you, my son," Eli said. "Go back to bed."

[7]Samuel did not yet know the Lord because he had never had a message from the Lord before. [8]So the Lord called a third time, and once more Samuel got up and went to Eli. "Here I am. Did you call me?"

Then Eli realized it was the Lord who was calling the boy. [9]So he said to Samuel, "Go and lie down again, and if someone calls again, say, 'Speak, Lord, your servant is listening.'" So Samuel went back to bed.

[10]And the Lord came and called as before, "Samuel! Samuel!"

And Samuel replied, "Speak, your servant is listening."

[11]Then the Lord said to Samuel, "I am about to do a shocking thing in Israel. [12]I am going to carry out all my threats against Eli and his family, from beginning to end. [13]I have warned him that judgment is coming upon his family forever, because his sons are blaspheming God and he hasn't disciplined them. [14]So I have vowed that the sins of Eli and his sons will never be forgiven by sacrifices or offerings." . . .

[19]As Samuel grew up, the Lord was with him, and everything Samuel said proved to be reliable. [20]And all Israel, from Dan in the north to Beersheba in the south, knew that Samuel was confirmed as a prophet of the Lord. [21]The Lord continued to appear at Shiloh and gave messages to Samuel there at the Tabernacle.

When you read God's Word, what do you expect him to say to you? Although this was a time when God still gave direct and audible messages to his people, such messages became rare in the days of Eli. Listening and responding are vital in a relationship with God. Although God may not use the sound of a human voice, he speaks just as clearly today through his Word. To receive his messages, we must be ready to listen and to act upon what he tells us. Like Samuel, be ready to say, "Speak, your servant is listening," when God speaks to you.

MARCH 21

Israel Wants a King

1 SAMUEL 8:1-22

As Samuel grew old, he appointed his sons to be judges over Israel. 2Joel and Abijah, his oldest
sons, held court in Beersheba. 3But they were not like their father, for they were greedy for
money. They accepted bribes and perverted justice.
4Finally, all the elders of Israel met at Ramah to discuss the matter with Samuel. 5"Look,"
they told him, "you are now old, and your sons are not like you. Give us a king to judge us
like all the other nations have."
6Samuel was displeased with their request and went to the LORD for guidance. 7"Do everything they say to you," the LORD replied, "for they are rejecting me, not you. They don't want
me to be their king any longer. 8Ever since I brought them from Egypt they have continually
abandoned me and followed other gods. And now they are giving you the same treatment.
9Do as they ask, but solemnly warn them about the way a king will reign over them."
10So Samuel passed on the LORD's warning to the people who were asking him for a king.
11"This is how a king will reign over you," Samuel said. "The king will draft your sons and
assign them to his chariots and his charioteers, making them run before his chariots. 12Some
will be generals and captains in his army, some will be forced to plow in his fields and harvest
his crops, and some will make his weapons and chariot equipment. 13The king will take your
daughters from you and force them to cook and bake and make perfumes for him. 14He will
take away the best of your fields and vineyards and olive groves and give them to his own
officials. 15He will take a tenth of your grain and your grape harvest and distribute it among
his officers and attendants. 16He will take your male and female slaves and demand the finest
of your cattle and donkeys for his own use. 17He will demand a tenth of your flocks, and
you will be his slaves. 18When that day comes, you will beg for relief from this king you are
demanding, but then the LORD will not help you."
19But the people refused to listen to Samuel's warning. "Even so, we still want a king,"
they said. 20"We want to be like the nations around us. Our king will judge us and lead us
into battle."
21So Samuel repeated to the LORD what the people had said, 22and the LORD replied, "Do
as they say, and give them a king." Then Samuel agreed and sent the people home.

What positive lessons have you learned from others' mistakes? Israel wanted a king for several reasons: (1) Samuel's sons were not fit to lead Israel. (2) It was hoped that a king would unite the tribes into one nation and one army. (3) The people wanted to be like the neighboring nations. This is exactly what God didn't want. Having a king would make it easy to forget that God was their real leader. We cannot ask God to lead our personal lives if we continue to live by the world's standards and values, for God requires obedience. Faith in God must touch all the practical areas of our lives. Is God the leader of your life?

Saul and the Lost Donkeys

MARCH 22

1 SAMUEL 9:1-17

There was a wealthy, influential man named Kish from the tribe of Benjamin. . . . 2His son Saul was the most handsome man in Israel—head and shoulders taller than anyone else in the land.

3One day Kish's donkeys strayed away, and he told Saul, "Take a servant with you, and go look for the donkeys." 4So Saul took one of the servants and traveled through the hill country of Ephraim, the land of Shalishah, the Shaalim area, and the entire land of Benjamin, but they couldn't find the donkeys anywhere. . . .

6But the servant said, "I've just thought of something! There is a man of God who lives here in this town. He is held in high honor by all the people because everything he says comes true. Let's go find him. Perhaps he can tell us which way to go."

7"But we don't have anything to offer him," Saul replied. "Even our food is gone, and we don't have a thing to give him."

8"Well," the servant said, "I have one small silver piece. We can at least offer it to the man of God and see what happens!" 9(In those days if people wanted a message from God, they would say, "Let's go and ask the seer," for prophets used to be called seers.)

10"All right," Saul agreed, "let's try it!" So they started into the town where the man of God lived.

11As they were climbing the hill to the town, they met some young women coming out to draw water. So Saul and his servant asked, "Is the seer here today?"

12"Yes," they replied. "Stay right on this road. He is at the town gates. He has just arrived to take part in a public sacrifice up at the place of worship. 13Hurry and catch him before he goes up there to eat. The guests won't begin eating until he arrives to bless the food."

14So they entered the town, and as they passed through the gates, Samuel was coming out toward them to go up to the place of worship.

15Now the LORD had told Samuel the previous day, 16"About this time tomorrow I will send you a man from the land of Benjamin. Anoint him to be the leader of my people, Israel. He will rescue them from the Philistines, for I have looked down on my people in mercy and have heard their cry."

17When Samuel saw Saul, the LORD said, "That's the man I told you about! He will rule my people."

What is God's part in your daily decisions? Often we think that events just happen to us, but as we learn from this story about Saul, God may use common occurrences to lead us where he wants. It is important to evaluate all situations as potential "divine appointments" designed to shape our lives. Think of all the good and bad circumstances that have affected you lately. Can you see God's purpose in them? Perhaps he is building a certain quality in you or leading you to serve him in a new area.

MARCH 23

Saul Becomes King

1 SAMUEL 10:1-24

Then Samuel took a flask of olive oil and poured it over Saul's head. He kissed Saul and said, "I am doing this because the LORD has appointed you to be the ruler over Israel, his special possession. . . .

3"When you get to the oak of Tabor, you will see three men coming toward you who are on their way to worship God at Bethel. One will be bringing three young goats, another will have three loaves of bread, and the third will be carrying a wineskin full of wine. 4They will greet you and offer you two of the loaves, which you are to accept.

5"When you arrive at Gibeah of God, where the garrison of the Philistines is located, you will meet a band of prophets coming down from the place of worship. They will be playing a harp, a tambourine, a flute, and a lyre, and they will be prophesying. 6At that time the Spirit of the LORD will come powerfully upon you, and you will prophesy with them. You will be changed into a different person. . . .

9As Saul turned and started to leave, God gave him a new heart, and all Samuel's signs were fulfilled that day. 10When Saul and his servant arrived at Gibeah, they saw a group of prophets coming toward them. Then the Spirit of God came powerfully upon Saul, and he, too, began to prophesy. 11When those who knew Saul heard about it, they exclaimed, "What? Is even Saul a prophet? How did the son of Kish become a prophet?" . . .

17Later Samuel called all the people of Israel to meet before the LORD at Mizpah. 18And he said, "This is what the LORD, the God of Israel, has declared: I brought you from Egypt and rescued you from the Egyptians and from all of the nations that were oppressing you. 19But though I have rescued you from your misery and distress, you have rejected your God today and have said, 'No, we want a king instead!' Now, therefore, present yourselves before the LORD by tribes and clans."

20So Samuel brought all the tribes of Israel before the LORD, and the tribe of Benjamin was chosen by lot. 21Then he brought each family of the tribe of Benjamin before the LORD, and the family of the Matrites was chosen. And finally Saul son of Kish was chosen from among them. But when they looked for him, he had disappeared! 22So they asked the LORD, "Where is he?"

And the LORD replied, "He is hiding among the baggage." 23So they found him and brought him out, and he stood head and shoulders above anyone else.

24Then Samuel said to all the people, "This is the man the LORD has chosen as your king. No one in all Israel is like him!"

And all the people shouted, "Long live the king!"

How do you evaluate people? Saul, who not long before was a farmer searching for donkeys, was now king. Although he was tall, handsome, and wealthy, it is surprising that he was God's choice to be king since he was not a deeply religious man. But God does not choose people according to our expectations. He may not even choose the one best qualified for the task but rather the one who will fulfill his larger purpose. God may want to use you for a great work, or he may choose someone else who seems less fit. In either case, try to look for God's greater purpose.

A Son to Make a Father Proud

MARCH 24

1 SAMUEL 14:1-23

One day Jonathan said to his armor bearer, "Come on, let's go over to where the Philistines
have their outpost." But Jonathan did not tell his father what he was doing. . . .
4To reach the Philistine outpost, Jonathan had to go down between two rocky cliffs that
were called Bozez and Seneh. 5The cliff on the north was in front of Micmash, and the one
on the south was in front of Geba. 6"Let's go across to the outpost of those pagans," Jonathan
said to his armor bearer. "Perhaps the LORD will help us, for nothing can hinder the LORD.
He can win a battle whether he has many warriors or only a few!"
7"Do what you think is best," the armor bearer replied. "I'm with you completely, whatever you decide."
8"All right, then," Jonathan told him. "We will cross over and let them see us. 9If they say
to us, 'Stay where you are or we'll kill you,' then we will stop and not go up to them. 10But
if they say, 'Come on up and fight,' then we will go up. That will be the LORD's sign that he
will help us defeat them."
11When the Philistines saw them coming, they shouted, "Look! The Hebrews are crawling
out of their holes!" 12Then the men from the outpost shouted to Jonathan, "Come on up
here, and we'll teach you a lesson!"
"Come on, climb right behind me," Jonathan said to his armor bearer, "for the LORD
will help us defeat them!"
13So they climbed up using both hands and feet, and the Philistines fell before Jonathan,
and his armor bearer killed those who came behind them. 14They killed some twenty men in
all, and their bodies were scattered over about half an acre.
15Suddenly, panic broke out in the Philistine army, both in the camp and in the field,
including even the outposts and raiding parties. And just then an earthquake struck, and
everyone was terrified.
16Saul's lookouts in Gibeah of Benjamin saw a strange sight—the vast army of Philistines
began to melt away in every direction. . . .
20Then Saul and all his men rushed out to the battle and found the Philistines killing each
other. There was terrible confusion everywhere. . . . 23So the LORD saved Israel that day, and
the battle continued to rage even beyond Beth-aven.

What would it mean to have a friend like Jonathan? Jonathan and his armor bearer weren't much of a force to attack the huge Philistine army. But while everyone else was afraid, they trusted God, knowing that the size of the enemy army had no relationship to God's ability to help them. God honored the faith and brave action of these two men with a tremendous victory. Have you ever felt surrounded by the "enemy" or faced overwhelming odds? God is never intimidated by the size of the enemy or the complexity of a problem. With him, there are always enough resources to resist the pressures and win your battles. If God has called you to action, then bravely commit what few resources you have to God, and rely upon him to give you the victory.

MARCH 25

Samuel Anoints David

1 SAMUEL 16:1-13

Now the LORD said to Samuel, "You have mourned long enough for Saul. I have rejected
him as king of Israel, so fill your flask with olive oil and go to Bethlehem. Find a man named
Jesse who lives there, for I have selected one of his sons to be my king."

2But Samuel asked, "How can I do that? If Saul hears about it, he will kill me."

"Take a heifer with you," the LORD replied, "and say that you have come to make a
sacrifice to the LORD. 3Invite Jesse to the sacrifice, and I will show you which of his sons to
anoint for me."

4So Samuel did as the LORD instructed. When he arrived at Bethlehem, the elders of the
town came trembling to meet him. "What's wrong?" they asked. "Do you come in peace?"

5"Yes," Samuel replied. "I have come to sacrifice to the LORD. Purify yourselves and come
with me to the sacrifice." Then Samuel performed the purification rite for Jesse and his sons
and invited them to the sacrifice, too.

6When they arrived, Samuel took one look at Eliab and thought, "Surely this is the LORD's
anointed!"

7But the LORD said to Samuel, "Don't judge by his appearance or height, for I have
rejected him. The LORD doesn't see things the way you see them. People judge by outward
appearance, but the LORD looks at the heart." . . .

11"There is still the youngest," Jesse replied. "But he's out in the fields watching the sheep
and goats."

"Send for him at once," Samuel said. "We will not sit down to eat until he arrives."

12So Jesse sent for him. He was dark and handsome, with beautiful eyes.

And the LORD said, "This is the one; anoint him."

13So as David stood there among his brothers, Samuel took the flask of olive oil he had
brought and anointed David with the oil. And the Spirit of the LORD came powerfully upon
David from that day on. Then Samuel returned to Ramah.

What do you appreciate in people other than their looks? Saul was tall and handsome; he was an impressive-looking man. Samuel may have been trying to find someone who looked like Saul to be Israel's next king, but God warned him against judging by appearance alone. Appearance doesn't reveal what people are really like or their true value. Fortunately, God judges by character, not appearance. And because only God can see on the inside, only he can accurately judge people. We spend hours each week maintaining our outward appearance, while we should be spending time developing our inner character. While everyone can see your face, only you and God know what your heart really looks like. Which is the more attractive part of you?

Jesus Teaches about Forgiveness

JULY 26

MATTHEW 18:10-22

10“Beware that you don’t look down on any of these little ones. For I tell you that in heaven
their angels are always in the presence of my heavenly Father.
12“If a man has a hundred sheep and one of them wanders away, what will he do? Won’t
he leave the ninety-nine others on the hills and go out to search for the one that is lost? 13And
if he finds it, I tell you the truth, he will rejoice over it more than over the ninety-nine that
didn’t wander away! 14In the same way, it is not my heavenly Father’s will that even one of
these little ones should perish.
15“If another believer sins against you, go privately and point out the offense. If the other
person listens and confesses it, you have won that person back. 16But if you are unsuccessful,
take one or two others with you and go back again, so that everything you say may be confirmed by two or three witnesses. 17If the person still refuses to listen, take your case to the
church. Then if he or she won’t accept the church’s decision, treat that person as a pagan or
a corrupt tax collector.
18“I tell you the truth, whatever you forbid on earth will be forbidden in heaven, and whatever
you permit on earth will be permitted in heaven.
19“I also tell you this: If two of you agree here on earth concerning anything you ask, my
Father in heaven will do it for you. 20For where two or three gather together as my followers,
I am there among them.”
21Then Peter came to him and asked, “Lord, how often should I forgive someone who
sins against me? Seven times?”
22“No, not seven times,” Jesus replied, “but seventy times seven!”

How do you react to the failures of others? The rabbis taught that people should forgive those who offend them—but only three times. Peter, trying to be especially generous, asked Jesus if seven (the “perfect” number) was enough times to forgive someone. But Jesus answered, “Seventy times seven,” meaning that we shouldn’t even keep track of how many times we forgive someone. We should always forgive those who are truly repentant, no matter how many times they ask.

MARCH 27

David Kills Goliath

1 SAMUEL 17:38-52

38 Then Saul gave David his own armor—a bronze helmet and a coat of mail. 39 David put
it on, strapped the sword over it, and took a step or two to see what it was like, for he had
never worn such things before.

"I can't go in these," he protested to Saul. "I'm not used to them." So David took them
off again. 40 He picked up five smooth stones from a stream and put them into his shepherd's
bag. Then, armed only with his shepherd's staff and sling, he started across the valley to fight
the Philistine.

41 Goliath walked out toward David with his shield bearer ahead of him, 42 sneering in
contempt at this ruddy-faced boy. 43 "Am I a dog," he roared at David, "that you come at me
with a stick?" And he cursed David by the names of his gods. 44 "Come over here, and I'll give
your flesh to the birds and wild animals!" Goliath yelled.

45 David replied to the Philistine, "You come to me with sword, spear, and javelin, but I
come to you in the name of the Lord of Heaven's Armies—the God of the armies of Israel,
whom you have defied. 46 Today the Lord will conquer you, and I will kill you and cut off
your head. And then I will give the dead bodies of your men to the birds and wild animals,
and the whole world will know that there is a God in Israel! 47 And everyone assembled here
will know that the Lord rescues his people, but not with sword and spear. This is the Lord's
battle, and he will give you to us!"

48 As Goliath moved closer to attack, David quickly ran out to meet him. 49 Reaching into
his shepherd's bag and taking out a stone, he hurled it with his sling and hit the Philistine
in the forehead. The stone sank in, and Goliath stumbled and fell face down on the ground.

50 So David triumphed over the Philistine with only a sling and a stone, for he had no
sword. 51 Then David ran over and pulled Goliath's sword from its sheath. David used it to
kill him and cut off his head.

When the Philistines saw that their champion was dead, they turned and ran. 52 Then the
men of Israel and Judah gave a great shout of triumph and rushed after the Philistines, chasing
them as far as Gath and the gates of Ekron. The bodies of the dead and wounded Philistines
were strewn all along the road from Shaaraim, as far as Gath and Ekron.

What "giants" need to be defeated in your life? David was an expert marksman with a sling, and as he advanced on Goliath, he stayed out of range of Goliath's huge weapons. What made David effective, however, was more than his ability with a sling; it was his courage and his faith in God. To fight like David, we need David's kind of fearlessness. When you face towering problems, recall how God has helped you in the past. Take heart, because God gives you strength. Use the skills God has already given you and move forward.

Wrong Conclusions

JULY 28

JOHN 7:32-52

[32]When the Pharisees heard that the crowds were whispering such things, they and the leading
priests sent Temple guards to arrest Jesus. [33]But Jesus told them, "I will be with you only a
little longer. Then I will return to the one who sent me. [34]You will search for me but not find
me. And you cannot go where I am going."

[35]The Jewish leaders were puzzled by this statement. "Where is he planning to go?" they
asked. "Is he thinking of leaving the country and going to the Jews in other lands? Maybe he
will even teach the Greeks! [36]What does he mean when he says, 'You will search for me but not
find me,' and 'You cannot go where I am going'?"

[37]On the last day, the climax of the festival, Jesus stood and shouted to the crowds,
"Anyone who is thirsty may come to me! [38]Anyone who believes in me may come and drink!
For the Scriptures declare, 'Rivers of living water will flow from his heart.'" [39](When he said
"living water," he was speaking of the Spirit, who would be given to everyone believing in
him. But the Spirit had not yet been given, because Jesus had not yet entered into his glory.)

[40]When the crowds heard him say this, some of them declared, "Surely this man is the
Prophet we've been expecting." [41]Others said, "He is the Messiah." Still others said, "But
he can't be! Will the Messiah come from Galilee? [42]For the Scriptures clearly state that the
Messiah will be born of the royal line of David, in Bethlehem, the village where King David
was born." [43]So the crowd was divided about him. [44]Some even wanted him arrested, but no
one laid a hand on him.

[45]When the Temple guards returned without having arrested Jesus, the leading priests and
Pharisees demanded, "Why didn't you bring him in?"

[46]"We have never heard anyone speak like this!" the guards responded.

[47]"Have you been led astray, too?" the Pharisees mocked. [48]"Is there a single one of us rulers or Pharisees who believes in him? [49]This foolish crowd follows him, but they are ignorant
of the law. God's curse is on them!"

[50]Then Nicodemus, the leader who had met with Jesus earlier, spoke up. [51]"Is it legal to
convict a man before he is given a hearing?" he asked.

[52]They replied, "Are you from Galilee, too? Search the Scriptures and see for yourself—no
prophet ever comes from Galilee!"

What does it mean to have "rivers of living water" flowing from within you? The crowd was asking questions about Jesus. Some believed, others were hostile, and others disqualified Jesus as the Messiah because he was from Nazareth, not Bethlehem (Micah 5:2). But he was born in Bethlehem (Luke 2:1-7), although he grew up in Nazareth. If they had looked more carefully, they would not have jumped to the wrong conclusions. When you search for God's truth, make sure you look carefully and thoughtfully at the Bible with an open heart and mind. Don't jump to conclusions before knowing more of what the Bible says.

MARCH 29

David and Jonathan

1 SAMUEL 20:1-17

David now fled from Naioth in Ramah and found Jonathan. "What have I done?" he
exclaimed. "What is my crime? How have I offended your father that he is so determined
to kill me?"

2"That's not true!" Jonathan protested. "You're not going to die. He always tells me everything he's going to do, even the little things. I know my father wouldn't hide something like
this from me. It just isn't so!"

3Then David took an oath before Jonathan and said, "Your father knows perfectly well
about our friendship, so he has said to himself, 'I won't tell Jonathan—why should I hurt
him?' But I swear to you that I am only a step away from death! I swear it by the LORD and
by your own soul!"

4"Tell me what I can do to help you," Jonathan exclaimed.

5David replied, "Tomorrow we celebrate the new moon festival. I've always eaten with
the king on this occasion, but tomorrow I'll hide in the field and stay there until the evening
of the third day. 6If your father asks where I am, tell him I asked permission to go home to
Bethlehem for an annual family sacrifice. 7If he says, 'Fine!' you will know all is well. But if
he is angry and loses his temper, you will know he is determined to kill me. 8Show me this
loyalty as my sworn friend—for we made a solemn pact before the LORD—or kill me yourself
if I have sinned against your father. But please don't betray me to him!"

9"Never!" Jonathan exclaimed. "You know that if I had the slightest notion my father was
planning to kill you, I would tell you at once."

10Then David asked, "How will I know whether or not your father is angry?"

11"Come out to the field with me," Jonathan replied. And they went out there together.
12Then Jonathan told David, "I promise by the LORD, the God of Israel, that by this time
tomorrow, or the next day at the latest, I will talk to my father and let you know at once how
he feels about you. If he speaks favorably about you, I will let you know. 13But if he is angry
and wants you killed, may the LORD strike me and even kill me if I don't warn you so you can
escape and live. May the LORD be with you as he used to be with my father. 14And may you
treat me with the faithful love of the LORD as long as I live. But if I die, 15treat my family with
this faithful love, even when the LORD destroys all your enemies from the face of the earth."

16So Jonathan made a solemn pact with David, saying, "May the LORD destroy all your
enemies!" 17And Jonathan made David reaffirm his vow of friendship again, for Jonathan
loved David as he loved himself.

How much can your friends trust you? Jonathan asked David to keep a promise to treat his children kindly in the future. Years later David took great pains to fulfill this promise: he invited Jonathan's son, Mephibosheth, into his palace to live (2 Samuel 9). When you make promises to your friends, do you keep them? Would you keep a promise you made many years earlier?

The Truth Will Set You Free

JULY 30

JOHN 8:21-32

21 Later Jesus said to them again, “I am going away. You will search for me but will die in your
sin. You cannot come where I am going.”
22 The people asked, “Is he planning to commit suicide? What does he mean, ‘You cannot
come where I am going’?”
23 Jesus continued, “You are from below; I am from above. You belong to this world; I do
not. 24 That is why I said that you will die in your sins; for unless you believe that I AM who
I claim to be, you will die in your sins.”
25 “Who are you?” they demanded.
Jesus replied, “The one I have always claimed to be. 26 I have much to say about you and
much to condemn, but I won’t. For I say only what I have heard from the one who sent me, and
he is completely truthful.” 27 But they still didn’t understand that he was talking about his Father.
28 So Jesus said, “When you have lifted up the Son of Man on the cross, then you will
understand that I AM he. I do nothing on my own but say only what the Father taught
me. 29 And the one who sent me is with me—he has not deserted me. For I always do what
pleases him.” 30 Then many who heard him say these things believed in him.
31 Jesus said to the people who believed in him, “You are truly my disciples if you remain
faithful to my teachings. 32 And you will know the truth, and the truth will set you free.”

How has Christ made you free? Jesus himself is the truth that makes us free. He is the source of truth, the perfect standard of what is right. He frees us from the consequences of sin, from self-deception, and from deception by Satan. He shows us clearly the way to everlasting life with God. Thus, Jesus does not give us freedom to do what we want but freedom to follow God. As you seek to serve God, Jesus’ perfect truth frees you to be all that God meant you to be.

MARCH 31

David Spares Saul's Life

1 SAMUEL 24:1-15

After Saul returned from fighting the Philistines, he was told that David had gone into the wilderness of En-gedi. 2So Saul chose 3,000 elite troops from all Israel and went to search for David and his men near the rocks of the wild goats.

3At the place where the road passes some sheepfolds, Saul went into a cave to relieve himself. But as it happened, David and his men were hiding farther back in that very cave!

4"Now's your opportunity!" David's men whispered to him. "Today the LORD is telling you, 'I will certainly put your enemy into your power, to do with as you wish.'" So David crept forward and cut off a piece of the hem of Saul's robe.

5But then David's conscience began bothering him because he had cut Saul's robe. 6He said to his men, "The LORD forbid that I should do this to my lord the king. I shouldn't attack the LORD's anointed one, for the LORD himself has chosen him." 7So David restrained his men and did not let them kill Saul.

After Saul had left the cave and gone on his way, 8David came out and shouted after him, "My lord the king!" And when Saul looked around, David bowed low before him.

9Then he shouted to Saul, "Why do you listen to the people who say I am trying to harm you? 10This very day you can see with your own eyes it isn't true. For the LORD placed you at my mercy back there in the cave. Some of my men told me to kill you, but I spared you. For I said, 'I will never harm the king—he is the LORD's anointed one.' 11Look, my father, at what I have in my hand. It is a piece of the hem of your robe! I cut it off, but I didn't kill you. This proves that I am not trying to harm you and that I have not sinned against you, even though you have been hunting for me to kill me.

12"May the LORD judge between us. Perhaps the LORD will punish you for what you are trying to do to me, but I will never harm you. 13As that old proverb says, 'From evil people come evil deeds.' So you can be sure I will never harm you. 14Who is the king of Israel trying to catch anyway? Should he spend his time chasing one who is as worthless as a dead dog or a single flea? 15May the LORD therefore judge which of us is right and punish the guilty one. He is my advocate, and he will rescue me from your power!"

Do you treat others the way you want to be treated? The means we use to accomplish a goal are just as important as the goal we are trying to accomplish. David's goal was to become king, so his men urged him to kill Saul when he had the chance. David's refusal was not an example of cowardice but of courage—the courage to stand against the group and do what he knew was right. Don't compromise your moral standards by giving in to group pressure or taking the easy way out. Be willing to do right, not what seems right. Being in tune with God will help you to know the difference.

April

APRIL 1

David and Abigail

1 SAMUEL 25:1-33

Then David moved down to the wilderness of Maon. 2There was a wealthy man from Maon who owned property near the town of Carmel. . . . 3This man's name was Nabal, and his wife, Abigail, was a sensible and beautiful woman. But Nabal, a descendant of Caleb, was crude and mean in all his dealings.

4When David heard that Nabal was shearing his sheep, 5he sent ten of his young men to Carmel with this message for Nabal: 6"Peace and prosperity to you, your family, and everything you own! 7I am told that it is sheep-shearing time. While your shepherds stayed among us near Carmel, we never harmed them, and nothing was ever stolen from them. 8Ask your own men, and they will tell you this is true. So would you be kind to us, since we have come at a time of celebration? Please share any provisions you might have on hand with us and with your friend David." 9David's young men gave this message to Nabal in David's name, and they waited for a reply.

10"Who is this fellow David?" Nabal sneered to the young men. "Who does this son of Jesse think he is? There are lots of servants these days who run away from their masters. 11Should I take my bread and my water and my meat that I've slaughtered for my shearers and give it to a band of outlaws who come from who knows where?"

12So David's young men returned and told him what Nabal had said. 13"Get your swords!" was David's reply as he strapped on his own. . . .

14Meanwhile, one of Nabal's servants went to Abigail and told her, "David sent messengers from the wilderness to greet our master, but he screamed insults at them. . . ."

18Abigail wasted no time. She quickly gathered 200 loaves of bread, two wineskins full of wine, five sheep that had been slaughtered, nearly a bushel of roasted grain, 100 clusters of raisins, and 200 fig cakes. She packed them on donkeys . . .

23When Abigail saw David, she quickly got off her donkey and bowed low before him. 24She fell at his feet and said, "I accept all blame in this matter, my lord. Please listen to what I have to say. 25I know Nabal is a wicked and ill-tempered man; please don't pay any attention to him. He is a fool, just as his name suggests. But I never even saw the young men you sent." . . .

32David replied to Abigail, "Praise the LORD, the God of Israel, who has sent you to meet me today! 33Thank God for your good sense! Bless you for keeping me from murder and from carrying out vengeance with my own hands."

How does God keep you from making big mistakes? David was in no mood to listen when he set out for Nabal's ranch. Nevertheless, he stopped to hear what Abigail had to say. If he had ignored her, he would have been guilty of taking vengeance into his own hands. No matter how right we think we are, we must always be careful to stop and listen to what others have to say. The extra time and effort can save us much pain and trouble in the long run.

Saul and the Occult

APRIL 2

1 SAMUEL 28:3-19

Saul had banned from the land of Israel all mediums and those who consult the spirits of the dead.

4 The Philistines set up their camp at Shunem, and Saul gathered all the army of Israel and camped at Gilboa. 5 When Saul saw the vast Philistine army, he became frantic with fear. 6 He asked the LORD what he should do, but the LORD refused to answer him, either by dreams or by sacred lots or by the prophets. 7 Saul then said to his advisers, "Find a woman who is a medium, so I can go and ask her what to do."

His advisers replied, "There is a medium at Endor."

8 So Saul disguised himself by wearing ordinary clothing instead of his royal robes. Then he went to the woman's home at night, accompanied by two of his men.

"I have to talk to a man who has died," he said. "Will you call up his spirit for me?"

9 "Are you trying to get me killed?" the woman demanded. "You know that Saul has outlawed all the mediums and all who consult the spirits of the dead. Why are you setting a trap for me?"

10 But Saul took an oath in the name of the LORD and promised, "As surely as the LORD lives, nothing bad will happen to you for doing this."

11 Finally, the woman said, "Well, whose spirit do you want me to call up?"

"Call up Samuel," Saul replied. . . .

15 "Why have you disturbed me by calling me back?" Samuel asked Saul.

"Because I am in deep trouble," Saul replied. "The Philistines are at war with me, and God has left me and won't reply by prophets or dreams. So I have called for you to tell me what to do."

16 But Samuel replied, "Why ask me, since the LORD has left you and has become your enemy? 17 The LORD has done just as he said he would. He has torn the kingdom from you and given it to your rival, David. 18 The LORD has done this to you today because you refused to carry out his fierce anger against the Amalekites. 19 What's more, the LORD will hand you and the army of Israel over to the Philistines tomorrow, and you and your sons will be here with me. The LORD will bring down the entire army of Israel in defeat."

What kinds of things could be considered "occult practices"? How would God feel about your involvement in such things? God had strictly forbidden the Israelites to have anything to do with divination, sorcery, witchcraft, mediums, spiritists, or anyone who consults the spirits of the dead (Deuteronomy 18:9-14). Practitioners of the occult have Satan and demons as the source of their information; God does not reveal his will to them. Instead he speaks through his own channels: the Bible; his Son, Jesus Christ; and the Holy Spirit. In this instance, God brought Samuel back, but this story in no way justifies efforts to contact the dead or communicate with persons or spirits from the past. God is against all such practices (Galatians 5:19-21).

APRIL 3

David Becomes King over Israel

2 SAMUEL 5:1-12

Then all the tribes of Israel went to David at Hebron and told him, "We are your own flesh and blood. [2]In the past, when Saul was our king, you were the one who really led the forces of Israel. And the LORD told you, 'You will be the shepherd of my people Israel. You will be Israel's leader.'"

[3]So there at Hebron, King David made a covenant before the LORD with all the elders of Israel. And they anointed him king of Israel.

[4]David was thirty years old when he began to reign, and he reigned forty years in all. [5]He had reigned over Judah from Hebron for seven years and six months, and from Jerusalem he reigned over all Israel and Judah for thirty-three years.

[6]David then led his men to Jerusalem to fight against the Jebusites, the original inhabitants of the land who were living there. The Jebusites taunted David, saying, "You'll never get in here! Even the blind and lame could keep you out!" For the Jebusites thought they were safe. [7]But David captured the fortress of Zion, which is now called the City of David.

[8]On the day of the attack, David said to his troops, "I hate those 'lame' and 'blind' Jebusites. Whoever attacks them should strike by going into the city through the water tunnel." That is the origin of the saying, "The blind and the lame may not enter the house."

[9]So David made the fortress his home, and he called it the City of David. He extended the city, starting at the supporting terraces and working inward. [10]And David became more and more powerful, because the LORD God of Heaven's Armies was with him.

[11]Then King Hiram of Tyre sent messengers to David, along with cedar timber and carpenters and stonemasons, and they built David a palace. [12]And David realized that the LORD had confirmed him as king over Israel and had blessed his kingdom for the sake of his people Israel.

How could you become a person who is pleasing to God, as David was? David now realized why the Lord had made him the king. Although the heathen kingdoms based their greatness on conquest, power, armies, and wealth, David knew that his greatness came only from God. To be great means keeping a close relationship with God personally and nationally. To do this, David had to keep his ambition under control. Although he was famous, successful, and well liked, he gave God first place in his life and served the people according to God's purposes. Do you seek greatness from God or from people? In the drive for success, remember to keep your ambition under God's control.

David Keeps His Promise

APRIL 4

2 SAMUEL 9:1-13

One day David asked, "Is anyone in Saul's family still alive—anyone to whom I can show kindness for Jonathan's sake?" 2He summoned a man named Ziba, who had been one of Saul's servants. "Are you Ziba?" the king asked.

"Yes sir, I am," Ziba replied.

3The king then asked him, "Is anyone still alive from Saul's family? If so, I want to show God's kindness to them."

Ziba replied, "Yes, one of Jonathan's sons is still alive. He is crippled in both feet."

4"Where is he?" the king asked.

"In Lo-debar," Ziba told him, "at the home of Makir son of Ammiel."

5So David sent for him and brought him from Makir's home. 6His name was Mephibosheth; he was Jonathan's son and Saul's grandson. When he came to David, he bowed low to the ground in deep respect. David said, "Greetings, Mephibosheth."

Mephibosheth replied, "I am your servant."

7"Don't be afraid!" David said. "I intend to show kindness to you because of my promise to your father, Jonathan. I will give you all the property that once belonged to your grandfather Saul, and you will eat here with me at the king's table!"

8Mephibosheth bowed respectfully and exclaimed, "Who is your servant, that you should show such kindness to a dead dog like me?"

9Then the king summoned Saul's servant Ziba and said, "I have given your master's grandson everything that belonged to Saul and his family. 10You and your sons and servants are to farm the land for him to produce food for your master's household. But Mephibosheth, your master's grandson, will eat here at my table." (Ziba had fifteen sons and twenty servants.)

11Ziba replied, "Yes, my lord the king; I am your servant, and I will do all that you have commanded." And from that time on, Mephibosheth ate regularly at David's table, like one of the king's own sons.

12Mephibosheth had a young son named Mica. From then on, all the members of Ziba's household were Mephibosheth's servants. 13And Mephibosheth, who was crippled in both feet, lived in Jerusalem and ate regularly at the king's table.

What promises need to be kept in your life? David had made a promise to his best friend, Jonathan, to take care of Jonathan's son, Mephibosheth (1 Samuel 20:14-17). David's treatment of Mephibosheth shows his integrity as a leader who accepted his obligation to show love and mercy. His generous provision for Jonathan's son goes beyond any political benefit he might have received for doing so. Do you keep your promises? Can you be generous with those less deserving? Each time you show compassion, your character is strengthened.

APRIL 5

David and Bathsheba

2 SAMUEL 11:1-27

In the spring of the year, when kings normally go out to war, David sent Joab and the Israelite army to fight the Ammonites. . . . David stayed behind in Jerusalem.

[2]Late one afternoon, after his midday rest, David got out of bed and was walking on the roof of the palace. As he looked out over the city, he noticed a woman of unusual beauty taking a bath. [3]He sent someone to find out who she was, and he was told, "She is Bathsheba, the daughter of Eliam and the wife of Uriah the Hittite." [4]Then David sent messengers to get her; and when she came to the palace, he slept with her. . . . [5]Later, when Bathsheba discovered that she was pregnant, she sent David a message, saying, "I'm pregnant."

[6]Then David sent word to Joab: "Send me Uriah the Hittite." So Joab sent him to David. [7]When Uriah arrived, David asked him how Joab and the army were getting along and how the war was progressing. [8]Then he told Uriah, "Go on home and relax." . . . [9]But Uriah didn't go home. He slept that night at the palace entrance with the king's palace guard.

[10]When David heard that Uriah had not gone home, he summoned him and asked, "What's the matter? Why didn't you go home last night after being away for so long?"

[11]Uriah replied, "The Ark and the armies of Israel and Judah are living in tents, and Joab and my master's men are camping in the open fields. How could I go home to wine and dine and sleep with my wife? I swear that I would never do such a thing." . . .

[14]So the next morning David wrote a letter to Joab and gave it to Uriah to deliver. [15]The letter instructed Joab, "Station Uriah on the front lines where the battle is fiercest. Then pull back so that he will be killed." [16]So Joab assigned Uriah to a spot close to the city wall where he knew the enemy's strongest men were fighting. [17]And when the enemy soldiers came out of the city to fight, Uriah the Hittite was killed along with several other Israelite soldiers. . . .

[26]When Uriah's wife heard that her husband was dead, she mourned for him. [27]When the period of mourning was over, David sent for her and brought her to the palace, and she became one of his wives. Then she gave birth to a son. But the LORD was displeased with what David had done.

How often are you tempted to correct one sin by committing another? In the episode with Bathsheba, David allowed himself to fall deeper and deeper into sin. (1) David abandoned his purpose, staying home from war (verse 1). (2) He focused on his own desires (verse 3). (3) When temptation came, David looked into it instead of turning away from it (verse 3). (4) He sinned deliberately (verse 4). (5) He tried to cover up his sin and basically committed murder (verses 6-17). David could have chosen to stop and turn from evil at any stage along the way. But once sin gets started, it is difficult to stop (James 1:14-15). It's much easier to stop sliding down a hill when you are near the top than when you are halfway down.

David and Nathan

APRIL 6

2 SAMUEL 12:1-25

So the LORD sent Nathan the prophet to tell David this story: "There were two men in a
certain town. One was rich, and one was poor. 2The rich man owned a great many sheep and
cattle. 3The poor man owned nothing but one little lamb he had bought. He raised that little
lamb, and it grew up with his children. It ate from the man's own plate and drank from his
cup. He cuddled it in his arms like a baby daughter. 4One day a guest arrived at the home of
the rich man. But instead of killing an animal from his own flock or herd, he took the poor
man's lamb and killed it and prepared it for his guest."

5David was furious. "As surely as the LORD lives," he vowed, "any man who would do
such a thing deserves to die! 6He must repay four lambs to the poor man for the one he stole
and for having no pity."

7Then Nathan said to David, "You are that man! The LORD, the God of Israel, says: I
anointed you king of Israel and saved you from the power of Saul. 8I gave you your master's
house and his wives and the kingdoms of Israel and Judah. And if that had not been enough,
I would have given you much, much more. 9Why, then, have you despised the word of the
LORD and done this horrible deed? For you have murdered Uriah the Hittite with the sword
of the Ammonites and stolen his wife. 10From this time on, your family will live by the sword
because you have despised me by taking Uriah's wife to be your own.

11"This is what the LORD says: Because of what you have done, I will cause your own
household to rebel against you. I will give your wives to another man before your very eyes,
and he will go to bed with them in public view. 12You did it secretly, but I will make this
happen to you openly in the sight of all Israel."

13Then David confessed to Nathan, "I have sinned against the LORD."

Nathan replied, "Yes, but the LORD has forgiven you, and you won't die for this sin.
14Nevertheless, because you have shown utter contempt for the word of the LORD by doing
this, your child will die." . . .

24Then David comforted Bathsheba, his wife, and slept with her. She became pregnant
and gave birth to a son, and David named him Solomon. The LORD loved the child 25and
sent word through Nathan the prophet that they should name him Jedidiah (which means
"beloved of the LORD"), as the LORD had commanded.

Which of your friends love you enough to correct you? David repented of his sin, but God's judgment was that his child would die. The consequences of David's sin were irreversible. Sometimes an apology isn't enough. When God forgives us and restores our relationship to him, he doesn't eliminate all the consequences of our wrongdoings. We may be tempted to say, "If this is wrong, I can always apologize to God," but we must remember that we may set into motion events with consequences that cannot be reversed.

APRIL 7

Sin in David's Family

2 SAMUEL 13:1-19

Now David's son Absalom had a beautiful sister named Tamar. And Amnon, her half brother, fell desperately in love with her. [2]Amnon became so obsessed with Tamar that he became ill. She was a virgin, and Amnon thought he could never have her.

[3]But Amnon had a very crafty friend—his cousin Jonadab. He was the son of David's brother Shimea. [4]One day Jonadab said to Amnon, "What's the trouble? Why should the son of a king look so dejected morning after morning?"

So Amnon told him, "I am in love with Tamar, my brother Absalom's sister."

[5]"Well," Jonadab said, "I'll tell you what to do. Go back to bed and pretend you are ill. When your father comes to see you, ask him to let Tamar come and prepare some food for you. Tell him you'll feel better if she prepares it as you watch and feeds you with her own hands."

[6]So Amnon lay down and pretended to be sick. And when the king came to see him, Amnon asked him, "Please let my sister Tamar come and cook my favorite dish as I watch. Then I can eat it from her own hands." [7]So David agreed and sent Tamar to Amnon's house to prepare some food for him. . . .

[11]But as she was feeding him, he grabbed her and demanded, "Come to bed with me, my darling sister."

[12]"No, my brother!" she cried. "Don't be foolish! Don't do this to me! . . ."

[14]But Amnon wouldn't listen to her, and since he was stronger than she was, he raped her. [15]Then suddenly Amnon's love turned to hate, and he hated her even more than he had loved her. "Get out of here!" he snarled at her.

[16]"No, no!" Tamar cried. "Sending me away now is worse than what you've already done to me."

But Amnon wouldn't listen to her. [17]He shouted for his servant and demanded, "Throw this woman out, and lock the door behind her!"

[18]So the servant put her out and locked the door behind her. She was wearing a long, beautiful robe, as was the custom in those days for the king's virgin daughters. [19]But now Tamar tore her robe and put ashes on her head. And then, with her face in her hands, she went away crying.

What actions do you take to avoid temptation? Love and lust are very different. After Amnon raped his half sister, his "love" turned to hate. Although he had claimed to be in love, he was actually overcome by lust. Love is patient; lust requires immediate sexual satisfaction. Love is kind; lust is harsh. Love does not demand its own way; lust does. And he yielded to the temptation to do evil. You can avoid this mistake: (1) Ask God in earnest prayer to help you stay away from people, places, and situations that offer temptation. (2) Memorize and meditate on portions of Scripture that combat your specific weaknesses. At the root of most temptation is a real need or desire that God can fill. (3) Find another believer with whom you can openly share your temptations, and call this person for help when temptation strikes.

Family Revenge

APRIL 8

2 SAMUEL 13:20-39

[20]Her brother Absalom saw her and asked, "Is it true that Amnon has been with you? Well, my sister, keep quiet for now, since he's your brother. Don't you worry about it." So Tamar lived as a desolate woman in her brother Absalom's house.

[21]When King David heard what had happened, he was very angry. [22]And though Absalom never spoke to Amnon about this, he hated Amnon deeply because of what he had done to his sister.

[23]Two years later, when Absalom's sheep were being sheared at Baal-hazor near Ephraim, Absalom invited all the king's sons to come to a feast. . . .

[28]Absalom told his men, "Wait until Amnon gets drunk; then at my signal, kill him! Don't be afraid. I'm the one who has given the command. Take courage and do it!" [29]So at Absalom's signal they murdered Amnon. Then the other sons of the king jumped on their mules and fled.

[30]As they were on the way back to Jerusalem, this report reached David: "Absalom has killed all the king's sons; not one is left alive!" [31]The king got up, tore his robe, and threw himself on the ground. His advisers also tore their clothes in horror and sorrow.

[32]But just then Jonadab, the son of David's brother Shimea, arrived and said, "No, don't believe that all the king's sons have been killed! It was only Amnon! Absalom has been plotting this ever since Amnon raped his sister Tamar. [33]No, my lord the king, your sons aren't all dead! It was only Amnon." [34]Meanwhile Absalom escaped.

Then the watchman on the Jerusalem wall saw a great crowd coming down the hill on the road from the west. He ran to tell the king, "I see a crowd of people coming from the Horonaim road along the side of the hill."

[35]"Look!" Jonadab told the king. "There they are now! The king's sons are coming, just as I said."

[36]They soon arrived, weeping and sobbing, and the king and all his servants wept bitterly with them. [37]And David mourned many days for his son Amnon.

Absalom fled to his grandfather, Talmai son of Ammihud, the king of Geshur. [38]He stayed there in Geshur for three years. [39]And King David, now reconciled to Amnon's death, longed to be reunited with his son Absalom.

Are you more likely to have committed David's sin or Absalom's? Absalom tried to comfort Tamar and persuade her not to turn the incident into a public scandal. Secretly, he planned to take revenge against Amnon himself, which he did two years later. Absalom told Tamar the rape was only a family matter. But God's standards for moral conduct are not suspended when we deal with family matters. Family problems must be dealt with openly and honestly. If you're facing a problem with a family member, ask God for wisdom as you deal with it. He will help you discover constructive ways to work through the matter.

APRIL 9

Family Betrayal

2 SAMUEL 15:1-23

After this, Absalom bought a chariot and horses, and he hired fifty bodyguards to run ahead
of him. 2He got up early every morning and went out to the gate of the city. When people
brought a case to the king for judgment, Absalom would ask where in Israel they were from,
and they would tell him their tribe. 3Then Absalom would say, "You've really got a strong
case here! It's too bad the king doesn't have anyone to hear it. 4I wish I were the judge. Then
everyone could bring their cases to me for judgment, and I would give them justice!"

5When people tried to bow before him, Absalom wouldn't let them. Instead, he took
them by the hand and kissed them. 6Absalom did this with everyone who came to the king
for judgment, and so he stole the hearts of all the people of Israel.

7After four years, Absalom said to the king, "Let me go to Hebron to offer a sacrifice to
the LORD and fulfill a vow I made to him. 8For while your servant was at Geshur in Aram, I
promised to sacrifice to the LORD in Hebron if he would bring me back to Jerusalem."

9"All right," the king told him. "Go and fulfill your vow."

So Absalom went to Hebron. 10But while he was there, he sent secret messengers to all
the tribes of Israel to stir up a rebellion against the king. . . .

13A messenger soon arrived in Jerusalem to tell David, "All Israel has joined Absalom in
a conspiracy against you!"

14"Then we must flee at once, or it will be too late!" David urged his men. "Hurry! If we
get out of the city before Absalom arrives, both we and the city of Jerusalem will be spared
from disaster."

15"We are with you," his advisers replied. "Do what you think is best."

16So the king and all his household set out at once. He left no one behind except ten of
his concubines to look after the palace. 17The king and all his people set out on foot, pausing
at the last house 18to let all the king's men move past to lead the way. There were 600 men
from Gath who had come with David, along with the king's bodyguard. . . .

23Everyone cried loudly as the king and his followers passed by. They crossed the Kidron
Valley and then went out toward the wilderness.

Who helps you keep your motives clear? Had David not escaped from Jerusalem, the ensuing fight might have destroyed both him and the innocent inhabitants of the city. Some fights that we think necessary may be costly and destructive to those around us. In such cases, it may be wise to back down and save the fight for another day—even if doing so hurts our pride. It takes courage to stand and fight, but it also takes courage to back down when you must for the sake of others.

The Death of Absalom

APRIL 10

2 SAMUEL 18:1-17

David now mustered the men who were with him and appointed generals and captains to lead them. [2]He sent the troops out in three groups, placing one group under Joab, one under Joab's brother Abishai son of Zeruiah, and one under Ittai, the man from Gath. The king told his troops, "I am going out with you."

[3]But his men objected strongly. "You must not go," they urged. "If we have to turn and run—and even if half of us die—it will make no difference to Absalom's troops; they will be looking only for you. You are worth 10,000 of us, and it is better that you stay here in the town and send help if we need it."

[4]"If you think that's the best plan, I'll do it," the king answered. So he stood alongside the gate of the town as all the troops marched out in groups of hundreds and of thousands.

[5]And the king gave this command to Joab, Abishai, and Ittai: "For my sake, deal gently with young Absalom." And all the troops heard the king give this order to his commanders.

. . . [9]During the battle, Absalom happened to come upon some of David's men. He tried to escape on his mule, but as he rode beneath the thick branches of a great tree, his hair got caught in the tree. His mule kept going and left him dangling in the air. [10]One of David's men saw what had happened and told Joab, "I saw Absalom dangling from a great tree."

[11]"What?" Joab demanded. "You saw him there and didn't kill him? I would have rewarded you with ten pieces of silver and a hero's belt!"

[12]"I would not kill the king's son for even a thousand pieces of silver," the man replied to Joab. "We all heard the king say to you and Abishai and Ittai, 'For my sake, please spare young Absalom.' [13]And if I had betrayed the king by killing his son—and the king would certainly find out who did it—you yourself would be the first to abandon me."

[14]"Enough of this nonsense," Joab said. Then he took three daggers and plunged them into Absalom's heart as he dangled, still alive, in the great tree. [15]Ten of Joab's young armor bearers then surrounded Absalom and killed him.

[16]Then Joab blew the ram's horn, and his men returned from chasing the army of Israel. [17]They threw Absalom's body into a deep pit in the forest and piled a great heap of stones over it. And all Israel fled to their homes.

In what situations are you most likely to lose control? The man who reported Absalom's predicament to Joab caught Joab in hypocrisy. He knew that if the king found out that his son had been killed, Joab would have turned on him instead of giving him a reward. Joab could not answer but only dismissed him. Those who do evil often do not take the time to consider what they are about to do. They don't care whether or not it is right or lawful. Don't rush into action without thinking. Consider whether what you are about to do is right or wrong.

APRIL 11

Conflict over the Throne

1 KINGS 1:5-27

5About that time David's son Adonijah, whose mother was Haggith, began boasting, "I will
make myself king." So he provided himself with chariots and charioteers and recruited fifty
men to run in front of him. 6Now his father, King David, had never disciplined him at any
time, even by asking, "Why are you doing that?" Adonijah had been born next after Absalom,
and he was very handsome.

7Adonijah took Joab son of Zeruiah and Abiathar the priest into his confidence, and they
agreed to help him become king. 8But Zadok the priest, Benaiah son of Jehoiada, Nathan the
prophet, Shimei, Rei, and David's personal bodyguard refused to support Adonijah.

9Adonijah went to the Stone of Zoheleth near the spring of En-rogel, where he sacrificed
sheep, cattle, and fattened calves. He invited all his brothers—the other sons of King David—
and all the royal officials of Judah. 10But he did not invite Nathan the prophet or Benaiah or
the king's bodyguard or his brother Solomon.

11Then Nathan went to Bathsheba, Solomon's mother, and asked her, "Haven't you heard
that Haggith's son, Adonijah, has made himself king, and our lord David doesn't even know
about it? 12If you want to save your own life and the life of your son Solomon, follow my
advice. 13Go at once to King David and say to him, 'My lord the king, didn't you make a vow
and say to me, "Your son Solomon will surely be the next king and will sit on my throne"?
Why then has Adonijah become king?' 14And while you are still talking with him, I will come
and confirm everything you have said." . . .

22While she was still speaking with the king, Nathan the prophet arrived. 23The king's
officials told him, "Nathan the prophet is here to see you."

Nathan went in and bowed before the king with his face to the ground. 24Nathan asked,
"My lord the king, have you decided that Adonijah will be the next king and that he will sit
on your throne? 25Today he has sacrificed many cattle, fattened calves, and sheep, and he has
invited all the king's sons to attend the celebration. He also invited the commanders of the
army and Abiathar the priest. They are feasting and drinking with him and shouting, 'Long
live King Adonijah!' . . . 27Has my lord the king really done this without letting any of his
officials know who should be the next king?"

What happens when you aren't self-disciplined? Because David had never interfered by opposing or even questioning his son, Adonijah did not know how to work within limits. The result was that he always wanted his own way, regardless of how it affected others. Adonijah did whatever he wanted and paid no respect to God's wishes. An undisciplined child may look cute to his parents, but an undisciplined adult destroys himself and others. Parents set limits so that their children will develop the self-restraint they will need later. A well-disciplined child becomes a self-disciplined adult. If your parents discipline you, be grateful that they love you. If you're a parent, do your children a favor and discipline them wisely.

David Gives Solomon the Crown

APRIL 12

1 KINGS 1:32-53

32Then King David ordered, "Call Zadok the priest, Nathan the prophet, and Benaiah son of
Jehoiada." When they came into the king's presence, 33the king said to them, "Take Solomon
and my officials down to Gihon Spring. Solomon is to ride on my own mule. 34There Zadok
the priest and Nathan the prophet are to anoint him king over Israel. Blow the ram's horn and
shout, 'Long live King Solomon!' 35Then escort him back here, and he will sit on my throne.
He will succeed me as king, for I have appointed him to be ruler over Israel and Judah." . . .

41Adonijah and his guests heard the celebrating and shouting just as they were finishing
their banquet. When Joab heard the sound of the ram's horn, he asked, "What's going on?
Why is the city in such an uproar?"

42And while he was still speaking, Jonathan son of Abiathar the priest arrived. "Come
in," Adonijah said to him, "for you are a good man. You must have good news."

43"Not at all!" Jonathan replied. "Our lord King David has just declared Solomon king!
. . . 47And all the royal officials have gone to King David and congratulated him, saying, 'May
your God make Solomon's fame even greater than your own, and may Solomon's reign be
even greater than yours!' Then the king bowed his head in worship as he lay in his bed, 48and
he said, 'Praise the Lord, the God of Israel, who today has chosen a successor to sit on my
throne while I am still alive to see it.'"

49Then all of Adonijah's guests jumped up in panic from the banquet table and quickly
scattered. 50Adonijah was afraid of Solomon, so he rushed to the sacred tent and grabbed on
to the horns of the altar. 51Word soon reached Solomon that Adonijah had seized the horns
of the altar in fear, and that he was pleading, "Let King Solomon swear today that he will
not kill me!"

52Solomon replied, "If he proves himself to be loyal, not a hair on his head will be
touched. But if he makes trouble, he will die." 53So King Solomon summoned Adonijah,
and they brought him down from the altar. He came and bowed respectfully before King
Solomon, who dismissed him, saying, "Go on home."

How often do you seek God's guidance before you act? Sometimes it takes getting caught before someone is willing to give up his scheme. When Adonijah learned that his plans had been exposed, he ran in panic to the sacred altar, the highest symbol of God's mercy and forgiveness. He went there, however, after his plans for treason were exposed. If Adonijah had first considered what God wanted, he might have avoided trouble. Don't wait until you have made a mess of things to run to God. Seek his direction before you act.

APRIL 13

Solomon's Wisdom

1 KINGS 3:1-15

Solomon made an alliance with Pharaoh, the king of Egypt, and married one of his daughters.
He brought her to live in the City of David until he could finish building his palace and the
Temple of the LORD and the wall around the city. 2At that time the people of Israel sacrificed
their offerings at local places of worship, for a temple honoring the name of the LORD had
not yet been built.

3Solomon loved the LORD and followed all the decrees of his father, David, except that
Solomon, too, offered sacrifices and burned incense at the local places of worship. 4The most
important of these places of worship was at Gibeon, so the king went there and sacrificed
1,000 burnt offerings. 5That night the LORD appeared to Solomon in a dream, and God said,
"What do you want? Ask, and I will give it to you!"

6Solomon replied, "You showed great and faithful love to your servant my father, David,
because he was honest and true and faithful to you. And you have continued to show this
great and faithful love to him today by giving him a son to sit on his throne.

7"Now, O LORD my God, you have made me king instead of my father, David, but I
am like a little child who doesn't know his way around. 8And here I am in the midst of your
own chosen people, a nation so great and numerous they cannot be counted! 9Give me an
understanding heart so that I can govern your people well and know the difference between
right and wrong. For who by himself is able to govern this great people of yours?"

10The Lord was pleased that Solomon had asked for wisdom. 11So God replied, "Because
you have asked for wisdom in governing my people with justice and have not asked for a long
life or wealth or the death of your enemies—12I will give you what you asked for! I will give
you a wise and understanding heart such as no one else has had or ever will have! 13And I will
also give you what you did not ask for—riches and fame! No other king in all the world will
be compared to you for the rest of your life! 14And if you follow me and obey my decrees and
my commands as your father, David, did, I will give you a long life."

15Then Solomon woke up and realized it had been a dream. He returned to Jerusalem and
stood before the Ark of the Lord's Covenant, where he sacrificed burnt offerings and peace
offerings. Then he invited all his officials to a great banquet.

Which of Solomon's choices would you have made? When given a chance to have anything in the world, Solomon asked for wisdom in order to lead well and make right decisions. We can ask God for this same wisdom (James 1:5). Notice that Solomon asked for wisdom to carry out his job. He did not ask God to do the job for him. We should not ask God to do for us what he wants to do through us. Instead, we should ask God to give us the wisdom to know what to do and the courage to follow through on it.

Solomon Solves a Problem

APRIL 14

1 KINGS 3:16-28

16Some time later two prostitutes came to the king to have an argument settled. 17"Please, my
lord," one of them began, "this woman and I live in the same house. I gave birth to a baby
while she was with me in the house. 18Three days later this woman also had a baby. We were
alone; there were only two of us in the house.

19"But her baby died during the night when she rolled over on it. 20Then she got up in the
night and took my son from beside me while I was asleep. She laid her dead child in my arms
and took mine to sleep beside her. 21And in the morning when I tried to nurse my son, he was
dead! But when I looked more closely in the morning light, I saw that it wasn't my son at all."

22Then the other woman interrupted, "It certainly was your son, and the living child is
mine."

"No," the first woman said, "the living child is mine, and the dead one is yours." And so they argued back and forth before the king.

23Then the king said, "Let's get the facts straight. Both of you claim the living child is
yours, and each says that the dead one belongs to the other. 24All right, bring me a sword."
So a sword was brought to the king.

25Then he said, "Cut the living child in two, and give half to one woman and half to the
other!"

26Then the woman who was the real mother of the living child, and who loved him very
much, cried out, "Oh no, my lord! Give her the child—please do not kill him!"

But the other woman said, "All right, he will be neither yours nor mine; divide him between us!"

27Then the king said, "Do not kill the child, but give him to the woman who wants him
to live, for she is his mother!"

28When all Israel heard the king's decision, the people were in awe of the king, for they
saw the wisdom God had given him for rendering justice.

In what situation in your life do you presently need God's wisdom? Solomon's settlement of this dispute was a classic example of his wisdom. This wise ruling was verification that God had answered Solomon's prayer and given him an understanding heart. We have God's wisdom available to us as we pray and request it. But, like Solomon, we must put it into action. Applying wisdom to life demonstrates our understanding.

APRIL 15 Solomon Builds the Temple

1 KINGS 6:1-38

It was in midspring, in the month of Ziv, during the fourth year of Solomon's reign, that he
began to construct the Temple of the Lord. This was 480 years after the people of Israel were
rescued from their slavery in the land of Egypt.
2 The Temple that King Solomon built for the Lord was 90 feet long, 30 feet wide, and
45 feet high. 3 The entry room at the front of the Temple was 30 feet wide, running across
the entire width of the Temple. It projected outward 15 feet from the front of the Temple.
4 Solomon also made narrow recessed windows throughout the Temple.
5 He built a complex of rooms against the outer walls of the Temple, all the way around
the sides and rear of the building. 6 The complex was three stories high, the bottom floor being
7½ feet wide, the second floor 9 feet wide, and the top floor 10½ feet wide. The rooms were
connected to the walls of the Temple by beams resting on ledges built out from the wall. So
the beams were not inserted into the walls themselves.
7 The stones used in the construction of the Temple were finished at the quarry, so there
was no sound of hammer, ax, or any other iron tool at the building site.
8 The entrance to the bottom floor was on the south side of the Temple. There were
winding stairs going up to the second floor, and another flight of stairs between the second
and third floors. 9 After completing the Temple structure, Solomon put in a ceiling made of
cedar beams and planks. 10 As already stated, he built a complex of rooms along the sides of
the building, attached to the Temple walls by cedar timbers. Each story of the complex was
7½ feet high.
11 Then the Lord gave this message to Solomon: 12 "Concerning this Temple you are
building, if you keep all my decrees and regulations and obey all my commands, I will fulfill
through you the promise I made to your father, David. 13 I will live among the Israelites and
will never abandon my people Israel." . . .
37 The foundation of the Lord's Temple was laid in midspring, in the month of Ziv,
during the fourth year of Solomon's reign. 38 The entire building was completed in every
detail by midautumn, in the month of Bul, during the eleventh year of his reign. So it took
seven years to build the Temple.

What can you learn from Solomon about making and carrying out plans? Verse 13 summarizes the Temple's main purpose. God promised that his eternal presence would never leave the Temple as long as one condition was met—the Israelites had to obey God's law. Knowing how many laws they had to follow, we may think this condition was difficult. But the Israelites' situation was much like ours today: they were not cut off from God for failing to keep some small subpoint of a law. Forgiveness was amply provided for all their sins, no matter how large or small. As you read the history of the kings, you will see that lawbreaking was the result, not the cause, of estrangement from God. The kings abandoned God in their hearts first and then failed to keep his laws. When we close our hearts to God, his power and presence soon leave us.

The Queen of Sheba Arrives

APRIL 16

1 KINGS 10:1-13

When the queen of Sheba heard of Solomon's fame, which brought honor to the name of the Lord, she came to test him with hard questions. 2She arrived in Jerusalem with a large group of attendants and a great caravan of camels loaded with spices, large quantities of gold, and precious jewels. When she met with Solomon, she talked with him about everything she had on her mind. 3Solomon had answers for all her questions; nothing was too hard for the king to explain to her. 4When the queen of Sheba realized how very wise Solomon was, and when she saw the palace he had built, 5she was overwhelmed. She was also amazed at the food on his tables, the organization of his officials and their splendid clothing, the cup-bearers, and the burnt offerings Solomon made at the Temple of the Lord.

6She exclaimed to the king, "Everything I heard in my country about your achievements and wisdom is true! 7I didn't believe what was said until I arrived here and saw it with my own eyes. In fact, I had not heard the half of it! Your wisdom and prosperity are far beyond what I was told. 8How happy your people must be! What a privilege for your officials to stand here day after day, listening to your wisdom! 9Praise the Lord your God, who delights in you and has placed you on the throne of Israel. Because of the Lord's eternal love for Israel, he has made you king so you can rule with justice and righteousness."

10Then she gave the king a gift of 9,000 pounds of gold, great quantities of spices, and precious jewels. Never again were so many spices brought in as those the queen of Sheba gave to King Solomon.

11(In addition, Hiram's ships brought gold from Ophir, and they also brought rich cargoes of red sandalwood and precious jewels. 12The king used the sandalwood to make railings for the Temple of the Lord and the royal palace, and to construct lyres and harps for the musicians. Never before or since has there been such a supply of sandalwood.)

13King Solomon gave the queen of Sheba whatever she asked for, besides all the customary gifts he had so generously given. Then she and all her attendants returned to their own land.

When have you noticed God's wisdom shining in your life? Because of Solomon's wisdom, the people were happy and the palace servants content. Wisdom's quality is shown by how well it works. In James 3:17 we learn that wisdom is peace loving. Are you seeking the kind of wisdom that establishes peace in your relationships?

APRIL 17 Solomon's Unwise Son

1 KINGS 12:1-19

Rehoboam went to Shechem, where all Israel had gathered to make him king. . . . 3The leaders
of Israel summoned him, and Jeroboam and the whole assembly of Israel went to speak with
Rehoboam. 4"Your father was a hard master," they said. "Lighten the harsh labor demands
and heavy taxes that your father imposed on us. Then we will be your loyal subjects."
5Rehoboam replied, "Give me three days to think this over. Then come back for my
answer." So the people went away.
6Then King Rehoboam discussed the matter with the older men who had counseled his
father, Solomon. "What is your advice?" he asked. "How should I answer these people?"
7The older counselors replied, "If you are willing to be a servant to these people today
and give them a favorable answer, they will always be your loyal subjects."
8But Rehoboam rejected the advice of the older men and instead asked the opinion of the
young men who had grown up with him and were now his advisers. 9"What is your advice?"
he asked them. "How should I answer these people who want me to lighten the burdens
imposed by my father?"
10The young men replied, "This is what you should tell those complainers who want a
lighter burden: 'My little finger is thicker than my father's waist! 11Yes, my father laid heavy
burdens on you, but I'm going to make them even heavier! My father beat you with whips,
but I will beat you with scorpions!'"
12Three days later Jeroboam and all the people returned to hear Rehoboam's decision,
just as the king had ordered. 13But Rehoboam spoke harshly to the people, for he rejected
the advice of the older counselors 14and followed the counsel of his younger advisers. He told
the people, "My father laid heavy burdens on you, but I'm going to make them even heavier!
My father beat you with whips, but I will beat you with scorpions!"
15So the king paid no attention to the people. This turn of events was the will of the
LORD, for it fulfilled the LORD's message to Jeroboam son of Nebat through the prophet
Ahijah from Shiloh. . . .
18King Rehoboam sent Adoniram, who was in charge of forced labor, to restore order,
but the people of Israel stoned him to death. When this news reached King Rehoboam, he
quickly jumped into his chariot and fled to Jerusalem. 19And to this day the northern tribes
of Israel have refused to be ruled by a descendant of David.

Who are the people you know will give you good advice? Rehoboam asked for advice, but he didn't carefully evaluate that advice. If he had, he would have realized that the advice offered by the older men was wiser than that of his peers. To evaluate advice, ask yourself if it is realistic, workable, and consistent with the Bible. Determine whether following the advice will be fair, make improvements, and result in a wise solution. Seek counsel from those more experienced and wise. Advice is helpful only if we evaluate it with God's standards in mind.

Lazarus Dies

AUGUST 18

JOHN 11:1-26

A man named Lazarus was sick. He lived in Bethany with his sisters, Mary and Martha. 2This is the Mary who later poured the expensive perfume on the Lord's feet and wiped them with her hair. Her brother, Lazarus, was sick. 3So the two sisters sent a message to Jesus telling him, "Lord, your dear friend is very sick."

4But when Jesus heard about it he said, "Lazarus's sickness will not end in death. No, it happened for the glory of God so that the Son of God will receive glory from this." 5So although Jesus loved Martha, Mary, and Lazarus, 6he stayed where he was for the next two days. 7Finally, he said to his disciples, "Let's go back to Judea."

8But his disciples objected. "Rabbi," they said, "only a few days ago the people in Judea were trying to stone you. Are you going there again?"

9Jesus replied, "There are twelve hours of daylight every day. During the day people can walk safely. They can see because they have the light of this world. 10But at night there is danger of stumbling because they have no light." 11Then he said, "Our friend Lazarus has fallen asleep, but now I will go and wake him up."

12The disciples said, "Lord, if he is sleeping, he will soon get better!" 13They thought Jesus meant Lazarus was simply sleeping, but Jesus meant Lazarus had died.

14So he told them plainly, "Lazarus is dead. 15And for your sakes, I'm glad I wasn't there, for now you will really believe. Come, let's go see him."

16Thomas, nicknamed the Twin, said to his fellow disciples, "Let's go, too—and die with Jesus."

17When Jesus arrived at Bethany, he was told that Lazarus had already been in his grave for four days. 18Bethany was only a few miles down the road from Jerusalem, 19and many of the people had come to console Martha and Mary in their loss. 20When Martha got word that Jesus was coming, she went to meet him. But Mary stayed in the house. 21Martha said to Jesus, "Lord, if only you had been here, my brother would not have died. 22But even now I know that God will give you whatever you ask."

23Jesus told her, "Your brother will rise again."

24"Yes," Martha said, "he will rise when everyone else rises, at the last day."

25Jesus told her, "I am the resurrection and the life. Anyone who believes in me will live, even after dying. 26Everyone who lives in me and believes in me will never ever die. Do you believe this, Martha?"

In what situations have you been disappointed with God? Jesus loved this family and often stayed with them. He knew their pain but did not respond immediately. His delay had a specific purpose. God's timing, especially his delays, may make us think that he is not answering or that he is not answering in the way we want. But he will meet all our needs according to his perfect schedule and purpose. Patiently await his timing.

The Prophets of Baal

APRIL 18

1 KINGS 18:17-29

17 When Ahab saw him, he exclaimed, "So, is it really you, you troublemaker of Israel?"
18 "I have made no trouble for Israel," Elijah replied. "You and your family are the troublemakers, for you have refused to obey the commands of the LORD and have worshiped the
images of Baal instead. 19 Now summon all Israel to join me at Mount Carmel, along with
the 450 prophets of Baal and the 400 prophets of Asherah who are supported by Jezebel."
20 So Ahab summoned all the people of Israel and the prophets to Mount Carmel. 21 Then
Elijah stood in front of them and said, "How much longer will you waver, hobbling between
two opinions? If the LORD is God, follow him! But if Baal is God, then follow him!" But the
people were completely silent.
22 Then Elijah said to them, "I am the only prophet of the LORD who is left, but Baal has
450 prophets. 23 Now bring two bulls. The prophets of Baal may choose whichever one they
wish and cut it into pieces and lay it on the wood of their altar, but without setting fire to it.
I will prepare the other bull and lay it on the wood on the altar, but not set fire to it. 24 Then
call on the name of your god, and I will call on the name of the LORD. The god who answers
by setting fire to the wood is the true God!" And all the people agreed.
25 Then Elijah said to the prophets of Baal, "You go first, for there are many of you.
Choose one of the bulls, and prepare it and call on the name of your god. But do not set fire
to the wood."
26 So they prepared one of the bulls and placed it on the altar. Then they called on the
name of Baal from morning until noontime, shouting, "O Baal, answer us!" But there was
no reply of any kind. Then they danced, hobbling around the altar they had made.
27 About noontime Elijah began mocking them. "You'll have to shout louder," he scoffed,
"for surely he is a god! Perhaps he is daydreaming, or is relieving himself. Or maybe he is
away on a trip, or is asleep and needs to be wakened!"
28 So they shouted louder, and following their normal custom, they cut themselves with
knives and swords until the blood gushed out. 29 They raved all afternoon until the time of
the evening sacrifice, but still there was no sound, no reply, no response.

How can you know God is real? Although the prophets of Baal "raved all afternoon," no one answered them. Their god was silent because it was not real. The gods we may be tempted to follow are not idols of wood or stone, but they are just as false and dangerous, because they cause us to depend on something other than God. Power, status, appearance, or material possessions can become our gods if we devote our lives to them. But when we reach times of crisis and desperately call out to these gods, there will only be silence. They can offer no true answers, no guidance, and no wisdom. The one true God, on the other hand, always hears and promises to answer.

Spiritual Burnout

APRIL 20

1 KINGS 19:1-13

When Ahab got home, he told Jezebel everything Elijah had done, including the way he had killed all the prophets of Baal. [2]So Jezebel sent this message to Elijah: "May the gods strike me and even kill me if by this time tomorrow I have not killed you just as you killed them."

[3]Elijah was afraid and fled for his life. He went to Beersheba, a town in Judah, and he left his servant there. [4]Then he went on alone into the wilderness, traveling all day. He sat down under a solitary broom tree and prayed that he might die. "I have had enough, LORD," he said. "Take my life, for I am no better than my ancestors who have already died."

[5]Then he lay down and slept under the broom tree. But as he was sleeping, an angel touched him and told him, "Get up and eat!" [6]He looked around and there beside his head was some bread baked on hot stones and a jar of water! So he ate and drank and lay down again.

[7]Then the angel of the LORD came again and touched him and said, "Get up and eat some more, or the journey ahead will be too much for you."

[8]So he got up and ate and drank, and the food gave him enough strength to travel forty days and forty nights to Mount Sinai, the mountain of God. [9]There he came to a cave, where he spent the night.

But the LORD said to him, "What are you doing here, Elijah?"

[10]Elijah replied, "I have zealously served the LORD God Almighty. But the people of Israel have broken their covenant with you, torn down your altars, and killed every one of your prophets. I am the only one left, and now they are trying to kill me, too."

[11]"Go out and stand before me on the mountain," the LORD told him. And as Elijah stood there, the LORD passed by, and a mighty windstorm hit the mountain. It was such a terrible blast that the rocks were torn loose, but the LORD was not in the wind. After the wind there was an earthquake, but the LORD was not in the earthquake. [12]And after the earthquake there was a fire, but the LORD was not in the fire. And after the fire there was the sound of a gentle whisper. [13]When Elijah heard it, he wrapped his face in his cloak and went out and stood at the entrance of the cave.

When was the last time you felt sorry for yourself? Elijah knew that the gentle whisper was God's voice. He realized that God doesn't reveal himself only in powerful, miraculous ways. To look for God only in something big (camps, churches, conferences, visible leaders) may be to miss him, because he is often found gently whispering in the quietness of a humbled heart. Are you listening for God? Step back from the noise and activity of your busy life and listen humbly and quietly for his guidance. It may come when you least expect it.

APRIL 21

The Stolen Vineyard

1 KINGS 21:1-16

Now there was a man named Naboth, from Jezreel, who owned a vineyard in Jezreel beside
the palace of King Ahab of Samaria. 2One day Ahab said to Naboth, "Since your vineyard
is so convenient to my palace, I would like to buy it to use as a vegetable garden. I will give
you a better vineyard in exchange, or if you prefer, I will pay you for it."

3But Naboth replied, "The Lord forbid that I should give you the inheritance that was
passed down by my ancestors."

4So Ahab went home angry and sullen because of Naboth's answer. The king went to bed
with his face to the wall and refused to eat!

5"What's the matter?" his wife Jezebel asked him. "What's made you so upset that you're
not eating?"

6"I asked Naboth to sell me his vineyard or trade it, but he refused!" Ahab told her.

7"Are you the king of Israel or not?" Jezebel demanded. "Get up and eat something, and
don't worry about it. I'll get you Naboth's vineyard!"

8So she wrote letters in Ahab's name, sealed them with his seal, and sent them to the elders
and other leaders of the town where Naboth lived. 9In her letters she commanded: "Call the
citizens together for a time of fasting, and give Naboth a place of honor. 10And then seat two
scoundrels across from him who will accuse him of cursing God and the king. Then take
him out and stone him to death."

11So the elders and other town leaders followed the instructions Jezebel had written in
the letters. 12They called for a fast and put Naboth at a prominent place before the people.
13Then the two scoundrels came and sat down across from him. And they accused Naboth
before all the people, saying, "He cursed God and the king." So he was dragged outside the
town and stoned to death. 14The town leaders then sent word to Jezebel, "Naboth has been
stoned to death."

15When Jezebel heard the news, she said to Ahab, "You know the vineyard Naboth
wouldn't sell you? Well, you can have it now! He's dead!" 16So Ahab immediately went down
to the vineyard of Naboth to claim it.

How important is justice in your life? Naboth was absolutely right to refuse to sell his land, because the land belonged to his family and was meant to be passed down. But that didn't concern Ahab or Jezebel in the least. Jezebel devised a scheme that appeared legal to get Naboth's land for her husband. Two witnesses were required to establish guilt of blasphemy, and the punishment was death by stoning. Those who twist the law and legal procedures to get what they want today may be more sophisticated in how they go about it, but they are guilty of the same sin.

Ahab Seeks Mercy

APRIL 22

1 KINGS 21:17-29

17 But the LORD said to Elijah, 18 "Go down to meet King Ahab of Israel, who rules in Samaria.
He will be at Naboth's vineyard in Jezreel, claiming it for himself. 19 Give him this message:
'This is what the LORD says: Wasn't it enough that you killed Naboth? Must you rob him,
too? Because you have done this, dogs will lick your blood at the very place where they licked
the blood of Naboth!'"

20 "So, my enemy, you have found me!" Ahab exclaimed to Elijah.

"Yes," Elijah answered, "I have come because you have sold yourself to what is evil in the
LORD's sight. 21 So now the LORD says, 'I will bring disaster on you and consume you. I will
destroy every one of your male descendants, slave and free alike, anywhere in Israel! 22 I am
going to destroy your family as I did the family of Jeroboam son of Nebat and the family of
Baasha son of Ahijah, for you have made me very angry and have led Israel into sin.'

23 "And regarding Jezebel, the LORD says, 'Dogs will eat Jezebel's body at the plot of land
in Jezreel.'

24 "The members of Ahab's family who die in the city will be eaten by dogs, and those
who die in the field will be eaten by vultures."

25 (No one else so completely sold himself to what was evil in the LORD's sight as Ahab
did under the influence of his wife Jezebel. 26 His worst outrage was worshiping idols just as
the Amorites had done—the people whom the LORD had driven out from the land ahead
of the Israelites.)

27 But when Ahab heard this message, he tore his clothing, dressed in burlap, and fasted.
He even slept in burlap and went about in deep mourning.

28 Then another message from the LORD came to Elijah: 29 "Do you see how Ahab has
humbled himself before me? Because he has done this, I will not do what I promised during
his lifetime. It will happen to his sons; I will destroy his dynasty."

Are you willing to admit when you've sinned? Ahab refused to admit his sin against God. Instead he accused Elijah of being his enemy. When we are blinded by envy and hatred, it is almost impossible to see our own sin. Ahab was more wicked than any other king of Israel, but when he repented in deep humility, God took notice and reduced his punishment. The same Lord who was merciful to Ahab wants to be merciful to you. No matter what you have done, it is never too late to humble yourself, turn to God, and ask for forgiveness.

APRIL 23

Elijah's Chariot

2 KINGS 2:1-12

When the LORD was about to take Elijah up to heaven in a whirlwind, Elijah and Elisha were traveling from Gilgal. 2And Elijah said to Elisha, "Stay here, for the LORD has told me to go to Bethel."

But Elisha replied, "As surely as the LORD lives and you yourself live, I will never leave you!" So they went down together to Bethel.

3The group of prophets from Bethel came to Elisha and asked him, "Did you know that the LORD is going to take your master away from you today?"

"Of course I know," Elisha answered. "But be quiet about it."

4Then Elijah said to Elisha, "Stay here, for the LORD has told me to go to Jericho."

But Elisha replied again, "As surely as the LORD lives and you yourself live, I will never leave you." So they went on together to Jericho.

5Then the group of prophets from Jericho came to Elisha and asked him, "Did you know that the LORD is going to take your master away from you today?"

"Of course I know," Elisha answered. "But be quiet about it."

6Then Elijah said to Elisha, "Stay here, for the LORD has told me to go to the Jordan River."

But again Elisha replied, "As surely as the LORD lives and you yourself live, I will never leave you." So they went on together.

7Fifty men from the group of prophets also went and watched from a distance as Elijah
and Elisha stopped beside the Jordan River. 8Then Elijah folded his cloak together and struck
the water with it. The river divided, and the two of them went across on dry ground!

9When they came to the other side, Elijah said to Elisha, "Tell me what I can do for you before I am taken away."

And Elisha replied, "Please let me inherit a double share of your spirit and become your successor."

10"You have asked a difficult thing," Elijah replied. "If you see me when I am taken from you, then you will get your request. But if not, then you won't."

11As they were walking along and talking, suddenly a chariot of fire appeared, drawn by
horses of fire. It drove between the two men, separating them, and Elijah was carried by a
whirlwind into heaven. 12Elisha saw it and cried out, "My father! My father! I see the chariots and charioteers of Israel!" And as they disappeared from sight, Elisha tore his clothes in
distress.

When you make a commitment, how far will you go to carry it out? Elisha asked for twice as much power as Elijah had. This was a bold request, but God granted it. Why? Because Elisha's motives were pure. His main goal was not to be better or more powerful than Elijah but to accomplish more for God. If our motives are pure, we don't have to be afraid to ask for great things from God. When we ask God for great power or ability, we need to examine our motives and get rid of any selfishness we find.

Elisha's Miracles

APRIL 24

2 KINGS 2:13-25

13Elisha picked up Elijah's cloak, which had fallen when he was taken up. Then Elisha
returned to the bank of the Jordan River. 14He struck the water with Elijah's cloak and cried
out, "Where is the LORD, the God of Elijah?" Then the river divided, and Elisha went across.
15When the group of prophets from Jericho saw from a distance what happened, they
exclaimed, "Elijah's spirit rests upon Elisha!" And they went to meet him and bowed to the
ground before him. 16"Sir," they said, "just say the word and fifty of our strongest men will
search the wilderness for your master. Perhaps the Spirit of the LORD has left him on some
mountain or in some valley."
"No," Elisha said, "don't send them." 17But they kept urging him until they shamed him
into agreeing, and he finally said, "All right, send them." So fifty men searched for three days
but did not find Elijah. 18Elisha was still at Jericho when they returned. "Didn't I tell you
not to go?" he asked.
19One day the leaders of the town of Jericho visited Elisha. "We have a problem, my lord,"
they told him. "This town is located in pleasant surroundings, as you can see. But the water
is bad, and the land is unproductive."
20Elisha said, "Bring me a new bowl with salt in it." So they brought it to him. 21Then he
went out to the spring that supplied the town with water and threw the salt into it. And he
said, "This is what the LORD says: I have purified this water. It will no longer cause death or
infertility." 22And the water has remained pure ever since, just as Elisha said.
23Elisha left Jericho and went up to Bethel. As he was walking along the road, a group of
boys from the town began mocking and making fun of him. "Go away, baldy!" they chanted.
"Go away, baldy!" 24Elisha turned around and looked at them, and he cursed them in the
name of the LORD. Then two bears came out of the woods and mauled forty-two of them.
25From there Elisha went to Mount Carmel and finally returned to Samaria.

How would someone else know that you have a deep respect for God? Some young men made fun of God's messenger and paid for it with their lives. Making fun of religious leaders has been a popular sport through the ages. To take a stand for God is to be different from the world and vulnerable to verbal abuse. When we are cynical and sarcastic toward religious leaders, we are in danger of mocking not just the person but also the spiritual message. We need to pray for leaders, not laugh at them. True leaders, those who follow God, need to be heard with respect and encouraged in their ministries.

APRIL 25

The Healing of Naaman

2 KINGS 5:1-14

The king of Aram had great admiration for Naaman, the commander of his army, because
through him the LORD had given Aram great victories. But though Naaman was a mighty
warrior, he suffered from leprosy.

2At this time Aramean raiders had invaded the land of Israel, and among their captives
was a young girl who had been given to Naaman's wife as a maid. 3One day the girl said to
her mistress, "I wish my master would go to see the prophet in Samaria. He would heal him
of his leprosy."

4So Naaman told the king what the young girl from Israel had said. 5"Go and visit the
prophet," the king of Aram told him. "I will send a letter of introduction. . . ." 6The letter
to the king of Israel said: "With this letter I present my servant Naaman. I want you to
heal him of his leprosy."

7When the king of Israel read the letter, he tore his clothes in dismay and said, "Am I
God, that I can give life and take it away? Why is this man asking me to heal someone with
leprosy? I can see that he's just trying to pick a fight with me."

8But when Elisha, the man of God, heard that the king of Israel had torn his clothes in
dismay, he sent this message to him: "Why are you so upset? Send Naaman to me, and he
will learn that there is a true prophet here in Israel."

9So Naaman went with his horses and chariots and waited at the door of Elisha's house.
10But Elisha sent a messenger out to him with this message: "Go and wash yourself seven
times in the Jordan River. Then your skin will be restored, and you will be healed of your
leprosy."

11But Naaman became angry and stalked away. "I thought he would certainly come out to
meet me!" he said. "I expected him to wave his hand over the leprosy and call on the name of
the LORD his God and heal me! 12Aren't the rivers of Damascus, the Abana and the Pharpar,
better than any of the rivers of Israel? Why shouldn't I wash in them and be healed?" So
Naaman turned and went away in a rage.

13But his officers tried to reason with him and said, "Sir, if the prophet had told you to
do something very difficult, wouldn't you have done it? So you should certainly obey him
when he says simply, 'Go and wash and be cured!'" 14So Naaman went down to the Jordan
River and dipped himself seven times, as the man of God had instructed him. And his skin
became as healthy as the skin of a young child, and he was healed!

What "small" things have you refused to do for God? Naaman, a great hero, was used to getting respect, and he was outraged when Elisha treated him like an ordinary person. To wash in a great river would be one thing, but the Jordan was small and dirty. Naaman had to humble himself and obey Elisha's commands in order to be healed. Obedience to God begins with humility. We may not always understand his ways of working, but by humbly obeying, we will receive his blessings. We must remember: (1) God's ways are best; (2) God wants our obedience more than anything; and (3) God can use anything to accomplish his purposes.

The Seven-Year-Old King

APRIL 26

2 KINGS 11:1-21

When Athaliah, the mother of King Ahaziah of Judah, learned that her son was dead, she
began to destroy the rest of the royal family. 2But Ahaziah's sister Jehosheba, the daughter of
King Jehoram, took Ahaziah's infant son, Joash, and stole him away from among the rest of
the king's children, who were about to be killed. She put Joash and his nurse in a bedroom,
and they hid him from Athaliah, so the child was not murdered. 3Joash remained hidden in
the Temple of the LORD for six years while Athaliah ruled over the land.
4In the seventh year of Athaliah's reign, Jehoiada the priest summoned the commanders,
the Carite mercenaries, and the palace guards to come to the Temple of the LORD. He made
a solemn pact with them . . . then he showed them the king's son. . . .
12Then Jehoiada brought out Joash, the king's son, placed the crown on his head, and
presented him with a copy of God's laws. They anointed him and proclaimed him king, and
everyone clapped their hands and shouted, "Long live the king!"
13When Athaliah heard the noise made by the palace guards and the people, she hurried
to the LORD's Temple to see what was happening. 14When she arrived, she saw the newly
crowned king standing in his place of authority by the pillar, as was the custom at times of
coronation. The commanders and trumpeters were surrounding him, and people from all
over the land were rejoicing and blowing trumpets. When Athaliah saw all this, she tore her
clothes in despair and shouted, "Treason! Treason!"
15Then Jehoiada the priest ordered the commanders who were in charge of the troops,
"Take her to the soldiers in front of the Temple, and kill anyone who tries to rescue her." For
the priest had said, "She must not be killed in the Temple of the LORD." 16So they seized her
and led her out to the gate where horses enter the palace grounds, and she was killed there.
17Then Jehoiada made a covenant between the LORD and the king and the people that
they would be the LORD's people. He also made a covenant between the king and the people.
18And all the people of the land went over to the temple of Baal and tore it down. . . .
21Joash was seven years old when he became king.

Who were your best examples in childhood? The covenant recorded in verse 17 was in fact a recommitment to a very old covenant—the one set up in the book of Deuteronomy for the righteous rule of the nation. It was meant to function as a constitution for the people. This covenant, however, had been virtually ignored for over a hundred years. The new king was only seven years old. But Jehoiada, the priest, wisely prepared for the king's future rule by recommitting the nation and the king to the Lord. What a godly example for the young king. Think of the people who have been good examples in your life. What effect did they have on you? How can you thank them?

APRIL 27

Discovery of the Lost Book

2 KINGS 22:1-13; 23:1-3

Josiah was eight years old when he became king, and he reigned in Jerusalem thirty-one years.
His mother was Jedidah, the daughter of Adaiah from Bozkath. 2He did what was pleasing
in the LORD's sight and followed the example of his ancestor David. He did not turn away
from doing what was right.

3In the eighteenth year of his reign, King Josiah sent Shaphan son of Azaliah and grandson
of Meshullam, the court secretary, to the Temple of the LORD. He told him, 4"Go to Hilkiah
the high priest and have him count the money the gatekeepers have collected from the people
at the LORD's Temple. 5Entrust this money to the men assigned to supervise the restoration
of the LORD's Temple. . . .

8Hilkiah the high priest said to Shaphan the court secretary, "I have found the Book of
the Law in the LORD's Temple!" Then Hilkiah gave the scroll to Shaphan, and he read it.

9Shaphan went to the king and reported, "Your officials have turned over the money
collected at the Temple of the LORD to the workers and supervisors at the Temple." 10Shaphan
also told the king, "Hilkiah the priest has given me a scroll." So Shaphan read it to the king.

11When the king heard what was written in the Book of the Law, he tore his clothes in
despair. 12Then he gave these orders to Hilkiah the priest, Ahikam son of Shaphan, Acbor son
of Micaiah, Shaphan the court secretary, and Asaiah the king's personal adviser: 13"Go to the
Temple and speak to the LORD for me and for the people and for all Judah. Inquire about
the words written in this scroll that has been found. For the LORD's great anger is burning
against us because our ancestors have not obeyed the words in this scroll. We have not been
doing everything it says we must do."

23:1Then the king summoned all the elders of Judah and Jerusalem. 2And the king went up to
the Temple of the LORD with all the people of Judah and Jerusalem, along with the priests
and the prophets—all the people from the least to the greatest. There the king read to them
the entire Book of the Covenant that had been found in the LORD's Temple. 3The king took
his place of authority beside the pillar and renewed the covenant in the LORD's presence. He
pledged to obey the LORD by keeping all his commands, laws, and decrees with all his heart
and soul. In this way, he confirmed all the terms of the covenant that were written in the
scroll, and all the people pledged themselves to the covenant.

What happens in your life when the Bible is a "lost book"? When Josiah heard the law, he tore his clothes in grief. He immediately instituted reforms. With just one reading of God's law, he changed the course of the nation. Today many people own Bibles, but few are affected by the truths found in God's Word. The Word of God should cause us, like Josiah, to take action immediately to reform our lives and bring them into harmony with God's will.

Rebuilding the Temple

EZRA 3:1-13

In early autumn, when the Israelites had settled in their towns, all the people assembled in
Jerusalem with a unified purpose. [2]Then Jeshua son of Jehozadak joined his fellow priests
and Zerubbabel son of Shealtiel with his family in rebuilding the altar of the God of Israel.
They wanted to sacrifice burnt offerings on it, as instructed in the Law of Moses, the man of
God. [3]Even though the people were afraid of the local residents, they rebuilt the altar at its
old site. Then they began to sacrifice burnt offerings on the altar to the LORD each morning
and evening. . . .

[7]Then the people hired masons and carpenters and bought cedar logs from the people of Tyre and Sidon, paying them with food, wine, and olive oil. The logs were brought down from the Lebanon mountains and floated along the coast of the Mediterranean Sea to Joppa, for King Cyrus had given permission for this.

[8]The construction of the Temple of God began in midspring, during the second year after they arrived in Jerusalem. . . .

[10]When the builders completed the foundation of the LORD's Temple, the priests put on
their robes and took their places to blow their trumpets. And the Levites, descendants of
Asaph, clashed their cymbals to praise the LORD, just as King David had prescribed. [11]With
praise and thanks, they sang this song to the LORD:

> "He is so good!
>   His faithful love for Israel endures forever!"

Then all the people gave a great shout, praising the LORD because the foundation of the LORD's Temple had been laid.

[12]But many of the older priests, Levites, and other leaders who had seen the first Temple
wept aloud when they saw the new Temple's foundation. The others, however, were shouting
for joy. [13]The joyful shouting and weeping mingled together in a loud noise that could be
heard far in the distance.

How do you feel when you're working on a large, important project? Fifty years after its destruction, the Temple was being rebuilt (536 BC). Some of the older people remembered Solomon's Temple and wept because the new Temple would not be as glorious as the first one. But the beauty of the building is not nearly so important to God as the attitudes of the builders and worshipers. God cares more about what we are than what we accomplish. Our world is always changing, and magnificent accomplishments decay and disappear. Do not be concerned if it seems as if your work for God is not as great as what others have done. Your relationship with him is more important than your works.

APRIL 29

Nehemiah Returns to Jerusalem

NEHEMIAH 2:1-12

Early the following spring, in the month of Nisan, during the twentieth year of King Artaxerxes' reign, I was serving the king his wine. I had never before appeared sad in his presence. [2]So the king asked me, "Why are you looking so sad? You don't look sick to me. You must be deeply troubled."

Then I was terrified, [3]but I replied, "Long live the king! How can I not be sad? For the city where my ancestors are buried is in ruins, and the gates have been destroyed by fire."

[4]The king asked, "Well, how can I help you?"

With a prayer to the God of heaven, [5]I replied, "If it please the king, and if you are pleased with me, your servant, send me to Judah to rebuild the city where my ancestors are buried."

[6]The king, with the queen sitting beside him, asked, "How long will you be gone? When will you return?" After I told him how long I would be gone, the king agreed to my request.

[7]I also said to the king, "If it please the king, let me have letters addressed to the governors of the province west of the Euphrates River, instructing them to let me travel safely through their territories on my way to Judah. [8]And please give me a letter addressed to Asaph, the manager of the king's forest, instructing him to give me timber. I will need it to make beams for the gates of the Temple fortress, for the city walls, and for a house for myself." And the king granted these requests, because the gracious hand of God was on me.

[9]When I came to the governors of the province west of the Euphrates River, I delivered the king's letters to them. The king, I should add, had sent along army officers and horsemen to protect me. [10]But when Sanballat the Horonite and Tobiah the Ammonite official heard of my arrival, they were very displeased that someone had come to help the people of Israel.

[11]So I arrived in Jerusalem. Three days later, [12]I slipped out during the night, taking only a few others with me. I had not told anyone about the plans God had put in my heart for Jerusalem.

What relationships in your past need to be rebuilt? After his prayer, Nehemiah asked the king for permission to go to Judah. As soon as he got a positive answer, he began asking for additional help. Sometimes when we have needs, we hesitate to ask the right people for help, because we are afraid to approach them. Not Nehemiah! He went directly to the person who could help him the most. Don't be reluctant to ask those to help who are most qualified. They may be more interested and approachable than you think. God's answers to prayer may come as a result of our asking others.

Nehemiah's Concern for the Poor

APRIL 30

NEHEMIAH 5:1-13

About this time some of the men and their wives raised a cry of protest against their fellow
Jews. 2They were saying, "We have such large families. We need more food to survive."

3Others said, "We have mortgaged our fields, vineyards, and homes to get food during
the famine."

4And others said, "We have had to borrow money on our fields and vineyards to pay our
taxes. 5We belong to the same family as those who are wealthy, and our children are just like
theirs. Yet we must sell our children into slavery just to get enough money to live. We have
already sold some of our daughters, and we are helpless to do anything about it, for our fields
and vineyards are already mortgaged to others."

6When I heard their complaints, I was very angry. 7After thinking it over, I spoke out
against these nobles and officials. I told them, "You are hurting your own relatives by charging
interest when they borrow money!" Then I called a public meeting to deal with the problem.

8At the meeting I said to them, "We are doing all we can to redeem our Jewish relatives
who have had to sell themselves to pagan foreigners, but you are selling them back into slavery again. How often must we redeem them?" And they had nothing to say in their defense.

9Then I pressed further, "What you are doing is not right! Should you not walk in the
fear of our God in order to avoid being mocked by enemy nations? 10I myself, as well as my
brothers and my workers, have been lending the people money and grain, but now let us
stop this business of charging interest. 11You must restore their fields, vineyards, olive groves,
and homes to them this very day. And repay the interest you charged when you lent them
money, grain, new wine, and olive oil."

12They replied, "We will give back everything and demand nothing more from the people.
We will do as you say." Then I called the priests and made the nobles and officials swear to
do what they had promised.

13I shook out the folds of my robe and said, "If you fail to keep your promise, may God
shake you like this from your homes and from your property!"

The whole assembly responded, "Amen," and they praised the LORD. And the people did
as they had promised.

How do you express your concern for the poor? God's concern for the poor is revealed in almost every book of the Bible. Here, Nehemiah insisted that fairness to the poor and oppressed was central to following God. The books of Moses clearly spelled out the Israelites' responsibility to care for the poor (Exodus 22:22-27; Leviticus 25:35-37; Deuteronomy 14:28-29; 15:7-11). The way we help those in need ought to mirror God's love and concern.

May

MAY 1

Reading God's Word

NEHEMIAH 8:1-18

All the people assembled with a unified purpose at the square just inside the Water Gate. They asked Ezra the scribe to bring out the Book of the Law of Moses, which the LORD had given for Israel to obey.

2So on October 8 Ezra the priest brought the Book of the Law before the assembly, which included the men and women and all the children old enough to understand. 3He faced the square just inside the Water Gate from early morning until noon and read aloud to everyone who could understand. All the people listened closely to the Book of the Law. . . .

8They read from the Book of the Law of God and clearly explained the meaning of what was being read, helping the people understand each passage.

9Then Nehemiah the governor, Ezra the priest and scribe, and the Levites who were interpreting for the people said to them, "Don't mourn or weep on such a day as this! For today is a sacred day before the LORD your God." For the people had all been weeping as they listened to the words of the Law.

10And Nehemiah continued, "Go and celebrate with a feast of rich foods and sweet drinks, and share gifts of food with people who have nothing prepared. This is a sacred day before our Lord. Don't be dejected and sad, for the joy of the LORD is your strength!"

11And the Levites, too, quieted the people, telling them, "Hush! Don't weep! For this is a sacred day." 12So the people went away to eat and drink at a festive meal, to share gifts of food, and to celebrate with great joy because they had heard God's words and understood them. . . .

18Ezra read from the Book of the Law of God on each of the seven days of the festival. Then on the eighth day they held a solemn assembly, as was required by law.

What are your expectations when you open God's Word? The people paid close attention to Ezra as he read God's Word, and their lives were changed. Because we hear the Bible so often, we can become dulled to its words and immune to its teachings. Instead, we should listen carefully to every verse and ask the Holy Spirit to help us answer the question, How does this apply to my life?

The Fall of a Queen

ESTHER 1:1-19

These events happened in the days of King Xerxes, who reigned over 127 provinces stretching from India to Ethiopia. 2At that time Xerxes ruled his empire from his royal throne at the fortress of Susa. 3In the third year of his reign, he gave a banquet for all his nobles and officials. He invited all the military officers of Persia and Media as well as the princes and nobles of the provinces. 4The celebration lasted 180 days—a tremendous display of the opulent wealth of his empire and the pomp and splendor of his majesty.

5When it was all over, the king gave a banquet for all the people, from the greatest to the least, who were in the fortress of Susa. It lasted for seven days and was held in the courtyard of the palace garden. . . .

9At the same time, Queen Vashti gave a banquet for the women in the royal palace of King Xerxes.

10On the seventh day of the feast, when King Xerxes was in high spirits because of the wine, he told the seven eunuchs who attended him . . . 11to bring Queen Vashti to him with the royal crown on her head. He wanted the nobles and all the other men to gaze on her beauty, for she was a very beautiful woman. 12But when they conveyed the king's order to Queen Vashti, she refused to come. This made the king furious, and he burned with anger.

13He immediately consulted with his wise advisers, who knew all the Persian laws and customs, for he always asked their advice. . . .

15"What must be done to Queen Vashti?" the king demanded. "What penalty does the law provide for a queen who refuses to obey the king's orders, properly sent through his eunuchs?"

16Memucan answered the king and his nobles, "Queen Vashti has wronged not only the king but also every noble and citizen throughout your empire. 17Women everywhere will begin to despise their husbands when they learn that Queen Vashti has refused to appear before the king. 18Before this day is out, the wives of all the king's nobles throughout Persia and Media will hear what the queen did and will start treating their husbands the same way. There will be no end to their contempt and anger.

19"So if it please the king, we suggest that you issue a written decree, a law of the Persians and Medes that cannot be revoked. It should order that Queen Vashti be forever banished from the presence of King Xerxes, and that the king should choose another queen more worthy than she."

How often do you take the important people in your life for granted? Xerxes made a rash, half-drunk decision, based purely on feelings. His self-restraint and practical wisdom were weakened by too much wine, and he later regretted his decision (Esther 2:1). Poor decisions are made when clear thinking is not involved. Make your decisions through careful thinking, not on the spur of the moment.

MAY 3 A Strange Way to Become Queen

ESTHER 2:1-18

But after Xerxes' anger had subsided, he began thinking about Vashti and what she had done and the decree he had made. 2So his personal attendants suggested, "Let us search the empire to find beautiful young virgins for the king. 3Let the king appoint agents in each province to bring these beautiful young women into the royal harem at the fortress of Susa. Hegai, the king's eunuch in charge of the harem, will see that they are all given beauty treatments. 4After that, the young woman who most pleases the king will be made queen instead of Vashti." This advice was very appealing to the king, so he put the plan into effect.

5At that time there was a Jewish man in the fortress of Susa whose name was Mordecai son of Jair. He was from the tribe of Benjamin and was a descendant of Kish and Shimei. 6His family had been among those who, with King Jehoiachin of Judah, had been exiled from Jerusalem to Babylon by King Nebuchadnezzar. 7This man had a very beautiful and lovely young cousin, Hadassah, who was also called Esther. When her father and mother died, Mordecai adopted her into his family and raised her as his own daughter.

8As a result of the king's decree, Esther, along with many other young women, was brought to the king's harem at the fortress of Susa and placed in Hegai's care. 9Hegai was very impressed with Esther and treated her kindly. He quickly ordered a special menu for her and provided her with beauty treatments. He also assigned her seven maids specially chosen from the king's palace, and he moved her and her maids into the best place in the harem.

10Esther had not told anyone of her nationality and family background, because Mordecai had directed her not to do so. 11Every day Mordecai would take a walk near the courtyard of the harem to find out about Esther and what was happening to her. . . .

16Esther was taken to King Xerxes at the royal palace in early winter of the seventh year of his reign. 17And the king loved Esther more than any of the other young women. He was so delighted with her that he set the royal crown on her head and declared her queen instead of Vashti. 18To celebrate the occasion, he gave a great banquet in Esther's honor for all his nobles and officials, declaring a public holiday for the provinces and giving generous gifts to everyone.

When have difficult or confusing events in your life actually been a preparation for something you would later experience? God placed Esther on the throne even before the Jews faced the possibility of complete destruction so that when trouble came, someone would be in a position to help. No human effort could thwart God's plan to send the Messiah to earth as a Jew. If you have to change jobs or move to a new location, you may not be able to see God's purpose in your situation. But remember that God is in control. He may be putting you in a special place for a special purpose. Ask him to help you discover it.

The Jews in Danger

MAY 4

ESTHER 3:1-14

Some time later King Xerxes promoted Haman son of Hammedatha the Agagite over all the
other nobles, making him the most powerful official in the empire. 2All the king's officials
would bow down before Haman to show him respect whenever he passed by, for so the king
had commanded. But Mordecai refused to bow down or show him respect.

3Then the palace officials at the king's gate asked Mordecai, "Why are you disobeying
the king's command?" 4They spoke to him day after day, but still he refused to comply with
the order. So they spoke to Haman about this to see if he would tolerate Mordecai's conduct,
since Mordecai had told them he was a Jew.

5When Haman saw that Mordecai would not bow down or show him respect, he was
filled with rage. 6He had learned of Mordecai's nationality, so he decided it was not enough to
lay hands on Mordecai alone. Instead, he looked for a way to destroy all the Jews throughout
the entire empire of Xerxes.

7So in the month of April, during the twelfth year of King Xerxes' reign, lots were cast in
Haman's presence (the lots were called *purim*) to determine the best day and month to take
action. And the day selected was March 7, nearly a year later.

8Then Haman approached King Xerxes and said, "There is a certain race of people scattered through all the provinces of your empire who keep themselves separate from everyone
else. Their laws are different from those of any other people, and they refuse to obey the laws
of the king. So it is not in the king's interest to let them live. 9If it please the king, issue a
decree that they be destroyed, and I will give 10,000 large sacks of silver to the government
administrators to be deposited in the royal treasury."

10The king agreed, confirming his decision by removing his signet ring from his finger
and giving it to Haman . . .

12So on April 17 the king's secretaries were summoned, and a decree was written exactly
as Haman dictated. . . . 13Dispatches were sent by swift messengers into all the provinces of
the empire, giving the order that all Jews—young and old, including women and children—
must be killed, slaughtered, and annihilated on a single day. This was scheduled to happen on
March 7 of the next year. The property of the Jews would be given to those who killed them.

14A copy of this decree was to be issued as law in every province and proclaimed to all
peoples, so that they would be ready to do their duty on the appointed day.

In what situations are you tempted to compromise your faith? Mordecai's faith was based on conviction. He did not first take a poll to determine the safest or most popular course of action; he had the courage to stand alone. Doing what is right is not always popular. Those who do right will be in the minority, but to obey God is more important than to obey people (Acts 5:29).

MAY 5 The Queen Decides to Help

ESTHER 4:3-17

3And as news of the king's decree reached all the provinces, there was great mourning among
the Jews. They fasted, wept, and wailed, and many people lay in burlap and ashes.
4When Queen Esther's maids and eunuchs came and told her about Mordecai, she was
deeply distressed. She sent clothing to him to replace the burlap, but he refused it. 5Then
Esther sent for Hathach, one of the king's eunuchs who had been appointed as her attendant.
She ordered him to go to Mordecai and find out what was troubling him and why he was
in mourning. 6So Hathach went out to Mordecai in the square in front of the palace gate.
7Mordecai told him the whole story, including the exact amount of money Haman had
promised to pay into the royal treasury for the destruction of the Jews. 8Mordecai gave
Hathach a copy of the decree issued in Susa that called for the death of all Jews. He asked
Hathach to show it to Esther and explain the situation to her. He also asked Hathach to
direct her to go to the king to beg for mercy and plead for her people. 9So Hathach returned
to Esther with Mordecai's message.
10Then Esther told Hathach to go back and relay this message to Mordecai: 11"All the
king's officials and even the people in the provinces know that anyone who appears before
the king in his inner court without being invited is doomed to die unless the king holds out
his gold scepter. And the king has not called for me to come to him for thirty days." 12So
Hathach gave Esther's message to Mordecai.
13Mordecai sent this reply to Esther: "Don't think for a moment that because you're in
the palace you will escape when all other Jews are killed. 14If you keep quiet at a time like
this, deliverance and relief for the Jews will arise from some other place, but you and your
relatives will die. Who knows if perhaps you were made queen for just such a time as this?"
15Then Esther sent this reply to Mordecai: 16"Go and gather together all the Jews of Susa
and fast for me. Do not eat or drink for three days, night or day. My maids and I will do the
same. And then, though it is against the law, I will go in to see the king. If I must die, I must
die." 17So Mordecai went away and did everything as Esther had ordered him.

In what ways has your faith cost you? Esther was preparing to risk her life for her people. Her courageous act is a model for us to follow in approaching a difficult or dangerous task. We should: (1) Calculate the cost. Esther realized her life was at stake. (2) Set priorities. She believed that the safety of the Jewish race was more important than her life. (3) Prepare. She gathered support and fasted. (4) Determine your course of action and move ahead boldly. She didn't think too long about it, allowing the interlude to lessen her commitment to what she had to do. Do you have to complete a difficult work assignment, confront a friend on a delicate subject, or make a difficult decision? Take action with confidence by following Esther's inspiring example.

Esther Risks Her Life

MAY 6

ESTHER 5:1-14

On the third day of the fast, Esther put on her royal robes and entered the inner court of the
palace, just across from the king's hall. The king was sitting on his royal throne, facing the
entrance. 2When he saw Queen Esther standing there in the inner court, he welcomed her
and held out the gold scepter to her. So Esther approached and touched the end of the scepter.
3Then the king asked her, "What do you want, Queen Esther? What is your request? I
will give it to you, even if it is half the kingdom!"
4And Esther replied, "If it please the king, let the king and Haman come today to a banquet I have prepared for the king."
5The king turned to his attendants and said, "Tell Haman to come quickly to a banquet,
as Esther has requested." So the king and Haman went to Esther's banquet.
6And while they were drinking wine, the king said to Esther, "Now tell me what you really
want. What is your request? I will give it to you, even if it is half the kingdom!"
7Esther replied, "This is my request and deepest wish. 8If I have found favor with the king,
and if it pleases the king to grant my request and do what I ask, please come with Haman
tomorrow to the banquet I will prepare for you. Then I will explain what this is all about."
9Haman was a happy man as he left the banquet! But when he saw Mordecai sitting at
the palace gate, not standing up or trembling nervously before him, Haman became furious.
10However, he restrained himself and went on home.
Then Haman gathered together his friends and Zeresh, his wife, 11and boasted to them
about his great wealth and his many children. He bragged about the honors the king had
given him and how he had been promoted over all the other nobles and officials.
12Then Haman added, "And that's not all! Queen Esther invited only me and the king himself to the banquet she prepared for us. And she has invited me to dine with her and the king
again tomorrow!" 13Then he added, "But this is all worth nothing as long as I see Mordecai the
Jew just sitting there at the palace gate."
14So Haman's wife, Zeresh, and all his friends suggested, "Set up a sharpened pole that
stands seventy-five feet tall, and in the morning ask the king to impale Mordecai on it. When
this is done, you can go on your merry way to the banquet with the king." This pleased
Haman, and he ordered the pole set up.

When was the last time you did something scary in order to obey God? God was in control, yet Mordecai and Esther had to act. We cannot understand how both can be true at the same time, and yet they are. God chooses to work through those willing to act for him. We should pray as if everything depended on God and act as if everything depended on us. But we should always avoid doing nothing.

MAY 7

God Protects His People

ESTHER 7:1-10

So the king and Haman went to Queen Esther's banquet. 2On this second occasion, while they were drinking wine, the king again said to Esther, "Tell me what you want, Queen Esther. What is your request? I will give it to you, even if it is half the kingdom!"

3Queen Esther replied, "If I have found favor with the king, and if it pleases the king to grant my request, I ask that my life and the lives of my people will be spared. 4For my people and I have been sold to those who would kill, slaughter, and annihilate us. If we had merely been sold as slaves, I could remain quiet, for that would be too trivial a matter to warrant disturbing the king."

5"Who would do such a thing?" King Xerxes demanded. "Who would be so presumptuous as to touch you?"

6Esther replied, "This wicked Haman is our adversary and our enemy." Haman grew pale with fright before the king and queen. 7Then the king jumped to his feet in a rage and went out into the palace garden.

Haman, however, stayed behind to plead for his life with Queen Esther, for he knew that the king intended to kill him. 8In despair he fell on the couch where Queen Esther was reclining, just as the king was returning from the palace garden.

The king exclaimed, "Will he even assault the queen right here in the palace, before my very eyes?" And as soon as the king spoke, his attendants covered Haman's face, signaling his doom.

9Then Harbona, one of the king's eunuchs, said, "Haman has set up a sharpened pole that stands seventy-five feet tall in his own courtyard. He intended to use it to impale Mordecai, the man who saved the king from assassination."

"Then impale Haman on it!" the king ordered. 10So they impaled Haman on the pole he had set up for Mordecai, and the king's anger subsided.

When is it helpful to remember that God is still in control of the world? Haman's hatred and evil plotting turned against him when the king discovered his true intentions. He was impaled on the pole he had set up for someone else. Proverbs 26:27 teaches that if you set a trap for others, you will get caught in it yourself. What happened to Haman shows the often violent results of setting any kind of trap for others.

The Testing of Job

MAY 8

JOB 1:1-19

There once was a man named Job who lived in the land of Uz. He was blameless—a man of complete integrity. . . .

6 One day the members of the heavenly court came to present themselves before the LORD, and the Accuser, Satan, came with them. 7 "Where have you come from?" the LORD asked Satan.

Satan answered the LORD, "I have been patrolling the earth, watching everything that's going on."

8 Then the LORD asked Satan, "Have you noticed my servant Job? He is the finest man in all the earth. He is blameless—a man of complete integrity. He fears God and stays away from evil."

9 Satan replied to the LORD, "Yes, but Job has good reason to fear God. 10 You have always put a wall of protection around him and his home and his property. You have made him prosper in everything he does. Look how rich he is! 11 But reach out and take away everything he has, and he will surely curse you to your face!"

12 "All right, you may test him," the LORD said to Satan. "Do whatever you want with everything he possesses, but don't harm him physically." So Satan left the LORD's presence.

13 One day when Job's sons and daughters were feasting at the oldest brother's house, 14 a messenger arrived at Job's home with this news: "Your oxen were plowing, with the donkeys feeding beside them, 15 when the Sabeans raided us. They stole all the animals and killed all the farmhands. . . ."

16 While he was still speaking, another messenger arrived with this news: "The fire of God has fallen from heaven and burned up your sheep and all the shepherds. I am the only one who escaped to tell you."

17 While he was still speaking, a third messenger arrived with this news: "Three bands of Chaldean raiders have stolen your camels and killed your servants. . . ."

18 While he was still speaking, another messenger arrived with this news: "Your sons and daughters were feasting in their oldest brother's home. 19 Suddenly, a powerful wind swept in from the wilderness and hit the house on all sides. The house collapsed, and all your children are dead."

In what situations do you most quickly question God's care? As we see calamity and suffering in the book of Job, we must remember that we live in a fallen world, where good behavior is not always rewarded and bad behavior is not always punished. Sin has twisted justice and made our world unpredictable and ugly. The book of Job shows a good man suffering for no apparent reason. Sadly, our world is like that. But Job's story does not end in despair. Through Job's life we can see that faith in God is justified even when our situations look hopeless. Faith based on rewards or prosperity is hollow. To be unshakable, faith must be built on the confidence that God's ultimate purpose will come to pass. Be sure that your faith is based on the unchangeable God who loves you.

MAY 9

Job and His Friends

JOB 2:1-13

One day the members of the heavenly court came again to present themselves before the LORD, and the Accuser, Satan, came with them. 2“Where have you come from?” the LORD asked Satan.

Satan answered the LORD, “I have been patrolling the earth, watching everything that’s going on.”

3Then the LORD asked Satan, “Have you noticed my servant Job? He is the finest man in all the earth. He is blameless—a man of complete integrity. He fears God and stays away from evil. And he has maintained his integrity, even though you urged me to harm him without cause.”

4Satan replied to the LORD, “Skin for skin! A man will give up everything he has to save his life. 5But reach out and take away his health, and he will surely curse you to your face!”

6“All right, do with him as you please,” the LORD said to Satan. “But spare his life.” 7So Satan left the LORD’s presence, and he struck Job with terrible boils from head to foot.

8Job scraped his skin with a piece of broken pottery as he sat among the ashes. 9His wife said to him, “Are you still trying to maintain your integrity? Curse God and die.”

10But Job replied, “You talk like a foolish woman. Should we accept only good things from the hand of God and never anything bad?” So in all this, Job said nothing wrong.

11When three of Job’s friends heard of the tragedy he had suffered, they got together and traveled from their homes to comfort and console him. Their names were Eliphaz the Temanite, Bildad the Shuhite, and Zophar the Naamathite. 12When they saw Job from a distance, they scarcely recognized him. Wailing loudly, they tore their robes and threw dust into the air over their heads to show their grief. 13Then they sat on the ground with him for seven days and nights. No one said a word to Job, for they saw that his suffering was too great for words.

How do you normally respond to someone else’s pain? How should you respond? Why did the friends arrive and then just sit quietly? According to Jewish tradition, people who come to comfort someone in mourning are not to speak until the mourner speaks. Often the best response to another person’s suffering is silence. Job’s friends realized that his pain was too deep to be healed with mere words, so they said nothing. (If only they had continued to just sit quietly!) Often, we feel we must say something spiritual and insightful to a hurting friend. Perhaps what he or she needs most is just our presence, showing that we care. Pat answers and trite quotations say much less than caring silence and loving companionship.

God Speaks to Job

JOB 38:1-27

Then the LORD answered Job from the whirlwind:

[2]"Who is this that questions my wisdom
with such ignorant words?
[3]Brace yourself like a man,
because I have some questions for you,
and you must answer them.

[4]"Where were you when I laid the foundations of the earth?
Tell me, if you know so much.
[5]Who determined its dimensions
and stretched out the surveying line?
[6]What supports its foundations,
and who laid its cornerstone
[7]as the morning stars sang together
and all the angels shouted for joy? . . .

[22]"Have you visited the storehouses of the snow
or seen the storehouses of hail?
[23](I have reserved them as weapons for the time of trouble,
for the day of battle and war.)
[24]Where is the path to the source of light?
Where is the home of the east wind?

[25]"Who created a channel for the torrents of rain?
Who laid out the path for the lightning?
[26]Who makes the rain fall on barren land,
in a desert where no one lives?
[27]Who sends rain to satisfy the parched ground
and make the tender grass spring up?"

What things around you remind you of God's greatness? God stated that he has all the forces of nature at his command and that he can unleash or restrain them at will. No one completely understands such common occurrences as rain or snow, and no one can command them—only God who created them has that power. God's point was that if Job could not explain such common events in nature, how could he possibly explain or question God? And if nature is beyond our grasp, God's moral purposes may not be what we imagine either. Your job is not to question God but to worship and serve him because of who he is and what he has done for you.

MAY 11

The Rest of Job's Story

JOB 42:1-17

Then Job replied to the LORD:

[2]"I know that you can do anything,
and no one can stop you.
[3]You asked, 'Who is this that questions my wisdom with such ignorance?'
It is I—and I was talking about things I knew nothing about,
things far too wonderful for me.
[4]You said, 'Listen and I will speak!
I have some questions for you,
and you must answer them.'
[5]I had only heard about you before,
but now I have seen you with my own eyes.
[6]I take back everything I said,
and I sit in dust and ashes to show my repentance."

[7]After the LORD had finished speaking to Job, he said to Eliphaz the Temanite: "I am
angry with you and your two friends, for you have not spoken accurately about me, as my
servant Job has. [8]So take seven bulls and seven rams and go to my servant Job and offer a
burnt offering for yourselves. My servant Job will pray for you, and I will accept his prayer
on your behalf. I will not treat you as you deserve, for you have not spoken accurately about
me, as my servant Job has." [9]So Eliphaz the Temanite, Bildad the Shuhite, and Zophar the
Naamathite did as the LORD commanded them, and the LORD accepted Job's prayer.

[10]When Job prayed for his friends, the LORD restored his fortunes. In fact, the LORD gave
him twice as much as before! [11]Then all his brothers, sisters, and former friends came and
feasted with him in his home. And they consoled him and comforted him because of all the
trials the LORD had brought against him. And each of them brought him a gift of money
and a gold ring.

[12]So the LORD blessed Job in the second half of his life even more than in the beginning.
. . . [16]Job lived 140 years after that, living to see four generations of his children and
grandchildren. [17]Then he died, an old man who had lived a long, full life.

What difference does it make to know and remember that God always has the last word? Job's friends had persistently asked him to admit his sin and ask for forgiveness, and eventually Job did indeed repent. Ironically, Job's repentance was not the kind called for by his friends. He did not ask for forgiveness for secret sins but forgiveness for questioning God's sovereignty and justice. Job repented of his attitude and acknowledged God's great power and perfect justice. We sin when we angrily ask, "If God is in control, how could he let this happen?" Since we are locked into time, unable to see beyond today, we cannot know the reasons for everything that happens. Thus, we must often choose between anger and trust. Will you trust God with your unanswered questions?

Two Kinds of Lives

PSALM 1:1-6

Oh, the joys of those who do not
follow the advice of the wicked,
or stand around with sinners,
or join in with mockers.
2But they delight in the law of the LORD,
meditating on it day and night.
3They are like trees planted along the riverbank,
bearing fruit each season.
Their leaves never wither,
and they prosper in all they do.

4But not the wicked!
They are like worthless chaff, scattered by the wind.
5They will be condemned at the time of judgment.
Sinners will have no place among the godly.
6For the LORD watches over the path of the godly,
but the path of the wicked leads to destruction.

What kind of person do you really want to be? God doesn't judge people on the basis of race, sex, or national origin. He judges them on the basis of their faith in him and their response to his revealed will. Those who diligently try to obey God are blessed. They are like healthy, fruit-bearing trees with strong roots, and God promises to watch over them. God's wisdom guides their lives. In contrast, those who don't trust and obey God have meaningless lives that blow away like dust. There are only two paths of life before you—God's way of obedience or the way of rebellion and destruction. Be sure to choose God's path, because the path you choose determines how you will spend eternity.

MAY 13

The Value of Humans

PSALM 8:1-9

For the choir director: A psalm of David, to be accompanied by a stringed instrument.

[1]O LORD, our Lord, your majestic name fills the earth!
Your glory is higher than the heavens.
[2]You have taught children and infants
to tell of your strength,
silencing your enemies
and all who oppose you.

[3]When I look at the night sky and see the work of your fingers—
the moon and the stars you set in place—
[4]what are mere mortals that you should think about them,
human beings that you should care for them?
[5]Yet you made them only a little lower than God
and crowned them with glory and honor.
[6]You gave them charge of everything you made,
putting all things under their authority—
[7]the flocks and the herds
and all the wild animals,
[8]the birds in the sky, the fish in the sea,
and everything that swims the ocean currents.

[9]O LORD, our Lord, your majestic name fills the earth!

How do you know you have worth? When we look at the marvels of creation, we wonder how God could be concerned for people who constantly disappoint him. Yet God created us only a little lower than the angels. The next time you question your worth as a person or feel down about yourself, remember that God considers you to be highly valuable. We have great worth because we bear the stamp of the Creator. Because God has already declared how valuable you are to him, you can be set free from feelings of worthlessness.

A Sheep's Song

PSALM 23:1-6

A psalm of David.

1 The LORD is my shepherd;
I have all that I need.
2 He lets me rest in green meadows;
he leads me beside peaceful streams.
3 He renews my strength.
He guides me along right paths,
bringing honor to his name.
4 Even when I walk
through the darkest valley,
I will not be afraid,
for you are close beside me.
Your rod and your staff
protect and comfort me.
5 You prepare a feast for me
in the presence of my enemies.
You honor me by anointing my head with oil.
My cup overflows with blessings.
6 Surely your goodness and unfailing love will pursue me
all the days of my life,
and I will live in the house of the LORD
forever.

What is the most comforting phrase to you in this psalm? When we allow God our Shepherd to guide us, we have contentment. When we choose to sin, however, we are choosing to go our own way, and we cannot blame God for the environment in which we find ourselves. Our Shepherd knows the "green meadows" and "peaceful streams" that will restore us. We will reach these places only by following him obediently. Rebelling against the Shepherd's leading is actually rebelling against our own best interests for the future. We must remember this the next time we are tempted to go our own way rather than the Shepherd's way.

MAY 15

A Confession

PSALM 51:1-17

For the choir director: A psalm of David, regarding the time Nathan the prophet came to him after David had committed adultery with Bathsheba.

1Have mercy on me, O God,
because of your unfailing love.
Because of your great compassion,
blot out the stain of my sins.
2Wash me clean from my guilt.
Purify me from my sin.
3For I recognize my rebellion;
it haunts me day and night.
4Against you, and you alone, have I sinned;
I have done what is evil in your sight.
You will be proved right in what you say,
and your judgment against me is just.
5For I was born a sinner—
yes, from the moment my mother conceived me.
6But you desire honesty from the womb,
teaching me wisdom even there.

7Purify me from my sins, and I will be clean;
wash me, and I will be whiter than snow.
8Oh, give me back my joy again;
you have broken me—
now let me rejoice.
9Don't keep looking at my sins.
Remove the stain of my guilt.
10Create in me a clean heart, O God.
Renew a loyal spirit within me.
11Do not banish me from your presence,
and don't take your Holy Spirit from me. . . .

16You do not desire a sacrifice, or I would offer one.
You do not want a burnt offering.
17The sacrifice you desire is a broken spirit.
You will not reject a broken and repentant heart, O God.

What examples of repentance have been part of your life? Because we are born as sinners (verse 5), our natural inclination is to please ourselves rather than God. Like David, we must ask God to purify us from within (verse 7), clearing our hearts and minds for new thoughts and desires. Right conduct can come only from a clean heart and mind. Ask God to create in you a clean heart and mind.

What God Is Like

PSALM 103:1-17

A psalm of David.

1 Let all that I am praise the LORD;
with my whole heart, I will praise his holy name.
2 Let all that I am praise the LORD;
may I never forget the good things he does for me.
3 He forgives all my sins
and heals all my diseases.
4 He redeems me from death
and crowns me with love and tender mercies.
5 He fills my life with good things.
My youth is renewed like the eagle's! . . .

7 He revealed his character to Moses
and his deeds to the people of Israel.
8 The LORD is compassionate and merciful,
slow to get angry and filled with unfailing love.
9 He will not constantly accuse us,
nor remain angry forever.
10 He does not punish us for all our sins;
he does not deal harshly with us, as we deserve.
11 For his unfailing love toward those who fear him
is as great as the height of the heavens above the earth.
12 He has removed our sins as far from us
as the east is from the west.
13 The LORD is like a father to his children,
tender and compassionate to those who fear him.
14 For he knows how weak we are;
he remembers we are only dust.
15 Our days on earth are like grass;
like wildflowers, we bloom and die.
16 The wind blows, and we are gone—
as though we had never been here.
17 But the love of the LORD remains forever
with those who fear him.

Which characteristic of God in this psalm helps you understand him better? David's praise focused on God's glorious acts. It is easy to complain about life, but David's list gives us plenty for which to praise God. No matter how difficult your life's journey, you can always count your blessings—past, present, and future. When you feel like you have nothing for which to praise God, read David's list.

MAY 17 How Well God Knows Us

PSALM 139:1-24

For the choir director: A psalm of David.

1O Lord, you have examined my heart
and know everything about me.
2You know when I sit down or stand up.
You know my thoughts even when I'm far away.
3You see me when I travel
and when I rest at home.
You know everything I do.
4You know what I am going to say
even before I say it, Lord.
5You go before me and follow me.
You place your hand of blessing on my head.
6Such knowledge is too wonderful for me,
too great for me to understand! . . .

13You made all the delicate, inner parts of my body
and knit me together in my mother's womb.
14Thank you for making me so wonderfully complex!
Your workmanship is marvelous—how well I know it.
15You watched me as I was being formed in utter seclusion,
as I was woven together in the dark of the womb.
16You saw me before I was born.
Every day of my life was recorded in your book.
Every moment was laid out
before a single day had passed.

17How precious are your thoughts about me, O God.
They cannot be numbered!
18I can't even count them;
they outnumber the grains of sand! . . .

23Search me, O God, and know my heart;
test me and know my anxious thoughts.
24Point out anything in me that offends you,
and lead me along the path of everlasting life.

What do you feel when you read this psalm? God's character goes into the creation of every person. When you feel worthless or even begin to hate yourself, remember that God's Spirit is ready and willing to work within you to make your character all God meant it to be. God thinks of you constantly (verses 17-18). We should have as much respect for ourselves as our Maker has for us.

God for All People and Time

MAY 18

PSALM 145:3-20

3 Great is the LORD! He is most worthy of praise!
No one can measure his greatness. . . .

5 I will meditate on your majestic, glorious splendor
and your wonderful miracles.
6 Your awe-inspiring deeds will be on every tongue;
I will proclaim your greatness.
7 Everyone will share the story of your wonderful goodness;
they will sing with joy about your righteousness.

8 The LORD is merciful and compassionate,
slow to get angry and filled with unfailing love.
9 The LORD is good to everyone.
He showers compassion on all his creation. . . .
13 For your kingdom is an everlasting kingdom.
You rule throughout all generations.

The LORD always keeps his promises;
he is gracious in all he does. . . .
15 The eyes of all look to you in hope;
you give them their food as they need it.
16 When you open your hand,
you satisfy the hunger and thirst of every living thing.
17 The LORD is righteous in everything he does;
he is filled with kindness.
18 The LORD is close to all who call on him,
yes, to all who call on him in truth.
19 He grants the desires of those who fear him;
he hears their cries for help and rescues them.
20 The LORD protects all those who love him,
but he destroys the wicked.

Which of God's qualities do you most need today? Sometimes our burdens seem more than we can bear, and we wonder how we can go on. God is able to lift us up because: (1) His greatness cannot be measured (verse 3). (2) He is full of splendor (verse 5). (3) He does wonderful and awe-inspiring deeds (verses 5-6). (4) He is righteous (verse 7). (5) He is merciful, compassionate, slow to anger, and full of love (verses 8-9). (6) His kingdom is everlasting (verse 13). (7) He provides for all our daily needs (verses 15-16). (8) He is righteous and filled with kindness (verse 17). (9) He remains close to all who call on him (verse 18). (10) He hears our cries and comes to rescue us (verses 19-20). If you are bending under a burden and feel that you are about to fall, turn to God for help. He is ready to lift you up and bear your burden.

MAY 19

Wise Words about Life

PROVERBS 4:4-23

4My father taught me,
"Take my words to heart.
Follow my commands, and you will live.
5Get wisdom; develop good judgment.
Don't forget my words or turn away from them.
6Don't turn your back on wisdom, for she will protect you.
Love her, and she will guard you.
7Getting wisdom is the wisest thing you can do!
And whatever else you do, develop good judgment.
8If you prize wisdom, she will make you great.
Embrace her, and she will honor you.
9She will place a lovely wreath on your head;
she will present you with a beautiful crown." . . .

14Don't do as the wicked do,
and don't follow the path of evildoers.
15Don't even think about it; don't go that way.
Turn away and keep moving.
16For evil people can't sleep until they've done their evil deed for the day.
They can't rest until they've caused someone to stumble.
17They eat the food of wickedness
and drink the wine of violence!

18The way of the righteous is like the first gleam of dawn,
which shines ever brighter until the full light of day.
19But the way of the wicked is like total darkness.
They have no idea what they are stumbling over.

20My child, pay attention to what I say.
Listen carefully to my words.
21Don't lose sight of them.
Let them penetrate deep into your heart,
22for they bring life to those who find them,
and healing to their whole body.

23Guard your heart above all else,
for it determines the course of your life.

What priority does finding wisdom have in your life? If you want wisdom, you must decide to go after it. This is not a once-in-a-lifetime step but a daily process of choosing between two paths—the way of the wicked (verses 14-17, 19) or the way of the righteous (verse 18). Nothing else is more important or more valuable. Choose your path wisely today.

Wise Words about Sex

MAY 20

PROVERBS 5:1-19

My son, pay attention to my wisdom;
listen carefully to my wise counsel.
2Then you will show discernment,
and your lips will express what you've learned.
3For the lips of an immoral woman are as sweet as honey,
and her mouth is smoother than oil.
4But in the end she is as bitter as poison,
as dangerous as a double-edged sword.
5Her feet go down to death;
her steps lead straight to the grave.
6For she cares nothing about the path to life.
She staggers down a crooked trail and doesn't realize it.

7So now, my sons, listen to me.
Never stray from what I am about to say:
8Stay away from her!
Don't go near the door of her house!
9If you do, you will lose your honor
and will lose to merciless people all you have achieved. . . .

15Drink water from your own well—
share your love only with your wife.
16Why spill the water of your springs in the streets,
having sex with just anyone?
17You should reserve it for yourselves.
Never share it with strangers.

18Let your wife be a fountain of blessing for you.
Rejoice in the wife of your youth.
19She is a loving deer, a graceful doe.
Let her breasts satisfy you always.
May you always be captivated by her love.

How does the above passage match what you hear around you every day? God does not intend marriage to be boring and dull. Sex is a gift that God gives to married people for their mutual enjoyment. Real happiness comes when we decide to find pleasure in the relationship God has given or will give us and to commit ourselves to making it pleasurable for the one God gives us to love. That may not be what you read online or what your friends think, but if you commit yourself to purity, you won't shortchange your future.

MAY 21

A Summary of Life

ECCLESIASTES 12:1-14

Don't let the excitement of youth cause you to forget your Creator. Honor him in your youth
before you grow old and say, "Life is not pleasant anymore." 2Remember him before the light
of the sun, moon, and stars is dim to your old eyes, and rain clouds continually darken your
sky. 3Remember him before your legs—the guards of your house—start to tremble; and
before your shoulders—the strong men—stoop. Remember him before your teeth—your
few remaining servants—stop grinding; and before your eyes—the women looking through
the windows—see dimly.

4Remember him before the door to life's opportunities is closed and the sound of work
fades. Now you rise at the first chirping of the birds, but then all their sounds will grow faint.

5Remember him before you become fearful of falling and worry about danger in the
streets; before your hair turns white like an almond tree in bloom, and you drag along
without energy like a dying grasshopper, and the caperberry no longer inspires sexual desire.
Remember him before you near the grave, your everlasting home, when the mourners will
weep at your funeral.

6Yes, remember your Creator now while you are young, before the silver cord of life snaps
and the golden bowl is broken. Don't wait until the water jar is smashed at the spring and
the pulley is broken at the well. 7For then the dust will return to the earth, and the spirit will
return to God who gave it.

8"Everything is meaningless," says the Teacher, "completely meaningless." . . .

11The words of the wise are like cattle prods—painful but helpful. Their collected sayings
are like a nail-studded stick with which a shepherd drives the sheep.

12But, my child, let me give you some further advice: Be careful, for writing books is
endless, and much study wears you out.

13That's the whole story. Here now is my final conclusion: Fear God and obey his commands, for this is everyone's duty. 14God will judge us for everything we do, including every
secret thing, whether good or bad.

In what way can you remember your Creator today? A life without God produces a bitter, lonely, and hopeless old person. A life centered around God is fulfilling; it makes the later years—when disabilities, sicknesses, and handicaps could cause barriers to enjoying life—satisfying because of the hope of eternal life. Being young is exciting, but the excitement of youth can become a barrier to closeness with God. However, those things that most young people live for (sports, sex, popularity) become increasingly unimportant with old age. Make your strength available to God when it is still yours—during your youthful years. Don't waste it on evil or meaningless activities that become bad habits and make you callous. Seek God now.

God Chooses Isaiah

MAY 22

ISAIAH 6:1-8

It was in the year King Uzziah died that I saw the Lord. He was sitting on a lofty throne, and
the train of his robe filled the Temple. 2Attending him were mighty seraphim, each having
six wings. With two wings they covered their faces, with two they covered their feet, and with
two they flew. 3They were calling out to each other,

> "Holy, holy, holy is the LORD of Heaven's Armies!
> The whole earth is filled with his glory!"

4Their voices shook the Temple to its foundations, and the entire building was filled with
smoke.

5Then I said, "It's all over! I am doomed, for I am a sinful man. I have filthy lips, and I
live among a people with filthy lips. Yet I have seen the King, the LORD of Heaven's Armies."

6Then one of the seraphim flew to me with a burning coal he had taken from the altar
with a pair of tongs. 7He touched my lips with it and said, "See, this coal has touched your
lips. Now your guilt is removed, and your sins are forgiven."

8Then I heard the Lord asking, "Whom should I send as a messenger to this people?
Who will go for us?"

I said, "Here I am. Send me."

When did you last realize your continuing need for God's forgiveness? Isaiah's lofty view of God in verses 1-4 gives us a sense of God's greatness, mystery, and power. His recognition of his sinfulness before God encourages us to confess our sin. His picture of forgiveness reminds us that we, too, are forgiven. When we recognize how great our God is, how sinful we are, and the extent of his forgiveness, we are energized to do his work. How does your concept of the greatness of God measure up to Isaiah's?

MAY 23

The Suffering Servant

ISAIAH 53:2-11

[2]My servant grew up in the LORD's presence like a tender green shoot,
like a root in dry ground.
There was nothing beautiful or majestic about his appearance,
nothing to attract us to him.
[3]He was despised and rejected—
a man of sorrows, acquainted with deepest grief.
We turned our backs on him and looked the other way.
He was despised, and we did not care.

[4]Yet it was our weaknesses he carried;
it was our sorrows that weighed him down. . . .
[5]But he was pierced for our rebellion,
crushed for our sins.
He was beaten so we could be whole.
He was whipped so we could be healed.
[6]All of us, like sheep, have strayed away.
We have left God's paths to follow our own.
Yet the LORD laid on him
the sins of us all.

[7]He was oppressed and treated harshly,
yet he never said a word.
He was led like a lamb to the slaughter.
And as a sheep is silent before the shearers,
he did not open his mouth. . . .

[10]But it was the LORD's good plan to crush him
and cause him grief. . . .
[11]When he sees all that is accomplished by his anguish,
he will be satisfied.
And because of his experience,
my righteous servant will make it possible
for many to be counted righteous,
for he will bear all their sins.

How would you describe what Jesus did for you? There was nothing beautiful or majestic in the physical appearance of this servant. Israel would miscalculate the servant's importance; they would consider him an ordinary man. But even though Jesus would not attract a large following based on his physical appearance, he would bring salvation and healing. Many people miscalculate the importance of Jesus' life and work, and they need faithful Christians to point out his extraordinary nature and his work.

God Chooses Jeremiah

MAY 24

JEREMIAH 1:1-9

These are the words of Jeremiah son of Hilkiah, one of the priests from the town of Anathoth in the land of Benjamin. 2The LORD first gave messages to Jeremiah during the thirteenth year of the reign of Josiah son of Amon, king of Judah. 3The LORD's messages continued throughout the reign of King Jehoiakim, Josiah's son, until the eleventh year of the reign of King Zedekiah, another of Josiah's sons. In August of that eleventh year the people of Jerusalem were taken away as captives.

4The LORD gave me this message:

5"I knew you before I formed you in your mother's womb.
    Before you were born I set you apart
    and appointed you as my prophet to the nations."

6"O Sovereign LORD," I said, "I can't speak for you! I'm too young!"

7The LORD replied, "Don't say, 'I'm too young,' for you must go wherever I send you and say whatever I tell you. 8And don't be afraid of the people, for I will be with you and will protect you. I, the LORD, have spoken!" 9Then the LORD reached out and touched my mouth and said,

"Look, I have put my words in your mouth!"

What is your reaction to the possibility of God using your life? Often people struggle with new challenges because they lack self-confidence, feeling that they have inadequate ability, training, or experience. Jeremiah thought he was "too young" and inexperienced to be God's spokesman to the world. But God promised to be with him. We should not allow feelings of inadequacy to keep us from obeying God's call. He will always be with us. When you find yourself avoiding something you know you should do, be careful not to use your lack of self-confidence as an excuse. If God gives you a job to do, he will provide all you need to do it.

MAY 25

The Book Burning

JEREMIAH 36:1-31

During the fourth year that Jehoiakim son of Josiah was king in Judah, the LORD gave this
message to Jeremiah: 2“Get a scroll, and write down all my messages against Israel, Judah, and
the other nations. Begin with the first message back in the days of Josiah, and write down
every message, right up to the present time. 3Perhaps the people of Judah will repent when
they hear again all the terrible things I have planned for them. Then I will be able to forgive
their sins and wrongdoings.”

4So Jeremiah sent for Baruch son of Neriah, and as Jeremiah dictated all the prophecies
that the LORD had given him, Baruch wrote them on a scroll. 5Then Jeremiah said to Baruch,
“I am a prisoner here and unable to go to the Temple. 6So you go to the Temple on the next
day of fasting, and read the messages from the LORD that I have had you write on this scroll.
Read them so the people who are there from all over Judah will hear them. 7Perhaps even yet
they will turn from their evil ways and ask the LORD’s forgiveness before it is too late. For the
LORD has threatened them with his terrible anger.”

8Baruch did as Jeremiah told him and read these messages from the LORD to the people
at the Temple. . . .

21The king sent Jehudi to get the scroll. Jehudi brought it from Elishama’s room and read
it to the king as all his officials stood by. 22It was late autumn, and the king was in a winterized
part of the palace, sitting in front of a fire to keep warm. 23Each time Jehudi finished reading
three or four columns, the king took a knife and cut off that section of the scroll. He then
threw it into the fire, section by section, until the whole scroll was burned up. . . .

27After the king had burned the scroll on which Baruch had written Jeremiah’s words, the
LORD gave Jeremiah another message. He said, 28“Get another scroll, and write everything
again just as you did on the scroll King Jehoiakim burned. 29Then say to the king, ‘This is
what the LORD says: You burned the scroll because it said the king of Babylon would destroy
this land and empty it of people and animals. 30Now this is what the LORD says about King
Jehoiakim of Judah: He will have no heirs to sit on the throne of David. His dead body will
be thrown out to lie unburied—exposed to the heat of the day and the frost of the night.
31I will punish him and his family and his attendants for their sins.’”

How much risk is involved in your relationship with God? God told Jeremiah to write his words on a scroll. Because he was not allowed to go to the Temple, Jeremiah asked his scribe, Baruch, to read it to the people gathered there. Baruch then read it to the officials, and finally Jehudi read it to the king himself. Although the king burned the scroll, he could not destroy God’s Word. Today many people try to put God’s Word aside or say that it contains errors and therefore cannot be trusted. People may reject God’s Word, but they cannot destroy it. God’s Word will stand forever (Psalm 119:89). As you read this book, realize that the words are God’s timeless message to all the world and to you personally.

Jeremiah in the Well

MAY 26

JEREMIAH 38:1-13

Now Shephatiah son of Mattan, Gedaliah son of Pashhur, Jehucal son of Shelemiah, and Pashhur son of Malkijah heard what Jeremiah had been telling the people. He had been saying, 2"This is what the LORD says: 'Everyone who stays in Jerusalem will die from war, famine, or disease, but those who surrender to the Babylonians will live. Their reward will be life. They will live!' 3The LORD also says: 'The city of Jerusalem will certainly be handed over to the army of the king of Babylon, who will capture it.'"

4So these officials went to the king and said, "Sir, this man must die! That kind of talk will undermine the morale of the few fighting men we have left, as well as that of all the people. This man is a traitor!"

5King Zedekiah agreed. "All right," he said. "Do as you like. I can't stop you."

6So the officials took Jeremiah from his cell and lowered him by ropes into an empty cistern in the prison yard. It belonged to Malkijah, a member of the royal family. There was no water in the cistern, but there was a thick layer of mud at the bottom, and Jeremiah sank down into it.

7But Ebed-melech the Ethiopian, an important court official, heard that Jeremiah was in the cistern. At that time the king was holding court at the Benjamin Gate, 8so Ebed-melech rushed from the palace to speak with him. 9"My lord the king," he said, "these men have done a very evil thing in putting Jeremiah the prophet into the cistern. He will soon die of hunger, for almost all the bread in the city is gone."

10So the king told Ebed-melech, "Take thirty of my men with you, and pull Jeremiah out of the cistern before he dies."

11So Ebed-melech took the men with him and went to a room in the palace beneath the treasury, where he found some old rags and discarded clothing. He carried these to the cistern and lowered them to Jeremiah on a rope. 12Ebed-melech called down to Jeremiah, "Put these rags under your armpits to protect you from the ropes." Then when Jeremiah was ready, 13they pulled him out. So Jeremiah was returned to the courtyard of the guard—the palace prison—where he remained.

What part of your life compares in any way with Jeremiah's time in the well? Ebed-melech feared God more than people. He alone among the palace officials stood up against the murder plot. His obedience could have cost him his life. Because he obeyed, however, he was spared when Jerusalem fell (Jeremiah 39:15-18). You can either go along with the crowd or speak up for God. When someone is treated unkindly or unjustly, for example, reach out to that person with God's love. You may be the only one who does. And when you're being treated unkindly yourself, be sure to thank God when he sends an "Ebed-melech" your way.

MAY 27

A Valley of Dry Bones

EZEKIEL 37:1-14

The Lord took hold of me, and I was carried away by the Spirit of the Lord to a valley filled with bones. 2He led me all around among the bones that covered the valley floor. They were scattered everywhere across the ground and were completely dried out. 3Then he asked me, "Son of man, can these bones become living people again?"

"O Sovereign Lord," I replied, "you alone know the answer to that."

4Then he said to me, "Speak a prophetic message to these bones and say, 'Dry bones, listen to the word of the Lord! 5This is what the Sovereign Lord says: Look! I am going to put breath into you and make you live again! 6I will put flesh and muscles on you and cover you with skin. I will put breath into you, and you will come to life. Then you will know that I am the Lord.'"

7So I spoke this message, just as he told me. Suddenly as I spoke, there was a rattling noise all across the valley. The bones of each body came together and attached themselves as complete skeletons. 8Then as I watched, muscles and flesh formed over the bones. Then skin formed to cover their bodies, but they still had no breath in them.

9Then he said to me, "Speak a prophetic message to the winds, son of man. Speak a prophetic message and say, 'This is what the Sovereign Lord says: Come, O breath, from the four winds! Breathe into these dead bodies so they may live again.'"

10So I spoke the message as he commanded me, and breath came into their bodies. They all came to life and stood up on their feet—a great army.

11Then he said to me, "Son of man, these bones represent the people of Israel. They are saying, 'We have become old, dry bones—all hope is gone. Our nation is finished.' 12Therefore, prophesy to them and say, 'This is what the Sovereign Lord says: O my people, I will open your graves of exile and cause you to rise again. Then I will bring you back to the land of Israel. 13When this happens, O my people, you will know that I am the Lord. 14I will put my Spirit in you, and you will live again and return home to your own land. Then you will know that I, the Lord, have spoken, and I have done what I said. Yes, the Lord has spoken!'"

What can you do to help you better understand God's plan for the world? The dry bones represented the people's spiritually dead condition. Your church may seem like a heap of dried-up bones to you, spiritually dead with no hope of vitality. But just as God promised to restore his nation, he can restore any church, no matter how dry or dead it may be. Rather than give up, pray for renewal, for God can restore it to life. The hope and prayer of every church should be that God will put his Spirit into it (verse 14). In fact, God is at work calling his people back to himself, bringing new life into dead churches.

Daniel and Three Friends

MAY 28

DANIEL 1:1-16

During the third year of King Jehoiakim's reign in Judah, King Nebuchadnezzar of Babylon
came to Jerusalem and besieged it. 2The Lord gave him victory over King Jehoiakim of
Judah and permitted him to take some of the sacred objects from the Temple of God. So
Nebuchadnezzar took them back to the land of Babylonia and placed them in the treasure-
house of his god.

3Then the king ordered Ashpenaz, his chief of staff, to bring to the palace some of
the young men of Judah's royal family and other noble families, who had been brought to
Babylon as captives. . . .

6Daniel, Hananiah, Mishael, and Azariah were four of the young men chosen, all from
the tribe of Judah. 7The chief of staff renamed them with these Babylonian names:

Daniel was called Belteshazzar.
Hananiah was called Shadrach.
Mishael was called Meshach.
Azariah was called Abednego.

8But Daniel was determined not to defile himself by eating the food and wine given to
them by the king. He asked the chief of staff for permission not to eat these unacceptable
foods. 9Now God had given the chief of staff both respect and affection for Daniel. 10But
he responded, "I am afraid of my lord the king, who has ordered that you eat this food and
wine. If you become pale and thin compared to the other youths your age, I am afraid the
king will have me beheaded."

11Daniel spoke with the attendant who had been appointed by the chief of staff to look
after Daniel, Hananiah, Mishael, and Azariah. 12"Please test us for ten days on a diet of
vegetables and water," Daniel said. 13"At the end of the ten days, see how we look compared
to the other young men who are eating the king's food. Then make your decision in light of
what you see." 14The attendant agreed to Daniel's suggestion and tested them for ten days.

15At the end of the ten days, Daniel and his three friends looked healthier and better nourished than the young men who had been eating the food assigned by the king. 16So after that,
the attendant fed them only vegetables instead of the food and wine provided for the others.

How might Daniel react to the pressure situations in your life? It is easier to resist temptation if you have thought through your convictions well before the temptation arises. Daniel and his friends made their decision to be faithful to the laws of their religion before they were faced with the king's delicacies, so they did not hesitate to stick with their convictions. Sometimes we get into trouble because we have not previously decided where to draw the line. Before such situations arise, decide on your commitments. Then when temptation comes, you will be ready and able to resist.

MAY 29

A King's Dream

DANIEL 2:1-24

One night during the second year of his reign, Nebuchadnezzar had such disturbing dreams
that he couldn't sleep. 2He called in his magicians, enchanters, sorcerers, and astrologers, and
he demanded that they tell him what he had dreamed. As they stood before the king, 3he said,
"I have had a dream that deeply troubles me, and I must know what it means."

4Then the astrologers answered the king in Aramaic, "Long live the king! Tell us the
dream, and we will tell you what it means."

5But the king said to the astrologers, "I am serious about this. If you don't tell me what
my dream was and what it means, you will be torn limb from limb, and your houses will be
turned into heaps of rubble! 6But if you tell me what I dreamed and what the dream means,
I will give you many wonderful gifts and honors. Just tell me the dream and what it means!"

7They said again, "Please, Your Majesty. Tell us the dream, and we will tell you what it
means."

8The king replied, "I know what you are doing! You're stalling for time because you know
I am serious when I say, 9'If you don't tell me the dream, you are doomed.' So you have
conspired to tell me lies, hoping I will change my mind. But tell me the dream, and then I'll
know that you can tell me what it means."

10The astrologers replied to the king, "No one on earth can tell the king his dream! And
no king, however great and powerful, has ever asked such a thing of any magician, enchanter,
or astrologer! 11The king's demand is impossible. No one except the gods can tell you your
dream, and they do not live here among people."

12The king was furious when he heard this, and he ordered that all the wise men of
Babylon be executed. 13And because of the king's decree, men were sent to find and kill Daniel
and his friends. . . .

17Then Daniel went home and told his friends Hananiah, Mishael, and Azariah what had
happened. 18He urged them to ask the God of heaven to show them his mercy by telling them
the secret, so they would not be executed along with the other wise men of Babylon. 19That
night the secret was revealed to Daniel in a vision. . . .

24Then Daniel went in to see Arioch, Daniel said to him, "Don't kill the wise men. Take
me to the king, and I will tell him the meaning of his dream."

What do you do in seemingly hopeless situations? Daniel was at a crisis point. Imagine going to see the powerful, temperamental king who had just angrily ordered your death! Daniel did not shrink back in fear, however, but he confidently believed that God would tell him all that the king wanted to know. When the king gave Daniel time to find the answer, Daniel found his three friends and they prayed. When you find yourself in a tight spot, share your needs with trusted friends who also believe in God's power. Prayer is more effective than panic. Panic confirms your hopelessness; prayer confirms your hope in God. Daniel's trust in God saved himself, his three friends, and all the wise men.

The Meaning of the Dream

MAY 30

DANIEL 2:27-49

[27]Daniel replied, "There are no wise men, enchanters, magicians, or fortune-tellers who can
reveal the king's secret. [28]But there is a God in heaven who reveals secrets, and he has shown
King Nebuchadnezzar what will happen in the future. Now I will tell you your dream and
the visions you saw as you lay on your bed.

[29]"While Your Majesty was sleeping, you dreamed about coming events. He who reveals
secrets has shown you what is going to happen. [30]And it is not because I am wiser than anyone
else that I know the secret of your dream, but because God wants you to understand what
was in your heart.

[31]"In your vision, Your Majesty, you saw standing before you a huge, shining statue of
a man. It was a frightening sight. [32]The head of the statue was made of fine gold. Its chest
and arms were silver, its belly and thighs were bronze, [33]its legs were iron, and its feet were a
combination of iron and baked clay. [34]As you watched, a rock was cut from a mountain, but
not by human hands. It struck the feet of iron and clay, smashing them to bits. [35]The whole
statue was crushed into small pieces of iron, clay, bronze, silver, and gold. Then the wind
blew them away without a trace, like chaff on a threshing floor. But the rock that knocked
the statue down became a great mountain that covered the whole earth.

[36]"That was the dream. Now we will tell the king what it means. . . ."

[46]Then King Nebuchadnezzar threw himself down before Daniel and worshiped him,
and he commanded his people to offer sacrifices and burn sweet incense before him. [47]The
king said to Daniel, "Truly, your God is the greatest of gods, the Lord over kings, a revealer
of mysteries, for you have been able to reveal this secret."

[48]Then the king appointed Daniel to a high position and gave him many valuable gifts.
He made Daniel ruler over the whole province of Babylon, as well as chief over all his wise
men. [49]At Daniel's request, the king appointed Shadrach, Meshach, and Abednego to be in
charge of all the affairs of the province of Babylon, while Daniel remained in the king's court.

Who gets the credit when things go right in your life? Nebuchadnezzar honored Daniel and Daniel's God. If Daniel had taken the credit himself, the king would have honored only Daniel. Because Daniel gave God the credit, the king honored both of them. Part of our mission in this world is to show nonbelievers what God is like. We can do that by giving God credit for the great things he does in our life. Our acts of love and compassion may make an impression on people, and if we give God credit for our actions, they will want to know more about him. Give thanks to God for what he is doing in and through you.

MAY 31 Three Friends in a Furnace

DANIEL 3:1-25

King Nebuchadnezzar made a gold statue ninety feet tall and nine feet wide and set it up on the plain of Dura in the province of Babylon. . . .

4Then a herald shouted out, “People of all races and nations and languages, listen to the king’s command! 5When you hear the sound of the horn, flute, zither, lyre, harp, pipes, and other musical instruments, bow to the ground to worship King Nebuchadnezzar’s gold statue. 6Anyone who refuses to obey will immediately be thrown into a blazing furnace.” . . .

8But some of the astrologers went to the king and informed on the Jews. 9They said to King Nebuchadnezzar, “Long live the king! 10You issued a decree requiring all the people to bow down and worship the gold statue . . . 12But there are some Jews—Shadrach, Meshach, and Abednego—whom you have put in charge of the province of Babylon. They pay no attention to you, Your Majesty. They refuse to serve your gods and do not worship the gold statue you have set up.”

13Then Nebuchadnezzar flew into a rage and ordered that Shadrach, Meshach, and Abednego be brought before him. When they were brought in, 14Nebuchadnezzar said to them, “Is it true, Shadrach, Meshach, and Abednego, that you refuse to serve my gods or to worship the gold statue I have set up? . . . ”

16Shadrach, Meshach, and Abednego replied, “O Nebuchadnezzar, we do not need to defend ourselves before you. 17If we are thrown into the blazing furnace, the God whom we serve is able to save us. He will rescue us from your power, Your Majesty. 18But even if he doesn’t, we want to make it clear to you, Your Majesty, that we will never serve your gods or worship the gold statue you have set up.”

19Nebuchadnezzar was so furious with Shadrach, Meshach, and Abednego that his face became distorted with rage. He commanded that the furnace be heated seven times hotter than usual. 20Then he ordered some of the strongest men of his army to bind Shadrach, Meshach, and Abednego and throw them into the blazing furnace. 21So they tied them up and threw them into the furnace, fully dressed in their pants, turbans, robes, and other garments.

25“Look!” Nebuchadnezzar shouted. “I see four men, unbound, walking around in the fire unharmed! And the fourth looks like a god!”

What examples can you give of God’s protection in your life? Why didn’t the three men just bow to the image and tell God that they didn’t mean it? They had determined never to worship another god, and they courageously took their stand. As a result, they were condemned and led away to be executed. They did not know whether they would be delivered from the fire; all they knew was that they would not bow to an idol. Are you ready to take a stand for God no matter what? When you stand for God, you will stand out. It may be painful, and it may not always have a happy ending. Be prepared to say, “If he delivers me, or if he doesn’t, I will serve only God.”

June

JUNE 1

The Writing on the Wall

DANIEL 5:1-30

Many years later King Belshazzar gave a great feast for 1,000 of his nobles, and he drank wine
with them. [2]While Belshazzar was drinking the wine, he gave orders to bring in the gold and
silver cups that his predecessor, Nebuchadnezzar, had taken from the Temple in Jerusalem. He
wanted to drink from them with his nobles, his wives, and his concubines. [3]So they brought
these gold cups taken from the Temple, the house of God in Jerusalem, and the king and his
nobles, his wives, and his concubines drank from them. [4]While they drank from them they
praised their idols made of gold, silver, bronze, iron, wood, and stone.

[5]Suddenly, they saw the fingers of a human hand writing on the plaster wall of the king's
palace, near the lampstand. The king himself saw the hand as it wrote, [6]and his face turned
pale with fright. His knees knocked together in fear and his legs gave way beneath him. . . .

[13]So Daniel was brought in before the king. The king asked him, "Are you Daniel, one of
the exiles brought from Judah by my predecessor, King Nebuchadnezzar? [14]I have heard that
you have the spirit of the gods within you and that you are filled with insight, understanding,
and wisdom. [15]My wise men and enchanters have tried to read the words on the wall and tell
me their meaning, but they cannot do it. [16]I am told that you can give interpretations and
solve difficult problems. If you can read these words and tell me their meaning, you will be
clothed in purple robes of royal honor, and you will have a gold chain placed around your
neck. You will become the third highest ruler in the kingdom."

[17]Daniel answered the king, "Keep your gifts or give them to someone else, but I will tell
you what the writing means. . . .

[25]"This is the message that was written: MENE, MENE, TEKEL, and PARSIN. [26]This is what
these words mean:

Mene means 'numbered'—God has numbered the days of your reign and has brought it to an end.

[27] *Tekel* means 'weighed'—you have been weighed on the balances and have not measured up.

[28] *Parsin* means 'divided'—your kingdom has been divided and given to the Medes and Persians." . . .

[30]That very night Belshazzar, the Babylonian king, was killed.

What reasons would God have for passing judgment on the society in which you live? The writing on the wall was a message for all those who defy God. Although Belshazzar had power and wealth, his kingdom was totally corrupt, and he could not withstand the judgment of God. God's time of judgment comes for all people. If you have forgotten God and slipped into a sinful way of life, turn away from your sin now before he denies you more opportunities to repent. Ask God to forgive you, and begin to live by his standards of justice.

Daniel and the Lions

JUNE 2

DANIEL 6:3-23

[3]Daniel soon proved himself more capable than all the other administrators and high officers. Because of Daniel's great ability, the king made plans to place him over the entire empire.

[4]Then the other administrators and high officers began searching for some fault in the way Daniel was handling government affairs, but they couldn't find anything to criticize or condemn. He was faithful, always responsible, and completely trustworthy. [5]So they concluded, "Our only chance of finding grounds for accusing Daniel will be in connection with the rules of his religion."

[6]So the administrators and high officers went to the king and said, "Long live King Darius! [7]We are all in agreement—we administrators, officials, high officers, advisers, and governors—that the king should make a law that will be strictly enforced. Give orders that for the next thirty days any person who prays to anyone, divine or human—except to you, Your Majesty—will be thrown into the den of lions. [8]And now, Your Majesty, issue and sign this law so it cannot be changed, an official law of the Medes and Persians that cannot be revoked." [9]So King Darius signed the law.

[10]But when Daniel learned that the law had been signed, he went home and knelt down as usual in his upstairs room, with its windows open toward Jerusalem. He prayed three times a day, just as he had always done, giving thanks to his God. . . .

[16]So at last the king gave orders for Daniel to be arrested and thrown into the den of lions. The king said to him, "May your God, whom you serve so faithfully, rescue you."

[17]A stone was brought and placed over the mouth of the den. The king sealed the stone with his own royal seal and the seals of his nobles, so that no one could rescue Daniel. . . .

[19]Very early the next morning, the king got up and hurried out to the lions' den. [20]When he got there, he called out in anguish, "Daniel, servant of the living God! Was your God, whom you serve so faithfully, able to rescue you from the lions?"

[21]Daniel answered, "Long live the king! [22]My God sent his angel to shut the lions' mouths so that they would not hurt me, for I have been found innocent in his sight. And I have not wronged you, Your Majesty."

[23]The king was overjoyed and ordered that Daniel be lifted from the den. Not a scratch was found on him, for he had trusted in his God.

When is your regular prayer time? Although Daniel knew about the law against praying, he still prayed three times a day, "just as he had always done." Daniel had a disciplined prayer life. Our prayers are not usually interrupted by threats but simply by the pressure of our schedules. Don't let threats or pressures interfere with your prayer time. Pray regularly, no matter what.

JUNE 3

Jonah Runs from God

JONAH 1:1-17

The LORD gave this message to Jonah son of Amittai: 2“Get up and go to the great city of Nineveh. Announce my judgment against it because I have seen how wicked its people are.”

3But Jonah got up and went in the opposite direction to get away from the LORD. He went down to the port of Joppa, where he found a ship leaving for Tarshish. He bought a ticket and went on board, hoping to escape from the LORD by sailing to Tarshish.

4But the LORD hurled a powerful wind over the sea, causing a violent storm that threatened to break the ship apart. 5Fearing for their lives, the desperate sailors shouted to their gods for help and threw the cargo overboard to lighten the ship.

But all this time Jonah was sound asleep down in the hold. 6So the captain went down after him. “How can you sleep at a time like this?” he shouted. “Get up and pray to your god! Maybe he will pay attention to us and spare our lives.”

7Then the crew cast lots to see which of them had offended the gods and caused the terrible storm. When they did this, the lots identified Jonah as the culprit. 8“Why has this awful storm come down on us?” they demanded. “Who are you? What is your line of work? What country are you from? What is your nationality?”

9Jonah answered, “I am a Hebrew, and I worship the LORD, the God of heaven, who made the sea and the land.”

10The sailors were terrified when they heard this, for he had already told them he was running away from the LORD. “Oh, why did you do it?” they groaned. 11And since the storm was getting worse all the time, they asked him, “What should we do to you to stop this storm?”

12“Throw me into the sea,” Jonah said, “and it will become calm again. I know that this terrible storm is all my fault.” . . .

15Then the sailors picked Jonah up and threw him into the raging sea, and the storm stopped at once! 16The sailors were awestruck by the LORD’s great power, and they offered him a sacrifice and vowed to serve him.

17Now the LORD had arranged for a great fish to swallow Jonah. And Jonah was inside the fish for three days and three nights.

When did you last try to avoid doing what you knew God wanted you to do? Jonah was afraid. He knew that God had a specific job for him, but he didn’t want to do it. When God gives us directions through his Word, sometimes we run in fear, claiming that God is asking too much. Fear made Jonah run, but running got him into worse trouble. In the end, Jonah knew that it was best to do what God had asked in the first place, but by then he had paid a costly price for running. It is far better to obey from the start.

Jonah's Attitude Check

JUNE 4

JONAH 3:1–4:11

Then the LORD spoke to Jonah a second time: 2“Get up and go to the great city of Nineveh, and deliver the message I have given you.”

3This time Jonah obeyed the LORD's command and went to Nineveh, a city so large that it took three days to see it all. 4On the day Jonah entered the city, he shouted to the crowds: “Forty days from now Nineveh will be destroyed!” 5The people of Nineveh believed God's message, and from the greatest to the least, they declared a fast and put on burlap to show their sorrow.

6When the king of Nineveh heard what Jonah was saying, he stepped down from his throne and took off his royal robes. He dressed himself in burlap and sat on a heap of ashes.

. . . 10When God saw what they had done and how they had put a stop to their evil ways, he changed his mind and did not carry out the destruction he had threatened.

4:1This change of plans greatly upset Jonah, and he became very angry. 2So he complained to the LORD about it: “Didn't I say before I left home that you would do this, LORD? That is why I ran away to Tarshish! I knew that you are a merciful and compassionate God, slow to get angry and filled with unfailing love. You are eager to turn back from destroying people. 3Just kill me now, LORD! I'd rather be dead than alive if what I predicted will not happen.” . . .

5Then Jonah went out to the east side of the city and made a shelter to sit under as he waited to see what would happen to the city. 6And the LORD God arranged for a leafy plant to grow there, and soon it spread its broad leaves over Jonah's head, shading him from the sun. . . .

7But God also arranged for a worm! The next morning at dawn the worm ate through the stem of the plant so that it withered away. 8And as the sun grew hot, God arranged for a scorching east wind to blow on Jonah. The sun beat down on his head until he grew faint and wished to die. “Death is certainly better than living like this!” he exclaimed. . . .

10Then the LORD said, “You feel sorry about the plant, though you did nothing to put it there. It came quickly and died quickly. 11But Nineveh has more than 120,000 people living in spiritual darkness, not to mention all the animals. Shouldn't I feel sorry for such a great city?”

About what things do you complain to God? Jonah revealed the reason for his reluctance to go to Nineveh (Jonah 4:2). He did not want the Ninevites forgiven; he wanted them destroyed. Jonah did not understand that the God of Israel is also the God of the whole world. Are you surprised when some unexpected person turns to God? Is it possible that your view is as narrow as Jonah's? We must not forget that, in reality, we do not deserve to be forgiven by God.

JUNE 5

Fully Human, Fully God

JOHN 1:1-18

In the beginning the Word already existed.
The Word was with God,
and the Word was God.
[2]He existed in the beginning with God.
[3]God created everything through him,
and nothing was created except through him.
[4]The Word gave life to everything that was created,
and his life brought light to everyone.
[5]The light shines in the darkness,
and the darkness can never extinguish it.

[6]God sent a man, John the Baptist, [7]to tell about the light so that everyone might believe because of his testimony. [8]John himself was not the light; he was simply a witness to tell about the light. [9]The one who is the true light, who gives light to everyone, was coming into the world.

[10]He came into the very world he created, but the world didn't recognize him. [11]He came to his own people, and even they rejected him. [12]But to all who believed him and accepted him, he gave the right to become children of God. [13]They are reborn—not with a physical birth resulting from human passion or plan, but a birth that comes from God.

[14]So the Word became human and made his home among us. He was full of unfailing love and faithfulness. And we have seen his glory, the glory of the Father's one and only Son.

[15]John testified about him when he shouted to the crowds, "This is the one I was talking about when I said, 'Someone is coming after me who is far greater than I am, for he existed long before me.'"

[16]From his abundance we have all received one gracious blessing after another. [17]For the law was given through Moses, but God's unfailing love and faithfulness came through Jesus Christ. [18]No one has ever seen God. But the unique One, who is himself God, is near to the Father's heart. He has revealed God to us.

Have you personally received Jesus as your Savior and become a child of God? What Jesus taught and what he did are tied inseparably to who he is. John shows Jesus as fully human and fully God. Although Jesus took upon himself full humanity and lived as a man, he never ceased to be the eternal God who has always existed, the Creator and Sustainer of all things, and the source of eternal life. This is the truth about Jesus, and the foundation of all truth. If we cannot or do not believe this basic truth, we will not have enough faith to trust our eternal destiny to him. That is why John wrote his Gospel; he wanted to build faith and confidence in Jesus Christ so that we may believe he truly was and is God's Son.

The Angel and Zechariah

JUNE 6

LUKE 1:5-25

5When Herod was king of Judea, there was a Jewish priest named Zechariah. He was a member of the priestly order of Abijah, and his wife, Elizabeth, was also from the priestly line
of Aaron. 6Zechariah and Elizabeth were righteous in God's eyes, careful to obey all of the
Lord's commandments and regulations. 7They had no children because Elizabeth was unable
to conceive, and they were both very old.

8One day Zechariah was serving God in the Temple, for his order was on duty that week.
9As was the custom of the priests, he was chosen by lot to enter the sanctuary of the Lord and
burn incense. 10While the incense was being burned, a great crowd stood outside, praying.

11While Zechariah was in the sanctuary, an angel of the Lord appeared to him, standing
to the right of the incense altar. 12Zechariah was shaken and overwhelmed with fear when he
saw him. 13But the angel said, "Don't be afraid, Zechariah! God has heard your prayer. Your
wife, Elizabeth, will give you a son, and you are to name him John. 14You will have great joy
and gladness, and many will rejoice at his birth, 15for he will be great in the eyes of the Lord.
He must never touch wine or other alcoholic drinks. He will be filled with the Holy Spirit,
even before his birth. 16And he will turn many Israelites to the Lord their God. 17He will be
a man with the spirit and power of Elijah. He will prepare the people for the coming of the
Lord. He will turn the hearts of the fathers to their children, and he will cause those who are
rebellious to accept the wisdom of the godly."

18Zechariah said to the angel, "How can I be sure this will happen? I'm an old man now,
and my wife is also well along in years."

19Then the angel said, "I am Gabriel! I stand in the very presence of God. It was he who
sent me to bring you this good news! 20But now, since you didn't believe what I said, you will
be silent and unable to speak until the child is born. For my words will certainly be fulfilled
at the proper time." . . .

23When Zechariah's week of service in the Temple was over, he returned home. 24Soon
afterward his wife, Elizabeth, became pregnant and went into seclusion for five months.
25"How kind the Lord is!" she exclaimed. "He has taken away my disgrace of having no
children."

How would you react to an angel's visit? When told he would have a son, Zechariah doubted the angel's word. From his human perspective, his doubts were understandable—but with God, anything is possible. Although Zechariah and Elizabeth were past the age of childbearing, God gave them a child. It is easy to doubt or misunderstand what God wants to do in our lives. Even God's people sometimes make the mistake of trusting their reason or experience instead of God. When tempted to think that one of God's promises is impossible, try to look at the situation from God's perspective. He is not bound by human limitations.

JUNE 7

Mary and Elizabeth

LUKE 1:26-45

26 In the sixth month of Elizabeth's pregnancy, God sent the angel Gabriel to Nazareth, a
village in Galilee, 27 to a virgin named Mary. She was engaged to be married to a man named
Joseph, a descendant of King David. 28 Gabriel appeared to her and said, "Greetings, favored
woman! The Lord is with you!"

29 Confused and disturbed, Mary tried to think what the angel could mean. 30 "Don't be
afraid, Mary," the angel told her, "for you have found favor with God! 31 You will conceive and
give birth to a son, and you will name him Jesus. 32 He will be very great and will be called the
Son of the Most High. The Lord God will give him the throne of his ancestor David. 33 And
he will reign over Israel forever; his Kingdom will never end!"

34 Mary asked the angel, "But how can this happen? I am a virgin."

35 The angel replied, "The Holy Spirit will come upon you, and the power of the Most
High will overshadow you. So the baby to be born will be holy, and he will be called the Son
of God. 36 What's more, your relative Elizabeth has become pregnant in her old age! People
used to say she was barren, but she has conceived a son and is now in her sixth month. 37 For
the word of God will never fail."

38 Mary responded, "I am the Lord's servant. May everything you have said about me come
true." And then the angel left her.

39 A few days later Mary hurried to the hill country of Judea, to the town 40 where Zechariah
lived. She entered the house and greeted Elizabeth. 41 At the sound of Mary's greeting,
Elizabeth's child leaped within her, and Elizabeth was filled with the Holy Spirit.

42 Elizabeth gave a glad cry and exclaimed to Mary, "God has blessed you above all women,
and your child is blessed. 43 Why am I so honored, that the mother of my Lord should visit
me? 44 When I heard your greeting, the baby in my womb jumped for joy. 45 You are blessed
because you believed that the Lord would do what he said."

How willingly do you offer yourself to God in risky situations? A young unmarried girl who became pregnant risked disaster. Unless the father of the child agreed to marry her, she would probably remain unmarried for life. If her own father rejected her, she could be forced into begging or prostitution in order to earn her living. And Mary, with her story about being made pregnant by the Holy Spirit, risked being considered crazy as well. Still Mary said, despite the possible risks, "May everything you have said about me come true." When Mary said that, she didn't know about the tremendous opportunity she would have. She only knew that God was asking her to serve him, and she willingly obeyed. Don't wait to see the bottom line before offering your life to God. Offer yourself willingly to God.

John the Baptist Is Born

LUKE 1:57-80

57When it was time for Elizabeth's baby to be born, she gave birth to a son. 58And when her
neighbors and relatives heard that the Lord had been very merciful to her, everyone rejoiced
with her. . . .

67Then his father, Zechariah, was filled with the Holy Spirit and gave this prophecy:

68"Praise the Lord, the God of Israel,
because he has visited and redeemed his people.
69He has sent us a mighty Savior
from the royal line of his servant David,
70just as he promised
through his holy prophets long ago.
71Now we will be saved from our enemies
and from all who hate us.
72He has been merciful to our ancestors
by remembering his sacred covenant—
73the covenant he swore with an oath
to our ancestor Abraham.
74We have been rescued from our enemies
so we can serve God without fear,
75in holiness and righteousness
for as long as we live.

76"And you, my little son,
will be called the prophet of the Most High,
because you will prepare the way for the Lord.
77You will tell his people how to find salvation
through forgiveness of their sins.
78Because of God's tender mercy,
the morning light from heaven is about to break upon us,
79to give light to those who sit in darkness and in the shadow of death,
and to guide us to the path of peace."

80John grew up and became strong in spirit. And he lived in the wilderness until he began
his public ministry to Israel.

When did you last say thank you to your parents for what they've done for you over the years? Zechariah had just recalled hundreds of years of God's sovereign work in history, beginning with Abraham and going on into eternity. Then, in tender contrast, he personalized the story. His son had been chosen for a key role in the drama of the ages. Although God has unlimited power, he chooses to work through frail humans who begin as helpless babies. Don't minimize what God can do through those who are faithful to him—even you.

JUNE 9

Jesus Is Born!

LUKE 2:1-20

At that time the Roman emperor, Augustus, decreed that a census should be taken throughout the Roman Empire. 2(This was the first census taken when Quirinius was governor of Syria.) 3All returned to their own ancestral towns to register for this census. 4And because Joseph was a descendant of King David, he had to go to Bethlehem in Judea, David's ancient home. He traveled there from the village of Nazareth in Galilee. 5He took with him Mary, to whom he was engaged, who was now expecting a child.

6And while they were there, the time came for her baby to be born. 7She gave birth to her firstborn son. She wrapped him snugly in strips of cloth and laid him in a manger, because there was no lodging available for them.

8That night there were shepherds staying in the fields nearby, guarding their flocks of sheep. 9Suddenly, an angel of the Lord appeared among them, and the radiance of the Lord's glory surrounded them. They were terrified, 10but the angel reassured them. "Don't be afraid!" he said. "I bring you good news that will bring great joy to all people. 11The Savior—yes, the Messiah, the Lord—has been born today in Bethlehem, the city of David! 12And you will recognize him by this sign: You will find a baby wrapped snugly in strips of cloth, lying in a manger."

13Suddenly, the angel was joined by a vast host of others—the armies of heaven—praising God and saying,

14"Glory to God in highest heaven,
and peace on earth to those with whom God is pleased."

15When the angels had returned to heaven, the shepherds said to each other, "Let's go to Bethlehem! Let's see this thing that has happened, which the Lord has told us about."

16They hurried to the village and found Mary and Joseph. And there was the baby, lying in the manger. 17After seeing him, the shepherds told everyone what had happened and what the angel had said to them about this child. 18All who heard the shepherds' story were astonished, 19but Mary kept all these things in her heart and thought about them often. 20The shepherds went back to their flocks, glorifying and praising God for all they had heard and seen. It was just as the angel had told them.

What does Christmas mean to you? The greatest event in history had just happened! The Messiah was born! For ages the Jews had waited for this, and when it finally happened, the announcement came to humble shepherds. The good news about Jesus is that he comes to all, including the plain and the ordinary. He comes to anyone with a heart humble enough to accept him. Whoever you are, whatever you do, you can have Jesus in your life. Don't think you need extraordinary qualifications—he accepts you as you are.

Jesus' First Trip to Church

JUNE 10

LUKE 2:21-38

[21]Eight days later, when the baby was circumcised, he was named Jesus, the name given him
by the angel even before he was conceived.
[22]Then it was time for their purification offering, as required by the law of Moses after
the birth of a child; so his parents took him to Jerusalem to present him to the Lord. [23]The
law of the Lord says, "If a woman's first child is a boy, he must be dedicated to the LORD."
[24]So they offered the sacrifice required in the law of the Lord—"either a pair of turtledoves
or two young pigeons."
[25]At that time there was a man in Jerusalem named Simeon. He was righteous and devout
and was eagerly waiting for the Messiah to come and rescue Israel. The Holy Spirit was upon
him [26]and had revealed to him that he would not die until he had seen the Lord's Messiah.
[27]That day the Spirit led him to the Temple. So when Mary and Joseph came to present the
baby Jesus to the Lord as the law required, [28]Simeon was there. He took the child in his arms
and praised God, saying,

[29]"Sovereign Lord, now let your servant die in peace,
as you have promised.
[30]I have seen your salvation,
[31] which you have prepared for all people.
[32]He is a light to reveal God to the nations,
and he is the glory of your people Israel!"

[33]Jesus' parents were amazed at what was being said about him. [34]Then Simeon blessed
them, and he said to Mary, the baby's mother, "This child is destined to cause many in Israel
to fall, and many others to rise. He has been sent as a sign from God, but many will oppose
him. [35]As a result, the deepest thoughts of many hearts will be revealed. And a sword will
pierce your very soul."
[36]Anna, a prophet, was also there in the Temple. She was the daughter of Phanuel from
the tribe of Asher, and she was very old. Her husband died when they had been married only
seven years. [37]Then she lived as a widow to the age of eighty-four. She never left the Temple
but stayed there day and night, worshiping God with fasting and prayer. [38]She came along
just as Simeon was talking with Mary and Joseph, and she began praising God. She talked
about the child to everyone who had been waiting expectantly for God to rescue Jerusalem.

How would you react to holding Jesus when he was a baby? Although Simeon and Anna were very old, they still hoped to see the Messiah. Led by the Holy Spirit, they were among the first to bear witness to Jesus. In the Jewish culture, elders were respected, so Simeon's and Anna's prophecies carried extra weight. Our society, however, values youthfulness over wisdom, and contributions by the elderly are often ignored. As Christians, we should reverse those values wherever we can. Encourage older people to share their wisdom and experience. Listen carefully when they speak. Help them find ways to continue to serve God.

JUNE 11

Wise Men from the East

MATTHEW 2:1-12

Jesus was born in Bethlehem in Judea, during the reign of King Herod. About that time some
wise men from eastern lands arrived in Jerusalem, asking, 2“Where is the newborn king of
the Jews? We saw his star as it rose, and we have come to worship him.”

3King Herod was deeply disturbed when he heard this, as was everyone in Jerusalem. 4He
called a meeting of the leading priests and teachers of religious law and asked, “Where is the
Messiah supposed to be born?”

5“In Bethlehem in Judea,” they said, “for this is what the prophet wrote:

6‘And you, O Bethlehem in the land of Judah,
  are not least among the ruling cities of Judah,
for a ruler will come from you
  who will be the shepherd for my people Israel.’”

7Then Herod called for a private meeting with the wise men, and he learned from them
the time when the star first appeared. 8Then he told them, “Go to Bethlehem and search
carefully for the child. And when you find him, come back and tell me so that I can go and
worship him, too!”

9After this interview the wise men went their way. And the star they had seen in the east
guided them to Bethlehem. It went ahead of them and stopped over the place where the child
was. 10When they saw the star, they were filled with joy! 11They entered the house and saw the
child with his mother, Mary, and they bowed down and worshiped him. Then they opened
their treasure chests and gave him gifts of gold, frankincense, and myrrh.

12When it was time to leave, they returned to their own country by another route, for
God had warned them in a dream not to return to Herod.

What gifts have you ever given Christ? The wise men traveled thousands of miles to see the King of the Jews. When they finally found him, they responded with joy, worship, and gifts. How different from the approach people often take today. We expect God to come looking for us, to explain himself, prove who he is, and give us gifts. But those who are wise still seek and worship Jesus today, not for what they can get, but for who he is.

Escape and Return

JUNE 12

MATTHEW 2:13-23

13 After the wise men were gone, an angel of the Lord appeared to Joseph in a dream. "Get
up! Flee to Egypt with the child and his mother," the angel said. "Stay there until I tell you
to return, because Herod is going to search for the child to kill him."
14 That night Joseph left for Egypt with the child and Mary, his mother, 15 and they stayed
there until Herod's death. This fulfilled what the Lord had spoken through the prophet: "I
called my Son out of Egypt."
16 Herod was furious when he realized that the wise men had outwitted him. He sent soldiers to kill all the boys in and around Bethlehem who were two years old and under, based
on the wise men's report of the star's first appearance. 17 Herod's brutal action fulfilled what
God had spoken through the prophet Jeremiah:

18 "A cry was heard in Ramah—
  weeping and great mourning.
Rachel weeps for her children,
  refusing to be comforted,
  for they are dead."

19 When Herod died, an angel of the Lord appeared in a dream to Joseph in Egypt. 20 "Get
up!" the angel said. "Take the child and his mother back to the land of Israel, because those
who were trying to kill the child are dead."
21 So Joseph got up and returned to the land of Israel with Jesus and his mother. 22 But
when he learned that the new ruler of Judea was Herod's son Archelaus, he was afraid to go
there. Then, after being warned in a dream, he left for the region of Galilee. 23 So the family
went and lived in a town called Nazareth. This fulfilled what the prophets had said: "He will
be called a Nazarene."

How has knowing God brought excitement into your life? Herod was afraid that this newborn King would one day take his throne. He completely misunderstood the reason for Christ's coming. Jesus didn't want Herod's throne—he wanted to be king of Herod's life. Jesus wanted to give Herod eternal life, not take away his present life. Today people are often afraid that Christ wants to take things away, when in reality he wants to give them real freedom, peace, and joy. Jesus wants to be King of your life. Have you let him sit on the throne of your life?

JUNE **13**

Jesus in the Temple Again

LUKE 2:41-52

[41]Every year Jesus' parents went to Jerusalem for the Passover festival. [42]When Jesus was twelve
years old, they attended the festival as usual. [43]After the celebration was over, they started
home to Nazareth, but Jesus stayed behind in Jerusalem. His parents didn't miss him at first,
[44]because they assumed he was among the other travelers. But when he didn't show up that
evening, they started looking for him among their relatives and friends.

[45]When they couldn't find him, they went back to Jerusalem to search for him there.
[46]Three days later they finally discovered him in the Temple, sitting among the religious
teachers, listening to them and asking questions. [47]All who heard him were amazed at his
understanding and his answers.

[48]His parents didn't know what to think. "Son," his mother said to him, "why have you
done this to us? Your father and I have been frantic, searching for you everywhere."

[49]"But why did you need to search?" he asked. "Didn't you know that I must be in my
Father's house?" [50]But they didn't understand what he meant.

[51]Then he returned to Nazareth with them and was obedient to them. And his mother
stored all these things in her heart.

[52]Jesus grew in wisdom and in stature and in favor with God and all the people.

What four words would summarize your teenage years? The second chapter of Luke shows us that although Jesus was unique, he had a normal childhood and adolescence. In terms of development, he went through the same progression we do. He grew physically and mentally, he related to other people, and he was loved by God. A full human life is not unbalanced. It was important to Jesus—and it should be important to all believers—to develop fully and harmoniously in these key areas: physical, mental, social, and spiritual. Make sure you're letting God help you grow in each of these areas.

Baptism and Temptation

JUNE 14

MARK 1:1-13

This is the Good News about Jesus the Messiah, the Son of God. It began 2just as the prophet
Isaiah had written:

> "Look, I am sending my messenger ahead of you,
> and he will prepare your way.
> 3He is a voice shouting in the wilderness,
> 'Prepare the way for the LORD's coming!
> Clear the road for him!'"

4This messenger was John the Baptist. He was in the wilderness and preached that people
should be baptized to show that they had repented of their sins and turned to God to be
forgiven. 5All of Judea, including all the people of Jerusalem, went out to see and hear John.
And when they confessed their sins, he baptized them in the Jordan River. 6His clothes were
woven from coarse camel hair, and he wore a leather belt around his waist. For food he ate
locusts and wild honey.

7John announced: "Someone is coming soon who is greater than I am—so much greater
that I'm not even worthy to stoop down like a slave and untie the straps of his sandals. 8I
baptize you with water, but he will baptize you with the Holy Spirit!"

9One day Jesus came from Nazareth in Galilee, and John baptized him in the Jordan
River. 10As Jesus came up out of the water, he saw the heavens splitting apart and the Holy
Spirit descending on him like a dove. 11And a voice from heaven said, "You are my dearly
loved Son, and you bring me great joy."

12The Spirit then compelled Jesus to go into the wilderness, 13where he was tempted by
Satan for forty days. He was out among the wild animals, and angels took care of him.

What are your most difficult temptations? Compare them to Jesus' temptations. To identify fully with human beings, Jesus had to endure Satan's temptations. Although Jesus is God, he is also man, and as a human being he was not exempt from Satan's attacks. Because Jesus faced temptations and overcame them, he can assist us in two important ways: (1) as an example of how to face temptation without sinning and (2) as our helper who knows just what we need because he went through the same experience. When you face temptation, trust Jesus to help you overcome it.

JUNE 15

John the Baptist and Jesus

JOHN 1:19-34

19This was John's testimony when the Jewish leaders sent priests and Temple assistants from
Jerusalem to ask John, "Who are you?" 20He came right out and said, "I am not the Messiah."

21"Well then, who are you?" they asked. "Are you Elijah?"

"No," he replied.

"Are you the Prophet we are expecting?"

"No."

22"Then who are you? We need an answer for those who sent us. What do you have to
say about yourself?"

23John replied in the words of the prophet Isaiah:

"I am a voice shouting in the wilderness,
'Clear the way for the LORD's coming!'"

24Then the Pharisees who had been sent 25asked him, "If you aren't the Messiah or Elijah
or the Prophet, what right do you have to baptize?"

26John told them, "I baptize with water, but right here in the crowd is someone you do
not recognize. 27Though his ministry follows mine, I'm not even worthy to be his slave and
untie the straps of his sandal."

28This encounter took place in Bethany, an area east of the Jordan River, where John was
baptizing.

29The next day John saw Jesus coming toward him and said, "Look! The Lamb of God
who takes away the sin of the world! 30He is the one I was talking about when I said, 'A
man is coming after me who is far greater than I am, for he existed long before me.' 31I did
not recognize him as the Messiah, but I have been baptizing with water so that he might be
revealed to Israel."

32Then John testified, "I saw the Holy Spirit descending like a dove from heaven and
resting upon him. 33I didn't know he was the one, but when God sent me to baptize with
water, he told me, 'The one on whom you see the Spirit descend and rest is the one who will
baptize with the Holy Spirit.' 34I saw this happen to Jesus, so I testify that he is the Chosen
One of God."

To whom did you last talk about Christ? Although John the Baptist was a well-known preacher and attracted large crowds, he was content to let Jesus take the higher place. This is true humility, the basis for greatness in preaching, teaching, or any other work we do for Christ. When you are content to do what God wants you to do and let Jesus Christ be honored for it, God will do great things through you.

Jesus' First Disciples

JUNE 16

JOHN 1:35-51

35The following day John was again standing with two of his disciples. 36As Jesus walked by,
John looked at him and declared, "Look! There is the Lamb of God!" 37When John's two
disciples heard this, they followed Jesus.

38Jesus looked around and saw them following. "What do you want?" he asked them.

They replied, "Rabbi" (which means "Teacher"), "where are you staying?"

39"Come and see," he said. It was about four o'clock in the afternoon when they went
with him to the place where he was staying, and they remained with him the rest of the day.

40Andrew, Simon Peter's brother, was one of these men who heard what John said and
then followed Jesus. 41Andrew went to find his brother, Simon, and told him, "We have found
the Messiah" (which means "Christ").

42Then Andrew brought Simon to meet Jesus. Looking intently at Simon, Jesus said,
"Your name is Simon, son of John—but you will be called Cephas" (which means "Peter").

43The next day Jesus decided to go to Galilee. He found Philip and said to him, "Come,
follow me." 44Philip was from Bethsaida, Andrew and Peter's hometown.

45Philip went to look for Nathanael and told him, "We have found the very person Moses
and the prophets wrote about! His name is Jesus, the son of Joseph from Nazareth."

46"Nazareth!" exclaimed Nathanael. "Can anything good come from Nazareth?"

"Come and see for yourself," Philip replied.

47As they approached, Jesus said, "Now here is a genuine son of Israel—a man of complete
integrity." 48"How do you know about me?" Nathanael asked.

Jesus replied, "I could see you under the fig tree before Philip found you."

49Then Nathanael exclaimed, "Rabbi, you are the Son of God—the King of Israel!"

50Jesus asked him, "Do you believe this just because I told you I had seen you under the
fig tree? You will see greater things than this." 51Then he said, "I tell you the truth, you will
all see heaven open and the angels of God going up and down on the Son of Man, the one
who is the stairway between heaven and earth."

How would someone know that you're a disciple of Jesus? As these new disciples got to know Jesus, their appreciation for him grew. The more time we spend getting to know Christ, the more we will understand and appreciate who he is. We may be drawn to him for his teaching, but we will come to know him as the Son of God. Although these disciples made this verbal shift in a few days, they would not fully understand Jesus until three years later (Acts 2). What they so easily professed had to be worked out in experience. We may find that words of faith come easily, but deep appreciation for Christ comes from living by faith.

JUNE 17

Water into Wine

JOHN 2:1-12

The next day there was a wedding celebration in the village of Cana in Galilee. Jesus' mother
was there, [2]and Jesus and his disciples were also invited to the celebration. [3]The wine supply
ran out during the festivities, so Jesus' mother told him, "They have no more wine."

[4]"Dear woman, that's not our problem," Jesus replied. "My time has not yet come."

[5]But his mother told the servants, "Do whatever he tells you."

[6]Standing nearby were six stone water jars, used for Jewish ceremonial washing. Each
could hold twenty to thirty gallons. [7]Jesus told the servants, "Fill the jars with water." When
the jars had been filled, [8]he said, "Now dip some out, and take it to the master of ceremonies."
So the servants followed his instructions.

[9]When the master of ceremonies tasted the water that was now wine, not knowing where
it had come from (though, of course, the servants knew), he called the bridegroom over. [10]"A
host always serves the best wine first," he said. "Then, when everyone has had a lot to drink,
he brings out the less expensive wine. But you have kept the best until now!"

[11]This miraculous sign at Cana in Galilee was the first time Jesus revealed his glory. And
his disciples believed in him.

[12]After the wedding he went to Capernaum for a few days with his mother, his brothers,
and his disciples.

How has Christ been unpredictable in your life? Jesus was on a mission to save the world, the greatest mission in the history of mankind. Yet he took time to attend a wedding and take part in its festivities. Jesus valued these wedding festivities because they involved people, and Jesus came to be with people. Our mission can often be accomplished in joyous times of celebration with others. Bring balance to your life by bringing Jesus into times of pleasure and play as well as times of school and work.

Jesus and Nicodemus

JUNE 18

JOHN 3:1-21

There was a man named Nicodemus, a Jewish religious leader who was a Pharisee. [2]After dark one evening, he came to speak with Jesus. “Rabbi,” he said, “we all know that God has sent you to teach us. Your miraculous signs are evidence that God is with you.”

[3]Jesus replied, “I tell you the truth, unless you are born again, you cannot see the Kingdom of God.”

[4]“What do you mean?” exclaimed Nicodemus. “How can an old man go back into his mother’s womb and be born again?”

[5]Jesus replied, “I assure you, no one can enter the Kingdom of God without being born of water and the Spirit. [6]Humans can reproduce only human life, but the Holy Spirit gives birth to spiritual life. [7]So don’t be surprised when I say, ‘You must be born again.’ [8]The wind blows wherever it wants. Just as you can hear the wind but can’t tell where it comes from or where it is going, so you can’t explain how people are born of the Spirit.”

[9]“How are these things possible?” Nicodemus asked.

[10]Jesus replied, “You are a respected Jewish teacher, and yet you don’t understand these things? [11]I assure you, we tell you what we know and have seen, and yet you won’t believe our testimony. [12]But if you don’t believe me when I tell you about earthly things, how can you possibly believe if I tell you about heavenly things? [13]No one has ever gone to heaven and returned. But the Son of Man has come down from heaven. [14]And as Moses lifted up the bronze snake on a pole in the wilderness, so the Son of Man must be lifted up, [15]so that everyone who believes in him will have eternal life.

[16]“For this is how God loved the world: He gave his one and only Son, so that everyone who believes in him will not perish but have eternal life. [17]God sent his Son into the world not to judge the world, but to save the world through him.

[18]“There is no judgment against anyone who believes in him. But anyone who does not believe in him has already been judged for not believing in God’s one and only Son. [19]And the judgment is based on this fact: God’s light came into the world, but people loved the darkness more than the light, for their actions were evil. [20]All who do evil hate the light and refuse to go near it for fear their sins will be exposed. [21]But those who do what is right come to the light so others can see that they are doing what God wants.”

When did you first meet Jesus? The entire gospel comes to a focus in verse 16. True love is not self-centered; it reaches out and draws others in. God sets the pattern of true love here, the basis for all love relationships. God paid with the life of his Son, the highest price he could pay. Jesus accepted our punishment, paid the price for our sins, and then offered us the new life that he bought for us. When we share the gospel with others, our love must be like his—we must willingly give up our own comfort and security so that others might join us in receiving God’s love.

JUNE 19 John the Baptist Gets into Trouble

JOHN 3:22-36; LUKE 3:19-20

22Then Jesus and his disciples left Jerusalem and went into the Judean countryside. Jesus spent
some time with them there, baptizing people.

23At this time John the Baptist was baptizing at Aenon, near Salim, because there was
plenty of water there; and people kept coming to him for baptism. 24(This was before John
was thrown into prison.) 25A debate broke out between John's disciples and a certain Jew over
ceremonial cleansing. 26So John's disciples came to him and said, "Rabbi, the man you met
on the other side of the Jordan River, the one you identified as the Messiah, is also baptizing
people. And everybody is going to him instead of coming to us."

27John replied, "No one can receive anything unless God gives it from heaven. 28You yourselves know how plainly I told you, 'I am not the Messiah. I am only here to prepare the way
for him.' 29It is the bridegroom who marries the bride, and the bridegroom's friend is simply
glad to stand with him and hear his vows. Therefore, I am filled with joy at his success. 30He
must become greater and greater, and I must become less and less.

31"He has come from above and is greater than anyone else. We are of the earth, and we
speak of earthly things, but he has come from heaven and is greater than anyone else. 32He
testifies about what he has seen and heard, but how few believe what he tells them! 33Anyone
who accepts his testimony can affirm that God is true. 34For he is sent by God. He speaks
God's words, for God gives him the Spirit without limit. 35The Father loves his Son and
has put everything into his hands. 36And anyone who believes in God's Son has eternal life.
Anyone who doesn't obey the Son will never experience eternal life but remains under God's
angry judgment."

LK 3:19John also publicly criticized Herod Antipas, the ruler of Galilee, for marrying Herodias,
his brother's wife, and for many other wrongs he had done. 20So Herod put John in prison,
adding this sin to his many others.

When has knowing Christ ever gotten you into trouble? In his Gospel, John has been demonstrating that Jesus is the true Son of God. Jesus sets before us the greatest choice in life. We are responsible to decide today whom we will obey (Joshua 24:15), and God wants us to choose him and life (Deuteronomy 30:15-20). The wrath of God is God's final judgment and rejection of the sinner. To put off the choice is to choose not to follow Christ. Indecision is a fatal decision.

The Woman at the Well

JUNE 20

JOHN 4:1-26

Jesus knew the Pharisees had heard that he was baptizing and making more disciples than John 2(though Jesus himself didn't baptize them—his disciples did). 3So he left Judea and returned to Galilee.

4He had to go through Samaria on the way. 5Eventually he came to the Samaritan village of Sychar, near the field that Jacob gave to his son Joseph. 6Jacob's well was there; and Jesus, tired from the long walk, sat wearily beside the well about noontime. 7Soon a Samaritan woman came to draw water, and Jesus said to her, "Please give me a drink." 8He was alone at the time because his disciples had gone into the village to buy some food.

9The woman was surprised, for Jews refuse to have anything to do with Samaritans. She said to Jesus, "You are a Jew, and I am a Samaritan woman. Why are you asking me for a drink?"

10Jesus replied, "If you only knew the gift God has for you and who you are speaking to, you would ask me, and I would give you living water."

11"But sir, you don't have a rope or a bucket," she said, "and this well is very deep. Where would you get this living water? 12And besides, do you think you're greater than our ancestor Jacob, who gave us this well? How can you offer better water than he and his sons and his animals enjoyed?"

13Jesus replied, "Anyone who drinks this water will soon become thirsty again. 14But those who drink the water I give will never be thirsty again. It becomes a fresh, bubbling spring within them, giving them eternal life."

15"Please, sir," the woman said, "give me this water! Then I'll never be thirsty again, and I won't have to come here to get water."

16"Go and get your husband," Jesus told her.

17"I don't have a husband," the woman replied.

Jesus said, "You're right! You don't have a husband—18for you have had five husbands, and you aren't even married to the man you're living with now. You certainly spoke the truth!" . . .

25The woman said, "I know the Messiah is coming—the one who is called Christ. When he comes, he will explain everything to us."

26Then Jesus told her, "I AM the Messiah!"

What barriers are you willing to cross to share the Good News? The woman had several strikes against her. She was (1) a Samaritan, a member of the hated mixed race, (2) known to be living in sin, and (3) in a public place. No respectable Jewish man would talk to a woman under such circumstances. But Jesus did. The Good News is for every person, no matter what his or her race, social position, or past sins. We must be prepared to share this Good News at any time and in any place. Jesus crossed all barriers to share the Good News, and we who follow him must do no less.

JUNE 21

Jesus Heals a Man's Son

JOHN 4:43-54

43At the end of the two days, Jesus went on to Galilee. 44He himself had said that a prophet
is not honored in his own hometown. 45Yet the Galileans welcomed him, for they had been
in Jerusalem at the Passover celebration and had seen everything he did there.

46As he traveled through Galilee, he came to Cana, where he had turned the water into
wine. There was a government official in nearby Capernaum whose son was very sick. 47When
he heard that Jesus had come from Judea to Galilee, he went and begged Jesus to come to
Capernaum to heal his son, who was about to die.

48Jesus asked, "Will you never believe in me unless you see miraculous signs and wonders?"

49The official pleaded, "Lord, please come now before my little boy dies."

50Then Jesus told him, "Go back home. Your son will live!" And the man believed what
Jesus said and started home.

51While the man was on his way, some of his servants met him with the news that his son
was alive and well. 52He asked them when the boy had begun to get better, and they replied,
"Yesterday afternoon at one o'clock his fever suddenly disappeared!" 53Then the father realized
that that was the very time Jesus had told him, "Your son will live." And he and his entire
household believed in Jesus. 54This was the second miraculous sign Jesus did in Galilee after
coming from Judea.

How do you show that you believe in Christ? This government official not only believed that Jesus could heal; he also obeyed Jesus by returning home, thus demonstrating his faith. It isn't enough for us to say we believe that Jesus can take care of our problems. We need to act as if he can. When you pray about a need or problem, live as though you believe Jesus can do what he says.

Jesus Visits the Synagogue

JUNE 22

LUKE 4:14-30

14 Then Jesus returned to Galilee, filled with the Holy Spirit's power. Reports about him
spread quickly through the whole region. 15 He taught regularly in their synagogues and was
praised by everyone.

16 When he came to the village of Nazareth, his boyhood home, he went as usual to the
synagogue on the Sabbath and stood up to read the Scriptures. 17 The scroll of Isaiah the
prophet was handed to him. He unrolled the scroll and found the place where this was
written:

> 18 "The Spirit of the LORD is upon me,
> for he has anointed me to bring Good News to the poor.
> He has sent me to proclaim that captives will be released,
> that the blind will see,
> that the oppressed will be set free,
> 19 and that the time of the LORD's favor has come."

20 He rolled up the scroll, handed it back to the attendant, and sat down. All eyes in the
synagogue looked at him intently. 21 Then he began to speak to them. "The Scripture you've
just heard has been fulfilled this very day!"

22 Everyone spoke well of him and was amazed by the gracious words that came from his
lips. "How can this be?" they asked. "Isn't this Joseph's son?"

23 Then he said, "You will undoubtedly quote me this proverb: 'Physician, heal yourself'—
meaning, 'Do miracles here in your hometown like those you did in Capernaum.' 24 But I tell
you the truth, no prophet is accepted in his own hometown.

25 "Certainly there were many needy widows in Israel in Elijah's time, when the heavens
were closed for three and a half years, and a severe famine devastated the land. 26 Yet Elijah
was not sent to any of them. He was sent instead to a foreigner—a widow of Zarephath in
the land of Sidon. 27 And many in Israel had leprosy in the time of the prophet Elisha, but
the only one healed was Naaman, a Syrian."

28 When they heard this, the people in the synagogue were furious. 29 Jumping up, they
mobbed him and forced him to the edge of the hill on which the town was built. They
intended to push him over the cliff, 30 but he passed right through the crowd and went on
his way.

How would Jesus be received in your church next Sunday? Jesus went to the synagogue "as usual." Even though he was the perfect Son of God and his local synagogue left much to be desired, he attended services every week. Jesus' example makes most excuses for not attending church sound weak and self-serving. Make regular worship a part of your life.

JUNE 23 Jesus Calls People to Follow

MARK 1:16-28; LUKE 5:27-32

16 One day as Jesus was walking along the shore of the Sea of Galilee, he saw Simon and his
brother Andrew throwing a net into the water, for they fished for a living. 17 Jesus called out
to them, "Come, follow me, and I will show you how to fish for people!" 18 And they left their
nets at once and followed him.

19 A little farther up the shore Jesus saw Zebedee's sons, James and John, in a boat repairing
their nets. 20 He called them at once, and they also followed him, leaving their father, Zebedee,
in the boat with the hired men.

21 Jesus and his companions went to the town of Capernaum. When the Sabbath day
came, he went into the synagogue and began to teach. 22 The people were amazed at his
teaching, for he taught with real authority—quite unlike the teachers of religious law.

23 Suddenly, a man in the synagogue who was possessed by an evil spirit cried out, 24 "Why
are you interfering with us, Jesus of Nazareth? Have you come to destroy us? I know who
you are—the Holy One of God!"

25 But Jesus reprimanded him. "Be quiet! Come out of the man," he ordered. 26 At that, the
evil spirit screamed, threw the man into a convulsion, and then came out of him.

27 Amazement gripped the audience, and they began to discuss what had happened. "What
sort of new teaching is this?" they asked excitedly. "It has such authority! Even evil spirits obey
his orders!" 28 The news about Jesus spread quickly throughout the entire region of Galilee.

LK 5:27 Later, as Jesus left the town, he saw a tax collector named Levi sitting at his tax collector's
booth. "Follow me and be my disciple," Jesus said to him. 28 So Levi got up, left everything,
and followed him.

29 Later, Levi held a banquet in his home with Jesus as the guest of honor. Many of Levi's
fellow tax collectors and other guests also ate with them. 30 But the Pharisees and their teachers of religious law complained bitterly to Jesus' disciples, "Why do you eat and drink with
such scum?"

31 Jesus answered them, "Healthy people don't need a doctor—sick people do. 32 I have
come to call not those who think they are righteous, but those who know they are sinners
and need to repent."

What specific things have you left behind to follow Christ? We often assume that Jesus' disciples were great men of faith from the first time they met Jesus. But they had to grow in their faith just as all believers do. (This was apparently not the only time Jesus called Peter, James, and John to follow him; see Luke 5:1-11 and John 1:35-42 for two other times.) Although it took time for Jesus' call and his message to get through, the disciples eventually followed. Levi (Matthew), however, followed immediately. Whether we question and falter or whether we willingly leave everything, we must never stop following Jesus.

Miracles and Questions

JUNE 24

LUKE 5:12-26

12 In one of the villages, Jesus met a man with an advanced case of leprosy. When the man saw
Jesus, he bowed with his face to the ground, begging to be healed. "Lord," he said, "if you
are willing, you can heal me and make me clean."

13 Jesus reached out and touched him. "I am willing," he said. "Be healed!" And instantly
the leprosy disappeared. 14 Then Jesus instructed him not to tell anyone what had happened.
He said, "Go to the priest and let him examine you. Take along the offering required in the
law of Moses for those who have been healed of leprosy. This will be a public testimony that
you have been cleansed."

15 But despite Jesus' instructions, the report of his power spread even faster, and vast
crowds came to hear him preach and to be healed of their diseases. 16 But Jesus often withdrew
to the wilderness for prayer.

17 One day while Jesus was teaching, some Pharisees and teachers of religious law were sitting nearby. (It seemed that these men showed up from every village in all Galilee and Judea,
as well as from Jerusalem.) And the Lord's healing power was strongly with Jesus.

18 Some men came carrying a paralyzed man on a sleeping mat. They tried to take him
inside to Jesus, 19 but they couldn't reach him because of the crowd. So they went up to the
roof and took off some tiles. Then they lowered the sick man on his mat down into the
crowd, right in front of Jesus. 20 Seeing their faith, Jesus said to the man, "Young man, your
sins are forgiven."

21 But the Pharisees and teachers of religious law said to themselves, "Who does he think
he is? That's blasphemy! Only God can forgive sins!"

22 Jesus knew what they were thinking, so he asked them, "Why do you question this in
your hearts? 23 Is it easier to say 'Your sins are forgiven,' or 'Stand up and walk'? 24 So I will
prove to you that the Son of Man has the authority on earth to forgive sins." Then Jesus
turned to the paralyzed man and said, "Stand up, pick up your mat, and go home!"

25 And immediately, as everyone watched, the man jumped up, picked up his mat, and
went home praising God. 26 Everyone was gripped with great wonder and awe, and they
praised God, exclaiming, "We have seen amazing things today!"

How do Jesus' miracles affect you today? It wasn't the sick man's faith that impressed Jesus but the faith of his friends. Jesus responded to their faith and healed the man. For better or worse, our faith affects others. We cannot make other people become Christians, but we can do much through our words, actions, and love to give them chances to respond. Look for opportunities to bring your friends to the living Christ.

JUNE 25 Jesus Is God's Son

JOHN 5:1-44

Afterward Jesus returned to Jerusalem for one of the Jewish holy days. 2Inside the city,
near the Sheep Gate, was the pool of Bethesda, with five covered porches. 3Crowds of sick
people—blind, lame, or paralyzed—lay on the porches. 5One of the men lying there had been
sick for thirty-eight years. 6When Jesus saw him and knew he had been ill for a long time, he
asked him, "Would you like to get well?"

7"I can't, sir," the sick man said, "for I have no one to put me into the pool when the water
bubbles up. Someone else always gets there ahead of me."

8Jesus told him, "Stand up, pick up your mat, and walk!"

9Instantly, the man was healed! He rolled up his sleeping mat and began walking! But
this miracle happened on the Sabbath, 10so the Jewish leaders objected. They said to the man
who was cured, "You can't work on the Sabbath! The law doesn't allow you to carry that
sleeping mat!"

11But he replied, "The man who healed me told me, 'Pick up your mat and walk.'"

12"Who said such a thing as that?" they demanded.

13The man didn't know, for Jesus had disappeared into the crowd. 14But afterward Jesus
found him in the Temple and told him, "Now you are well; so stop sinning, or something
even worse may happen to you." 15Then the man went and told the Jewish leaders that it was
Jesus who had healed him.

16So the Jewish leaders began harassing Jesus for breaking the Sabbath rules. 17But Jesus
replied, "My Father is always working, and so am I." 18So the Jewish leaders tried all the harder
to find a way to kill him. For he not only broke the Sabbath, he called God his Father, thereby
making himself equal with God.

19So Jesus explained, "I tell you the truth, the Son can do nothing by himself. He does
only what he sees the Father doing. Whatever the Father does, the Son also does. 20For the
Father loves the Son and shows him everything he is doing. In fact, the Father will show him
how to do even greater works than healing this man. Then you will truly be astonished. . . .

39"You search the Scriptures because you think they give you eternal life. But the Scriptures
point to me! 40Yet you refuse to come to me to receive this life.

41"Your approval means nothing to me, 42because I know you don't have God's love within
you. 43For I have come to you in my Father's name, and you have rejected me. Yet if others
come in their own name, you gladly welcome them. 44No wonder you can't believe!"

What do you find most attractive about Jesus? Whose approval do you seek? The Jewish religious leaders enjoyed great prestige in Israel, but their stamp of approval meant nothing to Jesus. He was concerned about God's approval. This is a good principle for us. If even the highest officials in the world approve of our actions and God does not, we should be concerned. But if God approves, even though others don't, we should be content.

Jesus and the Law

JUNE 26

MARK 2:23–3:6

23 One Sabbath day as Jesus was walking through some grainfields, his disciples began breaking off heads of grain to eat. 24 But the Pharisees said to Jesus, "Look, why are they breaking
the law by harvesting grain on the Sabbath?"
25 Jesus said to them, "Haven't you ever read in the Scriptures what David did when he
and his companions were hungry? 26 He went into the house of God (during the days when
Abiathar was high priest) and broke the law by eating the sacred loaves of bread that only the
priests are allowed to eat. He also gave some to his companions."
27 Then Jesus said to them, "The Sabbath was made to meet the needs of people, and not
people to meet the requirements of the Sabbath. 28 So the Son of Man is Lord, even over the
Sabbath!"

3:1 Jesus went into the synagogue again and noticed a man with a deformed hand. 2 Since it was
the Sabbath, Jesus' enemies watched him closely. If he healed the man's hand, they planned
to accuse him of working on the Sabbath.
3 Jesus said to the man with the deformed hand, "Come and stand in front of everyone."
4 Then he turned to his critics and asked, "Does the law permit good deeds on the Sabbath,
or is it a day for doing evil? Is this a day to save life or to destroy it?" But they wouldn't
answer him.
5 He looked around at them angrily and was deeply saddened by their hard hearts. Then
he said to the man, "Hold out your hand." So the man held out his hand, and it was restored!
6 At once the Pharisees went away and met with the supporters of Herod to plot how to kill
Jesus.

How would Jesus treat your personal traditions? Jesus used the example of David to point out how ridiculous the Pharisees' accusations were (this incident occurred in 1 Samuel 21:1-6). God created the Sabbath for our benefit, not his own. God derives no benefit from having us rest on the Sabbath, but we are restored both physically and spiritually when we take time to rest and to focus on God. For the Pharisees, Sabbath laws had become more important than Sabbath rest. Both David and Jesus understood that the intent of God's law is to promote love for God and others. When we apply a law to other people, we should make sure we understand its purpose so we don't make harmful or inappropriate judgments.

JUNE 27

Jesus Gives the Beatitudes

MATTHEW 5:1-16

One day as he saw the crowds gathering, Jesus went up on the mountainside and sat down. His disciples gathered around him, [2]and he began to teach them.

[3]"God blesses those who are poor and realize their need for him,
for the Kingdom of Heaven is theirs.
[4]God blesses those who mourn,
for they will be comforted.
[5]God blesses those who are humble,
for they will inherit the whole earth.
[6]God blesses those who hunger and thirst for justice,
for they will be satisfied.
[7]God blesses those who are merciful,
for they will be shown mercy.
[8]God blesses those whose hearts are pure,
for they will see God.
[9]God blesses those who work for peace,
for they will be called the children of God.
[10]God blesses those who are persecuted for doing right,
for the Kingdom of Heaven is theirs.

[11]"God blesses you when people mock you and persecute you and lie about you and say
all sorts of evil things against you because you are my followers. [12]Be happy about it! Be very
glad! For a great reward awaits you in heaven. And remember, the ancient prophets were persecuted in the same way.

[13]"You are the salt of the earth. But what good is salt if it has lost its flavor? Can you make it salty again? It will be thrown out and trampled underfoot as worthless.

[14]"You are the light of the world—like a city on a hilltop that cannot be hidden. [15]No one
lights a lamp and then puts it under a basket. Instead, a lamp is placed on a stand, where it
gives light to everyone in the house. [16]In the same way, let your good deeds shine out for all
to see, so that everyone will praise your heavenly Father.

Which of the Beatitudes can you claim? Jesus began his sermon with words that seem to contradict each other. But God's way of living usually contradicts the world's. If you want to live for God, you must be ready to say and do what seems strange to the world. You must be willing to give when others take, to love when others hate, to help when others abuse. In doing this, you will one day receive everything, while the others will end up with nothing.

Jesus on Law, Anger, and Lust

JUNE 28

MATTHEW 5:17-30

[17]"Don't misunderstand why I have come. I did not come to abolish the law of Moses or the writings of the prophets. No, I came to accomplish their purpose. [18]I tell you the truth, until heaven and earth disappear, not even the smallest detail of God's law will disappear until its purpose is achieved. [19]So if you ignore the least commandment and teach others to do the same, you will be called the least in the Kingdom of Heaven. But anyone who obeys God's laws and teaches them will be called great in the Kingdom of Heaven.

[20]"But I warn you—unless your righteousness is better than the righteousness of the teachers of religious law and the Pharisees, you will never enter the Kingdom of Heaven!

[21]"You have heard that our ancestors were told, 'You must not murder. If you commit murder, you are subject to judgment.' [22]But I say, if you are even angry with someone, you are subject to judgment! If you call someone an idiot, you are in danger of being brought before the court. And if you curse someone, you are in danger of the fires of hell.

[23]"So if you are presenting a sacrifice at the altar in the Temple and you suddenly remember that someone has something against you, [24]leave your sacrifice there at the altar. Go and be reconciled to that person. Then come and offer your sacrifice to God.

[25]"When you are on the way to court with your adversary, settle your differences quickly. Otherwise, your accuser may hand you over to the judge, who will hand you over to an officer, and you will be thrown into prison. [26]And if that happens, you surely won't be free again until you have paid the last penny.

[27]"You have heard the commandment that says, 'You must not commit adultery.' [28]But I say, anyone who even looks at a woman with lust has already committed adultery with her in his heart. [29]So if your eye—even your good eye—causes you to lust, gouge it out and throw it away. It is better for you to lose one part of your body than for your whole body to be thrown into hell. [30]And if your hand—even your stronger hand—causes you to sin, cut it off and throw it away. It is better for you to lose one part of your body than for your whole body to be thrown into hell."

How do Jesus' views compare with yours? Some believe that if lustful thoughts are sin, they might as well do the lustful actions, too. This is harmful in several ways: (1) It causes you to excuse your sin rather than eliminate it. (2) It destroys marriages. (3) It is deliberate rebellion against God's Word. (4) It always hurts someone else in addition to yourself. While desire is not as dangerous as action, it is just as damaging to righteousness. Left unchecked, wrong desires will result in wrong actions and turn you away from God.

JUNE 29 Growing toward Perfection

MATTHEW 5:31-48

31"You have heard the law that says, 'A man can divorce his wife by merely giving her a
written notice of divorce.' 32But I say that a man who divorces his wife, unless she has been
unfaithful, causes her to commit adultery. And anyone who marries a divorced woman also
commits adultery.

33"You have also heard that our ancestors were told, 'You must not break your vows; you
must carry out the vows you make to the LORD.' 34But I say, do not make any vows! Do not
say, 'By heaven!' because heaven is God's throne. 35And do not say, 'By the earth!' because the
earth is his footstool. And do not say, 'By Jerusalem!' for Jerusalem is the city of the great
King. 36Do not even say, 'By my head!' for you can't turn one hair white or black. 37Just say a
simple, 'Yes, I will,' or 'No, I won't.' Anything beyond this is from the evil one.

38"You have heard the law that says the punishment must match the injury: 'An eye for an
eye, and a tooth for a tooth.' 39But I say, do not resist an evil person! If someone slaps you on
the right cheek, offer the other cheek also. 40If you are sued in court and your shirt is taken
from you, give your coat, too. 41If a soldier demands that you carry his gear for a mile, carry
it two miles. 42Give to those who ask, and don't turn away from those who want to borrow.

43"You have heard the law that says, 'Love your neighbor' and hate your enemy. 44But I
say, love your enemies! Pray for those who persecute you! 45In that way, you will be acting as
true children of your Father in heaven. For he gives his sunlight to both the evil and the good,
and he sends rain on the just and the unjust alike. 46If you love only those who love you, what
reward is there for that? Even corrupt tax collectors do that much. 47If you are kind only to
your friends, how are you different from anyone else? Even pagans do that. 48But you are to
be perfect, even as your Father in heaven is perfect."

What part of your life could be most radically changed by these words? How can we be perfect? (1) In character. In this life we cannot be flawless, but we can aspire to be as much like Christ as possible. (2) In holiness. We are to separate ourselves from the world's sinful values and be devoted to God's desires rather than our own. (3) In maturity. We can't achieve Christlike character and holy living all at once, but we must grow toward maturity and wholeness. Just as we expect different behavior from a baby, a child, a teenager, and an adult, so God expects different behavior from us, depending on our stage of spiritual development. (4) In love. We can seek to love others as completely as God loves us. We can be "perfect" if our behavior is appropriate for our maturity level—perfect, yet with much room to grow. Our tendency to sin must never deter us from striving to be more like Christ. Christ calls all of his disciples to excel, to rise above mediocrity, and to mature in every area, becoming like him. Those who strive to become perfect will one day be perfect, even as Christ is perfect (1 John 3:2-3).

Motives for Doing Good

MATTHEW 6:1-18

"Watch out! Don't do your good deeds publicly, to be admired by others, for you will lose
the reward from your Father in heaven. [2]When you give to someone in need, don't do as
the hypocrites do . . . [4]Give your gifts in private, and your Father, who sees everything, will
reward you.

[5]"When you pray, don't be like the hypocrites who love to pray publicly on street corners
and in the synagogues where everyone can see them. I tell you the truth, that is all the reward
they will ever get. [6]But when you pray, go away by yourself, shut the door behind you, and
pray to your Father in private. Then your Father, who sees everything, will reward you.

[7]"When you pray, don't babble on and on as the Gentiles do. They think their prayers
are answered merely by repeating their words again and again. [8]Don't be like them, for your
Father knows exactly what you need even before you ask him! [9]Pray like this:

Our Father in heaven,
may your name be kept holy.
[10]May your Kingdom come soon.
May your will be done on earth,
as it is in heaven.
[11]Give us today the food we need,
[12]and forgive us our sins,
as we have forgiven those who sin against us.
[13]And don't let us yield to temptation,
but rescue us from the evil one.

[14]"If you forgive those who sin against you, your heavenly Father will forgive you. [15]But
if you refuse to forgive others, your Father will not forgive your sins.

[16]"And when you fast, don't make it obvious, as the hypocrites do, for they try to look
miserable and disheveled so people will admire them for their fasting. I tell you the truth,
that is the only reward they will ever get. [17]But when you fast, comb your hair and wash your
face. [18]Then no one will notice that you are fasting, except your Father, who knows what you
do in private. And your Father, who sees everything, will reward you."

How does your public life compare to your private life? To be sure our motives are not selfish, we should do our good works quietly or in secret, with no thought of reward. Jesus says we should check our motives when we give, pray, or fast. Those acts should not be self-centered but God-centered. The reward God promises is not material, and it is never given to those who seek it. Doing something only for ourselves is not a loving sacrifice. With your next good deed, ask yourself, Would I still do this if no one would ever know I did it?

July

JULY 1

Jesus on Money and Worry

MATTHEW 6:19-34

19“Don’t store up treasures here on earth, where moths eat them and rust destroys them,
and where thieves break in and steal. 20Store your treasures in heaven, where moths and rust
cannot destroy, and thieves do not break in and steal. 21Wherever your treasure is, there the
desires of your heart will also be.

22“Your eye is like a lamp that provides light for your body. When your eye is healthy,
your whole body is filled with light. 23But when your eye is unhealthy, your whole body is
filled with darkness. And if the light you think you have is actually darkness, how deep that
darkness is!

24“No one can serve two masters. For you will hate one and love the other; you will be
devoted to one and despise the other. You cannot serve God and be enslaved to money.

25“That is why I tell you not to worry about everyday life—whether you have enough
food and drink, or enough clothes to wear. Isn’t life more than food, and your body more
than clothing? 26Look at the birds. They don’t plant or harvest or store food in barns, for your
heavenly Father feeds them. And aren’t you far more valuable to him than they are? 27Can all
your worries add a single moment to your life?

28“And why worry about your clothing? Look at the lilies of the field and how they grow.
They don’t work or make their clothing, 29yet Solomon in all his glory was not dressed as
beautifully as they are. 30And if God cares so wonderfully for wildflowers that are here today
and thrown into the fire tomorrow, he will certainly care for you. Why do you have so little
faith?

31“So don’t worry about these things, saying, ‘What will we eat? What will we drink? What
will we wear?’ 32These things dominate the thoughts of unbelievers, but your heavenly Father
already knows all your needs. 33Seek the Kingdom of God above all else, and live righteously,
and he will give you everything you need.

34“So don’t worry about tomorrow, for tomorrow will bring its own worries. Today’s
trouble is enough for today.”

In what ways are money and worry related in your life? To live for God and make his Kingdom your primary concern means to turn to God first for help, to fill your thoughts with his desires, to take his character for your pattern, and to serve and obey him in everything. What is really important to you? People, objects, goals, and other desires all compete for priority. Any of these can quickly bump God out of first place if you don’t actively choose to give him first place in every area of your life.

Jesus on Judging and Praying

JULY 2

MATTHEW 7:1-12

“Do not judge others, and you will not be judged. 2For you will be treated as you treat others.
The standard you use in judging is the standard by which you will be judged.
3“And why worry about a speck in your friend’s eye when you have a log in your own?
4How can you think of saying to your friend, ‘Let me help you get rid of that speck in your
eye,’ when you can’t see past the log in your own eye? 5Hypocrite! First get rid of the log in
your own eye; then you will see well enough to deal with the speck in your friend’s eye.
6“Don’t waste what is holy on people who are unholy. Don’t throw your pearls to pigs!
They will trample the pearls, then turn and attack you.
7“Keep on asking, and you will receive what you ask for. Keep on seeking, and you will
find. Keep on knocking, and the door will be opened to you. 8For everyone who asks, receives.
Everyone who seeks, finds. And to everyone who knocks, the door will be opened.
9“You parents—if your children ask for a loaf of bread, do you give them a stone instead?
10Or if they ask for a fish, do you give them a snake? Of course not! 11So if you sinful people
know how to give good gifts to your children, how much more will your heavenly Father
give good gifts to those who ask him.
12“Do to others whatever you would like them to do to you. This is the essence of all that
is taught in the law and the prophets.”

Which do you do more of, criticizing or praying? Jesus tells us to examine our own motives and conduct instead of judging others. The traits that bother us in others are often those we dislike in ourselves. Our own bad habits and behavior patterns are the very ones that we most want to change in others. Do you find it easy to magnify others’ faults while excusing your own? If you are ready to criticize someone, check to see if you deserve the same criticism. Judge yourself first, and then lovingly forgive and help your neighbor.

JULY 3

Building on a Solid Foundation

MATTHEW 7:13-29

13“You can enter God’s Kingdom only through the narrow gate. The highway to hell is broad, and its gate is wide for the many who choose that way. 14But the gateway to life is very narrow and the road is difficult, and only a few ever find it.

15“Beware of false prophets who come disguised as harmless sheep but are really vicious wolves. 16You can identify them by their fruit, that is, by the way they act. Can you pick grapes from thornbushes, or figs from thistles? 17A good tree produces good fruit, and a bad tree produces bad fruit. 18A good tree can’t produce bad fruit, and a bad tree can’t produce good fruit. 19So every tree that does not produce good fruit is chopped down and thrown into the fire. 20Yes, just as you can identify a tree by its fruit, so you can identify people by their actions.

21“Not everyone who calls out to me, ‘Lord! Lord!’ will enter the Kingdom of Heaven. Only those who actually do the will of my Father in heaven will enter. 22On judgment day many will say to me, ‘Lord! Lord! We prophesied in your name and cast out demons in your name and performed many miracles in your name.’ 23But I will reply, ‘I never knew you. Get away from me, you who break God’s laws.’

24“Anyone who listens to my teaching and follows it is wise, like a person who builds a house on solid rock. 25Though the rain comes in torrents and the floodwaters rise and the winds beat against that house, it won’t collapse because it is built on bedrock. 26But anyone who hears my teaching and doesn’t obey it is foolish, like a person who builds a house on sand. 27When the rains and floods come and the winds beat against that house, it will collapse with a mighty crash.”

28When Jesus had finished saying these things, the crowds were amazed at his teaching, 29for he taught with real authority—quite unlike their teachers of religious law.

What is your foundation in life? Some sports fans can “talk” a great game, but that tells you nothing about their athletic skills. And not everyone who talks about heaven belongs to God’s Kingdom. Jesus is more concerned about our walk than our talk. He wants us to do right, not just say the right words. Your house, which represents your life (verse 25), will withstand storms only if you do what is right instead of just talking about it. What you do cannot be separated from what you believe.

Jesus and Foreigners

JULY 4

LUKE 7:1-17

When Jesus had finished saying all this to the people, he returned to Capernaum. 2At that
time the highly valued slave of a Roman officer was sick and near death. 3When the officer
heard about Jesus, he sent some respected Jewish elders to ask him to come and heal his slave.
4So they earnestly begged Jesus to help the man. "If anyone deserves your help, he does," they
said, 5"for he loves the Jewish people and even built a synagogue for us."

6So Jesus went with them. But just before they arrived at the house, the officer sent some
friends to say, "Lord, don't trouble yourself by coming to my home, for I am not worthy of
such an honor. 7I am not even worthy to come and meet you. Just say the word from where
you are, and my servant will be healed. 8I know this because I am under the authority of my
superior officers, and I have authority over my soldiers. I only need to say, 'Go,' and they go,
or 'Come,' and they come. And if I say to my slaves, 'Do this,' they do it."

9When Jesus heard this, he was amazed. Turning to the crowd that was following him,
he said, "I tell you, I haven't seen faith like this in all Israel!" 10And when the officer's friends
returned to his house, they found the slave completely healed.

11Soon afterward Jesus went with his disciples to the village of Nain, and a large crowd
followed him. 12A funeral procession was coming out as he approached the village gate. The
young man who had died was a widow's only son, and a large crowd from the village was
with her. 13When the Lord saw her, his heart overflowed with compassion. "Don't cry!" he
said. 14Then he walked over to the coffin and touched it, and the bearers stopped. "Young
man," he said, "I tell you, get up." 15Then the dead boy sat up and began to talk! And Jesus
gave him back to his mother.

16Great fear swept the crowd, and they praised God, saying, "A mighty prophet has risen
among us," and "God has visited his people today." 17And the news about Jesus spread throughout
Judea and the surrounding countryside.

What is your attitude toward foreigners? How can you show them God's love? The Roman officer didn't come to Jesus, and he didn't expect Jesus to come to him. Just as this officer did not need to be present to have his orders carried out, so Jesus didn't need to be present to heal. The officer's faith was especially amazing because he was a Gentile who had not been brought up to know a loving God. Jesus praised this man's faith. What would he say about yours?

JULY 5 Jesus Describes John the Baptist

MATTHEW 11:1-15

When Jesus had finished giving these instructions to his twelve disciples, he went out to teach and preach in towns throughout the region.

2John the Baptist, who was in prison, heard about all the things the Messiah was doing. So he sent his disciples to ask Jesus, 3"Are you the Messiah we've been expecting, or should we keep looking for someone else?"

4Jesus told them, "Go back to John and tell him what you have heard and seen—5the blind see, the lame walk, those with leprosy are cured, the deaf hear, the dead are raised to life, and the Good News is being preached to the poor." 6And he added, "God blesses those who do not fall away because of me."

7As John's disciples were leaving, Jesus began talking about him to the crowds. "What kind of man did you go into the wilderness to see? Was he a weak reed, swayed by every breath of wind? 8Or were you expecting to see a man dressed in expensive clothes? No, people with expensive clothes live in palaces. 9Were you looking for a prophet? Yes, and he is more than a prophet. 10John is the man to whom the Scriptures refer when they say,

'Look, I am sending my messenger ahead of you,
and he will prepare your way before you.'

11"I tell you the truth, of all who have ever lived, none is greater than John the Baptist. Yet even the least person in the Kingdom of Heaven is greater than he is! 12And from the time John the Baptist began preaching until now, the Kingdom of Heaven has been forcefully advancing, and violent people are attacking it. 13For before John came, all the prophets and the law of Moses looked forward to this present time. 14And if you are willing to accept what I say, he is Elijah, the one the prophets said would come. 15Anyone with ears to hear should listen and understand!"

How would you want Jesus to summarize your life? As John sat in prison, he began to have some doubts about whether Jesus really was the Messiah. Jesus answered John's doubts by pointing to the miracles in which the blind, lame, and deaf were healed, the lepers were cured, the dead were raised, and the gospel was preached to the poor. With so much evidence, Jesus' identity was obvious. If you sometimes doubt your salvation, the forgiveness of your sins, or God's work in your life, look at the evidence in Scripture and the changes in your life. When you doubt, don't turn away from Christ; turn to him.

Jesus and the Sinful Woman

LUKE 7:36-50

36One of the Pharisees asked Jesus to have dinner with him, so Jesus went to his home and
sat down to eat. 37When a certain immoral woman from that city heard he was eating there,
she brought a beautiful alabaster jar filled with expensive perfume. 38Then she knelt behind
him at his feet, weeping. Her tears fell on his feet, and she wiped them off with her hair. Then
she kept kissing his feet and putting perfume on them.

39When the Pharisee who had invited him saw this, he said to himself, "If this man were
a prophet, he would know what kind of woman is touching him. She's a sinner!"

40Then Jesus answered his thoughts. "Simon," he said to the Pharisee, "I have something
to say to you."

"Go ahead, Teacher," Simon replied.

41Then Jesus told him this story: "A man loaned money to two people—500 pieces of
silver to one and 50 pieces to the other. 42But neither of them could repay him, so he kindly
forgave them both, canceling their debts. Who do you suppose loved him more after that?"

43Simon answered, "I suppose the one for whom he canceled the larger debt."

"That's right," Jesus said. 44Then he turned to the woman and said to Simon, "Look at
this woman kneeling here. When I entered your home, you didn't offer me water to wash the
dust from my feet, but she has washed them with her tears and wiped them with her hair.
45You didn't greet me with a kiss, but from the time I first came in, she has not stopped kissing
my feet. 46You neglected the courtesy of olive oil to anoint my head, but she has anointed
my feet with rare perfume.

47"I tell you, her sins—and they are many—have been forgiven, so she has shown me
much love. But a person who is forgiven little shows only little love." 48Then Jesus said to the
woman, "Your sins are forgiven."

49The men at the table said among themselves, "Who is this man, that he goes around
forgiving sins?"

50And Jesus said to the woman, "Your faith has saved you; go in peace."

How would you have fit into the group that followed Jesus? Overflowing love is the natural response to forgiveness and the appropriate consequence of faith. But only those who realize the depth of their sin can appreciate the complete forgiveness God offers them. Jesus has rescued all of his followers from eternal death, regardless of whether they were once extremely wicked or conventionally good. Do you appreciate the wideness of God's mercy? Are you grateful for his forgiveness?

JULY 7

The Leaders Want a Sign

MATTHEW 12:22-42

22 Then a demon-possessed man, who was blind and couldn't speak, was brought to Jesus.
He healed the man so that he could both speak and see. 23 The crowd was amazed and asked,
"Could it be that Jesus is the Son of David, the Messiah?"

24 But when the Pharisees heard about the miracle, they said, "No wonder he can cast out
demons. He gets his power from Satan, the prince of demons."

25 Jesus knew their thoughts and replied, "Any kingdom divided by civil war is doomed.
A town or family splintered by feuding will fall apart. 26 And if Satan is casting out Satan,
he is divided and fighting against himself. His own kingdom will not survive. 27 And if I am
empowered by Satan, what about your own exorcists? They cast out demons, too, so they will
condemn you for what you have said. 28 But if I am casting out demons by the Spirit of God,
then the Kingdom of God has arrived among you. 29 For who is powerful enough to enter the
house of a strong man and plunder his goods? Only someone even stronger—someone who
could tie him up and then plunder his house.

30 "Anyone who isn't with me opposes me, and anyone who isn't working with me is
actually working against me. . . ."

38 One day some teachers of religious law and Pharisees came to Jesus and said, "Teacher,
we want you to show us a miraculous sign to prove your authority."

39 But Jesus replied, "Only an evil, adulterous generation would demand a miraculous
sign; but the only sign I will give them is the sign of the prophet Jonah. 40 For as Jonah was
in the belly of the great fish for three days and three nights, so will the Son of Man be in the
heart of the earth for three days and three nights.

41 "The people of Nineveh will stand up against this generation on judgment day and
condemn it, for they repented of their sins at the preaching of Jonah. Now someone greater
than Jonah is here—but you refuse to repent. 42 The queen of Sheba will also stand up against
this generation on judgment day and condemn it, for she came from a distant land to hear the
wisdom of Solomon. Now someone greater than Solomon is here—but you refuse to listen."

When are you tempted to have Jesus prove himself to you? Many people have thought, If I could just see a real miracle, then I could really believe in God. But Jesus' response to the Pharisees applies to us. Jesus knew that they had already seen enough miraculous proof to convince them that he was the Messiah—if they would just open their hearts. But the Pharisees had already decided not to believe in Jesus, and more miracles would not change that. We have plenty of evidence—Jesus' death, resurrection, ascension, and centuries of his work in the lives of believers around the world. Instead of looking for additional evidence or miracles, accept what God has already given and move forward. He may use your life as evidence to reach another person.

The Parable of the Soils

JULY 8

MARK 4:1-20

Once again Jesus began teaching by the lakeshore. A very large crowd soon gathered around him, so he got into a boat. Then he sat in the boat while all the people remained on the shore. 2He taught them by telling many stories in the form of parables, such as this one:

3"Listen! A farmer went out to plant some seed. 4As he scattered it across his field, some of the seed fell on a footpath, and the birds came and ate it. 5Other seed fell on shallow soil with underlying rock. The seed sprouted quickly because the soil was shallow. 6But the plant soon wilted under the hot sun, and since it didn't have deep roots, it died. 7Other seed fell among thorns that grew up and choked out the tender plants so they produced no grain. 8Still other seeds fell on fertile soil, and they sprouted, grew, and produced a crop that was thirty, sixty, and even a hundred times as much as had been planted!" 9Then he said, "Anyone with ears to hear should listen and understand."

10Later, when Jesus was alone with the twelve disciples and with the others who were gathered around, they asked him what the parables meant. . . .

13Then Jesus said to them, "If you can't understand the meaning of this parable, how will you understand all the other parables? 14The farmer plants seed by taking God's word to others. 15The seed that fell on the footpath represents those who hear the message, only to have Satan come at once and take it away. 16The seed on the rocky soil represents those who hear the message and immediately receive it with joy. 17But since they don't have deep roots, they don't last long. They fall away as soon as they have problems or are persecuted for believing God's word. 18The seed that fell among the thorns represents others who hear God's word, 19but all too quickly the message is crowded out by the worries of this life, the lure of wealth, and the desire for other things, so no fruit is produced. 20And the seed that fell on good soil represents those who hear and accept God's word and produce a harvest of thirty, sixty, or even a hundred times as much as had been planted!"

What kind of soil is your life right now? The four soils represent four different ways people respond to God's Word. Usually we think that Jesus was talking about four different kinds of people. But he may also have been talking about (1) different times or phases in a person's life or (2) how a person receives God's message in some areas of his life and resists it in others. For example, you may be open to God about your future but closed concerning how you spend your money. You may respond like good soil to God's demand for worship but like rocky soil to his demand to give to those in need. Ask God to help you strive to be like good soil in every area of your life at all times.

JULY 9

Weeds in the Field

MATTHEW 13:24-42

24 Here is another story Jesus told: "The Kingdom of Heaven is like a farmer who planted
good seed in his field. 25 But that night as the workers slept, his enemy came and planted
weeds among the wheat, then slipped away. 26 When the crop began to grow and produce
grain, the weeds also grew.

27 "The farmer's workers went to him and said, 'Sir, the field where you planted that good
seed is full of weeds! Where did they come from?'

28 " 'An enemy has done this!' the farmer exclaimed.

" 'Should we pull out the weeds?' they asked.

29 " 'No,' he replied, 'you'll uproot the wheat if you do. 30 Let both grow together until the
harvest. Then I will tell the harvesters to sort out the weeds, tie them into bundles, and burn
them, and to put the wheat in the barn.' "

31 Here is another illustration Jesus used: "The Kingdom of Heaven is like a mustard seed
planted in a field. 32 It is the smallest of all seeds, but it becomes the largest of garden plants; it
grows into a tree, and birds come and make nests in its branches." . . .

34 Jesus always used stories and illustrations like these when speaking to the crowds. In fact,
he never spoke to them without using such parables. 35 This fulfilled what God had spoken
through the prophet:

"I will speak to you in parables.
I will explain things hidden since the creation of the world."

36 Then, leaving the crowds outside, Jesus went into the house. His disciples said, "Please
explain to us the story of the weeds in the field."

37 Jesus replied, "The Son of Man is the farmer who plants the good seed. 38 The field is the
world, and the good seed represents the people of the Kingdom. The weeds are the people
who belong to the evil one. 39 The enemy who planted the weeds among the wheat is the devil.
The harvest is the end of the world, and the harvesters are the angels.

40 "Just as the weeds are sorted out and burned in the fire, so it will be at the end of the
world. 41 The Son of Man will send his angels, and they will remove from his Kingdom
everything that causes sin and all who do evil. 42 And the angels will throw them into the fiery
furnace, where there will be weeping and gnashing of teeth."

How concerned are you about the eternal fates of the people you know? The young weeds and the young blades of wheat look the same and can't be distinguished until they are grown and ready for harvest. Weeds (unbelievers) and wheat (believers) must live side by side in this world. God allows unbelievers to remain for a while, just as a farmer allows weeds to remain in his field so the surrounding wheat isn't uprooted with them. At the harvest, however, the weeds will be uprooted and thrown away. God's harvest (judgment) of all people is coming. Be certain you are ready by making sure that your faith is sincere.

Kingdom Parables

JULY 10

MATTHEW 13:44-52

44“The Kingdom of Heaven is like a treasure that a man discovered hidden in a field. In his excitement, he hid it again and sold everything he owned to get enough money to buy the field.

45“Again, the Kingdom of Heaven is like a merchant on the lookout for choice pearls. 46When he discovered a pearl of great value, he sold everything he owned and bought it!

47“Again, the Kingdom of Heaven is like a fishing net that was thrown into the water and caught fish of every kind. 48When the net was full, they dragged it up onto the shore, sat down, and sorted the good fish into crates, but threw the bad ones away. 49That is the way it will be at the end of the world. The angels will come and separate the wicked people from the righteous, 50throwing the wicked into the fiery furnace, where there will be weeping and gnashing of teeth. 51Do you understand all these things?”

“Yes,” they said, “we do.”

52Then he added, “Every teacher of religious law who becomes a disciple in the Kingdom of Heaven is like a homeowner who brings from his storeroom new gems of truth as well as old.”

How and where did you find the hidden treasure? The Kingdom of Heaven is more valuable than anything else we could have, and a person must be willing to give up everything to obtain it. The man who discovered the treasure in the field stumbled upon it by accident but knew its value when he found it. The merchant was earnestly searching for the pearl of great value, and when he found it, he sold everything he had to purchase it. If you have accepted Christ as your Savior, you, too, have found the treasure. Nothing is more valuable, and nothing is more important to share with others.

JULY 11

Calming a Storm and Demons

LUKE 8:22-37

[22]One day Jesus said to his disciples, "Let's cross to the other side of the lake." So they got into a boat and started out. [23]As they sailed across, Jesus settled down for a nap. But soon a fierce storm came down on the lake. The boat was filling with water, and they were in real danger.

[24]The disciples went and woke him up, shouting, "Master, Master, we're going to drown!"

When Jesus woke up, he rebuked the wind and the raging waves. Suddenly the storm stopped and all was calm. [25]Then he asked them, "Where is your faith?"

The disciples were terrified and amazed. "Who is this man?" they asked each other. "When he gives a command, even the wind and waves obey him!"

[26]So they arrived in the region of the Gerasenes, across the lake from Galilee. [27]As Jesus was climbing out of the boat, a man who was possessed by demons came out to meet him. For a long time he had been homeless and naked, living in the tombs outside the town.

[28]As soon as he saw Jesus, he shrieked and fell down in front of him. Then he screamed, "Why are you interfering with me, Jesus, Son of the Most High God? Please, I beg you, don't torture me!" [29]For Jesus had already commanded the evil spirit to come out of him. This spirit had often taken control of the man. Even when he was placed under guard and put in chains and shackles, he simply broke them and rushed out into the wilderness, completely under the demon's power.

[30]Jesus demanded, "What is your name?"

"Legion," he replied, for he was filled with many demons. [31]The demons kept begging Jesus not to send them into the bottomless pit.

[32]There happened to be a large herd of pigs feeding on the hillside nearby, and the demons begged him to let them enter into the pigs.

So Jesus gave them permission. [33]Then the demons came out of the man and entered the pigs, and the entire herd plunged down the steep hillside into the lake and drowned.

[34]When the herdsmen saw it, they fled to the nearby town and the surrounding countryside, spreading the news as they ran. [35]People rushed out to see what had happened. A crowd soon gathered around Jesus, and they saw the man who had been freed from the demons. He was sitting at Jesus' feet, fully clothed and perfectly sane, and they were all afraid. [36]Then those who had seen what happened told the others how the demon-possessed man had been healed. [37]And all the people in the region of the Gerasenes begged Jesus to go away and leave them alone, for a great wave of fear swept over them.

Which of these miracles gives you greatest comfort? When caught in the storms of life, it is easy to think that God has lost control and that we are at the mercy of the winds of fate. In reality, God controls the history of the world and our personal destinies. Just as Jesus calmed the waves and cast out demons, he can handle whatever problems you may face.

A Healing and a Resurrection

JULY 12

LUKE 8:40-56

40 On the other side of the lake the crowds welcomed Jesus, because they had been waiting
for him. 41 Then a man named Jairus, a leader of the local synagogue, came and fell at Jesus'
feet, pleading with him to come home with him. 42 His only daughter, who was about twelve
years old, was dying.

As Jesus went with him, he was surrounded by the crowds. 43 A woman in the crowd had
suffered for twelve years with constant bleeding, and she could find no cure. 44 Coming up
behind Jesus, she touched the fringe of his robe. Immediately, the bleeding stopped.

45 "Who touched me?" Jesus asked.

Everyone denied it, and Peter said, "Master, this whole crowd is pressing up against you."

46 But Jesus said, "Someone deliberately touched me, for I felt healing power go out from
me." 47 When the woman realized that she could not stay hidden, she began to tremble and
fell to her knees in front of him. The whole crowd heard her explain why she had touched
him and that she had been immediately healed. 48 "Daughter," he said to her, "your faith has
made you well. Go in peace."

49 While he was still speaking to her, a messenger arrived from the home of Jairus, the
leader of the synagogue. He told him, "Your daughter is dead. There's no use troubling the
Teacher now."

50 But when Jesus heard what had happened, he said to Jairus, "Don't be afraid. Just have
faith, and she will be healed."

51 When they arrived at the house, Jesus wouldn't let anyone go in with him except Peter,
John, James, and the little girl's father and mother. 52 The house was filled with people weeping and wailing, but he said, "Stop the weeping! She isn't dead; she's only asleep."

53 But the crowd laughed at him because they all knew she had died. 54 Then Jesus took
her by the hand and said in a loud voice, "My child, get up!" 55 And at that moment her life
returned, and she immediately stood up! Then Jesus told them to give her something to
eat. 56 Her parents were overwhelmed, but Jesus insisted that they not tell anyone what had
happened.

Where do you go when hope is gone? Anyone with a child can readily put himself or herself emotionally in Jairus's place. His daughter had died while they were on the way home. Luke did not record it, but the poor man probably cried out in grief. Jesus surely felt the father's very human sorrow. Jesus said, "Don't be afraid. Just have faith." Again, Luke didn't record Jairus's reaction to these words, but Jairus must have had at least some flicker of hope, because he did complete his mission in bringing Jesus to his house. When you experience intense grief over the loss of a loved one, the breakup of a marriage, the loss of a job, or the rejection of a close friend, don't abandon hope. Don't turn away from the one Person who can help you. Do what Jairus did: don't be afraid; just have faith. Your hope is found in the resurrected Lord, the one with power over life and death.

JULY 13

The Compassion of Jesus

MATTHEW 9:27-38

[27]After Jesus left the girl's home, two blind men followed along behind him, shouting, "Son of David, have mercy on us!"

[28]They went right into the house where he was staying, and Jesus asked them, "Do you believe I can make you see?"

"Yes, Lord," they told him, "we do."

[29]Then he touched their eyes and said, "Because of your faith, it will happen." [30]Then their eyes were opened, and they could see! Jesus sternly warned them, "Don't tell anyone about this." [31]But instead, they went out and spread his fame all over the region.

[32]When they left, a demon-possessed man who couldn't speak was brought to Jesus. [33]So Jesus cast out the demon, and then the man began to speak. The crowds were amazed. "Nothing like this has ever happened in Israel!" they exclaimed.

[34]But the Pharisees said, "He can cast out demons because he is empowered by the prince of demons."

[35]Jesus traveled through all the towns and villages of that area, teaching in the synagogues and announcing the Good News about the Kingdom. And he healed every kind of disease and illness. [36]When he saw the crowds, he had compassion on them because they were confused and helpless, like sheep without a shepherd. [37]He said to his disciples, "The harvest is great, but the workers are few. [38]So pray to the Lord who is in charge of the harvest; ask him to send more workers into his fields."

How do you picture Jesus caring for you? Jesus didn't respond immediately to the blind men's pleas. He waited to see how earnest they were. Not all people who say they want help really want it badly enough to do something about it. Jesus may have waited and questioned these men to make their desire and faith stronger. If it seems as if God is too slow in giving an answer to your prayers, maybe he is testing you as he did the blind men. Do you believe God can help you? Do you really want his help?

Some Don't Listen

JULY 14

MARK 6:1-13

Jesus left that part of the country and returned with his disciples to Nazareth, his hometown. 2The next Sabbath he began teaching in the synagogue, and many who heard him were amazed. They asked, "Where did he get all this wisdom and the power to perform such miracles?" 3Then they scoffed, "He's just a carpenter, the son of Mary and the brother of James, Joseph, Judas, and Simon. And his sisters live right here among us." They were deeply offended and refused to believe in him.

4Then Jesus told them, "A prophet is honored everywhere except in his own hometown and among his relatives and his own family." 5And because of their unbelief, he couldn't do any miracles among them except to place his hands on a few sick people and heal them. 6And he was amazed at their unbelief.

Then Jesus went from village to village, teaching the people. 7And he called his twelve disciples together and began sending them out two by two, giving them authority to cast out evil spirits. 8He told them to take nothing for their journey except a walking stick—no food, no traveler's bag, no money. 9He allowed them to wear sandals but not to take a change of clothes.

10"Wherever you go," he said, "stay in the same house until you leave town. 11But if any place refuses to welcome you or listen to you, shake its dust from your feet as you leave to show that you have abandoned those people to their fate."

12So the disciples went out, telling everyone they met to repent of their sins and turn to God. 13And they cast out many demons and healed many sick people, anointing them with olive oil.

Do you have an accurate picture of who Jesus really is? Jesus was teaching effectively and wisely, but the people of his hometown saw him as only a carpenter. "He's no better than us—he's just a common laborer," they said. They were offended that others could be impressed by him and follow him. They rejected his authority because he was one of their peers. They thought they knew him, but their preconceived notions about who he was made it impossible for them to accept his message. Don't let prejudice blind you to truth. As you learn more about Jesus, try to see him for who he really is.

JULY **15**

Jesus Prepares His Disciples

MATTHEW 10:16-33

16“Look, I am sending you out as sheep among wolves. So be as shrewd as snakes and harmless as doves. 17But beware! For you will be handed over to the courts and will be flogged with whips in the synagogues. 18You will stand trial before governors and kings because you are my followers. But this will be your opportunity to tell the rulers and other unbelievers about me. 19When you are arrested, don’t worry about how to respond or what to say. God will give you the right words at the right time. 20For it is not you who will be speaking—it will be the Spirit of your Father speaking through you.

21“A brother will betray his brother to death, a father will betray his own child, and children will rebel against their parents and cause them to be killed. 22And all nations will hate you because you are my followers. But everyone who endures to the end will be saved. 23When you are persecuted in one town, flee to the next. I tell you the truth, the Son of Man will return before you have reached all the towns of Israel.

24“Students are not greater than their teacher, and slaves are not greater than their master. 25Students are to be like their teacher, and slaves are to be like their master. And since I, the master of the household, have been called the prince of demons, the members of my household will be called by even worse names!

26“But don’t be afraid of those who threaten you. For the time is coming when everything that is covered will be revealed, and all that is secret will be made known to all. 27What I tell you now in the darkness, shout abroad when daybreak comes. What I whisper in your ear, shout from the housetops for all to hear!

28“Don’t be afraid of those who want to kill your body; they cannot touch your soul. Fear only God, who can destroy both soul and body in hell. 29What is the price of two sparrows—one copper coin? But not a single sparrow can fall to the ground without your Father knowing it. 30And the very hairs on your head are all numbered. 31So don’t be afraid; you are more valuable to God than a whole flock of sparrows.

32“Everyone who acknowledges me publicly here on earth, I will also acknowledge before my Father in heaven. 33But everyone who denies me here on earth, I will also deny before my Father in heaven.”

In what ways do Jesus’ words speak to the fears you have? Jesus said that God cares for the sparrows’ every need. We are far more valuable to God than these little birds, so valuable that God sent his only Son to die for us (John 3:16). You are of great worth to God. You are never lost in his inventory. Because God places such value on you, you need never be afraid in the face of personal threats or difficult trials. But don’t think that because you are valuable to God he will take away all your troubles. The real test of value is how well something holds up under the wear, tear, and abuse of everyday life. Those who stand up for Christ in spite of their troubles truly have lasting value and will receive great rewards.

Herod Kills John the Baptist

JULY 16

MARK 6:14-29

[14]Herod Antipas, the king, soon heard about Jesus, because everyone was talking about him.
Some were saying, "This must be John the Baptist raised from the dead. That is why he can
do such miracles." [15]Others said, "He's the prophet Elijah." Still others said, "He's a prophet
like the other great prophets of the past."

[16]When Herod heard about Jesus, he said, "John, the man I beheaded, has come back
from the dead."

[17]For Herod had sent soldiers to arrest and imprison John as a favor to Herodias. She had
been his brother Philip's wife, but Herod had married her. [18]John had been telling Herod, "It
is against God's law for you to marry your brother's wife." [19]So Herodias bore a grudge against
John and wanted to kill him. But without Herod's approval she was powerless, [20]for Herod
respected John; and knowing that he was a good and holy man, he protected him. Herod
was greatly disturbed whenever he talked with John, but even so, he liked to listen to him.

[21]Herodias's chance finally came on Herod's birthday. He gave a party for his high government officials, army officers, and the leading citizens of Galilee. [22]Then his daughter, also
named Herodias, came in and performed a dance that greatly pleased Herod and his guests.
"Ask me for anything you like," the king said to the girl, "and I will give it to you." [23]He even
vowed, "I will give you whatever you ask, up to half my kingdom!"

[24]She went out and asked her mother, "What should I ask for?"

Her mother told her, "Ask for the head of John the Baptist!"

[25]So the girl hurried back to the king and told him, "I want the head of John the Baptist,
right now, on a tray!"

[26]Then the king deeply regretted what he had said; but because of the vows he had made
in front of his guests, he couldn't refuse her. [27]So he immediately sent an executioner to the
prison to cut off John's head and bring it to him. The soldier beheaded John in the prison,
[28]brought his head on a tray, and gave it to the girl, who took it to her mother. [29]When John's
disciples heard what had happened, they came to get his body and buried it in a tomb.

How carefully do you choose your words? As a ruler under Roman authority, Herod had no kingdom to give. The offer of half his kingdom was Herod's way to say that he would give Herodias's daughter almost anything she wanted. When Herodias asked for John's head, Herod would have been greatly embarrassed in front of his guests if he had denied her request. Words are powerful. Because they can lead to great sin, we should use them with great care.

JULY 17

A Walk on the Water

MATTHEW 14:13-31

13As soon as Jesus heard the news, he left in a boat to a remote area to be alone. But the crowds
heard where he was headed and followed on foot from many towns. 14Jesus saw the huge
crowd as he stepped from the boat, and he had compassion on them and healed their sick.

15That evening the disciples came to him and said, "This is a remote place, and it's already
getting late. Send the crowds away so they can go to the villages and buy food for themselves."

16But Jesus said, "That isn't necessary—you feed them."

17"But we have only five loaves of bread and two fish!" they answered.

18"Bring them here," he said. 19Then he told the people to sit down on the grass. Jesus
took the five loaves and two fish, looked up toward heaven, and blessed them. Then, breaking
the loaves into pieces, he gave the bread to the disciples, who distributed it to the people.
20They all ate as much as they wanted, and afterward, the disciples picked up twelve baskets
of leftovers. 21About 5,000 men were fed that day, in addition to all the women and children!

22Immediately after this, Jesus insisted that his disciples get back into the boat and cross
to the other side of the lake, while he sent the people home. . . .

24Meanwhile, the disciples were in trouble far away from land, for a strong wind had risen,
and they were fighting heavy waves. 25About three o'clock in the morning Jesus came toward
them, walking on the water. 26When the disciples saw him walking on the water, they were
terrified. In their fear, they cried out, "It's a ghost!"

27But Jesus spoke to them at once. "Don't be afraid," he said. "Take courage. I am here!"

28Then Peter called to him, "Lord, if it's really you, tell me to come to you, walking on
the water."

29"Yes, come," Jesus said.

So Peter went over the side of the boat and walked on the water toward Jesus. 30But when
he saw the strong wind and the waves, he was terrified and began to sink. "Save me, Lord!"
he shouted.

31Jesus immediately reached out and grabbed him. "You have so little faith," Jesus said.
"Why did you doubt me?"

Would you have been more likely to step out with Peter or to stay in the boat? Peter was not testing Jesus; instead, he was the only one in the boat to react in faith. His impulsive request led him to experience a rather unusual demonstration of God's power. Peter started to sink because he took his eyes off Jesus and focused on the high waves around him. Then his faith wavered when he realized what he was doing. We may not walk on water, but we do walk through tough situations. If we focus on the waves of difficult circumstances around us without looking to Christ for help, we too may despair and sink. To maintain your faith in the midst of difficult situations, keep your eyes on Christ rather than on your inadequacies.

Jesus Is the Bread from Heaven

JULY 18

JOHN 6:22-40

22The next day the crowd that had stayed on the far shore saw that the disciples had taken the only boat, and they realized Jesus had not gone with them. 23Several boats from Tiberias landed near the place where the Lord had blessed the bread and the people had eaten. 24So when the crowd saw that neither Jesus nor his disciples were there, they got into the boats and went across to Capernaum to look for him. 25They found him on the other side of the lake and asked, "Rabbi, when did you get here?"

26Jesus replied, "I tell you the truth, you want to be with me because I fed you, not because you understood the miraculous signs. 27But don't be so concerned about perishable things like food. Spend your energy seeking the eternal life that the Son of Man can give you. For God the Father has given me the seal of his approval."

28They replied, "We want to perform God's works, too. What should we do?"

29Jesus told them, "This is the only work God wants from you: Believe in the one he has sent."

30They answered, "Show us a miraculous sign if you want us to believe in you. What can you do? 31After all, our ancestors ate manna while they journeyed through the wilderness! The Scriptures say, 'Moses gave them bread from heaven to eat.'"

32Jesus said, "I tell you the truth, Moses didn't give you bread from heaven. My Father did. And now he offers you the true bread from heaven. 33The true bread of God is the one who comes down from heaven and gives life to the world."

34"Sir," they said, "give us that bread every day."

35Jesus replied, "I am the bread of life. Whoever comes to me will never be hungry again. Whoever believes in me will never be thirsty. 36But you haven't believed in me even though you have seen me. 37However, those the Father has given me will come to me, and I will never reject them. 38For I have come down from heaven to do the will of God who sent me, not to do my own will. 39And this is the will of God, that I should not lose even one of all those he has given me, but that I should raise them up at the last day. 40For it is my Father's will that all who see his Son and believe in him should have eternal life. I will raise them up at the last day."

How is Jesus "bread" to you? People eat bread to satisfy physical hunger and to sustain physical life. We can satisfy spiritual hunger and sustain spiritual life only by having a right relationship with Jesus Christ. It is no wonder that he called himself the Bread of Life. But bread must be eaten to sustain life, and Christ must be invited into our daily walk to sustain spiritual life.

JULY 19

Jesus Criticized and Deserted

JOHN 6:41-71

41 Then the people began to murmur in disagreement because he had said, "I am the bread
that came down from heaven." 42 They said, "Isn't this Jesus, the son of Joseph? We know his
father and mother. How can he say, 'I came down from heaven'?" . . .

47 "I tell you the truth, anyone who believes has eternal life. . . ."

53 So Jesus said again, "I tell you the truth, unless you eat the flesh of the Son of Man and
drink his blood, you cannot have eternal life within you. 54 But anyone who eats my flesh and
drinks my blood has eternal life, and I will raise that person at the last day. 55 For my flesh
is true food, and my blood is true drink. 56 Anyone who eats my flesh and drinks my blood
remains in me, and I in him. 57 I live because of the living Father who sent me; in the same
way, anyone who feeds on me will live because of me. 58 I am the true bread that came down
from heaven. Anyone who eats this bread will not die as your ancestors did (even though
they ate the manna) but will live forever."

59 He said these things while he was teaching in the synagogue in Capernaum.

60 Many of his disciples said, "This is very hard to understand. How can anyone accept it?"

61 Jesus was aware that his disciples were complaining, so he said to them, "Does this
offend you? 62 Then what will you think if you see the Son of Man ascend to heaven again?
63 The Spirit alone gives eternal life. Human effort accomplishes nothing. And the very words
I have spoken to you are spirit and life. 64 But some of you do not believe me." (For Jesus knew
from the beginning which ones didn't believe, and he knew who would betray him.) 65 Then
he said, "That is why I said that people can't come to me unless the Father gives them to me."

66 At this point many of his disciples turned away and deserted him. 67 Then Jesus turned
to the Twelve and asked, "Are you also going to leave?"

68 Simon Peter replied, "Lord, to whom would we go? You have the words that give eternal
life. 69 We believe, and we know you are the Holy One of God."

70 Then Jesus said, "I chose the twelve of you, but one is a devil." 71 He was speaking of
Judas, son of Simon Iscariot, one of the Twelve, who would later betray him.

How do you react when you hear critical or derogatory comments about Jesus? After many of Jesus' followers had deserted him, he asked the twelve disciples if they were also going to leave. Peter responded, "To whom would we go?" In his straightforward way, Peter answered for all of us—there is no other way. Jesus alone gives life. People look everywhere for eternal life and miss Christ, the only source. Stay with him, especially when you are confused or feel alone.

Jesus Teaches about Purity

JULY 20

MARK 7:1-23

One day some Pharisees and teachers of religious law arrived from Jerusalem to see Jesus.
[2]They noticed that some of his disciples failed to follow the Jewish ritual of hand washing
before eating. [3](The Jews, especially the Pharisees, do not eat until they have poured water
over their cupped hands, as required by their ancient traditions. [4]Similarly, they don't eat anything from the market until they immerse their hands in water. This is but one of many traditions they have clung to—such as their ceremonial washing of cups, pitchers, and kettles.)
[5]So the Pharisees and teachers of religious law asked him, "Why don't your disciples follow our age-old tradition? They eat without first performing the hand-washing ceremony."
[6]Jesus replied, "You hypocrites! Isaiah was right when he prophesied about you, for he
wrote,

'These people honor me with their lips,
    but their hearts are far from me.
[7]Their worship is a farce,
    for they teach man-made ideas as commands from God.'

[8]For you ignore God's law and substitute your own tradition." . . .
[14]Then Jesus called to the crowd to come and hear. "All of you listen," he said, "and try
to understand. [15]It's not what goes into your body that defiles you; you are defiled by what
comes from your heart."
[17]Then Jesus went into a house to get away from the crowd, and his disciples asked him
what he meant by the parable he had just used. [18]"Don't you understand either?" he asked.
"Can't you see that the food you put into your body cannot defile you? [19]Food doesn't go into
your heart, but only passes through the stomach and then goes into the sewer." (By saying
this, he declared that every kind of food is acceptable in God's eyes.)
[20]And then he added, "It is what comes from inside that defiles you. [21]For from within,
out of a person's heart, come evil thoughts, sexual immorality, theft, murder, [22]adultery, greed,
wickedness, deceit, lustful desires, envy, slander, pride, and foolishness. [23]All these vile things
come from within; they are what defile you."

In what area of your life do you most need God's purifying work? An evil action begins with a single thought. Our thoughts can pollute us, leading us into sin. Allowing our thoughts to dwell on lust, envy, hate, or revenge will lead to evil actions. Don't be made unfit for God. Instead, "fix your thoughts on what is true, and honorable, and right, and pure, and lovely, and admirable. Think about things that are excellent and worthy of praise" (Philippians 4:8).

JULY 21

Jesus Feeds and Warns

MATTHEW 15:32-39; 16:5-12

32 Then Jesus called his disciples and told them, “I feel sorry for these people. They have been here with me for three days, and they have nothing left to eat. I don’t want to send them away hungry, or they will faint along the way.”

33 The disciples replied, “Where would we get enough food here in the wilderness for such a huge crowd?”

34 Jesus asked, “How much bread do you have?”

They replied, “Seven loaves, and a few small fish.”

35 So Jesus told all the people to sit down on the ground. 36 Then he took the seven loaves and the fish, thanked God for them, and broke them into pieces. He gave them to the disciples, who distributed the food to the crowd.

37 They all ate as much as they wanted. Afterward, the disciples picked up seven large baskets of leftover food. 38 There were 4,000 men who were fed that day, in addition to all the women and children. 39 Then Jesus sent the people home, and he got into a boat and crossed over to the region of Magadan.

16:5 Later, after they crossed to the other side of the lake, the disciples discovered they had forgotten to bring any bread. 6 “Watch out!” Jesus warned them. “Beware of the yeast of the Pharisees and Sadducees.”

7 At this they began to argue with each other because they hadn’t brought any bread. 8 Jesus knew what they were saying, so he said, “You have so little faith! Why are you arguing with each other about having no bread? 9 Don’t you understand even yet? Don’t you remember the 5,000 I fed with five loaves, and the baskets of leftovers you picked up? 10 Or the 4,000 I fed with seven loaves, and the large baskets of leftovers you picked up? 11 Why can’t you understand that I’m not talking about bread? So again I say, ‘Beware of the yeast of the Pharisees and Sadducees.’”

12 Then at last they understood that he wasn’t speaking about the yeast in bread, but about the deceptive teaching of the Pharisees and Sadducees.

How do you evaluate what you hear? Yeast is put into bread to make it rise, and it takes only a little bit to affect a whole batch of dough. Jesus used yeast as an example of how a small amount of evil can affect a large group of people. The wrong teachings of the Pharisees and Sadducees were leading many people astray. Beware of the tendency to say, “How can this small wrong possibly affect anyone?”

"You Are the Messiah"

JULY 22

MARK 8:22-38

22 When they arrived at Bethsaida, some people brought a blind man to Jesus, and they begged
him to touch the man and heal him. 23 Jesus took the blind man by the hand and led him out
of the village. Then, spitting on the man's eyes, he laid his hands on him and asked, "Can
you see anything now?"

24 The man looked around. "Yes," he said, "I see people, but I can't see them very clearly.
They look like trees walking around."

25 Then Jesus placed his hands on the man's eyes again, and his eyes were opened. His sight
was completely restored, and he could see everything clearly. 26 Jesus sent him away, saying,
"Don't go back into the village on your way home."

27 Jesus and his disciples left Galilee and went up to the villages near Caesarea Philippi. As
they were walking along, he asked them, "Who do people say I am?"

28 "Well," they replied, "some say John the Baptist, some say Elijah, and others say you
are one of the other prophets."

29 Then he asked them, "But who do you say I am?"

Peter replied, "You are the Messiah."

30 But Jesus warned them not to tell anyone about him.

31 Then Jesus began to tell them that the Son of Man must suffer many terrible things
and be rejected by the elders, the leading priests, and the teachers of religious law. He would
be killed, but three days later he would rise from the dead. 32 As he talked about this openly
with his disciples, Peter took him aside and began to reprimand him for saying such things.

33 Jesus turned around and looked at his disciples, then reprimanded Peter. "Get away
from me, Satan!" he said. "You are seeing things merely from a human point of view, not
from God's."

34 Then, calling the crowd to join his disciples, he said, "If any of you wants to be my
follower, you must give up your own way, take up your cross, and follow me. 35 If you try to
hang on to your life, you will lose it. But if you give up your life for my sake and for the sake
of the Good News, you will save it. 36 And what do you benefit if you gain the whole world
but lose your own soul? 37 Is anything worth more than your soul? 38 If anyone is ashamed of
me and my message in these adulterous and sinful days, the Son of Man will be ashamed of
that person when he returns in the glory of his Father with the holy angels."

In what specific ways have you come to understand Jesus better in the last few weeks? Jesus asked the disciples who others thought he was; then he focused on them: "Who do you say I am?" It is not enough to know what others say about Jesus. You must know, understand, and accept for yourself that he is the Messiah. You must move from curiosity to commitment, from admiration to adoration.

Jesus Is Transfigured

LUKE 9:28-45

28 About eight days later Jesus took Peter, John, and James up on a mountain to pray. 29 And as
he was praying, the appearance of his face was transformed, and his clothes became dazzling
white. 30 Suddenly, two men, Moses and Elijah, appeared and began talking with Jesus. 31 They
were glorious to see. And they were speaking about his exodus from this world, which was
about to be fulfilled in Jerusalem.

32 Peter and the others had fallen asleep. When they woke up, they saw Jesus' glory and
the two men standing with him. 33 As Moses and Elijah were starting to leave, Peter, not even
knowing what he was saying, blurted out, "Master, it's wonderful for us to be here! Let's
make three shelters as memorials—one for you, one for Moses, and one for Elijah." 34 But
even as he was saying this, a cloud overshadowed them, and terror gripped them as the cloud
covered them.

35 Then a voice from the cloud said, "This is my Son, my Chosen One. Listen to him."
36 When the voice finished, Jesus was there alone. They didn't tell anyone at that time what
they had seen.

37 The next day, after they had come down the mountain, a large crowd met Jesus. 38 A man
in the crowd called out to him, "Teacher, I beg you to look at my son, my only child. 39 An
evil spirit keeps seizing him, making him scream. It throws him into convulsions so that he
foams at the mouth. It batters him and hardly ever leaves him alone. 40 I begged your disciples
to cast out the spirit, but they couldn't do it."

41 Jesus said, "You faithless and corrupt people! How long must I be with you and put up
with you?" Then he said to the man, "Bring your son here."

42 As the boy came forward, the demon knocked him to the ground and threw him into
a violent convulsion. But Jesus rebuked the evil spirit and healed the boy. Then he gave him
back to his father. 43 Awe gripped the people as they saw this majestic display of God's power.

While everyone was marveling at everything he was doing, Jesus said to his disciples,
44 "Listen to me and remember what I say. The Son of Man is going to be betrayed into the
hands of his enemies." 45 But they didn't know what he meant. Its significance was hidden
from them, so they couldn't understand it, and they were afraid to ask him about it.

Would you rather leave the world and be with Christ or be with Christ in the world? Peter, James, and John experienced a wonderful moment on the mountain, and they didn't want to leave. Sometimes we, too, have such an exciting experience that we want to stay where we are—away from the reality and problems of our daily lives. Knowing that struggles await us in the valley encourages us to retreat from reality. Yet staying on the mountaintop does not allow us to minister to others. Instead of becoming spiritual giants, we would soon become giants of self-centeredness. We need times of retreat and renewal, but only so we can return to minister to the world. Our faith must make sense off the mountain as well as on it.

Who's the Greatest?

JULY **24**

MATTHEW 17:24–18:6

24On their arrival in Capernaum, the collectors of the Temple tax came to Peter and asked
him, "Doesn't your teacher pay the Temple tax?"
25"Yes, he does," Peter replied. Then he went into the house.
But before he had a chance to speak, Jesus asked him, "What do you think, Peter? Do
kings tax their own people or the people they have conquered?"
26"They tax the people they have conquered," Peter replied.
"Well, then," Jesus said, "the citizens are free! 27However, we don't want to offend them,
so go down to the lake and throw in a line. Open the mouth of the first fish you catch, and
you will find a large silver coin. Take it and pay the tax for both of us."

18:1About that time the disciples came to Jesus and asked, "Who is greatest in the Kingdom
of Heaven?"
2Jesus called a little child to him and put the child among them. 3Then he said, "I tell
you the truth, unless you turn from your sins and become like little children, you will never
get into the Kingdom of Heaven. 4So anyone who becomes as humble as this little child is
the greatest in the Kingdom of Heaven.
5"And anyone who welcomes a little child like this on my behalf is welcoming me. 6But if
you cause one of these little ones who trusts in me to fall into sin, it would be better for you
to have a large millstone tied around your neck and be drowned in the depths of the sea."

When do you worry about status? The disciples had become so preoccupied with the organization of Jesus' earthly kingdom that they had lost sight of its divine purpose. Instead of seeking a place of service, they sought positions of advantage. Jesus used a child to help his self-centered disciples get the point. We are not to be childish (like the disciples, arguing over petty issues) but rather childlike, with humble and sincere hearts. Are you being childlike or childish?

JULY 25

Who's on Our Side?

MARK 9:38-50

38John said to Jesus, "Teacher, we saw someone using your name to cast out demons, but we
told him to stop because he wasn't in our group."

39"Don't stop him!" Jesus said. "No one who performs a miracle in my name will soon
be able to speak evil of me. 40Anyone who is not against us is for us. 41If anyone gives you
even a cup of water because you belong to the Messiah, I tell you the truth, that person will
surely be rewarded.

42"But if you cause one of these little ones who trusts in me to fall into sin, it would be
better for you to be thrown into the sea with a large millstone hung around your neck. 43If
your hand causes you to sin, cut it off. It's better to enter eternal life with only one hand than
to go into the unquenchable fires of hell with two hands. 45If your foot causes you to sin, cut
it off. It's better to enter eternal life with only one foot than to be thrown into hell with two
feet. 47And if your eye causes you to sin, gouge it out. It's better to enter the Kingdom of God
with only one eye than to have two eyes and be thrown into hell, 48'where the maggots never
die and the fire never goes out.'

49"For everyone will be tested with fire. 50Salt is good for seasoning. But if it loses its
flavor, how do you make it salty again? You must have the qualities of salt among yourselves
and live in peace with each other."

Is there a sin in your life that would be painful but necessary to cut off? Jesus used startling language to stress the importance of cutting sin out of our lives. Painful self-discipline is sometimes required of his true followers. Giving up a relationship, attitude, or habit that is against God's will may seem just as painful as cutting off a hand. Our high goal, however, is worth any sacrifice; Christ is worth any possible loss. Nothing should stand in the way of faith and obedience. We must be ruthless in removing sin from our lives now in order to avoid being stuck with it for eternity. Make your choices from an eternal perspective.

Jesus Teaches about Forgiveness

JULY 26

MATTHEW 18:10-22

10“Beware that you don’t look down on any of these little ones. For I tell you that in heaven
their angels are always in the presence of my heavenly Father.

12“If a man has a hundred sheep and one of them wanders away, what will he do? Won’t
he leave the ninety-nine others on the hills and go out to search for the one that is lost? 13And
if he finds it, I tell you the truth, he will rejoice over it more than over the ninety-nine that
didn’t wander away! 14In the same way, it is not my heavenly Father’s will that even one of
these little ones should perish.

15“If another believer sins against you, go privately and point out the offense. If the other
person listens and confesses it, you have won that person back. 16But if you are unsuccessful,
take one or two others with you and go back again, so that everything you say may be confirmed by two or three witnesses. 17If the person still refuses to listen, take your case to the
church. Then if he or she won’t accept the church’s decision, treat that person as a pagan or
a corrupt tax collector.

18“I tell you the truth, whatever you forbid on earth will be forbidden in heaven, and whatever
you permit on earth will be permitted in heaven.

19“I also tell you this: If two of you agree here on earth concerning anything you ask, my
Father in heaven will do it for you. 20For where two or three gather together as my followers,
I am there among them.”

21Then Peter came to him and asked, “Lord, how often should I forgive someone who
sins against me? Seven times?”

22“No, not seven times,” Jesus replied, “but seventy times seven!”

How do you react to the failures of others? The rabbis taught that people should forgive those who offend them—but only three times. Peter, trying to be especially generous, asked Jesus if seven (the “perfect” number) was enough times to forgive someone. But Jesus answered, “Seventy times seven,” meaning that we shouldn’t even keep track of how many times we forgive someone. We should always forgive those who are truly repentant, no matter how many times they ask.

JULY 27

Jesus Out in the Open

JOHN 7:1-18

After this, Jesus traveled around Galilee. He wanted to stay out of Judea, where the Jewish
leaders were plotting his death. [2]But soon it was time for the Jewish Festival of Shelters, [3]and
Jesus' brothers said to him, "Leave here and go to Judea, where your followers can see your
miracles! [4]You can't become famous if you hide like this! If you can do such wonderful things,
show yourself to the world!" [5]For even his brothers didn't believe in him.

[6]Jesus replied, "Now is not the right time for me to go, but you can go anytime. [7]The
world can't hate you, but it does hate me because I accuse it of doing evil. [8]You go on. I'm
not going to this festival, because my time has not yet come." [9]After saying these things, Jesus
remained in Galilee.

[10]But after his brothers left for the festival, Jesus also went, though secretly, staying out of
public view. [11]The Jewish leaders tried to find him at the festival and kept asking if anyone had
seen him. [12]There was a lot of grumbling about him among the crowds. Some argued, "He's
a good man," but others said, "He's nothing but a fraud who deceives the people." [13]But no
one had the courage to speak favorably about him in public, for they were afraid of getting
in trouble with the Jewish leaders.

[14]Then, midway through the festival, Jesus went up to the Temple and began to teach.
[15]The people were surprised when they heard him. "How does he know so much when he
hasn't been trained?" they asked.

[16]So Jesus told them, "My message is not my own; it comes from God who sent me.
[17]Anyone who wants to do the will of God will know whether my teaching is from God or
is merely my own. [18]Those who speak for themselves want glory only for themselves, but a
person who seeks to honor the one who sent him speaks truth, not lies."

Which of Jesus' teachings are difficult for you to accept? Jesus' brothers had a difficult time believing in him. Some of these brothers would eventually become leaders in the church (James, for example), but for several years they were embarrassed by Jesus. After Jesus died and rose again, they finally believed. We today have every reason to believe, because we have the full record of Jesus' miracles, death, and resurrection. We also have the evidence of what the gospel has done in people's lives through the centuries. Don't miss this opportunity to believe in God's Son.

Wrong Conclusions

JULY 28

JOHN 7:32-52

32 When the Pharisees heard that the crowds were whispering such things, they and the leading priests sent Temple guards to arrest Jesus. 33 But Jesus told them, "I will be with you only a little longer. Then I will return to the one who sent me. 34 You will search for me but not find me. And you cannot go where I am going."

35 The Jewish leaders were puzzled by this statement. "Where is he planning to go?" they asked. "Is he thinking of leaving the country and going to the Jews in other lands? Maybe he will even teach the Greeks! 36 What does he mean when he says, 'You will search for me but not find me,' and 'You cannot go where I am going'?"

37 On the last day, the climax of the festival, Jesus stood and shouted to the crowds, "Anyone who is thirsty may come to me! 38 Anyone who believes in me may come and drink! For the Scriptures declare, 'Rivers of living water will flow from his heart.'" 39 (When he said "living water," he was speaking of the Spirit, who would be given to everyone believing in him. But the Spirit had not yet been given, because Jesus had not yet entered into his glory.)

40 When the crowds heard him say this, some of them declared, "Surely this man is the Prophet we've been expecting." 41 Others said, "He is the Messiah." Still others said, "But he can't be! Will the Messiah come from Galilee? 42 For the Scriptures clearly state that the Messiah will be born of the royal line of David, in Bethlehem, the village where King David was born." 43 So the crowd was divided about him. 44 Some even wanted him arrested, but no one laid a hand on him.

45 When the Temple guards returned without having arrested Jesus, the leading priests and Pharisees demanded, "Why didn't you bring him in?"

46 "We have never heard anyone speak like this!" the guards responded.

47 "Have you been led astray, too?" the Pharisees mocked. 48 "Is there a single one of us rulers or Pharisees who believes in him? 49 This foolish crowd follows him, but they are ignorant of the law. God's curse is on them!"

50 Then Nicodemus, the leader who had met with Jesus earlier, spoke up. 51 "Is it legal to convict a man before he is given a hearing?" he asked.

52 They replied, "Are you from Galilee, too? Search the Scriptures and see for yourself—no prophet ever comes from Galilee!"

What does it mean to have "rivers of living water" flowing from within you? The crowd was asking questions about Jesus. Some believed, others were hostile, and others disqualified Jesus as the Messiah because he was from Nazareth, not Bethlehem (Micah 5:2). But he was born in Bethlehem (Luke 2:1-7), although he grew up in Nazareth. If they had looked more carefully, they would not have jumped to the wrong conclusions. When you search for God's truth, make sure you look carefully and thoughtfully at the Bible with an open heart and mind. Don't jump to conclusions before knowing more of what the Bible says.

JULY 29

The Woman Caught in Adultery

JOHN 8:1-19

Jesus returned to the Mount of Olives, 2but early the next morning he was back again at the Temple. A crowd soon gathered, and he sat down and taught them. 3As he was speaking, the teachers of religious law and the Pharisees brought a woman who had been caught in the act of adultery. They put her in front of the crowd.

4"Teacher," they said to Jesus, "this woman was caught in the act of adultery. 5The law of Moses says to stone her. What do you say?"

6They were trying to trap him into saying something they could use against him, but Jesus stooped down and wrote in the dust with his finger. 7They kept demanding an answer, so he stood up again and said, "All right, but let the one who has never sinned throw the first stone!" 8Then he stooped down again and wrote in the dust.

9When the accusers heard this, they slipped away one by one, beginning with the oldest, until only Jesus was left in the middle of the crowd with the woman. 10Then Jesus stood up again and said to the woman, "Where are your accusers? Didn't even one of them condemn you?"

11"No, Lord," she said.

And Jesus said, "Neither do I. Go and sin no more."

12Jesus spoke to the people once more and said, "I am the light of the world. If you follow me, you won't have to walk in darkness, because you will have the light that leads to life."

13The Pharisees replied, "You are making those claims about yourself! Such testimony is not valid."

14Jesus told them, "These claims are valid even though I make them about myself. For I know where I came from and where I am going, but you don't know this about me. 15You judge me by human standards, but I do not judge anyone. 16And if I did, my judgment would be correct in every respect because I am not alone. The Father who sent me is with me. 17Your own law says that if two people agree about something, their witness is accepted as fact. 18I am one witness, and my Father who sent me is the other."

19"Where is your father?" they asked.

Jesus answered, "Since you don't know who I am, you don't know who my Father is. If you knew me, you would also know my Father."

Who is the last person you had to forgive? This passage makes a significant statement about judging others. Because Jesus upheld the legal penalty for adultery, stoning, he could not be accused of being against the law. But by saying that only a sinless person could throw the first stone, he highlighted the importance of compassion and forgiveness. When others are caught in sin, are you quick to pass judgment? To do so is to act as though you have never sinned. It is God's role to judge, not yours. Your role is to show forgiveness and compassion.

The Truth Will Set You Free

JULY 30

JOHN 8:21-32

21Later Jesus said to them again, "I am going away. You will search for me but will die in your
sin. You cannot come where I am going."

22The people asked, "Is he planning to commit suicide? What does he mean, 'You cannot
come where I am going'?"

23Jesus continued, "You are from below; I am from above. You belong to this world; I do
not. 24That is why I said that you will die in your sins; for unless you believe that I Am who
I claim to be, you will die in your sins."

25"Who are you?" they demanded.

Jesus replied, "The one I have always claimed to be. 26I have much to say about you and
much to condemn, but I won't. For I say only what I have heard from the one who sent me, and
he is completely truthful." 27But they still didn't understand that he was talking about his Father.

28So Jesus said, "When you have lifted up the Son of Man on the cross, then you will
understand that I Am he. I do nothing on my own but say only what the Father taught
me. 29And the one who sent me is with me—he has not deserted me. For I always do what
pleases him." 30Then many who heard him say these things believed in him.

31Jesus said to the people who believed in him, "You are truly my disciples if you remain
faithful to my teachings. 32And you will know the truth, and the truth will set you free."

How has Christ made you free? Jesus himself is the truth that makes us free. He is the source of truth, the perfect standard of what is right. He frees us from the consequences of sin, from self-deception, and from deception by Satan. He shows us clearly the way to everlasting life with God. Thus, Jesus does not give us freedom to do what we want but freedom to follow God. As you seek to serve God, Jesus' perfect truth frees you to be all that God meant you to be.

JULY 31

Jesus Sends Out Messengers

LUKE 10:1-24

The Lord now chose seventy-two other disciples and sent them ahead in pairs to all the towns and places he planned to visit. 2These were his instructions to them: "The harvest is great, but the workers are few. So pray to the Lord who is in charge of the harvest; ask him to send more workers into his fields. 3Now go, and remember that I am sending you out as lambs among wolves. 4Don't take any money with you, nor a traveler's bag, nor an extra pair of sandals. And don't stop to greet anyone on the road.

5"Whenever you enter someone's home, first say, 'May God's peace be on this house.' 6If those who live there are peaceful, the blessing will stand; if they are not, the blessing will return to you. 7Don't move around from home to home. Stay in one place, eating and drinking what they provide. Don't hesitate to accept hospitality, because those who work deserve their pay.

8"If you enter a town and it welcomes you, eat whatever is set before you. 9Heal the sick, and tell them, 'The Kingdom of God is near you now.' 10But if a town refuses to welcome you, go out into its streets and say, 11'We wipe even the dust of your town from our feet to show that we have abandoned you to your fate. And know this—the Kingdom of God is near!' 12I assure you, even wicked Sodom will be better off than such a town on judgment day. . . ."

16Then he said to the disciples, "Anyone who accepts your message is also accepting me. And anyone who rejects you is rejecting me. And anyone who rejects me is rejecting God, who sent me."

17When the seventy-two disciples returned, they joyfully reported to him, "Lord, even the demons obey us when we use your name!" . . .

21At that same time Jesus was filled with the joy of the Holy Spirit, and he said, "O Father, Lord of heaven and earth, thank you for hiding these things from those who think themselves wise and clever, and for revealing them to the childlike. Yes, Father, it pleased you to do it this way.

22"My Father has entrusted everything to me. No one truly knows the Son except the Father, and no one truly knows the Father except the Son and those to whom the Son chooses to reveal him."

23Then when they were alone, he turned to the disciples and said, "Blessed are the eyes that see what you have seen. 24I tell you, many prophets and kings longed to see what you see, but they didn't see it. And they longed to hear what you hear, but they didn't hear it."

What would have been most exciting about this trip for you? Jesus thanked God that spiritual truth was for everyone, not just the elite. We come to Jesus, not through strength or brains, but through childlike trust. Jesus is not against those engaged in scholarly pursuits; he is against spiritual pride (being wise in your own eyes). We can thank God that we all have equal access to him through Jesus Christ. Trust in God, not in your personal qualifications, for your citizenship in the Kingdom.

August

AUGUST 1 — The Good Samaritan

LUKE 10:25-37

25One day an expert in religious law stood up to test Jesus by asking him this question: "Teacher, what should I do to inherit eternal life?"

26Jesus replied, "What does the law of Moses say? How do you read it?"

27The man answered, "'You must love the LORD your God with all your heart, all your soul, all your strength, and all your mind.' And, 'Love your neighbor as yourself.'"

28"Right!" Jesus told him. "Do this and you will live!"

29The man wanted to justify his actions, so he asked Jesus, "And who is my neighbor?"

30Jesus replied with a story: "A Jewish man was traveling from Jerusalem down to Jericho, and he was attacked by bandits. They stripped him of his clothes, beat him up, and left him half dead beside the road.

31"By chance a priest came along. But when he saw the man lying there, he crossed to the
other side of the road and passed him by. 32A Temple assistant walked over and looked at him
lying there, but he also passed by on the other side.

33"Then a despised Samaritan came along, and when he saw the man, he felt compassion
for him. 34Going over to him, the Samaritan soothed his wounds with olive oil and wine and
bandaged them. Then he put the man on his own donkey and took him to an inn, where
he took care of him. 35The next day he handed the innkeeper two silver coins, telling him,
'Take care of this man. If his bill runs higher than this, I'll pay you the next time I'm here.'

36"Now which of these three would you say was a neighbor to the man who was attacked by bandits?" Jesus asked.

37The man replied, "The one who showed him mercy."

Then Jesus said, "Yes, now go and do the same."

Who has been a Good Samaritan to you? From this parable we learn three principles about loving our neighbors: (1) Lack of love is often easy to justify. (2) Our neighbor is anyone of any race or creed or social background who is in need. (3) Love means acting to meet a need. Wherever you live, there are needy people close by. There are no good reasons for refusing to help.

Jesus Teaches about Prayer

AUGUST 2

LUKE 11:1-13

Once Jesus was in a certain place praying. As he finished, one of his disciples came to him
and said, "Lord, teach us to pray, just as John taught his disciples."
2Jesus said, "This is how you should pray:

"Father, may your name be kept holy.
    May your Kingdom come soon.
3Give us each day the food we need,
4and forgive us our sins,
    as we forgive those who sin against us.
And don't let us yield to temptation."

5Then, teaching them more about prayer, he used this story: "Suppose you went to a
friend's house at midnight, wanting to borrow three loaves of bread. You say to him, 6'A
friend of mine has just arrived for a visit, and I have nothing for him to eat.' 7And suppose
he calls out from his bedroom, 'Don't bother me. The door is locked for the night, and my
family and I are all in bed. I can't help you.' 8But I tell you this—though he won't do it for
friendship's sake, if you keep knocking long enough, he will get up and give you whatever
you need because of your shameless persistence.
9"And so I tell you, keep on asking, and you will receive what you ask for. Keep on
seeking, and you will find. Keep on knocking, and the door will be opened to you. 10For
everyone who asks, receives. Everyone who seeks, finds. And to everyone who knocks, the
door will be opened.
11"You fathers—if your children ask for a fish, do you give them a snake instead? 12Or
if they ask for an egg, do you give them a scorpion? Of course not! 13So if you sinful people
know how to give good gifts to your children, how much more will your heavenly Father
give the Holy Spirit to those who ask him."

How could your prayer habits be improved? When Jesus taught his disciples to pray, he made forgiveness the cornerstone of their relationship with God. God has forgiven our sins, so we must forgive those who have wronged us. To remain unforgiving shows we have not understood that we ourselves, along with all other human beings, need to be forgiven. Think of some people who have wronged you. Have you truly forgiven them, or do you still carry a grudge against them? How will God deal with you if he treats you as you treat others?

AUGUST 3

Accusations and Unbelief

LUKE 11:14-32

14One day Jesus cast out a demon from a man who couldn't speak, and when the demon was
gone, the man began to speak. The crowds were amazed, 15but some of them said, "No wonder he can cast out demons. He gets his power from Satan, the prince of demons." 16Others,
trying to test Jesus, demanded that he show them a miraculous sign from heaven to prove
his authority.

17He knew their thoughts, so he said, "Any kingdom divided by civil war is doomed. A
family splintered by feuding will fall apart. 18You say I am empowered by Satan. But if Satan is
divided and fighting against himself, how can his kingdom survive? 19And if I am empowered
by Satan, what about your own exorcists? They cast out demons, too, so they will condemn
you for what you have said. 20But if I am casting out demons by the power of God, then the
Kingdom of God has arrived among you. 21For when a strong man is fully armed and guards
his palace, his possessions are safe—22until someone even stronger attacks and overpowers
him, strips him of his weapons, and carries off his belongings.

23"Anyone who isn't with me opposes me, and anyone who isn't working with me is
actually working against me. . . ."

27As he was speaking, a woman in the crowd called out, "God bless your mother—the
womb from which you came, and the breasts that nursed you!"

28Jesus replied, "But even more blessed are all who hear the word of God and put it into
practice."

29As the crowd pressed in on Jesus, he said, "This evil generation keeps asking me to
show them a miraculous sign. But the only sign I will give them is the sign of Jonah. 30What
happened to him was a sign to the people of Nineveh that God had sent him. What happens
to the Son of Man will be a sign to these people that he was sent by God.

31"The queen of Sheba will stand up against this generation on judgment day and condemn it, for she came from a distant land to hear the wisdom of Solomon. Now someone
greater than Solomon is here—but you refuse to listen. 32The people of Nineveh will also
stand up against this generation on judgment day and condemn it, for they repented of their
sins at the preaching of Jonah. Now someone greater than Jonah is here—but you refuse to
repent."

What are your strongest reasons for being a faithful follower of Christ? Jesus says, "Anyone who isn't with me opposes me." People may be neutral toward Christians, but they cannot be neutral in their relationship to Jesus. You can't be neutral in the battle between Jesus and Satan. You can't be aloof or noncommittal, because there are only two sides. Since God has already won the battle, why be on the losing side? If you aren't actively for Christ, you are against him.

Real Versus Unreal Spirituality

AUGUST 4

LUKE 11:37-52

37 As Jesus was speaking, one of the Pharisees invited him home for a meal. So he went in and
took his place at the table. 38 His host was amazed to see that he sat down to eat without first
performing the hand-washing ceremony required by Jewish custom. 39 Then the Lord said
to him, "You Pharisees are so careful to clean the outside of the cup and the dish, but inside
you are filthy—full of greed and wickedness! 40 Fools! Didn't God make the inside as well as
the outside? 41 So clean the inside by giving gifts to the poor, and you will be clean all over.

42 "What sorrow awaits you Pharisees! For you are careful to tithe even the tiniest income
from your herb gardens, but you ignore justice and the love of God. You should tithe, yes,
but do not neglect the more important things.

43 "What sorrow awaits you Pharisees! For you love to sit in the seats of honor in the synagogues and receive respectful greetings as you walk in the marketplaces. 44 Yes, what sorrow
awaits you! For you are like hidden graves in a field. People walk over them without knowing
the corruption they are stepping on."

45 "Teacher," said an expert in religious law, "you have insulted us, too, in what you just
said."

46 "Yes," said Jesus, "what sorrow also awaits you experts in religious law! For you crush
people with unbearable religious demands, and you never lift a finger to ease the burden.
47 What sorrow awaits you! For you build monuments for the prophets your own ancestors
killed long ago. 48 But in fact, you stand as witnesses who agree with what your ancestors did.
They killed the prophets, and you join in their crime by building the monuments! 49 This is
what God in his wisdom said about you: 'I will send prophets and apostles to them, but they
will kill some and persecute the others.'

50 "As a result, this generation will be held responsible for the murder of all God's prophets
from the creation of the world—51 from the murder of Abel to the murder of Zechariah, who
was killed between the altar and the sanctuary. Yes, it will certainly be charged against this
generation.

52 "What sorrow awaits you experts in religious law! For you remove the key to knowledge from the people. You don't enter the Kingdom yourselves, and you prevent others from
entering."

What is real spirituality? Jesus criticized the Pharisees because they (1) washed the outside but were not clean inside, (2) tithed but forgot justice, (3) loved people's praise, (4) made impossible religious demands, and (5) would not accept the truth about Jesus and prevented others from believing. They focused on outward appearances and ignored the condition of their hearts. We do the same when our service is motivated by a desire to be seen rather than by a pure heart and love for others. Others may be fooled, but God isn't. Bring your inner life under God's control; then your outer life will naturally reflect him.

AUGUST 5

Guard Against Greed

LUKE 12:1-21

Meanwhile, the crowds grew until thousands were milling about and stepping on each other.
Jesus turned first to his disciples and warned them, “Beware of the yeast of the Pharisees—
their hypocrisy. . . .
4“Dear friends, don’t be afraid of those who want to kill your body; they cannot do any
more to you after that. 5But I’ll tell you whom to fear. Fear God, who has the power to kill
you and then throw you into hell. Yes, he’s the one to fear.
6“What is the price of five sparrows—two copper coins? Yet God does not forget a single
one of them. 7And the very hairs on your head are all numbered. So don’t be afraid; you are
more valuable to God than a whole flock of sparrows.
8“I tell you the truth, everyone who acknowledges me publicly here on earth, the Son of
Man will also acknowledge in the presence of God’s angels. 9But anyone who denies me here
on earth will be denied before God’s angels. 10Anyone who speaks against the Son of Man can
be forgiven, but anyone who blasphemes the Holy Spirit will not be forgiven.
11“And when you are brought to trial in the synagogues and before rulers and authorities,
don’t worry about how to defend yourself or what to say, 12for the Holy Spirit will teach you
at that time what needs to be said.”
13Then someone called from the crowd, “Teacher, please tell my brother to divide our
father’s estate with me.”
14Jesus replied, “Friend, who made me a judge over you to decide such things as that?”
15Then he said, “Beware! Guard against every kind of greed. Life is not measured by how
much you own.”
16Then he told them a story: “A rich man had a fertile farm that produced fine crops.
17He said to himself, ‘What should I do? I don’t have room for all my crops.’ 18Then he said,
‘I know! I’ll tear down my barns and build bigger ones. Then I’ll have room enough to store
all my wheat and other goods. 19And I’ll sit back and say to myself, “My friend, you have
enough stored away for years to come. Now take it easy! Eat, drink, and be merry!”’
20“But God said to him, ‘You fool! You will die this very night. Then who will get everything you worked for?’
21“Yes, a person is a fool to store up earthly wealth but not have a rich relationship with
God.”

In what situations do you get too caught up in the goals of this world? Jesus says that the good life has nothing to do with being wealthy. This is the exact opposite of what society usually says. Advertisers spend millions of dollars to entice us to think that if we buy more and more of their products, we will be happier or more comfortable. How do you respond to the constant pressure to buy? Learn to tune out expensive enticements and concentrate on the truly good life—living in a relationship with God and doing his work.

Jesus Warns about Worry

AUGUST 6

LUKE 12:22-40

22 Then, turning to his disciples, Jesus said, "That is why I tell you not to worry about everyday life—whether you have enough food to eat or enough clothes to wear. 23 For life is more than food, and your body more than clothing. 24 Look at the ravens. They don't plant or harvest or store food in barns, for God feeds them. And you are far more valuable to him than any birds! 25 Can all your worries add a single moment to your life? 26 And if worry can't accomplish a little thing like that, what's the use of worrying over bigger things?

27 "Look at the lilies and how they grow. They don't work or make their clothing, yet Solomon in all his glory was not dressed as beautifully as they are. 28 And if God cares so wonderfully for flowers that are here today and thrown into the fire tomorrow, he will certainly care for you. Why do you have so little faith?

29 "And don't be concerned about what to eat and what to drink. Don't worry about such things. 30 These things dominate the thoughts of unbelievers all over the world, but your Father already knows your needs. 31 Seek the Kingdom of God above all else, and he will give you everything you need.

32 "So don't be afraid, little flock. For it gives your Father great happiness to give you the Kingdom.

33 "Sell your possessions and give to those in need. This will store up treasure for you in heaven! And the purses of heaven never get old or develop holes. Your treasure will be safe; no thief can steal it and no moth can destroy it. 34 Wherever your treasure is, there the desires of your heart will also be.

35 "Be dressed for service and keep your lamps burning, 36 as though you were waiting for your master to return from the wedding feast. Then you will be ready to open the door and let him in the moment he arrives and knocks. 37 The servants who are ready and waiting for his return will be rewarded. I tell you the truth, he himself will seat them, put on an apron, and serve them as they sit and eat! 38 He may come in the middle of the night or just before dawn. But whenever he comes, he will reward the servants who are ready.

39 "Understand this: If a homeowner knew exactly when a burglar was coming, he would not permit his house to be broken into. 40 You also must be ready all the time, for the Son of Man will come when least expected."

Do you feel worried or hopeful when you think about the future? Seeking the Kingdom of God means making Jesus the Lord and King of your life. He must control every area—your work, play, plans, and relationships. Is the Kingdom only one of your many concerns, or is it central to all you do? Are you holding back any areas of your life from God's control? As Lord and Creator, he wants to help provide what you need as well as guide how you use what he provides.

AUGUST 7

Jesus Warns about Troubles

LUKE 12:49-59

49“I have come to set the world on fire, and I wish it were already burning! 50I have a terrible baptism of suffering ahead of me, and I am under a heavy burden until it is accomplished. 51Do you think I have come to bring peace to the earth? No, I have come to divide people against each other! 52From now on families will be split apart, three in favor of me, and two against—or two in favor and three against.

53‘Father will be divided against son
  and son against father;
mother against daughter
  and daughter against mother;
and mother-in-law against daughter-in-law
  and daughter-in-law against mother-in-law.’”

54Then Jesus turned to the crowd and said, “When you see clouds beginning to form in the west, you say, ‘Here comes a shower.’ And you are right. 55When the south wind blows, you say, ‘Today will be a scorcher.’ And it is. 56You fools! You know how to interpret the weather signs of the earth and sky, but you don’t know how to interpret the present times.

57“Why can’t you decide for yourselves what is right? 58When you are on the way to court with your accuser, try to settle the matter before you get there. Otherwise, your accuser may drag you before the judge, who will hand you over to an officer, who will throw you into prison. 59And if that happens, you won’t be free again until you have paid the very last penny.”

What examples have you seen of the problems Jesus mentions? In these strange and unsettling words, Jesus revealed that his coming often results in conflict. He demands a response, and even close groups can be torn apart when some choose to follow him and others refuse to do so. There is no middle ground with Jesus. Loyalties must be declared and commitments made, sometimes to the severing of other relationships. Life is easiest when a family unitedly believes in Christ, of course; but this often does not happen. Are you willing to risk your family’s approval in order to gain eternal life?

Fruitful for the Kingdom

AUGUST 8

LUKE 13:6-21

[6]Then Jesus told this story: "A man planted a fig tree in his garden and came again and
again to see if there was any fruit on it, but he was always disappointed. [7]Finally, he said to
his gardener, 'I've waited three years, and there hasn't been a single fig! Cut it down. It's just
taking up space in the garden.'

[8]"The gardener answered, 'Sir, give it one more chance. Leave it another year, and I'll
give it special attention and plenty of fertilizer. [9]If we get figs next year, fine. If not, then you
can cut it down.'"

[10]One Sabbath day as Jesus was teaching in a synagogue, [11]he saw a woman who had
been crippled by an evil spirit. She had been bent double for eighteen years and was unable
to stand up straight. [12]When Jesus saw her, he called her over and said, "Dear woman, you
are healed of your sickness!" [13]Then he touched her, and instantly she could stand straight.
How she praised God!

[14]But the leader in charge of the synagogue was indignant that Jesus had healed her on
the Sabbath day. "There are six days of the week for working," he said to the crowd. "Come
on those days to be healed, not on the Sabbath."

[15]But the Lord replied, "You hypocrites! Each of you works on the Sabbath day! Don't you
untie your ox or your donkey from its stall on the Sabbath and lead it out for water? [16]This
dear woman, a daughter of Abraham, has been held in bondage by Satan for eighteen years.
Isn't it right that she be released, even on the Sabbath?"

[17]This shamed his enemies, but all the people rejoiced at the wonderful things he did.

[18]Then Jesus said, "What is the Kingdom of God like? How can I illustrate it? [19]It is like a
tiny mustard seed that a man planted in a garden; it grows and becomes a tree, and the birds
make nests in its branches."

[20]He also asked, "What else is the Kingdom of God like? [21]It is like the yeast a woman
used in making bread. Even though she put only a little yeast in three measures of flour, it
permeated every part of the dough."

Is your life producing godly fruit? In the Old Testament a fruitful tree was often used as a symbol of godly living (see Psalm 1:3). Jesus pointed out what would happen to the other kind of tree—the kind that took valuable time and space and still produced nothing for the patient gardener. This was one way Jesus warned his listeners that God would not tolerate forever their lack of productivity. Have you been enjoying God's special treatment without giving anything in return? If so, respond to the Gardener's patient care, and begin to bear the fruit God has created you to produce.

AUGUST 9

Jesus and a Blind Man

JOHN 9:1-38

As Jesus was walking along, he saw a man who had been blind from birth. 2“Rabbi,” his disciples asked him, “why was this man born blind? Was it because of his own sins or his parents’ sins?”

3“It was not because of his sins or his parents’ sins,” Jesus answered. “This happened so the power of God could be seen in him. . . .”

6Then he spit on the ground, made mud with the saliva, and spread the mud over the blind man’s eyes. 7He told him, “Go wash yourself in the pool of Siloam” (Siloam means “sent”). So the man went and washed and came back seeing!

8His neighbors and others who knew him as a blind beggar asked each other, “Isn’t this the man who used to sit and beg?” 9Some said he was, and others said, “No, he just looks like him!”

But the beggar kept saying, “Yes, I am the same one!” . . .

13Then they took the man who had been blind to the Pharisees, 14because it was on the Sabbath that Jesus had made the mud and healed him. . . .

16Some of the Pharisees said, “This man Jesus is not from God, for he is working on the Sabbath.” Others said, “But how could an ordinary sinner do such miraculous signs?” So there was a deep division of opinion among them.

17Then the Pharisees again questioned the man who had been blind and demanded, “What’s your opinion about this man who healed you?”

The man replied, “I think he must be a prophet.” . . .

24So for the second time they called in the man who had been blind and told him, “God should get the glory for this, because we know this man Jesus is a sinner.” . . .

30“Why, that’s very strange!” the man replied. “He healed my eyes, and yet you don’t know where he comes from? 31We know that God doesn’t listen to sinners, but he is ready to hear those who worship him and do his will. 32Ever since the world began, no one has been able to open the eyes of someone born blind. 33If this man were not from God, he couldn’t have done it.” . . .

35When Jesus heard what had happened, he found the man and asked, “Do you believe in the Son of Man?”

36The man answered, “Who is he, sir? I want to believe in him.”

37“You have seen him,” Jesus said, “and he is speaking to you!”

38“Yes, Lord, I believe!” the man said. And he worshiped Jesus.

What different stages of “seeing” have been part of your life? The longer this man experienced his new life through Christ, the more confident he became in the one who had healed him. He gained not only physical sight but also spiritual sight as he recognized Jesus first as a prophet, then as his Lord. When you turn to Christ, you begin to see him differently. The longer you walk with him, the better you will understand who he is.

Jesus Is the Good Shepherd

AUGUST 10

JOHN 10:1-18

"I tell you the truth, anyone who sneaks over the wall of a sheepfold, rather than going through the gate, must surely be a thief and a robber! [2]But the one who enters through the gate is the shepherd of the sheep. [3]The gatekeeper opens the gate for him, and the sheep recognize his voice and come to him. He calls his own sheep by name and leads them out. [4]After he has gathered his own flock, he walks ahead of them, and they follow him because they know his voice. [5]They won't follow a stranger; they will run from him because they don't know his voice."

[6]Those who heard Jesus use this illustration didn't understand what he meant, [7]so he explained it to them: "I tell you the truth, I am the gate for the sheep. [8]All who came before me were thieves and robbers. But the true sheep did not listen to them. [9]Yes, I am the gate. Those who come in through me will be saved. They will come and go freely and will find good pastures. [10]The thief's purpose is to steal and kill and destroy. My purpose is to give them a rich and satisfying life.

[11]"I am the good shepherd. The good shepherd sacrifices his life for the sheep. [12]A hired hand will run when he sees a wolf coming. He will abandon the sheep because they don't belong to him and he isn't their shepherd. And so the wolf attacks them and scatters the flock. [13]The hired hand runs away because he's working only for the money and doesn't really care about the sheep.

[14]"I am the good shepherd; I know my own sheep, and they know me, [15]just as my Father knows me and I know the Father. So I sacrifice my life for the sheep. [16]I have other sheep, too, that are not in this sheepfold. I must bring them also. They will listen to my voice, and there will be one flock with one shepherd.

[17]"The Father loves me because I sacrifice my life so I may take it back again. [18]No one can take my life from me. I sacrifice it voluntarily. For I have the authority to lay it down when I want to and also to take it up again. For this is what my Father has commanded."

How have you experienced God's guidance in your life? With the sheepfold the shepherd functioned as a door, letting the sheep in and protecting them. Jesus is the door to God's salvation for us. He is our protector and offers us safety and security. Some people resent that Jesus is the door, the only way to God. But Jesus is God's Son. Why should we seek any other way or want to customize a different approach to God?

AUGUST 11

Kingdom Surprises

LUKE 13:22-35

22Jesus went through the towns and villages, teaching as he went, always pressing on toward
Jerusalem. 23Someone asked him, "Lord, will only a few be saved?"
He replied, 24"Work hard to enter the narrow door to God's Kingdom, for many will try
to enter but will fail. 25When the master of the house has locked the door, it will be too late.
You will stand outside knocking and pleading, 'Lord, open the door for us!' But he will reply,
'I don't know you or where you come from.' 26Then you will say, 'But we ate and drank with
you, and you taught in our streets.' 27And he will reply, 'I tell you, I don't know you or where
you come from. Get away from me, all you who do evil.'
28"There will be weeping and gnashing of teeth, for you will see Abraham, Isaac, Jacob,
and all the prophets in the Kingdom of God, but you will be thrown out. 29And people will
come from all over the world—from east and west, north and south—to take their places
in the Kingdom of God. 30And note this: Some who seem least important now will be the
greatest then, and some who are the greatest now will be least important then."
31At that time some Pharisees said to him, "Get away from here if you want to live! Herod
Antipas wants to kill you!"
32Jesus replied, "Go tell that fox that I will keep on casting out demons and healing people
today and tomorrow; and the third day I will accomplish my purpose. 33Yes, today, tomorrow,
and the next day I must proceed on my way. For it wouldn't do for a prophet of God to be
killed except in Jerusalem!
34"O Jerusalem, Jerusalem, the city that kills the prophets and stones God's messengers!
How often I have wanted to gather your children together as a hen protects her chicks
beneath her wings, but you wouldn't let me. 35And now, look, your house is abandoned. And
you will never see me again until you say, 'Blessings on the one who comes in the name of
the LORD!'"

How do you feel about those around you who don't know Christ? There will be many surprises in God's Kingdom. Some who are despised now will be greatly honored then; some influential people here will be left outside the gates. Many "great" people on this earth (in God's eyes) are virtually ignored by the rest of the world. What matters to God is not a person's earthly popularity, status, wealth, heritage, or power but his or her commitment to Christ. How do your values match what the Bible tells you to value? Put God first, and you will join people from all over the world who will take their places at the feast in the Kingdom of Heaven.

Jesus on Seeking Honor

AUGUST 12

LUKE 14:1-14

One Sabbath day Jesus went to eat dinner in the home of a leader of the Pharisees, and the people were watching him closely. 2There was a man there whose arms and legs were swollen. 3Jesus asked the Pharisees and experts in religious law, “Is it permitted in the law to heal people on the Sabbath day, or not?” 4When they refused to answer, Jesus touched the sick man and healed him and sent him away. 5Then he turned to them and said, “Which of you doesn’t work on the Sabbath? If your son or your cow falls into a pit, don’t you rush to get him out?” 6Again they could not answer.

7When Jesus noticed that all who had come to the dinner were trying to sit in the seats of honor near the head of the table, he gave them this advice: 8“When you are invited to a wedding feast, don’t sit in the seat of honor. What if someone who is more distinguished than you has also been invited? 9The host will come and say, ‘Give this person your seat.’ Then you will be embarrassed, and you will have to take whatever seat is left at the foot of the table!

10“Instead, take the lowest place at the foot of the table. Then when your host sees you, he will come and say, ‘Friend, we have a better place for you!’ Then you will be honored in front of all the other guests. 11For those who exalt themselves will be humbled, and those who humble themselves will be exalted.”

12Then he turned to his host. “When you put on a luncheon or a banquet,” he said, “don’t invite your friends, brothers, relatives, and rich neighbors. For they will invite you back, and that will be your only reward. 13Instead, invite the poor, the crippled, the lame, and the blind. 14Then at the resurrection of the righteous, God will reward you for inviting those who could not repay you.”

When would others say that you look out for yourself too much? Jesus advised people not to rush for the best seats at a feast. People today are just as eager to raise their social status, whether by being with the right people, dressing in the right clothes, or driving the right car. Dressing nicely or striving to be successful in school or in sports is not wrong in itself—it is wrong only when you want these things just to impress others. Whom do you try to impress? Rather than aiming for prestige, look for a place where you can serve.

AUGUST 13

Count the Cost

LUKE 14:15-33

15 Hearing this, a man sitting at the table with Jesus exclaimed, "What a blessing it will be to
attend a banquet in the Kingdom of God!"
16 Jesus replied with this story: "A man prepared a great feast and sent out many invitations. 17 When the banquet was ready, he sent his servant to tell the guests, 'Come, the banquet
is ready.' 18 But they all began making excuses. One said, 'I have just bought a field and must
inspect it. Please excuse me.' 19 Another said, 'I have just bought five pairs of oxen, and I want
to try them out. Please excuse me.' 20 Another said, 'I just got married, so I can't come.'
21 "The servant returned and told his master what they had said. His master was furious
and said, 'Go quickly into the streets and alleys of the town and invite the poor, the crippled,
the blind, and the lame.' 22 After the servant had done this, he reported, 'There is still room for
more.' 23 So his master said, 'Go out into the country lanes and behind the hedges and urge
anyone you find to come, so that the house will be full. 24 For none of those I first invited will
get even the smallest taste of my banquet.'"
25 A large crowd was following Jesus. He turned around and said to them, 26 "If you want to
be my disciple, you must, by comparison, hate everyone else—your father and mother, wife
and children, brothers and sisters—yes, even your own life. Otherwise, you cannot be my
disciple. 27 And if you do not carry your own cross and follow me, you cannot be my disciple.
28 "But don't begin until you count the cost. For who would begin construction of a building without first calculating the cost to see if there is enough money to finish it? 29 Otherwise,
you might complete only the foundation before running out of money, and then everyone
would laugh at you. 30 They would say, 'There's the person who started that building and
couldn't afford to finish it!'
31 "Or what king would go to war against another king without first sitting down with his
counselors to discuss whether his army of 10,000 could defeat the 20,000 soldiers marching
against him? 32 And if he can't, he will send a delegation to discuss terms of peace while the
enemy is still far away. 33 So you cannot become my disciple without giving up everything
you own."

What is it going to cost you to be a follower of Jesus? Are you willing to pay the price? When a builder doesn't count the costs or estimates them inaccurately, his building may be left half completed. Will your Christian life be only half built and then abandoned because you did not count the cost of commitment to Jesus? What are those costs? Christians may face loss of social status or wealth. They may have to give up control over their money, their time, or their careers. They may be hated, separated from their families, and even put to death. Following Christ does not mean a trouble-free life. We must carefully count the cost of becoming Christ's disciples so that we will know what we are getting into and won't be tempted later to turn back.

Losing and Finding

AUGUST 14

LUKE 15:1-10

Tax collectors and other notorious sinners often came to listen to Jesus teach. [2]This made
the Pharisees and teachers of religious law complain that he was associating with such sinful
people—even eating with them!

[3]So Jesus told them this story: [4]"If a man has a hundred sheep and one of them gets lost,
what will he do? Won't he leave the ninety-nine others in the wilderness and go to search for
the one that is lost until he finds it? [5]And when he has found it, he will joyfully carry it home
on his shoulders. [6]When he arrives, he will call together his friends and neighbors, saying,
'Rejoice with me because I have found my lost sheep.' [7]In the same way, there is more joy
in heaven over one lost sinner who repents and returns to God than over ninety-nine others
who are righteous and haven't strayed away!

[8]"Or suppose a woman has ten silver coins and loses one. Won't she light a lamp and
sweep the entire house and search carefully until she finds it? [9]And when she finds it, she will
call in her friends and neighbors and say, 'Rejoice with me because I have found my lost coin.'
[10]In the same way, there is joy in the presence of God's angels when even one sinner repents."

How do these stories help you understand God's love for you? It may seem foolish for the shepherd to leave ninety-nine sheep to go and search for just one. But the shepherd knew that the ninety-nine would be safe in the sheepfold, whereas the lost sheep was in danger. Because each sheep was of high value, the shepherd knew that it was worthwhile to search diligently for the lost one. God's love for each individual is so great that he seeks each one out and rejoices when he or she is "found." Jesus associated with sinners because he wanted to bring the lost sheep—people considered beyond hope—into God's Kingdom. Before you were a believer, God sought you; his love is still seeking those who are yet lost.

AUGUST 15

A Son Who Was Found

LUKE 15:11-32

Jesus told them this story: "A man had two sons. 12The younger son told his father, 'I want
my share of your estate now before you die.' So his father agreed to divide his wealth between
his sons.

13"A few days later this younger son packed all his belongings and moved to a distant land,
and there he wasted all his money in wild living. 14About the time his money ran out, a great
famine swept over the land, and he began to starve. 15He persuaded a local farmer to hire him,
and the man sent him into his fields to feed the pigs. 16The young man became so hungry that
even the pods he was feeding the pigs looked good to him. But no one gave him anything.

17"When he finally came to his senses, he said to himself, 'At home even the hired servants
have food enough to spare, and here I am dying of hunger! 18I will go home to my father and
say, "Father, I have sinned against both heaven and you, 19and I am no longer worthy of being
called your son. Please take me on as a hired servant."'

20"So he returned home to his father. And while he was still a long way off, his father saw
him coming. Filled with love and compassion, he ran to his son, embraced him, and kissed him.
21His son said to him, 'Father, I have sinned against both heaven and you, and I am no longer
worthy of being called your son.'

22"But his father said to the servants, 'Quick! Bring the finest robe in the house and
put it on him. Get a ring for his finger and sandals for his feet. 23And kill the calf we have
been fattening. We must celebrate with a feast, 24for this son of mine was dead and has now
returned to life. He was lost, but now he is found.' So the party began.

25"Meanwhile, the older son was in the fields working. When he returned home, he heard
music and dancing in the house, 26and he asked one of the servants what was going on. 27'Your
brother is back,' he was told, 'and your father has killed the fattened calf. We are celebrating
because of his safe return.'

28"The older brother was angry and wouldn't go in. His father came out and begged him, 29but
he replied, 'All these years I've slaved for you and never once refused to do a single thing you told
me to. And in all that time you never gave me even one young goat for a feast with my friends.
30Yet when this son of yours comes back after squandering your money on prostitutes, you celebrate
by killing the fattened calf!'

31"His father said to him, 'Look, dear son, you have always stayed by me, and everything I
have is yours. 32We had to celebrate this happy day. For your brother was dead and has come
back to life! He was lost, but now he is found!'"

What is important to you? The younger son's attitude was based on a desire to live as he pleased. That is not so different from the desires of most people in our world today. It may take great sorrow and tragedy to cause them to look up to the only one who can help them. Are you trying to live life your way, selfishly pushing aside anything that gets in your way?

The Shrewd Manager

AUGUST 16

LUKE 16:1-13

Jesus told this story to his disciples: "There was a certain rich man who had a manager handling his affairs. One day a report came that the manager was wasting his employer's money.
2So the employer called him in and said, 'What's this I hear about you? Get your report in
order, because you are going to be fired.'

3"The manager thought to himself, 'Now what? My boss has fired me. I don't have the
strength to dig ditches, and I'm too proud to beg. 4Ah, I know how to ensure that I'll have
plenty of friends who will give me a home when I am fired.'

5"So he invited each person who owed money to his employer to come and discuss the
situation. He asked the first one, 'How much do you owe him?' 6The man replied, 'I owe
him 800 gallons of olive oil.' So the manager told him, 'Take the bill and quickly change it
to 400 gallons.'

7" 'And how much do you owe my employer?' he asked the next man. 'I owe him 1,000
bushels of wheat,' was the reply. 'Here,' the manager said, 'take the bill and change it to
800 bushels.'

8"The rich man had to admire the dishonest rascal for being so shrewd. And it is true that
the children of this world are more shrewd in dealing with the world around them than are
the children of the light. 9Here's the lesson: Use your worldly resources to benefit others and
make friends. Then, when your possessions are gone, they will welcome you to an eternal
home.

10"If you are faithful in little things, you will be faithful in large ones. But if you are
dishonest in little things, you won't be honest with greater responsibilities. 11And if you are
untrustworthy about worldly wealth, who will trust you with the true riches of heaven? 12And
if you are not faithful with other people's things, why should you be trusted with things of
your own?

13"No one can serve two masters. For you will hate one and love the other; you will be
devoted to one and despise the other. You cannot serve God and be enslaved to money."

What does it mean to be an honest person? Our integrity is often tested in regard to money matters. God calls us to be honest even in small details we could easily rationalize away. Heaven's riches are far more valuable than earthly wealth. But if we are not trustworthy with our money here (no matter how much or how little we have), we will be unfit to handle the vast riches of God's Kingdom. Don't let your integrity slip in small matters, and it will not be compromised in crucial decisions.

AUGUST 17 The Rich Man and the Beggar

LUKE 16:19-31

19Jesus said, "There was a certain rich man who was splendidly clothed in purple and fine linen and who lived each day in luxury. 20At his gate lay a poor man named Lazarus who was covered with sores. 21As Lazarus lay there longing for scraps from the rich man's table, the dogs would come and lick his open sores.

22"Finally, the poor man died and was carried by the angels to sit beside Abraham at the heavenly banquet. The rich man also died and was buried, 23and he went to the place of the dead. There, in torment, he saw Abraham in the far distance with Lazarus at his side.

24"The rich man shouted, 'Father Abraham, have some pity! Send Lazarus over here to dip the tip of his finger in water and cool my tongue. I am in anguish in these flames.'

25"But Abraham said to him, 'Son, remember that during your lifetime you had everything you wanted, and Lazarus had nothing. So now he is here being comforted, and you are in anguish. 26And besides, there is a great chasm separating us. No one can cross over to you from here, and no one can cross over to us from there.'

27"Then the rich man said, 'Please, Father Abraham, at least send him to my father's home. 28For I have five brothers, and I want him to warn them so they don't end up in this place of torment.'

29"But Abraham said, 'Moses and the prophets have warned them. Your brothers can read what they wrote.'

30"The rich man replied, 'No, Father Abraham! But if someone is sent to them from the dead, then they will repent of their sins and turn to God.'

31"But Abraham said, 'If they won't listen to Moses and the prophets, they won't be persuaded even if someone rises from the dead.'"

Where are the poor people in your community? Whom do you know who is poor? How can you help the poor? The Pharisees considered wealth to be a proof of a person's righteousness. Jesus startled them with this story in which a diseased beggar is rewarded and a rich man is punished. The rich man did not go to hell because of his wealth but because he was selfish, refusing to feed Lazarus, take him in, or care for him. The rich man was hard hearted in spite of his great blessings. The amount of money we have is not as important as the way we use it. What is your attitude toward your money and possessions? Do you hoard them selfishly, or do you use them to help others?

Lazarus Dies

AUGUST 18

JOHN 11:1-26

A man named Lazarus was sick. He lived in Bethany with his sisters, Mary and Martha. [2]This is the Mary who later poured the expensive perfume on the Lord's feet and wiped them with her hair. Her brother, Lazarus, was sick. [3]So the two sisters sent a message to Jesus telling him, "Lord, your dear friend is very sick."

[4]But when Jesus heard about it he said, "Lazarus's sickness will not end in death. No, it happened for the glory of God so that the Son of God will receive glory from this." [5]So although Jesus loved Martha, Mary, and Lazarus, [6]he stayed where he was for the next two days. [7]Finally, he said to his disciples, "Let's go back to Judea."

[8]But his disciples objected. "Rabbi," they said, "only a few days ago the people in Judea were trying to stone you. Are you going there again?"

[9]Jesus replied, "There are twelve hours of daylight every day. During the day people can walk safely. They can see because they have the light of this world. [10]But at night there is danger of stumbling because they have no light." [11]Then he said, "Our friend Lazarus has fallen asleep, but now I will go and wake him up."

[12]The disciples said, "Lord, if he is sleeping, he will soon get better!" [13]They thought Jesus meant Lazarus was simply sleeping, but Jesus meant Lazarus had died.

[14]So he told them plainly, "Lazarus is dead. [15]And for your sakes, I'm glad I wasn't there, for now you will really believe. Come, let's go see him."

[16]Thomas, nicknamed the Twin, said to his fellow disciples, "Let's go, too—and die with Jesus."

[17]When Jesus arrived at Bethany, he was told that Lazarus had already been in his grave for four days. [18]Bethany was only a few miles down the road from Jerusalem, [19]and many of the people had come to console Martha and Mary in their loss. [20]When Martha got word that Jesus was coming, she went to meet him. But Mary stayed in the house. [21]Martha said to Jesus, "Lord, if only you had been here, my brother would not have died. [22]But even now I know that God will give you whatever you ask."

[23]Jesus told her, "Your brother will rise again."

[24]"Yes," Martha said, "he will rise when everyone else rises, at the last day."

[25]Jesus told her, "I am the resurrection and the life. Anyone who believes in me will live, even after dying. [26]Everyone who lives in me and believes in me will never ever die. Do you believe this, Martha?"

In what situations have you been disappointed with God? Jesus loved this family and often stayed with them. He knew their pain but did not respond immediately. His delay had a specific purpose. God's timing, especially his delays, may make us think that he is not answering or that he is not answering in the way we want. But he will meet all our needs according to his perfect schedule and purpose. Patiently await his timing.

AUGUST 19

Jesus Raises Lazarus

JOHN 11:33-53

33When Jesus saw her weeping and saw the other people wailing with her, a deep anger welled
up within him, and he was deeply troubled. 34"Where have you put him?" he asked them.
They told him, "Lord, come and see." 35Then Jesus wept. 36The people who were standing
nearby said, "See how much he loved him!" 37But some said, "This man healed a blind man.
Couldn't he have kept Lazarus from dying?"
38Jesus was still angry as he arrived at the tomb, a cave with a stone rolled across its
entrance. 39"Roll the stone aside," Jesus told them.
But Martha, the dead man's sister, protested, "Lord, he has been dead for four days. The
smell will be terrible."
40Jesus responded, "Didn't I tell you that you would see God's glory if you believe?" 41So
they rolled the stone aside. Then Jesus looked up to heaven and said, "Father, thank you for
hearing me. 42You always hear me, but I said it out loud for the sake of all these people standing here, so that they will believe you sent me." 43Then Jesus shouted, "Lazarus, come out!"
44And the dead man came out, his hands and feet bound in graveclothes, his face wrapped in
a headcloth. Jesus told them, "Unwrap him and let him go!"
45Many of the people who were with Mary believed in Jesus when they saw this happen.
46But some went to the Pharisees and told them what Jesus had done. 47Then the leading
priests and Pharisees called the high council together. "What are we going to do?" they asked
each other. "This man certainly performs many miraculous signs. 48If we allow him to go on
like this, soon everyone will believe in him. Then the Roman army will come and destroy
both our Temple and our nation."
49Caiaphas, who was high priest at that time, said, "You don't know what you're talking
about! 50You don't realize that it's better for you that one man should die for the people than
for the whole nation to be destroyed."
51He did not say this on his own; as high priest at that time he was led to prophesy that
Jesus would die for the entire nation. 52And not only for that nation, but to bring together
and unite all the children of God scattered around the world.
53So from that time on, the Jewish leaders began to plot Jesus' death.

How would you have felt watching Lazarus walk out of the tomb? John stresses that we have a God who cares. This portrait contrasts with the popular concept of God—a God with no emotions and no involvement with humans. Here we see many of Jesus' emotions—compassion, indignation, sorrow, even frustration. He often expressed deep emotion, so we need never be afraid to reveal our true feelings to him. He understands them, for he experienced them. Be honest, and don't try to hide anything from your Savior. He cares.

Jesus and Ten Lepers

AUGUST 20

LUKE 17:1-19

One day Jesus said to his disciples, "There will always be temptations to sin, but what sorrow awaits the person who does the tempting! 2It would be better to be thrown into the sea with a millstone hung around your neck than to cause one of these little ones to fall into sin. 3So watch yourselves!

"If another believer sins, rebuke that person; then if there is repentance, forgive. 4Even if that person wrongs you seven times a day and each time turns again and asks forgiveness, you must forgive."

5The apostles said to the Lord, "Show us how to increase our faith."

6The Lord answered, "If you had faith even as small as a mustard seed, you could say to this mulberry tree, 'May you be uprooted and be planted in the sea,' and it would obey you!

7"When a servant comes in from plowing or taking care of sheep, does his master say, 'Come in and eat with me'? 8No, he says, 'Prepare my meal, put on your apron, and serve me while I eat. Then you can eat later.' 9And does the master thank the servant for doing what he was told to do? Of course not. 10In the same way, when you obey me you should say, 'We are unworthy servants who have simply done our duty.'"

11As Jesus continued on toward Jerusalem, he reached the border between Galilee and Samaria. 12As he entered a village there, ten men with leprosy stood at a distance, 13crying out, "Jesus, Master, have mercy on us!"

14He looked at them and said, "Go show yourselves to the priests." And as they went, they were cleansed of their leprosy.

15One of them, when he saw that he was healed, came back to Jesus, shouting, "Praise God!" 16He fell to the ground at Jesus' feet, thanking him for what he had done. This man was a Samaritan.

17Jesus asked, "Didn't I heal ten men? Where are the other nine? 18Has no one returned to give glory to God except this foreigner?" 19And Jesus said to the man, "Stand up and go. Your faith has healed you."

For what are you thankful to God? Jesus healed all ten lepers, but only one returned to thank him. It is possible to receive God's great gifts with an ungrateful spirit—nine of the ten men did so. Only the thankful man, however, learned that his faith had played a role in his healing; in the same way, only grateful Christians grow in understanding God's grace. God does not demand that we thank him, but he is pleased when we do so. And he uses our responsiveness to teach us more about himself.

AUGUST 21

The Coming Kingdom

LUKE 17:20-37

20 One day the Pharisees asked Jesus, "When will the Kingdom of God come?"
Jesus replied, "The Kingdom of God can't be detected by visible signs. 21 You won't be
able to say, 'Here it is!' or 'It's over there!' For the Kingdom of God is already among you."
22 Then he said to his disciples, "The time is coming when you will long to see the day
when the Son of Man returns, but you won't see it. 23 People will tell you, 'Look, there is the
Son of Man,' or 'Here he is,' but don't go out and follow them. 24 For as the lightning flashes
and lights up the sky from one end to the other, so it will be on the day when the Son of
Man comes. 25 But first the Son of Man must suffer terribly and be rejected by this generation.
26 "When the Son of Man returns, it will be like it was in Noah's day. 27 In those days, the
people enjoyed banquets and parties and weddings right up to the time Noah entered his
boat and the flood came and destroyed them all.
28 "And the world will be as it was in the days of Lot. People went about their daily business—eating and drinking, buying and selling, farming and building— 29 until the morning
Lot left Sodom. Then fire and burning sulfur rained down from heaven and destroyed them
all. 30 Yes, it will be 'business as usual' right up to the day when the Son of Man is revealed.
31 On that day a person out on the deck of a roof must not go down into the house to pack.
A person out in the field must not return home. 32 Remember what happened to Lot's wife!
33 If you cling to your life, you will lose it, and if you let your life go, you will save it. 34 That
night two people will be asleep in one bed; one will be taken, the other left. 35 Two women
will be grinding flour together at the mill; one will be taken, the other left."
37 "Where will this happen, Lord?" the disciples asked.
Jesus replied, "Just as the gathering of vultures shows there is a carcass nearby, so these signs indicate that the end is near."

What difference would it make in your life if Jesus returned today? Life will be going on as usual on the day Christ returns. There will be no warning. Most people will be going about their everyday tasks, indifferent to the things of God. They will be as surprised by Christ's return as the people in Noah's day were by the Flood (Genesis 6–8) or the people in Lot's day by the destruction of Sodom (Genesis 19). We don't know the time of Christ's return, but we do know that he is coming. He may come today, tomorrow, or centuries in the future. Whenever he comes, we must be spiritually ready. Live as if Jesus was returning today.

Persistence in Prayer

AUGUST 22

LUKE 18:1-14

One day Jesus told his disciples a story to show that they should always pray and never give up. 2“There was a judge in a certain city,” he said, “who neither feared God nor cared about people. 3A widow of that city came to him repeatedly, saying, ‘Give me justice in this dispute with my enemy.’ 4The judge ignored her for a while, but finally he said to himself, ‘I don’t fear God or care about people, 5but this woman is driving me crazy. I’m going to see that she gets justice, because she is wearing me out with her constant requests!’ ”

6Then the Lord said, “Learn a lesson from this unjust judge. 7Even he rendered a just decision in the end. So don’t you think God will surely give justice to his chosen people who cry out to him day and night? Will he keep putting them off? 8I tell you, he will grant justice to them quickly! But when the Son of Man returns, how many will he find on the earth who have faith?”

9Then Jesus told this story to some who had great confidence in their own righteousness and scorned everyone else: 10“Two men went to the Temple to pray. One was a Pharisee, and the other was a despised tax collector. 11The Pharisee stood by himself and prayed this prayer: ‘I thank you, God, that I am not like other people—cheaters, sinners, adulterers. I’m certainly not like that tax collector! 12I fast twice a week, and I give you a tenth of my income.’

13“But the tax collector stood at a distance and dared not even lift his eyes to heaven as he prayed. Instead, he beat his chest in sorrow, saying, ‘O God, be merciful to me, for I am a sinner.’ 14I tell you, this sinner, not the Pharisee, returned home justified before God. For those who exalt themselves will be humbled, and those who humble themselves will be exalted.”

What is the tone of your prayers? To repeat our prayers until the answer comes does not mean endless repetition or painfully long prayer sessions. Constant prayer means keeping our requests continually before God as we live for him day by day, always believing he will answer. When we thus live by faith, we are not to give up. God may delay answering, but his delays always have good reasons. We must not confuse them with neglect. As we persist in prayer, we grow in character, faith, and hope.

AUGUST 23

Jesus on Family Matters

MARK 10:1-16

Then Jesus left Capernaum and went down to the region of Judea and into the area east of the
Jordan River. Once again crowds gathered around him, and as usual he was teaching them.
2Some Pharisees came and tried to trap him with this question: "Should a man be allowed
to divorce his wife?"
3Jesus answered them with a question: "What did Moses say in the law about divorce?"
4"Well, he permitted it," they replied. "He said a man can give his wife a written notice
of divorce and send her away."
5But Jesus responded, "He wrote this commandment only as a concession to your hard
hearts. 6But 'God made them male and female' from the beginning of creation. 7'This
explains why a man leaves his father and mother and is joined to his wife, 8and the two are
united into one.' Since they are no longer two but one, 9let no one split apart what God has
joined together."
10Later, when he was alone with his disciples in the house, they brought up the subject again. 11He told them, "Whoever divorces his wife and marries someone else commits
adultery against her. 12And if a woman divorces her husband and marries someone else, she
commits adultery."
13One day some parents brought their children to Jesus so he could touch and bless them.
But the disciples scolded the parents for bothering him.
14When Jesus saw what was happening, he was angry with his disciples. He said to them,
"Let the children come to me. Don't stop them! For the Kingdom of God belongs to those
who are like these children. 15I tell you the truth, anyone who doesn't receive the Kingdom
of God like a child will never enter it." 16Then he took the children in his arms and placed
his hands on their heads and blessed them.

To what extent do you trust God with a childlike faith? Adults are not as trusting as little children. To feel secure, all children need is a loving look and gentle touch from someone who cares. Complete intellectual understanding is not one of their requirements. If they trust us, they believe us. Jesus said that people should believe in him with this kind of childlike faith. We should not have to understand all the mysteries of the universe; it should be enough to know that God loves us and provides forgiveness for our sin. This doesn't mean that we should be childish or immature, but we should trust God with a childlike simplicity and receptivity.

Jesus and the Rich Man

AUGUST 24

MARK 10:17-31

17 As Jesus was starting out on his way to Jerusalem, a man came running up to him, knelt
down, and asked, "Good Teacher, what must I do to inherit eternal life?"
18 "Why do you call me good?" Jesus asked. "Only God is truly good. 19 But to answer
your question, you know the commandments: 'You must not murder. You must not commit
adultery. You must not steal. You must not testify falsely. You must not cheat anyone. Honor
your father and mother.'"
20 "Teacher," the man replied, "I've obeyed all these commandments since I was young."
21 Looking at the man, Jesus felt genuine love for him. "There is still one thing you haven't
done," he told him. "Go and sell all your possessions and give the money to the poor, and
you will have treasure in heaven. Then come, follow me."
22 At this the man's face fell, and he went away sad, for he had many possessions.
23 Jesus looked around and said to his disciples, "How hard it is for the rich to enter the
Kingdom of God!" 24 This amazed them. But Jesus said again, "Dear children, it is very hard
to enter the Kingdom of God. 25 In fact, it is easier for a camel to go through the eye of a
needle than for a rich person to enter the Kingdom of God!"
26 The disciples were astounded. "Then who in the world can be saved?" they asked.
27 Jesus looked at them intently and said, "Humanly speaking, it is impossible. But not
with God. Everything is possible with God."
28 Then Peter began to speak up. "We've given up everything to follow you," he said.
29 "Yes," Jesus replied, "and I assure you that everyone who has given up house or brothers
or sisters or mother or father or children or property, for my sake and for the Good News,
30 will receive now in return a hundred times as many houses, brothers, sisters, mothers,
children, and property—along with persecution. And in the world to come that person will
have eternal life. 31 But many who are the greatest now will be least important then, and those
who seem least important now will be the greatest then."

What is the most difficult thing Jesus could ask you to give up? This young man said he'd never once broken any of God's laws, but Jesus broke through his pride with a challenge that brought out his true motives: "Sell all your possessions and give the money to the poor." Love of money was the barrier that could keep this man out of the Kingdom. Ironically, the man's attitude made him unable to keep the first commandment, to let nothing be more important than God (Exodus 20:3). He could not turn his whole heart and life over to God. The man came to Jesus wondering what he could do; he left knowing what he was unable to do. What barriers are keeping you from turning your life over to Christ?

AUGUST 25

A Parable about Equal Pay

MATTHEW 20:1-19

"For the Kingdom of Heaven is like the landowner who went out early one morning to hire workers for his vineyard. 2He agreed to pay the normal daily wage and sent them out to work.

3"At nine o'clock in the morning he was passing through the marketplace and saw some people standing around doing nothing. 4So he hired them, telling them he would pay them whatever was right at the end of the day. 5So they went to work in the vineyard. At noon and again at three o'clock he did the same thing.

6"At five o'clock that afternoon he was in town again and saw some more people standing around. He asked them, 'Why haven't you been working today?'

7"They replied, 'Because no one hired us.'

"The landowner told them, 'Then go out and join the others in my vineyard.'

8"That evening he told the foreman to call the workers in and pay them, beginning with the last workers first. 9When those hired at five o'clock were paid, each received a full day's wage. 10When those hired first came to get their pay, they assumed they would receive more. But they, too, were paid a day's wage. 11When they received their pay, they protested to the owner, 12'Those people worked only one hour, and yet you've paid them just as much as you paid us who worked all day in the scorching heat.'

13"He answered one of them, 'Friend, I haven't been unfair! Didn't you agree to work all day for the usual wage? 14Take your money and go. I wanted to pay this last worker the same as you. 15Is it against the law for me to do what I want with my money? Should you be jealous because I am kind to others?'

16"So those who are last now will be first then, and those who are first will be last."

17As Jesus was going up to Jerusalem, he took the twelve disciples aside privately and told them what was going to happen to him. 18"Listen," he said, "we're going up to Jerusalem, where the Son of Man will be betrayed to the leading priests and the teachers of religious law. They will sentence him to die. 19Then they will hand him over to the Romans to be mocked, flogged with a whip, and crucified. But on the third day he will be raised from the dead."

How often are you jealous of what God has given to someone else? This parable is a strong teaching about grace, which is God's generosity. We shouldn't begrudge those who turn to God in the last moments of life, because in reality, no one deserves eternal life. Many people we don't expect to see in the Kingdom may be there. The person who accepts Christ at the end of life will be there as well as the person who has believed and served God for many years. Do you resent God's gracious acceptance of the despised, the outcast, and the sinners who have turned to him for forgiveness? Are you ever jealous of what God has given to another person? Focus on God's gracious benefits to you, and be thankful for what you have.

Jesus on Serving Others

AUGUST 26

MARK 10:35-52

[35]Then James and John, the sons of Zebedee, came over and spoke to him. "Teacher," they said, "we want you to do us a favor."

[36]"What is your request?" he asked.

[37]They replied, "When you sit on your glorious throne, we want to sit in places of honor next to you, one on your right and the other on your left."

[38]But Jesus said to them, "You don't know what you are asking! Are you able to drink from the bitter cup of suffering I am about to drink? Are you able to be baptized with the baptism of suffering I must be baptized with?"

[39]"Oh yes," they replied, "we are able!"

Then Jesus told them, "You will indeed drink from my bitter cup and be baptized with
my baptism of suffering. [40]But I have no right to say who will sit on my right or my left. God
has prepared those places for the ones he has chosen."

[41]When the ten other disciples heard what James and John had asked, they were indignant. [42]So Jesus called them together and said, "You know that the rulers in this world lord
it over their people, and officials flaunt their authority over those under them. [43]But among
you it will be different. Whoever wants to be a leader among you must be your servant, [44]and
whoever wants to be first among you must be the slave of everyone else. [45]For even the Son
of Man came not to be served but to serve others and to give his life as a ransom for many."

[46]Then they reached Jericho, and as Jesus and his disciples left town, a large crowd followed him. A blind beggar named Bartimaeus (son of Timaeus) was sitting beside the road.
[47]When Bartimaeus heard that Jesus of Nazareth was nearby, he began to shout, "Jesus, Son
of David, have mercy on me!"

[48]"Be quiet!" many of the people yelled at him.

But he only shouted louder, "Son of David, have mercy on me!"

[49]When Jesus heard him, he stopped and said, "Tell him to come here."

So they called the blind man. "Cheer up," they said. "Come on, he's calling you!"
[50]Bartimaeus threw aside his coat, jumped up, and came to Jesus.

[51]"What do you want me to do for you?" Jesus asked.

"My Rabbi," the blind man said, "I want to see!"

[52]And Jesus said to him, "Go, for your faith has healed you." Instantly the man could see, and he followed Jesus down the road.

In what ways are you learning to be a servant? James and John said they were willing to face any trial for Christ. Both did suffer: James died as a martyr (Acts 12:2), and John was forced to live in exile (Revelation 1:9). It is easy to say we will endure anything for Christ, and yet most of us complain over the most minor problems. If we say we are willing to suffer on a large scale for Christ, we must also be willing to suffer the irritations that may come with serving others.

AUGUST 27

Jesus and Zacchaeus

LUKE 19:1-10

Jesus entered Jericho and made his way through the town. 2There was a man there named
Zacchaeus. He was the chief tax collector in the region, and he had become very rich. 3He
tried to get a look at Jesus, but he was too short to see over the crowd. 4So he ran ahead and
climbed a sycamore-fig tree beside the road, for Jesus was going to pass that way.

5When Jesus came by, he looked up at Zacchaeus and called him by name. "Zacchaeus!"
he said. "Quick, come down! I must be a guest in your home today."

6Zacchaeus quickly climbed down and took Jesus to his house in great excitement and
joy. 7But the people were displeased. "He has gone to be the guest of a notorious sinner,"
they grumbled.

8Meanwhile, Zacchaeus stood before the Lord and said, "I will give half my wealth to
the poor, Lord, and if I have cheated people on their taxes, I will give them back four times
as much!"

9Jesus responded, "Salvation has come to this home today, for this man has shown himself
to be a true son of Abraham. 10For the Son of Man came to seek and save those who are lost."

Has your faith resulted in action? What changes do you need to make? Judging from the crowd's reaction to him, Zacchaeus must have been a very crooked tax collector. But after he met Jesus, he realized that his life needed straightening out. By giving to the poor and making restitution—with generous interest—to those he had cheated, Zacchaeus demonstrated inward change by outward action. It is not enough to follow Jesus in your head or heart alone. You must show your faith by changed behavior.

A Woman Anoints Jesus

AUGUST 28

JOHN 12:1-11

Six days before the Passover celebration began, Jesus arrived in Bethany, the home of Lazarus—the man he had raised from the dead. [2]A dinner was prepared in Jesus' honor. Martha served, and Lazarus was among those who ate with him. [3]Then Mary took a twelve-ounce jar of expensive perfume made from essence of nard, and she anointed Jesus' feet with it, wiping his feet with her hair. The house was filled with the fragrance.

[4]But Judas Iscariot, the disciple who would soon betray him, said, [5]"That perfume was worth a year's wages. It should have been sold and the money given to the poor." [6]Not that he cared for the poor—he was a thief, and since he was in charge of the disciples' money, he often stole some for himself.

[7]Jesus replied, "Leave her alone. She did this in preparation for my burial. [8]You will always have the poor among you, but you will not always have me."

[9]When all the people heard of Jesus' arrival, they flocked to see him and also to see Lazarus, the man Jesus had raised from the dead. [10]Then the leading priests decided to kill Lazarus, too, [11]for it was because of him that many of the people had deserted them and believed in Jesus.

What have you ever "wasted" as an expression of love for Christ? This act and Jesus' response to it do not teach us to ignore the poor so we can spend money extravagantly for Christ. This was a unique act for a specific occasion—an anointing that anticipated Jesus' burial and a public declaration of faith in him as Messiah. Jesus' words should have taught Judas a valuable lesson about the worth of money. Unfortunately, Judas did not take heed; soon he would sell his Master's life for thirty pieces of silver.

AUGUST 29 Jesus Rides into Jerusalem

MATTHEW 21:1-15

As Jesus and the disciples approached Jerusalem, they came to the town of Bethphage on the Mount of Olives. Jesus sent two of them on ahead. [2]"Go into the village over there," he said. "As soon as you enter it, you will see a donkey tied there, with its colt beside it. Untie them and bring them to me. [3]If anyone asks what you are doing, just say, 'The Lord needs them,' and he will immediately let you take them."

[4]This took place to fulfill the prophecy that said,

[5]"Tell the people of Jerusalem,
'Look, your King is coming to you.
He is humble, riding on a donkey—
riding on a donkey's colt.'"

[6]The two disciples did as Jesus commanded. [7]They brought the donkey and the colt to him and threw their garments over the colt, and he sat on it.

[8]Most of the crowd spread their garments on the road ahead of him, and others cut branches from the trees and spread them on the road. [9]Jesus was in the center of the procession, and the people all around him were shouting,

"Praise God for the Son of David!
Blessings on the one who comes in the name of the LORD!
Praise God in highest heaven!"

[10]The entire city of Jerusalem was in an uproar as he entered. "Who is this?" they asked.

[11]And the crowds replied, "It's Jesus, the prophet from Nazareth in Galilee."

[12]Jesus entered the Temple and began to drive out all the people buying and selling animals for sacrifice. He knocked over the tables of the money changers and the chairs of those selling doves. [13]He said to them, "The Scriptures declare, 'My Temple will be called a house of prayer,' but you have turned it into a den of thieves!"

[14]The blind and the lame came to him in the Temple, and he healed them. [15]The leading priests and the teachers of religious law saw these wonderful miracles and heard even the children in the Temple shouting, "Praise God for the Son of David."

If you were part of the crowd that day, what would have been your most lasting memory? This passage is one of the few places where the Gospels record that Jesus' glory is recognized on earth. Jesus boldly declared himself King, and the crowd gladly joined him. But these same people would bow to political pressure and desert him in just a few days. Today we celebrate this event on Palm Sunday. That day should remind us to guard against superficial acclaim for Christ. Think about this next time you celebrate Palm Sunday.

Jesus Explains Why He Must Die

AUGUST 30

JOHN 12:20-36

[20]Some Greeks who had come to Jerusalem for the Passover celebration [21]paid a visit to Philip,
who was from Bethsaida in Galilee. They said, "Sir, we want to meet Jesus." [22]Philip told
Andrew about it, and they went together to ask Jesus.

[23]Jesus replied, "Now the time has come for the Son of Man to enter into his glory. [24]I
tell you the truth, unless a kernel of wheat is planted in the soil and dies, it remains alone.
But its death will produce many new kernels—a plentiful harvest of new lives. [25]Those who
love their life in this world will lose it. Those who care nothing for their life in this world will
keep it for eternity. [26]Anyone who wants to serve me must follow me, because my servants
must be where I am. And the Father will honor anyone who serves me.

[27]"Now my soul is deeply troubled. Should I pray, 'Father, save me from this hour'? But
this is the very reason I came! [28]Father, bring glory to your name."

Then a voice spoke from heaven, saying, "I have already brought glory to my name, and
I will do so again." [29]When the crowd heard the voice, some thought it was thunder, while
others declared an angel had spoken to him.

[30]Then Jesus told them, "The voice was for your benefit, not mine. [31]The time for judging
this world has come, when Satan, the ruler of this world, will be cast out. [32]And when I am
lifted up from the earth, I will draw everyone to myself." [33]He said this to indicate how he
was going to die.

[34]The crowd responded, "We understood from Scripture that the Messiah would live
forever. How can you say the Son of Man will die? Just who is this Son of Man, anyway?"

[35]Jesus replied, "My light will shine for you just a little longer. Walk in the light while you
can, so the darkness will not overtake you. Those who walk in the darkness cannot see where
they are going. [36]Put your trust in the light while there is still time; then you will become
children of the light."

After saying these things, Jesus went away and was hidden from them.

How would you explain to someone why Jesus had to die on the cross? The crowd could not believe what Jesus was saying about the Messiah. They were waving palm branches for a victorious Messiah who would set up a political, earthly kingdom that would never end. From their reading of certain Scriptures, they thought the Messiah would never die (Psalms 89:35-36; 110:4; Isaiah 9:7). Other passages, however, showed that he would (Isaiah 53:5-9). Jesus' words did not mesh with their concept of the Messiah. First he had to suffer and die—then he would one day set up his eternal Kingdom. What kind of Messiah, or Savior, are you seeking? Beware of trying to force Jesus into your own mold—he won't fit.

AUGUST 31

Jesus and His Message

JOHN 12:37-50

37 But despite all the miraculous signs Jesus had done, most of the people still did not believe in him. 38 This is exactly what Isaiah the prophet had predicted:

> "Lord, who has believed our message?
> To whom has the Lord revealed his powerful arm?"

39 But the people couldn't believe, for as Isaiah also said,

> 40 "The Lord has blinded their eyes
> and hardened their hearts—
> so that their eyes cannot see,
> and their hearts cannot understand,
> and they cannot turn to me
> and have me heal them."

41 Isaiah was referring to Jesus when he said this, because he saw the future and spoke of the Messiah's glory. 42 Many people did believe in him, however, including some of the Jewish leaders. But they wouldn't admit it for fear that the Pharisees would expel them from the synagogue. 43 For they loved human praise more than the praise of God.

44 Jesus shouted to the crowds, "If you trust me, you are trusting not only me, but also God who sent me. 45 For when you see me, you are seeing the one who sent me. 46 I have come as a light to shine in this dark world, so that all who put their trust in me will no longer remain in the dark. 47 I will not judge those who hear me but don't obey me, for I have come to save the world and not to judge it. 48 But all who reject me and my message will be judged on the day of judgment by the truth I have spoken. 49 I don't speak on my own authority. The Father who sent me has commanded me what to say and how to say it. 50 And I know his commands lead to eternal life; so I say whatever the Father tells me to say."

What kinds of pressures make you hesitant to tell others about your belief in Christ? Jesus had performed many miracles, but most people still didn't believe in him. Likewise, many today won't believe, despite all God does. Don't be discouraged if your witness for Christ doesn't turn as many to him as you'd like. Your job is to continue as a faithful witness. You are responsible not for the decisions of others but simply to reach out to them.

September

SEPTEMBER 1

Bold Prayers

MARK 11:20-33

[20]The next morning as they passed by the fig tree he had cursed, the disciples noticed it
had withered from the roots up. [21]Peter remembered what Jesus had said to the tree on the
previous day and exclaimed, "Look, Rabbi! The fig tree you cursed has withered and died!"
[22]Then Jesus said to the disciples, "Have faith in God. [23]I tell you the truth, you can say
to this mountain, 'May you be lifted up and thrown into the sea,' and it will happen. But you
must really believe it will happen and have no doubt in your heart. [24]I tell you, you can pray
for anything, and if you believe that you've received it, it will be yours. [25]But when you are
praying, first forgive anyone you are holding a grudge against, so that your Father in heaven
will forgive your sins, too."
[27]Again they entered Jerusalem. As Jesus was walking through the Temple area, the leading
priests, the teachers of religious law, and the elders came up to him. [28]They demanded, "By
what authority are you doing all these things? Who gave you the right to do them?"
[29]"I'll tell you by what authority I do these things if you answer one question," Jesus
replied. [30]"Did John's authority to baptize come from heaven, or was it merely human?
Answer me!"
[31]They talked it over among themselves. "If we say it was from heaven, he will ask why
we didn't believe John. [32]But do we dare say it was merely human?" For they were afraid of
what the people would do, because everyone believed that John was a prophet. [33]So they
finally replied, "We don't know."

And Jesus responded, "Then I won't tell you by what authority I do these things."

How bold is your prayer life? Jesus, our example for prayer, once prayed, "Everything is possible for you. . . . Yet I want your will to be done, not mine" (Mark 14:36). Often when we pray, we are motivated by our own interests and desires. We like to hear that we can have anything. But Jesus prayed with God's interests in mind. When we pray, we are to express our desires, but we should want his will above ours. Check yourself to see if your prayers are focusing on your interests or on God's.

Two Parables

MATTHEW 21:28-43

SEPTEMBER 2

28“But what do you think about this? A man with two sons told the older boy, ‘Son, go out
and work in the vineyard today.’ 29The son answered, ‘No, I won’t go,’ but later he changed
his mind and went anyway. 30Then the father told the other son, ‘You go,’ and he said, ‘Yes,
sir, I will.’ But he didn’t go.

31“Which of the two obeyed his father?”

They replied, “The first.”

Then Jesus explained his meaning: “I tell you the truth, corrupt tax collectors and prostitutes will get into the Kingdom of God before you do. 32For John the Baptist came and
showed you the right way to live, but you didn’t believe him, while tax collectors and prostitutes did. And even when you saw this happening, you refused to believe him and repent
of your sins.

33“Now listen to another story. A certain landowner planted a vineyard, built a wall
around it, dug a pit for pressing out the grape juice, and built a lookout tower. Then he
leased the vineyard to tenant farmers and moved to another country. 34At the time of the
grape harvest, he sent his servants to collect his share of the crop. 35But the farmers grabbed
his servants, beat one, killed one, and stoned another. 36So the landowner sent a larger group
of his servants to collect for him, but the results were the same.

37“Finally, the owner sent his son, thinking, ‘Surely they will respect my son.’

38“But when the tenant farmers saw his son coming, they said to one another, ‘Here comes
the heir to this estate. Come on, let’s kill him and get the estate for ourselves!’ 39So they grabbed
him, dragged him out of the vineyard, and murdered him.

40“When the owner of the vineyard returns,” Jesus asked, “what do you think he will do
to those farmers?”

41The religious leaders replied, “He will put the wicked men to a horrible death and lease
the vineyard to others who will give him his share of the crop after each harvest.”

42Then Jesus asked them, “Didn’t you ever read this in the Scriptures?

‘The stone that the builders rejected
    has now become the cornerstone.
This is the LORD’s doing,
    and it is wonderful to see.’

43I tell you, the Kingdom of God will be taken away from you and given to a nation that will
produce the proper fruit.”

Which son do you resemble most? The son who said he would obey and then didn’t represented the nation of Israel in Jesus’ day. They said they wanted to do God’s will, but they constantly disobeyed. It is dangerous to pretend to obey God when our hearts are far from him, because God knows the intentions of our hearts. Our actions must match our words.

SEPTEMBER 3 — The Wedding Banquet

MATTHEW 22:1-14

Jesus also told them other parables. He said, 2"The Kingdom of Heaven can be illustrated by
the story of a king who prepared a great wedding feast for his son. 3When the banquet was
ready, he sent his servants to notify those who were invited. But they all refused to come!
4"So he sent other servants to tell them, 'The feast has been prepared. The bulls and
fattened cattle have been killed, and everything is ready. Come to the banquet!' 5But the
guests he had invited ignored them and went their own way, one to his farm, another to his
business. 6Others seized his messengers and insulted them and killed them.
7"The king was furious, and he sent out his army to destroy the murderers and burn
their town. 8And he said to his servants, 'The wedding feast is ready, and the guests I invited
aren't worthy of the honor. 9Now go out to the street corners and invite everyone you see.'
10So the servants brought in everyone they could find, good and bad alike, and the banquet
hall was filled with guests.
11"But when the king came in to meet the guests, he noticed a man who wasn't wearing the
proper clothes for a wedding. 12'Friend,' he asked, 'how is it that you are here without wedding
clothes?' But the man had no reply. 13Then the king said to his aides, 'Bind his hands and feet
and throw him into the outer darkness, where there will be weeping and gnashing of teeth.'
14"For many are called, but few are chosen."

At what point in your life did you realize that you were invited to God's table? How did you respond? In this culture, two invitations were expected when banquets were given. The first invitation asked the guests to attend; the second announced that all was ready. Here the king (God) invited his guests three times—and each time they refused to come. God wants us to join him at his banquet that will last for eternity. That's why he sends us invitations again and again. Have you accepted his invitation?

Jesus Answers Questions

SEPTEMBER 4

LUKE 20:20-40

20Watching for their opportunity, the leaders sent spies pretending to be honest men. They
tried to get Jesus to say something that could be reported to the Roman governor so he would
arrest Jesus. 21"Teacher," they said, "we know that you speak and teach what is right and are
not influenced by what others think. You teach the way of God truthfully. 22Now tell us—is
it right for us to pay taxes to Caesar or not?"

23He saw through their trickery and said, 24"Show me a Roman coin. Whose picture and
title are stamped on it?"

"Caesar's," they replied.

25"Well then," he said, "give to Caesar what belongs to Caesar, and give to God what
belongs to God."

26So they failed to trap him by what he said in front of the people. Instead, they were
amazed by his answer, and they became silent.

27Then Jesus was approached by some Sadducees—religious leaders who say there is no
resurrection from the dead. 28They posed this question: "Teacher, Moses gave us a law that
if a man dies, leaving a wife but no children, his brother should marry the widow and have
a child who will carry on the brother's name. 29Well, suppose there were seven brothers. The
oldest one married and then died without children. 30So the second brother married the
widow, but he also died. 31Then the third brother married her. This continued with all seven
of them, who died without children. 32Finally, the woman also died. 33So tell us, whose wife
will she be in the resurrection? For all seven were married to her!"

34Jesus replied, "Marriage is for people here on earth. 35But in the age to come, those
worthy of being raised from the dead will neither marry nor be given in marriage. 36And they
will never die again. In this respect they will be like angels. They are children of God and
children of the resurrection.

37"But now, as to whether the dead will be raised—even Moses proved this when he wrote
about the burning bush. Long after Abraham, Isaac, and Jacob had died, he referred to the
Lord as 'the God of Abraham, the God of Isaac, and the God of Jacob.' 38So he is the God of
the living, not the dead, for they are all alive to him."

39"Well said, Teacher!" remarked some of the teachers of religious law who were standing
there. 40And then no one dared to ask him any more questions.

How do you answer tough questions? The Sadducees came to Jesus with a trick question. Not believing in the Resurrection, they wanted Jesus to say something they could refute. Jesus answered the question and then went beyond it to the real issue. When people ask you tough questions, such as "How can a loving God allow people to suffer?" you should follow Jesus' example. Answer the question to the best of your ability, then look for the real issue—hurt over a personal tragedy, for example. Often the spoken question is only a test, not of your ability to answer hard questions, but of your willingness to listen and care.

SEPTEMBER 5 — Questions Given and Taken

MARK 12:28-37

[28]One of the teachers of religious law was standing there listening to the debate. He realized that Jesus had answered well, so he asked, "Of all the commandments, which is the most important?"

[29]Jesus replied, "The most important commandment is this: 'Listen, O Israel! The LORD our God is the one and only LORD. [30]And you must love the LORD your God with all your heart, all your soul, all your mind, and all your strength.' [31]The second is equally important: 'Love your neighbor as yourself.' No other commandment is greater than these."

[32]The teacher of religious law replied, "Well said, Teacher. You have spoken the truth by saying that there is only one God and no other. [33]And I know it is important to love him with all my heart and all my understanding and all my strength, and to love my neighbor as myself. This is more important than to offer all of the burnt offerings and sacrifices required in the law."

[34]Realizing how much the man understood, Jesus said to him, "You are not far from the Kingdom of God." And after that, no one dared to ask him any more questions.

[35]Later, as Jesus was teaching the people in the Temple, he asked, "Why do the teachers of religious law claim that the Messiah is the son of David? [36]For David himself, speaking under the inspiration of the Holy Spirit, said,

'The LORD said to my Lord,
Sit in the place of honor at my right hand
until I humble your enemies beneath your feet.'

[37]Since David himself called the Messiah 'my Lord,' how can the Messiah be his son?" The large crowd listened to him with great delight.

Whom do you know who is not far from the Kingdom of God? God's laws are not burdensome in number or detail. They can be reduced to two simple rules for life: love God, and love others. These commands are from the Old Testament (Leviticus 19:18; Deuteronomy 6:5). When you love God completely and care for others as you care for yourself, then you have fulfilled the intent of the Ten Commandments and the other Old Testament laws. According to Jesus, these two rules summarize all of God's laws. Let them rule your thoughts, decisions, and actions. When you are uncertain about what to do, ask yourself which course of action best demonstrates love for God and love for others.

Warning and Grieving

SEPTEMBER 6

MATTHEW 23:1-28

Then Jesus said to the crowds and to his disciples, 2“The teachers of religious law and the
Pharisees are the official interpreters of the law of Moses. 3So practice and obey whatever
they tell you, but don’t follow their example. For they don’t practice what they teach. 4They
crush people with unbearable religious demands and never lift a finger to ease the burden.

5“Everything they do is for show. . . .

16“Blind guides! What sorrow awaits you! For you say that it means nothing to swear
‘by God’s Temple,’ but that it is binding to swear ‘by the gold in the Temple.’ 17Blind fools!
Which is more important—the gold or the Temple that makes the gold sacred? 18And you say
that to swear ‘by the altar’ is not binding, but to swear ‘by the gifts on the altar’ is binding.
19How blind! For which is more important—the gift on the altar or the altar that makes the
gift sacred? 20When you swear ‘by the altar,’ you are swearing by it and by everything on it.
21And when you swear ‘by the Temple,’ you are swearing by it and by God, who lives in it.
22And when you swear ‘by heaven,’ you are swearing by the throne of God and by God, who
sits on the throne.

23“What sorrow awaits you teachers of religious law and you Pharisees. Hypocrites! For
you are careful to tithe even the tiniest income from your herb gardens, but you ignore the
more important aspects of the law—justice, mercy, and faith. You should tithe, yes, but do
not neglect the more important things. 24Blind guides! You strain your water so you won’t
accidentally swallow a gnat, but you swallow a camel!

25“What sorrow awaits you teachers of religious law and you Pharisees. Hypocrites! For
you are so careful to clean the outside of the cup and the dish, but inside you are filthy—full
of greed and self-indulgence! 26You blind Pharisee! First wash the inside of the cup and the
dish, and then the outside will become clean, too.

27“What sorrow awaits you teachers of religious law and you Pharisees. Hypocrites! For
you are like whitewashed tombs—beautiful on the outside but filled on the inside with dead
people’s bones and all sorts of impurity. 28Outwardly you look like righteous people, but
inwardly your hearts are filled with hypocrisy and lawlessness.”

Which of these warnings most directly relates to your life? Jesus condemned the Pharisees and religious leaders for appearing saintly and holy but remaining full of corruption and greed on the inside. Living out our Christianity merely as a show for others is like washing a cup on the outside only. When we are clean on the inside, our cleanliness on the outside won’t be phony.

SEPTEMBER 7

Jesus Talks about the Future

LUKE 21:5-24

5Some of his disciples began talking about the majestic stonework of the Temple and the
memorial decorations on the walls. But Jesus said, 6"The time is coming when all these things
will be completely demolished. Not one stone will be left on top of another!"
7"Teacher," they asked, "when will all this happen? What sign will show us that these
things are about to take place?"
8He replied, "Don't let anyone mislead you, for many will come in my name, claiming,
'I am the Messiah,' and saying, 'The time has come!' But don't believe them. 9And when you
hear of wars and insurrections, don't panic. Yes, these things must take place first, but the
end won't follow immediately." 10Then he added, "Nation will go to war against nation, and
kingdom against kingdom. 11There will be great earthquakes, and there will be famines and
plagues in many lands, and there will be terrifying things and great miraculous signs from
heaven.
12"But before all this occurs, there will be a time of great persecution. You will be dragged
into synagogues and prisons, and you will stand trial before kings and governors because you
are my followers. 13But this will be your opportunity to tell them about me. 14So don't worry
in advance about how to answer the charges against you, 15for I will give you the right words
and such wisdom that none of your opponents will be able to reply or refute you! 16Even those
closest to you—your parents, brothers, relatives, and friends—will betray you. They will even
kill some of you. 17And everyone will hate you because you are my followers. 18But not a hair
of your head will perish! 19By standing firm, you will win your souls.
20"And when you see Jerusalem surrounded by armies, then you will know that the time
of its destruction has arrived. 21Then those in Judea must flee to the hills. Those in Jerusalem
must get out, and those out in the country should not return to the city. 22For those will be
days of God's vengeance, and the prophetic words of the Scriptures will be fulfilled. 23How
terrible it will be for pregnant women and for nursing mothers in those days. For there will
be disaster in the land and great anger against this people. 24They will be killed by the sword
or sent away as captives to all the nations of the world. And Jerusalem will be trampled down
by the Gentiles until the period of the Gentiles comes to an end."

What do you believe about the future? The picture of natural disasters and coming persecutions is gloomy, but ultimately it is a cause not for worry but for great joy. As believers see these events happening, we will know that the return of our Messiah is near, and we can look forward to his reign of justice and peace. Rather than being terrified by what is happening in our world, we should confidently await Christ's return to bring justice and restoration to his people.

Jesus on Being Prepared

SEPTEMBER 8

LUKE 21:25-38

25 “And there will be strange signs in the sun, moon, and stars. And here on earth the nations
will be in turmoil, perplexed by the roaring seas and strange tides. 26 People will be terrified
at what they see coming upon the earth, for the powers in the heavens will be shaken. 27 Then
everyone will see the Son of Man coming on a cloud with power and great glory. 28 So when
all these things begin to happen, stand and look up, for your salvation is near!”

29 Then he gave them this illustration: “Notice the fig tree, or any other tree. 30 When the
leaves come out, you know without being told that summer is near. 31 In the same way, when
you see all these things taking place, you can know that the Kingdom of God is near. 32 I tell
you the truth, this generation will not pass from the scene until all these things have taken
place. 33 Heaven and earth will disappear, but my words will never disappear.

34 “Watch out! Don’t let your hearts be dulled by carousing and drunkenness, and by the
worries of this life. Don’t let that day catch you unaware, 35 like a trap. For that day will come
upon everyone living on the earth. 36 Keep alert at all times. And pray that you might be strong
enough to escape these coming horrors and stand before the Son of Man.”

37 Every day Jesus went to the Temple to teach, and each evening he returned to spend
the night on the Mount of Olives. 38 The crowds gathered at the Temple early each morning
to hear him.

What does your schedule today say about your watchfulness? Jesus told the disciples to keep a constant watch for his return. Although nearly two thousand years have passed since he spoke these words, their truth remains: Christ is coming again, and we need to watch and be spiritually fit. This means working faithfully at the tasks God has given us. Don’t let your mind and spirit be dulled by careless living, drinking, or the foolish pursuit of pleasure. Don’t let life’s anxieties overburden you. Instead, be ready to move at God’s command.

SEPTEMBER 9

Fruit for the Kingdom

MATTHEW 25:14-30

14“Again, the Kingdom of Heaven can be illustrated by the story of a man going on a long
trip. He called together his servants and entrusted his money to them while he was gone.
15He gave five bags of silver to one, two bags of silver to another, and one bag of silver to the
last—dividing it in proportion to their abilities. He then left on his trip.

16“The servant who received the five bags of silver began to invest the money and earned
five more. 17The servant with two bags of silver also went to work and earned two more.
18But the servant who received the one bag of silver dug a hole in the ground and hid the
master’s money.

19“After a long time their master returned from his trip and called them to give an account
of how they had used his money. 20The servant to whom he had entrusted the five bags of
silver came forward with five more and said, ‘Master, you gave me five bags of silver to invest,
and I have earned five more.’

21“The master was full of praise. ‘Well done, my good and faithful servant. You have been
faithful in handling this small amount, so now I will give you many more responsibilities.
Let’s celebrate together!’

22“The servant who had received the two bags of silver came forward and said, ‘Master,
you gave me two bags of silver to invest, and I have earned two more.’

23“The master said, ‘Well done, my good and faithful servant. You have been faithful in
handling this small amount, so now I will give you many more responsibilities. Let’s celebrate
together!’

24“Then the servant with the one bag of silver came and said, ‘Master, I knew you were
a harsh man, harvesting crops you didn’t plant and gathering crops you didn’t cultivate. 25I
was afraid I would lose your money, so I hid it in the earth. Look, here is your money back.’

26“But the master replied, ‘You wicked and lazy servant! If you knew I harvested crops I
didn’t plant and gathered crops I didn’t cultivate, 27why didn’t you deposit my money in the
bank? At least I could have gotten some interest on it.’

28“Then he ordered, ‘Take the money from this servant, and give it to the one with the
ten bags of silver. 29To those who use well what they are given, even more will be given, and
they will have an abundance. But from those who do nothing, even what little they have
will be taken away. 30Now throw this useless servant into outer darkness, where there will be
weeping and gnashing of teeth.’”

With which of the servants in this story do you identify most? This parable describes the consequences of different attitudes toward Christ’s return. The person who diligently prepares for it by investing his or her time and talent to serve God will be rewarded. The person who has no heart for the work of the Kingdom will be punished. God rewards faithfulness. Those who bear no fruit for God’s Kingdom cannot expect to be treated the same as those who are faithful.

Final Judgment

SEPTEMBER 10

MATTHEW 25:31-46

31“But when the Son of Man comes in his glory, and all the angels with him, then he will sit upon his glorious throne. 32All the nations will be gathered in his presence, and he will separate the people as a shepherd separates the sheep from the goats. 33He will place the sheep at his right hand and the goats at his left.

34“Then the King will say to those on his right, ‘Come, you who are blessed by my Father, inherit the Kingdom prepared for you from the creation of the world. 35For I was hungry, and you fed me. I was thirsty, and you gave me a drink. I was a stranger, and you invited me into your home. 36I was naked, and you gave me clothing. I was sick, and you cared for me. I was in prison, and you visited me.’

37“Then these righteous ones will reply, ‘Lord, when did we ever see you hungry and feed you? Or thirsty and give you something to drink? 38Or a stranger and show you hospitality? Or naked and give you clothing? 39When did we ever see you sick or in prison and visit you?’

40“And the King will say, ‘I tell you the truth, when you did it to one of the least of these my brothers and sisters, you were doing it to me!’

41“Then the King will turn to those on the left and say, ‘Away with you, you cursed ones, into the eternal fire prepared for the devil and his demons. 42For I was hungry, and you didn’t feed me. I was thirsty, and you didn’t give me a drink. 43I was a stranger, and you didn’t invite me into your home. I was naked, and you didn’t give me clothing. I was sick and in prison, and you didn’t visit me.’

44“Then they will reply, ‘Lord, when did we ever see you hungry or thirsty or a stranger or naked or sick or in prison, and not help you?’

45“And he will answer, ‘I tell you the truth, when you refused to help the least of these my brothers and sisters, you were refusing to help me.’

46“And they will go away into eternal punishment, but the righteous will go into eternal life.”

Are you treating the people in your life the same way you would treat Christ? God will separate his obedient followers from pretenders and unbelievers. The real evidence of our belief is the way we act. To treat all persons we encounter as if they were Jesus is no easy task. What we do for others demonstrates what we really think about Jesus’ words to us—feed the hungry, give the homeless a place to stay, visit the sick. How well do your actions separate you from pretenders and unbelievers?

SEPTEMBER 11

Final Hours

LUKE 22:1-13

The Festival of Unleavened Bread, which is also called Passover, was approaching. 2The leading priests and teachers of religious law were plotting how to kill Jesus, but they were afraid
of the people's reaction.
3Then Satan entered into Judas Iscariot, who was one of the twelve disciples, 4and he went
to the leading priests and captains of the Temple guard to discuss the best way to betray Jesus
to them. 5They were delighted, and they promised to give him money. 6So he agreed and
began looking for an opportunity to betray Jesus so they could arrest him when the crowds
weren't around.
7Now the Festival of Unleavened Bread arrived, when the Passover lamb is sacrificed.
8Jesus sent Peter and John ahead and said, "Go and prepare the Passover meal, so we can eat
it together."
9"Where do you want us to prepare it?" they asked him.
10He replied, "As soon as you enter Jerusalem, a man carrying a pitcher of water will
meet you. Follow him. At the house he enters, 11say to the owner, 'The Teacher asks: Where
is the guest room where I can eat the Passover meal with my disciples?' 12He will take you
upstairs to a large room that is already set up. That is where you should prepare our meal."
13They went off to the city and found everything just as Jesus had said, and they prepared
the Passover meal there.

How do you prepare yourself for Communion? Satan's part in the betrayal of Jesus does not remove any of the responsibility from Judas. Disillusioned because Jesus was talking about dying rather than about setting up his Kingdom, Judas may have been trying to force Jesus' hand and make him use his power to prove he was the Messiah. Or perhaps Judas, not understanding Jesus' mission, no longer believed that Jesus was God's chosen one. Whatever Judas thought, Satan assumed that Jesus' death would end Jesus' mission and thwart God's plan. Like Judas, he did not know that Jesus' death and resurrection were the most important parts of God's plan all along. Jesus gave the ultimate sacrifice for you. The next time you take Communion at church, remember what Jesus did on the cross for you.

Jesus Washes His Disciples' Feet

SEPTEMBER 12

JOHN 13:1-17

Before the Passover celebration, Jesus knew that his hour had come to leave this world and return to his Father. He had loved his disciples during his ministry on earth, and now he loved them to the very end. [2]It was time for supper, and the devil had already prompted Judas, son of Simon Iscariot, to betray Jesus. [3]Jesus knew that the Father had given him authority over everything and that he had come from God and would return to God. [4]So he got up from the table, took off his robe, wrapped a towel around his waist, [5]and poured water into a basin. Then he began to wash the disciples' feet, drying them with the towel he had around him.

[6]When Jesus came to Simon Peter, Peter said to him, "Lord, are you going to wash my feet?"

[7]Jesus replied, "You don't understand now what I am doing, but someday you will."

[8]"No," Peter protested, "you will never ever wash my feet!"

Jesus replied, "Unless I wash you, you won't belong to me."

[9]Simon Peter exclaimed, "Then wash my hands and head as well, Lord, not just my feet!"

[10]Jesus replied, "A person who has bathed all over does not need to wash, except for the feet, to be entirely clean. And you disciples are clean, but not all of you." [11]For Jesus knew who would betray him. That is what he meant when he said, "Not all of you are clean."

[12]After washing their feet, he put on his robe again and sat down and asked, "Do you understand what I was doing? [13]You call me 'Teacher' and 'Lord,' and you are right, because that's what I am. [14]And since I, your Lord and Teacher, have washed your feet, you ought to wash each other's feet. [15]I have given you an example to follow. Do as I have done to you. [16]I tell you the truth, slaves are not greater than their master. Nor is the messenger more important than the one who sends the message. [17]Now that you know these things, God will bless you for doing them."

What is the greatest act of service someone has done for you? How do you serve others? Jesus was the model servant, and he showed this attitude to his disciples. Washing guests' feet was a job for a household servant to do when guests arrived. But Jesus wrapped a towel around himself, as the lowliest slave would do, and washed his disciples' feet. If even God in the flesh was willing to serve, then we as his followers must also be servants who are willing to serve in any way in order to glorify God. Are you willing to follow Christ's example of serving? Whom can you serve today?

SEPTEMBER 13

Sad Predictions

JOHN 13:21-38

21 Now Jesus was deeply troubled, and he exclaimed, "I tell you the truth, one of you will
betray me!"
22 The disciples looked at each other, wondering whom he could mean. 23 The disciple
Jesus loved was sitting next to Jesus at the table. 24 Simon Peter motioned to him to ask,
"Who's he talking about?" 25 So that disciple leaned over to Jesus and asked, "Lord, who is it?"
26 Jesus responded, "It is the one to whom I give the bread I dip in the bowl." And when
he had dipped it, he gave it to Judas, son of Simon Iscariot. 27 When Judas had eaten the
bread, Satan entered into him. Then Jesus told him, "Hurry and do what you're going to do."
28 None of the others at the table knew what Jesus meant. 29 Since Judas was their treasurer,
some thought Jesus was telling him to go and pay for the food or to give some money to the
poor. 30 So Judas left at once, going out into the night.
31 As soon as Judas left the room, Jesus said, "The time has come for the Son of Man
to enter into his glory, and God will be glorified because of him. 32 And since God receives
glory because of the Son, he will give his own glory to the Son, and he will do so at once.
33 Dear children, I will be with you only a little longer. And as I told the Jewish leaders, you
will search for me, but you can't come where I am going. 34 So now I am giving you a new
commandment: Love each other. Just as I have loved you, you should love each other. 35 Your
love for one another will prove to the world that you are my disciples."
36 Simon Peter asked, "Lord, where are you going?"
And Jesus replied, "You can't go with me now, but you will follow me later."
37 "But why can't I come now, Lord?" he asked. "I'm ready to die for you."
38 Jesus answered, "Die for me? I tell you the truth, Peter—before the rooster crows tomorrow morning, you will deny three times that you even know me."

How well do you feel Christ knows you? John describes these few moments in clear detail. We can see that Jesus knew exactly what was going to happen. He knew about Judas and about Peter, but he did not change the situation, nor did he stop loving them. In the same way, Jesus knows exactly what you will do to hurt him. Yet he still loves you unconditionally and will forgive you whenever you ask. Judas couldn't understand this, and his life ended tragically. Peter understood, and despite his shortcomings, his life ended triumphantly because he never let go of his faith in the one who loved him.

Jesus Is the Way

JOHN 14:1-14

"Don't let your hearts be troubled. Trust in God, and trust also in me. [2]There is more than
enough room in my Father's home. If this were not so, would I have told you that I am going
to prepare a place for you? [3]When everything is ready, I will come and get you, so that you
will always be with me where I am. [4]And you know the way to where I am going."

[5]"No, we don't know, Lord," Thomas said. "We have no idea where you are going, so
how can we know the way?"

[6]Jesus told him, "I am the way, the truth, and the life. No one can come to the Father
except through me. [7]If you had really known me, you would know who my Father is. From
now on, you do know him and have seen him!"

[8]Philip said, "Lord, show us the Father, and we will be satisfied."

[9]Jesus replied, "Have I been with you all this time, Philip, and yet you still don't know
who I am? Anyone who has seen me has seen the Father! So why are you asking me to show
him to you? [10]Don't you believe that I am in the Father and the Father is in me? The words
I speak are not my own, but my Father who lives in me does his work through me. [11]Just
believe that I am in the Father and the Father is in me. Or at least believe because of the
work you have seen me do.

[12]"I tell you the truth, anyone who believes in me will do the same works I have done,
and even greater works, because I am going to be with the Father. [13]You can ask for anything
in my name, and I will do it, so that the Son can bring glory to the Father. [14]Yes, ask me for
anything in my name, and I will do it!"

How would you rate your present level of understanding of Christ and his teachings? Jesus says he is the only way to God the Father. Some people may argue that this is too narrow. In reality, it is wide enough for the whole world if the world chooses to accept it. Instead of worrying about how limited it sounds to have only one way, we should be saying, "Thank you, God, for providing a sure way to get to you!"

SEPTEMBER 15

The Holy Spirit is Promised

JOHN 14:15-31

15“If you love me, obey my commandments. 16And I will ask the Father, and he will give you another Advocate, who will never leave you. 17He is the Holy Spirit, who leads into all truth. The world cannot receive him, because it isn’t looking for him and doesn’t recognize him. But you know him, because he lives with you now and later will be in you. 18No, I will not abandon you as orphans—I will come to you. 19Soon the world will no longer see me, but you will see me. Since I live, you also will live. 20When I am raised to life again, you will know that I am in my Father, and you are in me, and I am in you. 21Those who accept my commandments and obey them are the ones who love me. And because they love me, my Father will love them. And I will love them and reveal myself to each of them.”

22Judas (not Judas Iscariot, but the other disciple with that name) said to him, “Lord, why are you going to reveal yourself only to us and not to the world at large?”

23Jesus replied, “All who love me will do what I say. My Father will love them, and we will come and make our home with each of them. 24Anyone who doesn’t love me will not obey me. And remember, my words are not my own. What I am telling you is from the Father who sent me. 25I am telling you these things now while I am still with you. 26But when the Father sends the Advocate as my representative—that is, the Holy Spirit—he will teach you everything and will remind you of everything I have told you.

27“I am leaving you with a gift—peace of mind and heart. And the peace I give is a gift the world cannot give. So don’t be troubled or afraid. 28Remember what I told you: I am going away, but I will come back to you again. If you really loved me, you would be happy that I am going to the Father, who is greater than I am. 29I have told you these things before they happen so that when they do happen, you will believe.

30“I don’t have much more time to talk to you, because the ruler of this world approaches. He has no power over me, 31but I will do what the Father requires of me, so that the world will know that I love the Father. Come, let’s be going.”

How have you experienced the Advocate? The end result of the Holy Spirit’s work in our lives is deep and lasting peace. Unlike worldly peace, which is usually defined as the absence of conflict, this peace is confident assurance in any circumstance; with Christ’s peace, we have no need to fear the present or the future. If your life is full of stress, allow the Holy Spirit to fill you with Christ’s peace.

The Vine and the Branches

SEPTEMBER 16

JOHN 15:1-16

"I am the true grapevine, and my Father is the gardener. 2He cuts off every branch of mine
that doesn't produce fruit, and he prunes the branches that do bear fruit so they will produce
even more. 3You have already been pruned and purified by the message I have given you.
4Remain in me, and I will remain in you. For a branch cannot produce fruit if it is severed
from the vine, and you cannot be fruitful unless you remain in me.

5"Yes, I am the vine; you are the branches. Those who remain in me, and I in them, will
produce much fruit. For apart from me you can do nothing. 6Anyone who does not remain
in me is thrown away like a useless branch and withers. Such branches are gathered into a
pile to be burned. 7But if you remain in me and my words remain in you, you may ask for
anything you want, and it will be granted! 8When you produce much fruit, you are my true
disciples. This brings great glory to my Father.

9"I have loved you even as the Father has loved me. Remain in my love. 10When you obey
my commandments, you remain in my love, just as I obey my Father's commandments and
remain in his love. 11I have told you these things so that you will be filled with my joy. Yes,
your joy will overflow! 12This is my commandment: Love each other in the same way I have
loved you. 13There is no greater love than to lay down one's life for one's friends. 14You are
my friends if you do what I command. 15I no longer call you slaves, because a master doesn't
confide in his slaves. Now you are my friends, since I have told you everything the Father
told me. 16You didn't choose me. I chose you. I appointed you to go and produce lasting fruit,
so that the Father will give you whatever you ask for, using my name."

What kind of fruit has the Gardener produced in you? Many people try to be good, honest people who do what is right. But Jesus says that the only way to live a truly good life is to stay close to him, like a branch attached to the vine. Apart from Christ our efforts are unfruitful. Are you receiving the nourishment and life offered by Christ, the Vine? If not, you are missing a special gift he has for you.

SEPTEMBER 17

Love Each Other

JOHN 15:17–16:4

17This is my command: Love each other.
18“If the world hates you, remember that it hated me first. 19The world would love you as
one of its own if you belonged to it, but you are no longer part of the world. I chose you to
come out of the world, so it hates you. 20Do you remember what I told you? ‘A slave is not
greater than the master.’ Since they persecuted me, naturally they will persecute you. And
if they had listened to me, they would listen to you. 21They will do all this to you because
of me, for they have rejected the one who sent me. 22They would not be guilty if I had not
come and spoken to them. But now they have no excuse for their sin. 23Anyone who hates
me also hates my Father. 24If I hadn’t done such miraculous signs among them that no one
else could do, they would not be guilty. But as it is, they have seen everything I did, yet they
still hate me and my Father. 25This fulfills what is written in their Scriptures: ‘They hated
me without cause.’
26“But I will send you the Advocate—the Spirit of truth. He will come to you from the
Father and will testify all about me. 27And you must also testify about me because you have
been with me from the beginning of my ministry.

16:1“I have told you these things so that you won’t abandon your faith. 2For you will be expelled
from the synagogues, and the time is coming when those who kill you will think they are
doing a holy service for God. 3This is because they have never known the Father or me. 4Yes,
I’m telling you these things now, so that when they happen, you will remember my warning.
I didn’t tell you earlier because I was going to be with you for a while longer.”

What have you learned recently about loving others? Christians will get plenty of hatred from the world; from one another we need love and support. Do you allow small problems to get in the way of loving other believers? Jesus commands that you love them, and he will give you the strength to do it.

Overcoming the World

SEPTEMBER 18

JOHN 16:13-33

13When the Spirit of truth comes, he will guide you into all truth. He will not speak on his
own but will tell you what he has heard. He will tell you about the future. 14He will bring me
glory by telling you whatever he receives from me. . . .

16"In a little while you won't see me anymore. But a little while after that, you will see
me again."

17Some of the disciples asked each other, "What does he mean when he says, 'In a little
while you won't see me, but then you will see me,' and 'I am going to the Father'? 18And what
does he mean by 'a little while'? We don't understand."

19Jesus realized they wanted to ask him about it, so he said, "Are you asking yourselves
what I meant? I said in a little while you won't see me, but a little while after that you will
see me again. 20I tell you the truth, you will weep and mourn over what is going to happen
to me, but the world will rejoice. You will grieve, but your grief will suddenly turn to wonderful joy. 21It will be like a woman suffering the pains of labor. When her child is born, her
anguish gives way to joy because she has brought a new baby into the world. 22So you have
sorrow now, but I will see you again; then you will rejoice, and no one can rob you of that
joy. 23At that time you won't need to ask me for anything. I tell you the truth, you will ask
the Father directly, and he will grant your request because you use my name. 24You haven't
done this before. Ask, using my name, and you will receive, and you will have abundant joy.

25"I have spoken of these matters in figures of speech, but soon I will stop speaking figuratively and will tell you plainly all about the Father. 26Then you will ask in my name. I'm not
saying I will ask the Father on your behalf, 27for the Father himself loves you dearly because
you love me and believe that I came from God. 28Yes, I came from the Father into the world,
and now I will leave the world and return to the Father."

29Then his disciples said, "At last you are speaking plainly and not figuratively. 30Now we
understand that you know everything, and there's no need to question you. From this we
believe that you came from God."

31Jesus asked, "Do you finally believe? 32But the time is coming—indeed it's here now—
when you will be scattered, each one going his own way, leaving me alone. Yet I am not
alone because the Father is with me. 33I have told you all this so that you may have peace
in me. Here on earth you will have many trials and sorrows. But take heart, because I have
overcome the world."

Which of these verses give you peace of heart and mind? What a contrast between the disciples and the world! The world rejoiced as the disciples wept, but the disciples would see Jesus again (in three days) and rejoice. The world's values are often the opposite of God's values. This can cause Christians to feel like misfits. But even if life is difficult now, one day we will rejoice. Keep your eye on the future and on God's promises!

SEPTEMBER 19

Jesus Prays

JOHN 17:1-26

After saying all these things, Jesus looked up to heaven and said, "Father, the hour has come. Glorify your Son so he can give glory back to you. . . .

6"I have revealed you to the ones you gave me from this world. They were always yours. You gave them to me, and they have kept your word. 7Now they know that everything I have is a gift from you, 8for I have passed on to them the message you gave me. They accepted it and know that I came from you, and they believe you sent me.

9"My prayer is not for the world, but for those you have given me, because they belong to you. 10All who are mine belong to you, and you have given them to me, so they bring me glory. 11Now I am departing from the world; they are staying in this world, but I am coming to you. Holy Father, you have given me your name; now protect them by the power of your name so that they will be united just as we are. 12During my time here, I protected them by the power of the name you gave me. I guarded them so that not one was lost, except the one headed for destruction, as the Scriptures foretold.

13"Now I am coming to you. I told them many things while I was with them in this world so they would be filled with my joy. 14I have given them your word. And the world hates them because they do not belong to the world, just as I do not belong to the world. 15I'm not asking you to take them out of the world, but to keep them safe from the evil one. 16They do not belong to this world any more than I do. 17Make them holy by your truth; teach them your word, which is truth. 18Just as you sent me into the world, I am sending them into the world. 19And I give myself as a holy sacrifice for them so they can be made holy by your truth.

20"I am praying not only for these disciples but also for all who will ever believe in me through their message. 21I pray that they will all be one, just as you and I are one—as you are in me, Father, and I am in you. And may they be in us so that the world will believe you sent me.

22"I have given them the glory you gave me, so they may be one as we are one. 23I am in them and you are in me. May they experience such perfect unity that the world will know that you sent me and that you love them as much as you love me. 24Father, I want these whom you have given me to be with me where I am. Then they can see all the glory you gave me because you loved me even before the world began!

25"O righteous Father, the world doesn't know you, but I do; and these disciples know you sent me. 26I have revealed you to them, and I will continue to do so. Then your love for me will be in them, and I will be in them."

Where do you find yourself in this prayer? Jesus didn't ask God to take believers out of the world but instead to use them in the world. Because Jesus sends us into the world, we should not try to escape from the world or avoid all relationships with non-Christians. We are called to be salt and light (Matthew 5:13-16), and we are to do the work God sent us to do.

The Cup of Suffering

SEPTEMBER 20

MARK 14:26-42

26 Then they sang a hymn and went out to the Mount of Olives.

27 On the way, Jesus told them, "All of you will desert me. For the Scriptures say,

'God will strike the Shepherd,
and the sheep will be scattered.'

28 But after I am raised from the dead, I will go ahead of you to Galilee and meet you there."
29 Peter said to him, "Even if everyone else deserts you, I never will."
30 Jesus replied, "I tell you the truth, Peter—this very night, before the rooster crows twice,
you will deny three times that you even know me."
31 "No!" Peter declared emphatically. "Even if I have to die with you, I will never deny
you!" And all the others vowed the same.
32 They went to the olive grove called Gethsemane, and Jesus said, "Sit here while I go
and pray." 33 He took Peter, James, and John with him, and he became deeply troubled and
distressed. 34 He told them, "My soul is crushed with grief to the point of death. Stay here
and keep watch with me."
35 He went on a little farther and fell to the ground. He prayed that, if it were possible,
the awful hour awaiting him might pass him by. 36 "Abba, Father," he cried out, "everything
is possible for you. Please take this cup of suffering away from me. Yet I want your will to
be done, not mine."
37 Then he returned and found the disciples asleep. He said to Peter, "Simon, are you
asleep? Couldn't you watch with me even one hour? 38 Keep watch and pray, so that you will
not give in to temptation. For the spirit is willing, but the body is weak."
39 Then Jesus left them again and prayed the same prayer as before. 40 When he returned
to them again, he found them sleeping, for they couldn't keep their eyes open. And they
didn't know what to say.
41 When he returned to them the third time, he said, "Go ahead and sleep. Have your rest.
But no—the time has come. The Son of Man is betrayed into the hands of sinners. 42 Up, let's
be going. Look, my betrayer is here!"

What does your commitment to God cost you? While praying, Jesus was aware of what doing the Father's will would cost him. He understood the suffering he was about to encounter, and he did not want to have to endure the horrible experience. But Jesus prayed, "I want your will to be done, not mine." Anything worth having costs something. Be willing to pay the price to gain something worthwhile in the end.

SEPTEMBER 21

Abandoned and Denied

JOHN 18:1-14; MATTHEW 26:69-74

After saying these things, Jesus crossed the Kidron Valley with his disciples and entered a grove of olive trees. [2]Judas, the betrayer, knew this place, because Jesus had often gone there with his disciples. [3]The leading priests and Pharisees had given Judas a contingent of Roman soldiers and Temple guards to accompany him. Now with blazing torches, lanterns, and weapons, they arrived at the olive grove.

[4]Jesus fully realized all that was going to happen to him, so he stepped forward to meet them. "Who are you looking for?" he asked.

[5]"Jesus the Nazarene," they replied.

"I AM he," Jesus said. (Judas, who betrayed him, was standing with them.) [6]As Jesus said "I AM he," they all drew back and fell to the ground! . . .

[10]Then Simon Peter drew a sword and slashed off the right ear of Malchus, the high priest's slave. [11]But Jesus said to Peter, "Put your sword back into its sheath. Shall I not drink from the cup of suffering the Father has given me?"

[12]So the soldiers, their commanding officer, and the Temple guards arrested Jesus and tied him up. [13]First they took him to Annas, since he was the father-in-law of Caiaphas, the high priest at that time. [14]Caiaphas was the one who had told the other Jewish leaders, "It's better that one man should die for the people."

[MT 26:69]Meanwhile, Peter was sitting outside in the courtyard. A servant girl came over and said to him, "You were one of those with Jesus the Galilean."

[70]But Peter denied it in front of everyone. "I don't know what you're talking about," he said.

[71]Later, out by the gate, another servant girl noticed him and said to those standing around, "This man was with Jesus of Nazareth."

[72]Again Peter denied it, this time with an oath. "I don't even know the man," he said.

[73]A little later some of the other bystanders came over to Peter and said, "You must be one of them; we can tell by your Galilean accent."

[74]Peter swore, "A curse on me if I'm lying—I don't know the man!" And immediately the rooster crowed.

How close have you come to denying Christ? There were three stages to Peter's denial. First, he acted confused and tried to divert attention from himself by changing the subject. Second, he vehemently denied Jesus. Third, he denied Jesus with an oath. Believers who deny Christ often begin doing so by subtly pretending not to know him. When opportunities to discuss religious issues come up, they walk away or pretend they don't know the answers. With only a little more pressure, they can be induced to flatly deny their relationship with Christ. If you find yourself subtly avoiding occasions to talk about Christ, watch out. You may be on the road to denying him.

Trial and Judgment

SEPTEMBER 22

MATTHEW 26:57-68

57 Then the people who had arrested Jesus led him to the home of Caiaphas, the high priest,
where the teachers of religious law and the elders had gathered. 58 Meanwhile, Peter followed
him at a distance and came to the high priest's courtyard. He went in and sat with the guards
and waited to see how it would all end.

59 Inside, the leading priests and the entire high council were trying to find witnesses who
would lie about Jesus, so they could put him to death. 60 But even though they found many
who agreed to give false witness, they could not use anyone's testimony. Finally, two men
came forward 61 who declared, "This man said, 'I am able to destroy the Temple of God and
rebuild it in three days.'"

62 Then the high priest stood up and said to Jesus, "Well, aren't you going to answer these
charges? What do you have to say for yourself?" 63 But Jesus remained silent. Then the high
priest said to him, "I demand in the name of the living God—tell us if you are the Messiah,
the Son of God."

64 Jesus replied, "You have said it. And in the future you will see the Son of Man seated in
the place of power at God's right hand and coming on the clouds of heaven."

65 Then the high priest tore his clothing to show his horror and said, "Blasphemy! Why do
we need other witnesses? You have all heard his blasphemy. 66 What is your verdict?"

"Guilty!" they shouted. "He deserves to die!"

67 Then they began to spit in Jesus' face and beat him with their fists. And some slapped
him, 68 jeering, "Prophesy to us, you Messiah! Who hit you that time?"

What do you believe about Jesus' claim that he is God? The high priest accused Jesus of blasphemy—calling himself God. To the Jews, this was a great crime, punishable by death (Leviticus 24:16). The religious leaders refused even to consider that Jesus' words might be true. They had decided to kill Jesus, and in so doing, they sealed their own fate as well as his. Like the members of the high council, you must decide whether Jesus' words are blasphemy or truth. Your decision has eternal implications.

SEPTEMBER 23

The Death of Judas

MATTHEW 27:1-10

Very early in the morning the leading priests and the elders of the people met again to lay
plans for putting Jesus to death. [2]Then they bound him, led him away, and took him to
Pilate, the Roman governor.

[3]When Judas, who had betrayed him, realized that Jesus had been condemned to die, he
was filled with remorse. So he took the thirty pieces of silver back to the leading priests and
the elders. [4]"I have sinned," he declared, "for I have betrayed an innocent man."

"What do we care?" they retorted. "That's your problem."

[5]Then Judas threw the silver coins down in the Temple and went out and hanged himself.

[6]The leading priests picked up the coins. "It wouldn't be right to put this money in the
Temple treasury," they said, "since it was payment for murder." [7]After some discussion they
finally decided to buy the potter's field, and they made it into a cemetery for foreigners. [8]That
is why the field is still called the Field of Blood. [9]This fulfilled the prophecy of Jeremiah that
says,

"They took the thirty pieces of silver—
the price at which he was valued by the people of Israel,
[10]and purchased the potter's field,
as the LORD directed."

When you think of sin's consequences, what personal examples come to mind? Jesus' formal accuser wanted to drop his charges, but the religious leaders refused to halt the trial. When Judas first betrayed Jesus, perhaps he was trying to force Jesus' hand to get him to lead a revolt against Rome. This did not work, of course. Whatever his reason, Judas changed his mind, but it was too late. Many of the plans we set into motion cannot be reversed. It is best to think of the potential consequences before we launch into an action we may later regret.

Two Political Trials

SEPTEMBER 24

LUKE 23:1-12

Then the entire council took Jesus to Pilate, the Roman governor. 2They began to state their
case: "This man has been leading our people astray by telling them not to pay their taxes to
the Roman government and by claiming he is the Messiah, a king."

3So Pilate asked him, "Are you the king of the Jews?"

Jesus replied, "You have said it."

4Pilate turned to the leading priests and to the crowd and said, "I find nothing wrong
with this man!"

5Then they became insistent. "But he is causing riots by his teaching wherever he goes—
all over Judea, from Galilee to Jerusalem!"

6"Oh, is he a Galilean?" Pilate asked. 7When they said that he was, Pilate sent him to
Herod Antipas, because Galilee was under Herod's jurisdiction, and Herod happened to be
in Jerusalem at the time.

8Herod was delighted at the opportunity to see Jesus, because he had heard about him
and had been hoping for a long time to see him perform a miracle. 9He asked Jesus question
after question, but Jesus refused to answer. 10Meanwhile, the leading priests and the teachers
of religious law stood there shouting their accusations. 11Then Herod and his soldiers began
mocking and ridiculing Jesus. Finally, they put a royal robe on him and sent him back to
Pilate. 12(Herod and Pilate, who had been enemies before, became friends that day.)

In what ways did your childhood and background prepare you to respond to Jesus? Pilate was the Roman governor of Judea, where Jerusalem was located. He seemed to take special pleasure in harassing the Jews. For example, Pilate had taken money from the Temple treasury and had used it to build an aqueduct. And he had insulted the Jewish religion by bringing imperial images into the city. As Pilate well knew, such acts could backfire. If the people were to lodge a formal complaint against his administration, Rome might remove him from his post. Pilate was already beginning to feel insecure in his position when the Jewish leaders brought Jesus to trial. Would he continue to badger the Jews and risk his political future, or would he give in to their demands and condemn a man who, he was quite sure, was innocent? That was the question facing Pilate that springtime Friday morning nearly two thousand years ago. Under the circumstances, how would you have responded?

SEPTEMBER 25

Sentencing and Torture

MARK 15:6-24

6Now it was the governor's custom each year during the Passover celebration to release one
prisoner—anyone the people requested. 7One of the prisoners at that time was Barabbas, a
revolutionary who had committed murder in an uprising. 8The crowd went to Pilate and
asked him to release a prisoner as usual.

9"Would you like me to release to you this 'King of the Jews'?" Pilate asked. 10(For he
realized by now that the leading priests had arrested Jesus out of envy.) 11But at this point
the leading priests stirred up the crowd to demand the release of Barabbas instead of Jesus.
12Pilate asked them, "Then what should I do with this man you call the king of the Jews?"

13They shouted back, "Crucify him!"

14"Why?" Pilate demanded. "What crime has he committed?"

But the mob roared even louder, "Crucify him!"

15So to pacify the crowd, Pilate released Barabbas to them. He ordered Jesus flogged with
a lead-tipped whip, then turned him over to the Roman soldiers to be crucified.

16The soldiers took Jesus into the courtyard of the governor's headquarters (called the
Praetorium) and called out the entire regiment. 17They dressed him in a purple robe, and
they wove thorn branches into a crown and put it on his head. 18Then they saluted him and
taunted, "Hail! King of the Jews!" 19And they struck him on the head with a reed stick, spit
on him, and dropped to their knees in mock worship. 20When they were finally tired of
mocking him, they took off the purple robe and put his own clothes on him again. Then
they led him away to be crucified.

21A passerby named Simon, who was from Cyrene, was coming in from the countryside
just then, and the soldiers forced him to carry Jesus' cross. (Simon was the father of Alexander
and Rufus.) 22And they brought Jesus to a place called Golgotha (which means "Place of the
Skull"). 23They offered him wine drugged with myrrh, but he refused it.

24Then the soldiers nailed him to the cross. They divided his clothes and threw dice to
decide who would get each piece.

Was there a time when you chose to do the wrong thing on purpose? Why? What happened? Although Jesus was innocent according to Roman law, Pilate caved in under political pressure. He abandoned what he knew was right. He tried to second-guess the Jewish leaders and give a decision that would please everyone while keeping himself safe. When we ignore God's clear statements of right and wrong and make decisions based on our audiences, we fall into compromise and lawlessness. God promises to honor those who do right, not those who make everyone happy.

Jesus Crucified

SEPTEMBER 26

LUKE 23:32-49

32 Two others, both criminals, were led out to be executed with him. 33 When they came to a place called The Skull, they nailed him to the cross. And the criminals were also crucified—one on his right and one on his left.

34 Jesus said, "Father, forgive them, for they don't know what they are doing." And the soldiers gambled for his clothes by throwing dice.

35 The crowd watched and the leaders scoffed. "He saved others," they said, "let him save himself if he is really God's Messiah, the Chosen One." 36 The soldiers mocked him, too, by offering him a drink of sour wine. 37 They called out to him, "If you are the King of the Jews, save yourself!" 38 A sign was fastened above him with these words: "This is the King of the Jews."

39 One of the criminals hanging beside him scoffed, "So you're the Messiah, are you? Prove it by saving yourself—and us, too, while you're at it!"

40 But the other criminal protested, "Don't you fear God even when you have been sentenced to die? 41 We deserve to die for our crimes, but this man hasn't done anything wrong." 42 Then he said, "Jesus, remember me when you come into your Kingdom."

43 And Jesus replied, "I assure you, today you will be with me in paradise."

44 By this time it was about noon, and darkness fell across the whole land until three o'clock. 45 The light from the sun was gone. And suddenly, the curtain in the sanctuary of the Temple was torn down the middle. 46 Then Jesus shouted, "Father, I entrust my spirit into your hands!" And with those words he breathed his last.

47 When the Roman officer overseeing the execution saw what had happened, he worshiped God and said, "Surely this man was innocent." 48 And when all the crowd that came to see the crucifixion saw what had happened, they went home in deep sorrow. 49 But Jesus' friends, including the women who had followed him from Galilee, stood at a distance watching.

What do you feel as you read this description of the Crucifixion? Jesus asked God to forgive the people who were putting him to death—the Jewish leaders, Roman politicians and soldiers, bystanders—and God answered that prayer by opening up the way of salvation even to Jesus' murderers. The Roman officer and soldiers who witnessed the Crucifixion said, "This man truly was the Son of God!" (Matthew 27:54). Soon many priests were converted to the Christian faith (Acts 6:7). Since we are all sinners, we all played a part in putting Jesus to death. The good news is that God is gracious. He will forgive us and give us new life through his Son.

SEPTEMBER 27

A Guarded Tomb

MATTHEW 27:57-66

[57]As evening approached, Joseph, a rich man from Arimathea who had become a follower of Jesus, [58]went to Pilate and asked for Jesus' body. And Pilate issued an order to release it to him. [59]Joseph took the body and wrapped it in a long sheet of clean linen cloth. [60]He placed it in his own new tomb, which had been carved out of the rock. Then he rolled a great stone across the entrance and left. [61]Both Mary Magdalene and the other Mary were sitting across from the tomb and watching.

[62]The next day, on the Sabbath, the leading priests and Pharisees went to see Pilate. [63]They told him, "Sir, we remember what that deceiver once said while he was still alive: 'After three days I will rise from the dead.' [64]So we request that you seal the tomb until the third day. This will prevent his disciples from coming and stealing his body and then telling everyone he was raised from the dead! If that happens, we'll be worse off than we were at first."

[65]Pilate replied, "Take guards and secure it the best you can." [66]So they sealed the tomb and posted guards to protect it.

What have you seen people do in their resistance to Christ? The religious leaders took Jesus' resurrection claims more seriously than the disciples did. The Pharisees were so afraid of Jesus' predictions about his resurrection that they made sure the tomb was thoroughly sealed and guarded. Because the tomb was hewn out of rock in the side of a hill, there was only one entrance. The tomb was sealed by stringing a cord over the stone that was rolled across the entrance and sealing it at each end with clay. But the religious leaders took a further precaution, asking that guards be placed at the tomb's entrance. The disciples didn't remember Jesus' teaching about his resurrection, but the religious leaders did. Because of his claims, the religious leaders were almost as afraid of Jesus after his death as when he was alive. They tried to take every precaution to see that his body would remain in the tomb. If you had been one of the disciples, what would you have been thinking? How would you have felt knowing that Jesus' body was in a sealed and guarded tomb? How would you have explained Jesus' words about rising again?

Jesus Is Alive!

SEPTEMBER 28

JOHN 20:1-18

Early on Sunday morning, while it was still dark, Mary Magdalene came to the tomb and
found that the stone had been rolled away from the entrance. 2She ran and found Simon
Peter and the other disciple, the one whom Jesus loved. She said, "They have taken the Lord's
body out of the tomb, and we don't know where they have put him!"

3Peter and the other disciple started out for the tomb. 4They were both running, but the
other disciple outran Peter and reached the tomb first. 5He stooped and looked in and saw the
linen wrappings lying there, but he didn't go in. 6Then Simon Peter arrived and went inside.
He also noticed the linen wrappings lying there, 7while the cloth that had covered Jesus'
head was folded up and lying apart from the other wrappings. 8Then the disciple who had
reached the tomb first also went in, and he saw and believed—9for until then they still hadn't
understood the Scriptures that said Jesus must rise from the dead. 10Then they went home.

11Mary was standing outside the tomb crying, and as she wept, she stooped and looked
in. 12She saw two white-robed angels, one sitting at the head and the other at the foot of
the place where the body of Jesus had been lying. 13"Dear woman, why are you crying?" the
angels asked her.

"Because they have taken away my Lord," she replied, "and I don't know where they have
put him."

14She turned to leave and saw someone standing there. It was Jesus, but she didn't recognize him. 15"Dear woman, why are you crying?" Jesus asked her. "Who are you looking for?"

She thought he was the gardener. "Sir," she said, "if you have taken him away, tell me
where you have put him, and I will go and get him."

16"Mary!" Jesus said.

She turned to him and cried out, "Rabboni!" (which is Hebrew for "Teacher").

17"Don't cling to me," Jesus said, "for I haven't yet ascended to the Father. But go find
my brothers and tell them, 'I am ascending to my Father and your Father, to my God and
your God.'"

18Mary Magdalene found the disciples and told them, "I have seen the Lord!" Then she
gave them his message.

What makes Easter an important celebration in your life? Jesus' resurrection is the key to the Christian faith. Why? (1) Just as he said, Jesus rose from the dead. We can be confident that he will accomplish everything he has promised. (2) Jesus' bodily resurrection shows us that the living Christ is ruler of God's eternal Kingdom. (3) We can be certain of our own resurrection, because Jesus was resurrected. Death is not the end—there is a future life. (4) The divine power that brought Jesus back to life is now available to bring spiritually dead people back to life. (5) The Resurrection is the basis for the church's witness to the world. When you go to church on Easter Sunday, rejoice in what the Resurrection means for you.

SEPTEMBER 29 Reactions to the Resurrection

MATTHEW 28:8-15

8The women ran quickly from the tomb. They were very frightened but also filled with great
joy, and they rushed to give the disciples the angel's message. 9And as they went, Jesus met
them and greeted them. And they ran to him, grasped his feet, and worshiped him. 10Then
Jesus said to them, "Don't be afraid! Go tell my brothers to leave for Galilee, and they will
see me there."

11As the women were on their way, some of the guards went into the city and told the
leading priests what had happened. 12A meeting with the elders was called, and they decided
to give the soldiers a large bribe. 13They told the soldiers, "You must say, 'Jesus' disciples
came during the night while we were sleeping, and they stole his body.' 14If the governor
hears about it, we'll stand up for you so you won't get in trouble." 15So the guards accepted
the bribe and said what they were told to say. Their story spread widely among the Jews,
and they still tell it today.

What would be your first words to Jesus if he appeared to you? Jesus' resurrection was already causing a great stir in Jerusalem. A group of women was moving quickly through the streets, looking for the disciples to tell them the amazing news that Jesus was alive. At the same time, a group of religious leaders was plotting how to cover up the Resurrection. Today there is still a great stir over the Resurrection, and there are still only two choices—to believe that Jesus rose from the dead or to be closed to the truth, denying it, ignoring it, or rationalizing it away. What is your choice? Why?

On the Road to Emmaus

SEPTEMBER 30

LUKE 24:13-34

13 That same day two of Jesus' followers were walking to the village of Emmaus, seven miles from Jerusalem. 14 As they walked along they were talking about everything that had happened. 15 As they talked and discussed these things, Jesus himself suddenly came and began walking with them. 16 But God kept them from recognizing him.

17 He asked them, "What are you discussing so intently as you walk along?"

They stopped short, sadness written across their faces. 18 Then one of them, Cleopas, replied, "You must be the only person in Jerusalem who hasn't heard about all the things that have happened there the last few days."

19 "What things?" Jesus asked.

"The things that happened to Jesus, the man from Nazareth," they said. "He was a prophet who did powerful miracles, and he was a mighty teacher in the eyes of God and all the people. 20 But our leading priests and other religious leaders handed him over to be condemned to death, and they crucified him. 21 We had hoped he was the Messiah who had come to rescue Israel. This all happened three days ago.

22 "Then some women from our group of his followers were at his tomb early this morning, and they came back with an amazing report. 23 They said his body was missing, and they had seen angels who told them Jesus is alive! 24 Some of our men ran out to see, and sure enough, his body was gone, just as the women had said."

25 Then Jesus said to them, "You foolish people! You find it so hard to believe all that the prophets wrote in the Scriptures. 26 Wasn't it clearly predicted that the Messiah would have to suffer all these things before entering his glory?" 27 Then Jesus took them through the writings of Moses and all the prophets, explaining from all the Scriptures the things concerning himself.

28 By this time they were nearing Emmaus and the end of their journey. Jesus acted as if he were going on, 29 but they begged him, "Stay the night with us, since it is getting late." So he went home with them. 30 As they sat down to eat, he took the bread and blessed it. Then he broke it and gave it to them. 31 Suddenly, their eyes were opened, and they recognized him. And at that moment he disappeared!

32 They said to each other, "Didn't our hearts burn within us as he talked with us on the road and explained the Scriptures to us?" 33 And within the hour they were on their way back to Jerusalem. There they found the eleven disciples and the others who had gathered with them, 34 who said, "The Lord has really risen! He appeared to Peter."

Would you recognize Jesus if you saw him today? The two disciples missed Jesus because they were too focused on their disappointment. In addition, they were walking in the wrong direction—away from the fellowship of believers. When we become preoccupied with our dashed hopes and frustrated plans, and when we withdraw from the strength found in other believers, we are likely to miss Jesus and the power and help he can bring.

October

OCTOBER 1 More Appearances of Jesus

JOHN 20:24–21:14

[24]One of the twelve disciples, Thomas (nicknamed the Twin), was not with the others when
Jesus came. [25]They told him, "We have seen the Lord!"

But he replied, "I won't believe it unless I see the nail wounds in his hands, put my fingers
into them, and place my hand into the wound in his side."

[26]Eight days later the disciples were together again, and this time Thomas was with them.
The doors were locked; but suddenly, as before, Jesus was standing among them. "Peace be
with you," he said. [27]Then he said to Thomas, "Put your finger here, and look at my hands.
Put your hand into the wound in my side. Don't be faithless any longer. Believe!"

[28]"My Lord and my God!" Thomas exclaimed.

[29]Then Jesus told him, "You believe because you have seen me. Blessed are those who
believe without seeing me."

[30]The disciples saw Jesus do many other miraculous signs in addition to the ones recorded
in this book. [31]But these are written so that you may continue to believe that Jesus is the
Messiah, the Son of God, and that by believing in him you will have life by the power of
his name.

[21:1]Later, Jesus appeared again to the disciples beside the Sea of Galilee. This is how it happened. [2]Several of the disciples were there—Simon Peter, Thomas (nicknamed the Twin),
Nathanael from Cana in Galilee, the sons of Zebedee, and two other disciples.

[3]Simon Peter said, "I'm going fishing."

"We'll come, too," they all said. So they went out in the boat, but they caught nothing
all night.

[4]At dawn Jesus was standing on the beach, but the disciples couldn't see who he was. [5]He
called out, "Fellows, have you caught any fish?"

"No," they replied.

[6]Then he said, "Throw out your net on the right-hand side of the boat, and you'll get
some!" So they did, and they couldn't haul in the net because there were so many fish in it.

[7]Then the disciple Jesus loved said to Peter, "It's the Lord!" . . .

[14]This was the third time Jesus had appeared to his disciples since he had been raised
from the dead.

How has Christ dispelled your doubts? Jesus wasn't hard on Thomas for his doubts. Despite his skepticism, Thomas was still loyal to the believers and to Jesus himself. Some people need to doubt before they believe. If doubt leads to questions, and questions lead to answers, and the answers are accepted, then doubt has done good work. It is when doubt becomes stubbornness, and stubbornness becomes a lifestyle that doubt harms faith. When you doubt, don't stop there, but let your doubt deepen your faith as you continue to search for the answer.

Jesus Talks with Peter

OCTOBER 2

JOHN 21:15-25

15After breakfast Jesus asked Simon Peter, "Simon son of John, do you love me more than these?"

"Yes, Lord," Peter replied, "you know I love you."

"Then feed my lambs," Jesus told him.

16Jesus repeated the question: "Simon son of John, do you love me?"

"Yes, Lord," Peter said, "you know I love you."

"Then take care of my sheep," Jesus said.

17A third time he asked him, "Simon son of John, do you love me?"

Peter was hurt that Jesus asked the question a third time. He said, "Lord, you know everything. You know that I love you."

Jesus said, "Then feed my sheep.

18"I tell you the truth, when you were young, you were able to do as you liked; you dressed
yourself and went wherever you wanted to go. But when you are old, you will stretch out your
hands, and others will dress you and take you where you don't want to go." 19Jesus said this to
let him know by what kind of death he would glorify God. Then Jesus told him, "Follow me."

20Peter turned around and saw behind them the disciple Jesus loved—the one who had
leaned over to Jesus during supper and asked, "Lord, who will betray you?" 21Peter asked
Jesus, "What about him, Lord?"

22Jesus replied, "If I want him to remain alive until I return, what is that to you? As for
you, follow me." 23So the rumor spread among the community of believers that this disciple
wouldn't die. But that isn't what Jesus said at all. He only said, "If I want him to remain alive
until I return, what is that to you?"

24This disciple is the one who testifies to these events and has recorded them here. And we know that his account of these things is accurate.

25Jesus also did many other things. If they were all written down, I suppose the whole world could not contain the books that would be written.

What difference would it make to you to read these verses with your name in the place of Simon Peter's? Peter asked Jesus how John would die. Jesus replied that Peter should not concern himself with that. We tend to compare our lives to others', whether to rationalize our own level of devotion to Christ or to question God's justice. Jesus responds to us as he did to Peter: "What is that to you? As for you, follow me."

OCTOBER 3

The Great Commission

MATTHEW 28:16-20

16Then the eleven disciples left for Galilee, going to the mountain where Jesus had told them
to go. 17When they saw him, they worshiped him—but some of them doubted!

18Jesus came and told his disciples, "I have been given all authority in heaven and on earth.
19Therefore, go and make disciples of all the nations, baptizing them in the name of the Father
and the Son and the Holy Spirit. 20Teach these new disciples to obey all the commands I have
given you. And be sure of this: I am with you always, even to the end of the age."

What are you doing specifically to obey Christ's words? When someone is dying or leaving us, that person's last words are very important. Jesus left the disciples with these last words of instruction: they were under his authority, they were to make more disciples, they were to baptize and teach them to obey him, and he would be with them always. Whereas in previous missions Jesus had sent his disciples only to the Jews, their mission from now on would be worldwide. Jesus is Lord of the earth, and he died for the sins of all those who trust him, everywhere. We are to go—whether it is next door or to another country—and make disciples. It is not an option but a command to all who call Jesus Lord. All of us are not evangelists, but we have all received gifts that we can use in helping to fulfill the great commission. As we obey, we have comfort in the knowledge that Jesus is always with us.

Jesus Ascends to Heaven

OCTOBER 4

LUKE 24:44-53

[44]Then he said, "When I was with you before, I told you that everything written about me
in the law of Moses and the prophets and in the Psalms must be fulfilled." [45]Then he opened
their minds to understand the Scriptures. [46]And he said, "Yes, it was written long ago that
the Messiah would suffer and die and rise from the dead on the third day. [47]It was also written that this message would be proclaimed in the authority of his name to all the nations,
beginning in Jerusalem: 'There is forgiveness of sins for all who repent.' [48]You are witnesses
of all these things.

[49]"And now I will send the Holy Spirit, just as my Father promised. But stay here in the
city until the Holy Spirit comes and fills you with power from heaven."

[50]Then Jesus led them to Bethany, and lifting his hands to heaven, he blessed them.
[51]While he was blessing them, he left them and was taken up to heaven. [52]So they worshiped
him and then returned to Jerusalem filled with great joy. [53]And they spent all of their time
in the Temple, praising God.

How do you find Christ opening your mind as you read the Bible? Jesus opened these people's minds to understand the Scriptures. The Holy Spirit does this in our lives today when we study the Bible. Have you ever wondered what a difficult Bible passage meant? Besides reading surrounding passages, asking other people, and consulting reference works, pray that the Holy Spirit will open your mind to understand, giving you the needed insight to put God's Word into action in your life.

OCTOBER 5

He Will Return

ACTS 1:1-11

In my first book I told you, Theophilus, about everything Jesus began to do and teach
2until the day he was taken up to heaven after giving his chosen apostles further instructions
through the Holy Spirit. 3During the forty days after he suffered and died, he appeared to the
apostles from time to time, and he proved to them in many ways that he was actually alive.
And he talked to them about the Kingdom of God.

4Once when he was eating with them, he commanded them, "Do not leave Jerusalem
until the Father sends you the gift he promised, as I told you before. 5John baptized with
water, but in just a few days you will be baptized with the Holy Spirit."

6So when the apostles were with Jesus, they kept asking him, "Lord, has the time come
for you to free Israel and restore our kingdom?"

7He replied, "The Father alone has the authority to set those dates and times, and they are
not for you to know. 8But you will receive power when the Holy Spirit comes upon you. And
you will be my witnesses, telling people about me everywhere—in Jerusalem, throughout
Judea, in Samaria, and to the ends of the earth."

9After saying this, he was taken up into a cloud while they were watching, and they could
no longer see him. 10As they strained to see him rising into heaven, two white-robed men
suddenly stood among them. 11"Men of Galilee," they said, "why are you standing here staring
into heaven? Jesus has been taken from you into heaven, but someday he will return from
heaven in the same way you saw him go!"

What one thing would you be sure to do if you knew Jesus was coming back today? Today there are still people who doubt Jesus' resurrection. But Jesus appeared to the apostles on many occasions after his resurrection, proving that he was alive. Look at the change the Resurrection made in the disciples' lives. At Jesus' death, they scattered. They were disillusioned and feared for their lives. After seeing the resurrected Christ, they were fearless and risked everything to spread the Good News about him around the world. They faced imprisonment, beatings, rejection, and martyrdom, yet they never compromised their mission. These men would not have risked their lives for something they knew was a fraud. They knew Jesus was raised from the dead, and the early church was fired up with enthusiasm to tell others.

First Things First

OCTOBER 6

ACTS 1:12-26

[12]Then the apostles returned to Jerusalem from the Mount of Olives, a distance of half a mile.
[13]When they arrived, they went to the upstairs room of the house where they were staying.

Here are the names of those who were present: Peter, John, James, Andrew, Philip, Thomas, Bartholomew, Matthew, James (son of Alphaeus), Simon (the zealot), and Judas
(son of James). [14]They all met together and were constantly united in prayer, along with Mary the mother of Jesus, several other women, and the brothers of Jesus.

[15]During this time, when about 120 believers were together in one place, Peter stood
up and addressed them. [16]"Brothers," he said, "the Scriptures had to be fulfilled concerning Judas, who guided those who arrested Jesus. This was predicted long ago by the Holy Spirit,
speaking through King David. [17]Judas was one of us and shared in the ministry with us."

[18](Judas had bought a field with the money he received for his treachery. Falling headfirst
there, his body split open, spilling out all his intestines. [19]The news of his death spread to all the people of Jerusalem, and they gave the place the Aramaic name *Akeldama,* which means "Field of Blood.")

[20]Peter continued, "This was written in the book of Psalms, where it says, 'Let his home become desolate, with no one living in it.' It also says, 'Let someone else take his position.'

[21]"So now we must choose a replacement for Judas from among the men who were with
us the entire time we were traveling with the Lord Jesus—[22]from the time he was baptized
by John until the day he was taken from us. Whoever is chosen will join us as a witness of Jesus' resurrection."

[23]So they nominated two men: Joseph called Barsabbas (also known as Justus) and
Matthias. [24]Then they all prayed, "O Lord, you know every heart. Show us which of these
men you have chosen [25]as an apostle to replace Judas in this ministry, for he has deserted us
and gone where he belongs." [26]Then they cast lots, and Matthias was selected to become an apostle with the other eleven.

How much time do you spend in prayer when facing a difficult situation? After Christ was taken up into heaven, the disciples immediately returned to Jerusalem and had a prayer meeting. Jesus had said they would be baptized with the Holy Spirit in a few days, so they waited and prayed. When you face a difficult task, an important decision, or a baffling dilemma, don't rush, hoping it will come out right. Instead, your first step should be to pray for the Holy Spirit's power and guidance.

OCTOBER 7

An Amazing Gift

ACTS 2:1-13

On the day of Pentecost all the believers were meeting together in one place. 2Suddenly, there was a sound from heaven like the roaring of a mighty windstorm, and it filled the house where they were sitting. 3Then, what looked like flames or tongues of fire appeared and settled on each of them. 4And everyone present was filled with the Holy Spirit and began speaking in other languages, as the Holy Spirit gave them this ability.

5At that time there were devout Jews from every nation living in Jerusalem. 6When they heard the loud noise, everyone came running, and they were bewildered to hear their own languages being spoken by the believers.

7They were completely amazed. "How can this be?" they exclaimed. "These people are all from Galilee, 8and yet we hear them speaking in our own native languages! 9Here we are—Parthians, Medes, Elamites, people from Mesopotamia, Judea, Cappadocia, Pontus, the province of Asia, 10Phrygia, Pamphylia, Egypt, and the areas of Libya around Cyrene, visitors from Rome 11(both Jews and converts to Judaism), Cretans, and Arabs. And we all hear these people speaking in our own languages about the wonderful things God has done!" 12They stood there amazed and perplexed. "What can this mean?" they asked each other.

13But others in the crowd ridiculed them, saying, "They're just drunk, that's all!"

What is the main purpose of each gift God has given you? God made his presence known to this group of believers in a spectacular way—a mighty windstorm, tongues of fire, and his Holy Spirit. Would you like God to reveal himself to you in such recognizable ways? He may do so, but be wary of forcing your expectations on God. In 1 Kings 19:10-13, Elijah also needed a message from God. There was a great wind, then an earthquake, and finally a fire. But God's message came in a "gentle whisper." God may use dramatic methods to work in your life—or he may speak in a gentle whisper. Wait patiently and listen.

Peter's First Sermon

OCTOBER 8

ACTS 2:14-38

[14]Then Peter stepped forward with the eleven other apostles and shouted to the crowd,
"Listen carefully, all of you, fellow Jews and residents of Jerusalem! Make no mistake about
this. [15]These people are not drunk, as some of you are assuming. Nine o'clock in the morning
is much too early for that. [16]No, what you see was predicted long ago by the prophet Joel:

[17]'In the last days,' God says,
'I will pour out my Spirit upon all people.
Your sons and daughters will prophesy.
Your young men will see visions,
and your old men will dream dreams.
[18]In those days I will pour out my Spirit
even on my servants—men and women alike—
and they will prophesy.
[19]And I will cause wonders in the heavens above
and signs on the earth below—
blood and fire and clouds of smoke.
[20]The sun will become dark,
and the moon will turn blood red
before that great and glorious day of the LORD arrives.
[21]But everyone who calls on the name of the LORD
will be saved.'

[22]"People of Israel, listen! God publicly endorsed Jesus the Nazarene by doing powerful
miracles, wonders, and signs through him, as you well know. [23]But God knew what would
happen, and his prearranged plan was carried out when Jesus was betrayed. With the help of
lawless Gentiles, you nailed him to a cross and killed him. [24]But God released him from the
horrors of death and raised him back to life, for death could not keep him in its grip." . . .

[37]Peter's words pierced their hearts, and they said to him and to the other apostles,
"Brothers, what should we do?"

[38]Peter replied, "Each of you must repent of your sins and turn to God, and be baptized
in the name of Jesus Christ for the forgiveness of your sins. Then you will receive the gift of
the Holy Spirit."

Have you ever felt as though you've made such bad mistakes that God could never forgive and use you? Peter had been an unstable leader during Jesus' ministry, even denying that he knew Jesus. But Christ forgave and restored Peter after his denial. This was a new Peter, humble but bold. His confidence came from the Holy Spirit, who made him a powerful and dynamic speaker. No matter what sins you have committed, God says he will forgive you and make you useful for his Kingdom. Confess your sins and allow God to use you effectively to serve him.

OCTOBER 9 Miracles in the Early Church

ACTS 2:41–3:11

41 Those who believed what Peter said were baptized and added to the church that day—about
3,000 in all.
42 All the believers devoted themselves to the apostles' teaching, and to fellowship, and to
sharing in meals (including the Lord's Supper), and to prayer.
43 A deep sense of awe came over them all, and the apostles performed many miraculous
signs and wonders. 44 And all the believers met together in one place and shared everything
they had. 45 They sold their property and possessions and shared the money with those in
need. 46 They worshiped together at the Temple each day, met in homes for the Lord's Supper,
and shared their meals with great joy and generosity—47 all the while praising God and enjoying the goodwill of all the people. And each day the Lord added to their fellowship those
who were being saved.

3:1 Peter and John went to the Temple one afternoon to take part in the three o'clock prayer
service. 2 As they approached the Temple, a man lame from birth was being carried in. Each
day he was put beside the Temple gate, the one called the Beautiful Gate, so he could beg
from the people going into the Temple. 3 When he saw Peter and John about to enter, he
asked them for some money.
4 Peter and John looked at him intently, and Peter said, "Look at us!" 5 The lame man
looked at them eagerly, expecting some money. 6 But Peter said, "I don't have any silver or
gold for you. But I'll give you what I have. In the name of Jesus Christ the Nazarene, get up
and walk!"
7 Then Peter took the lame man by the right hand and helped him up. And as he did, the
man's feet and ankles were instantly healed and strengthened. 8 He jumped up, stood on his
feet, and began to walk! Then, walking, leaping, and praising God, he went into the Temple
with them.
9 All the people saw him walking and heard him praising God. 10 When they realized he was
the lame beggar they had seen so often at the Beautiful Gate, they were absolutely astounded!
11 They all rushed out in amazement to Solomon's Colonnade, where the man was holding
tightly to Peter and John.

When have you experienced God giving you what you need, even if it wasn't what you thought you wanted? The lame beggar asked for money, but Peter gave him something much better—the use of his legs. We often ask God to solve a small problem, but he wants to give us a new life and help for all our problems. When we ask God for help, he may say, "I've got something even better for you." Ask God for what you want, but don't be surprised when he gives you what you really need.

Peter's Second Sermon

OCTOBER 10

ACTS 3:12–4:4

[12]Peter saw his opportunity and addressed the crowd. "People of Israel," he said, "what is so
surprising about this? And why stare at us as though we had made this man walk by our
own power or godliness? [13]For it is the God of Abraham, Isaac, and Jacob—the God of all
our ancestors—who has brought glory to his servant Jesus by doing this. This is the same
Jesus whom you handed over and rejected before Pilate, despite Pilate's decision to release
him. [14]You rejected this holy, righteous one and instead demanded the release of a murderer.
[15]You killed the author of life, but God raised him from the dead. And we are witnesses of
this fact! . . .

[17]"Friends, I realize that what you and your leaders did to Jesus was done in ignorance.
[18]But God was fulfilling what all the prophets had foretold about the Messiah—that he must
suffer these things. [19]Now repent of your sins and turn to God, so that your sins may be wiped
away. [20]Then times of refreshment will come from the presence of the Lord, and he will again
send you Jesus, your appointed Messiah. [21]For he must remain in heaven until the time for the
final restoration of all things, as God promised long ago through his holy prophets. [22]Moses
said, 'The LORD your God will raise up for you a Prophet like me from among your own
people. Listen carefully to everything he tells you.' [23]Then Moses said, 'Anyone who will not
listen to that Prophet will be completely cut off from God's people.'

[24]"Starting with Samuel, every prophet spoke about what is happening today. [25]You are
the children of those prophets, and you are included in the covenant God promised to your
ancestors. For God said to Abraham, 'Through your descendants all the families on earth
will be blessed.' [26]When God raised up his servant, Jesus, he sent him first to you people of
Israel, to bless you by turning each of you back from your sinful ways."

[4:1]While Peter and John were speaking to the people, they were confronted by the priests, the
captain of the Temple guard, and some of the Sadducees. [2]These leaders were very disturbed
that Peter and John were teaching the people that through Jesus there is a resurrection of the
dead. [3]They arrested them and, since it was already evening, put them in jail until morning.
[4]But many of the people who heard their message believed it, so the number of men who
believed now totaled about 5,000.

What do you risk in witnessing about Christ and sharing your faith—rejection, persecution? Not often will sharing the gospel send us to jail as it did for Peter and John. Still, we run risks in trying to win others to Christ. We might be willing to face a night in jail if it would bring five thousand people to Christ, but shouldn't we also be willing to suffer for the sake of even one? Whatever the risks, realize that nothing done for God is ever wasted.

OCTOBER 11

Hostile Reactions

ACTS 4:5-22

5The next day the council of all the rulers and elders and teachers of religious law met in
Jerusalem. . . . 7They brought in the two disciples and demanded, "By what power, or in
whose name, have you done this?"

8Then Peter, filled with the Holy Spirit, said to them, "Rulers and elders of our people,
9are we being questioned today because we've done a good deed for a crippled man? Do you
want to know how he was healed? 10Let me clearly state to all of you and to all the people
of Israel that he was healed by the powerful name of Jesus Christ the Nazarene, the man
you crucified but whom God raised from the dead. 11For Jesus is the one referred to in the
Scriptures, where it says,

> 'The stone that you builders rejected
> has now become the cornerstone.'

12There is salvation in no one else! God has given no other name under heaven by which we
must be saved."

13The members of the council were amazed when they saw the boldness of Peter and John,
for they could see that they were ordinary men with no special training in the Scriptures.
They also recognized them as men who had been with Jesus. 14But since they could see the
man who had been healed standing right there among them, there was nothing the council
could say. 15So they ordered Peter and John out of the council chamber and conferred among
themselves.

16"What should we do with these men?" they asked each other. "We can't deny that they
have performed a miraculous sign, and everybody in Jerusalem knows about it. 17But to keep
them from spreading their propaganda any further, we must warn them not to speak to anyone in Jesus' name again." 18So they called the apostles back in and commanded them never
again to speak or teach in the name of Jesus.

19But Peter and John replied, "Do you think God wants us to obey you rather than him?
20We cannot stop telling about everything we have seen and heard."

21The council then threatened them further, but they finally let them go because they
didn't know how to punish them without starting a riot. For everyone was praising God 22for
this miraculous sign—the healing of a man who had been lame for more than forty years.

What excuses are you most likely to use to keep from sharing your faith? Although the evidence was overwhelming and irrefutable (changed lives and a healed man), the religious leaders refused to believe in Christ and continued to try to suppress the truth. Don't be surprised if some people reject you and your positive witness for Christ. When minds are closed, even the clearest presentation of the facts can't open them. But don't give up. Pray for those people and continue to spread the gospel. Peter and John's zeal for the Lord was so strong that they could not keep quiet. If your courage to witness for God has weakened, pray that your boldness may increase.

Praying and Sharing

OCTOBER 12

ACTS 4:23-37

23As soon as they were freed, Peter and John returned to the other believers and told them what the leading priests and elders had said. 24When they heard the report, all the believers lifted their voices together in prayer to God: "O Sovereign Lord, Creator of heaven and earth, the sea, and everything in them—25you spoke long ago by the Holy Spirit through our ancestor David, your servant, saying,

'Why were the nations so angry?
    Why did they waste their time with futile plans?
26The kings of the earth prepared for battle;
    the rulers gathered together
against the LORD
    and against his Messiah.'

27"In fact, this has happened here in this very city! For Herod Antipas, Pontius Pilate the governor, the Gentiles, and the people of Israel were all united against Jesus, your holy servant, whom you anointed. 28But everything they did was determined beforehand according to your will. 29And now, O Lord, hear their threats, and give us, your servants, great boldness in preaching your word. 30Stretch out your hand with healing power; may miraculous signs and wonders be done through the name of your holy servant Jesus."

31After this prayer, the meeting place shook, and they were all filled with the Holy Spirit. Then they preached the word of God with boldness.

32All the believers were united in heart and mind. And they felt that what they owned was not their own, so they shared everything they had. 33The apostles testified powerfully to the resurrection of the Lord Jesus, and God's great blessing was upon them all. 34There were no needy people among them, because those who owned land or houses would sell them 35and bring the money to the apostles to give to those in need.

36For instance, there was Joseph, the one the apostles nicknamed Barnabas (which means "Son of Encouragement"). He was from the tribe of Levi and came from the island of Cyprus. 37He sold a field he owned and brought the money to the apostles.

When was the last time you sacrificially shared with someone else? None of these Christians felt that what they had was their own, and so they were able to give and share, eliminating poverty among them. They would not let a brother or sister suffer when others had plenty. How do you feel about your possessions? We should adopt the attitude that everything we have comes from God, and we are sharing only what is already his.

OCTOBER 13 Ananias and Sapphira

ACTS 5:1-16

But there was a certain man named Ananias who, with his wife, Sapphira, sold some property.
2He brought part of the money to the apostles, claiming it was the full amount. With his
wife's consent, he kept the rest.

3Then Peter said, "Ananias, why have you let Satan fill your heart? You lied to the Holy
Spirit, and you kept some of the money for yourself. 4The property was yours to sell or not
sell, as you wished. And after selling it, the money was also yours to give away. How could
you do a thing like this? You weren't lying to us but to God!"

5As soon as Ananias heard these words, he fell to the floor and died. Everyone who heard
about it was terrified. 6Then some young men got up, wrapped him in a sheet, and took him
out and buried him.

7About three hours later his wife came in, not knowing what had happened. 8Peter asked
her, "Was this the price you and your husband received for your land?"

"Yes," she replied, "that was the price."

9And Peter said, "How could the two of you even think of conspiring to test the Spirit of
the Lord like this? The young men who buried your husband are just outside the door, and
they will carry you out, too."

10Instantly, she fell to the floor and died. When the young men came in and saw that she
was dead, they carried her out and buried her beside her husband. 11Great fear gripped the
entire church and everyone else who heard what had happened.

12The apostles were performing many miraculous signs and wonders among the people.
And all the believers were meeting regularly at the Temple in the area known as Solomon's
Colonnade. 13But no one else dared to join them, even though all the people had high regard
for them. 14Yet more and more people believed and were brought to the Lord—crowds of
both men and women. 15As a result of the apostles' work, sick people were brought out into
the streets on beds and mats so that Peter's shadow might fall across some of them as he went
by. 16Crowds came from the villages around Jerusalem, bringing their sick and those possessed
by evil spirits, and they were all healed.

How often are you tempted to take God lightly? The sin that Ananias and Sapphira committed was not stinginess or holding back part of the money. It was their choice whether or not to sell the land and how much to give. Their sin was lying to God and to God's people—saying they gave the whole amount but holding back some for themselves and trying to make themselves appear more generous than they really were. This act was judged harshly because dishonesty, greed, and covetousness are destructive in a church, preventing the Holy Spirit from working effectively. All lying is bad, but when we lie to try to deceive God and his people about our relationship with him, we destroy our testimony about Christ.

Arrested!

OCTOBER 14

ACTS 5:17-42

17The high priest and his officials, who were Sadducees, were filled with jealousy. 18They arrested the apostles and put them in the public jail. 19But an angel of the Lord came at night, opened the gates of the jail, and brought them out. Then he told them, 20"Go to the Temple and give the people this message of life!"

21So at daybreak the apostles entered the Temple, as they were told, and immediately began teaching. . . .

26The captain went with his Temple guards and arrested the apostles, but without violence, for they were afraid the people would stone them. 27Then they brought the apostles before the high council, where the high priest confronted them. 28"We gave you strict orders never again to teach in this man's name!" he said. "Instead, you have filled all Jerusalem with your teaching about him, and you want to make us responsible for his death!"

29But Peter and the apostles replied, "We must obey God rather than any human authority."

. . . 33When they heard this, the high council was furious and decided to kill them. 34But one member, a Pharisee named Gamaliel, who was an expert in religious law and respected by all the people, stood up and ordered that the men be sent outside the council chamber for a while. 35Then he said to his colleagues, "Men of Israel, take care what you are planning to do to these men! 36Some time ago there was that fellow Theudas, who pretended to be someone great. About 400 others joined him, but he was killed, and all his followers went their various ways. The whole movement came to nothing. . . .

38"So my advice is, leave these men alone. Let them go. If they are planning and doing these things merely on their own, it will soon be overthrown. 39But if it is from God, you will not be able to overthrow them. You may even find yourselves fighting against God!"

40The others accepted his advice. They called in the apostles and had them flogged. Then they ordered them never again to speak in the name of Jesus, and they let them go.

41The apostles left the high council rejoicing that God had counted them worthy to suffer disgrace for the name of Jesus. 42And every day, in the Temple and from house to house, they continued to teach and preach this message: "Jesus is the Messiah."

How do you react when you are treated unfairly? Have you ever thought of persecution as a blessing? This beating suffered by Peter and John was the first time any of the apostles had been physically abused for their faith. These men knew how Jesus had suffered, and they praised God that he allowed them to be persecuted like their Lord. If you are mocked or persecuted for your faith, it isn't because you are doing something wrong but because God has counted you "worthy to suffer disgrace for the name of Jesus."

OCTOBER 15 Stephen: Special Servant

ACTS 6:1-15

But as the believers rapidly multiplied, there were rumblings of discontent. The Greek-speaking believers complained about the Hebrew-speaking believers, saying that their widows were being discriminated against in the daily distribution of food.

2So the Twelve called a meeting of all the believers. They said, "We apostles should spend our time teaching the word of God, not running a food program. 3And so, brothers, select seven men who are well respected and are full of the Spirit and wisdom. We will give them this responsibility. 4Then we apostles can spend our time in prayer and teaching the word."

5Everyone liked this idea, and they chose the following: Stephen (a man full of faith and the Holy Spirit), Philip, Procorus, Nicanor, Timon, Parmenas, and Nicolas of Antioch (an earlier convert to the Jewish faith). 6These seven were presented to the apostles, who prayed for them as they laid their hands on them.

7So God's message continued to spread. The number of believers greatly increased in Jerusalem, and many of the Jewish priests were converted, too.

8Stephen, a man full of God's grace and power, performed amazing miracles and signs among the people. 9But one day some men from the Synagogue of Freed Slaves, as it was called, started to debate with him. They were Jews from Cyrene, Alexandria, Cilicia, and the province of Asia. 10None of them could stand against the wisdom and the Spirit with which Stephen spoke.

11So they persuaded some men to lie about Stephen, saying, "We heard him blaspheme Moses, and even God." 12This roused the people, the elders, and the teachers of religious law. So they arrested Stephen and brought him before the high council.

13The lying witnesses said, "This man is always speaking against the holy Temple and against the law of Moses. 14We have heard him say that this Jesus of Nazareth will destroy the Temple and change the customs Moses handed down to us."

15At this point everyone in the high council stared at Stephen, because his face became as bright as an angel's.

What specific responsibilities do you have in your local church? As the early church increased in size, so did its needs. One great need was to organize the distribution of food to the poor. The apostles needed to focus on preaching, so they chose others to administer the food program. Each person has a vital part to play in the life of the church. If you are in a position of leadership and find yourself overwhelmed by responsibilities, determine your God-given abilities and priorities, and then find others to help. If you are not in leadership, offer your God-given gifts for service in various areas of your church's ministry.

History Review, Part 1

OCTOBER 16

ACTS 7:1-25

Then the high priest asked Stephen, "Are these accusations true?"
2This was Stephen's reply: "Brothers and fathers, listen to me. Our glorious God appeared
to our ancestor Abraham in Mesopotamia before he settled in Haran. 3God told him, 'Leave
your native land and your relatives, and come into the land that I will show you.' 4So Abraham
left the land of the Chaldeans and lived in Haran until his father died. Then God brought
him here to the land where you now live. . . .
8"God also gave Abraham the covenant of circumcision at that time. . . . And the practice
was continued when Isaac became the father of Jacob, and when Jacob became the father of
the twelve patriarchs of the Israelite nation.
9"These patriarchs were jealous of their brother Joseph, and they sold him to be a slave in
Egypt. But God was with him 10and rescued him . . .
14Then Joseph sent for his father, Jacob, and all his relatives to come to Egypt, seventy-five
persons in all. 15So Jacob went to Egypt. He died there, as did our ancestors. 16Their bodies
were taken to Shechem and buried in the tomb Abraham had bought for a certain price from
Hamor's sons in Shechem.
17"As the time drew near when God would fulfill his promise to Abraham, the number of
our people in Egypt greatly increased. 18But then a new king came to the throne of Egypt who
knew nothing about Joseph. 19This king exploited our people and oppressed them, forcing
parents to abandon their newborn babies so they would die.
20"At that time Moses was born—a beautiful child in God's eyes. His parents cared for
him at home for three months. 21When they had to abandon him, Pharaoh's daughter adopted
him and raised him as her own son. 22Moses was taught all the wisdom of the Egyptians, and
he was powerful in both speech and action.
23"One day when Moses was forty years old, he decided to visit his relatives, the people
of Israel. 24He saw an Egyptian mistreating an Israelite. So Moses came to the man's defense
and avenged him, killing the Egyptian. 25Moses assumed his fellow Israelites would realize
that God had sent him to rescue them, but they didn't."

How familiar are you becoming with "his story" in history? Stephen's review of Jewish history gives a clear testimony of God's faithfulness and sovereignty. Despite the continued failures of his chosen people and the swirling world events, God was working out his plan. When faced by a confusing array of circumstances, remember: (1) God is in control—nothing surprises him. (2) This world is not all there is—it will pass away, but God is eternal. (3) God is just, and he will make things right—punishing the wicked and rewarding the faithful. (4) God wants to use you (like Joseph, Moses, and Stephen) to make a difference in the world.

OCTOBER 17 — History Review, Part 2

ACTS 7:30-60

30 “Forty years later, in the desert near Mount Sinai, an angel appeared to Moses in the flame of a burning bush. 31 When Moses saw it, he was amazed at the sight. As he went to take a closer look, the voice of the LORD called out to him, 32 ‘I am the God of your ancestors—the God of Abraham, Isaac, and Jacob.’ Moses shook with terror and did not dare to look.

33 “Then the LORD said to him, ‘Take off your sandals, for you are standing on holy ground. 34 I have certainly seen the oppression of my people in Egypt. I have heard their groans and have come down to rescue them. Now go, for I am sending you back to Egypt.’ . . .

39 “But our ancestors refused to listen to Moses. They rejected him and wanted to return to Egypt. 40 They told Aaron, ‘Make us some gods who can lead us, for we don’t know what has become of this Moses, who brought us out of Egypt.’ 41 So they made an idol shaped like a calf, and they sacrificed to it and celebrated over this thing they had made. . . .

51 “You stubborn people! You are heathen at heart and deaf to the truth. Must you forever resist the Holy Spirit? That’s what your ancestors did, and so do you! 52 Name one prophet your ancestors didn’t persecute! They even killed the ones who predicted the coming of the Righteous One—the Messiah whom you betrayed and murdered. 53 You deliberately disobeyed God’s law, even though you received it from the hands of angels.”

54 The Jewish leaders were infuriated by Stephen’s accusation, and they shook their fists at him in rage. 55 But Stephen, full of the Holy Spirit, gazed steadily into heaven and saw the glory of God, and he saw Jesus standing in the place of honor at God’s right hand. 56 And he told them, “Look, I see the heavens opened and the Son of Man standing in the place of honor at God’s right hand!”

57 Then they put their hands over their ears and began shouting. They rushed at him 58 and dragged him out of the city and began to stone him. His accusers took off their coats and laid them at the feet of a young man named Saul.

59 As they stoned him, Stephen prayed, “Lord Jesus, receive my spirit.” 60 He fell to his knees, shouting, “Lord, don’t charge them with this sin!” And with that, he died.

In what ways would you want to be more like Stephen? Stephen saw the glory of God and Jesus the Messiah standing at God’s right hand. Stephen’s vision supported Jesus’ claim of being the Messiah and angered the Jewish leaders who had condemned Jesus to death for blasphemy. They would not tolerate Stephen’s words, so they dragged him out of the city and killed him. People may not kill us for witnessing about Christ, but they will let us know they don’t want to hear the truth and try to silence us. Keep honoring God in your conduct and your words; though many may turn against you and your message, some will follow Christ. Remember, Stephen’s death made a profound impact on Paul, who later became the world’s greatest missionary. Even those who oppose you now may later turn to Christ.

Benefits of Persecution

OCTOBER 18

ACTS 8:1-25

A great wave of persecution began that day, sweeping over the church in Jerusalem; and all
the believers except the apostles were scattered through the regions of Judea and Samaria. . . .
4But the believers who were scattered preached the Good News about Jesus wherever
they went. 5Philip, for example, went to the city of Samaria and told the people there about
the Messiah. 6Crowds listened intently to Philip because they were eager to hear his message
and see the miraculous signs he did. 7Many evil spirits were cast out, screaming as they left
their victims. And many who had been paralyzed or lame were healed. 8So there was great
joy in that city.
9A man named Simon had been a sorcerer there for many years, amazing the people of
Samaria and claiming to be someone great. . . .
12But now the people believed Philip's message of Good News concerning the Kingdom of
God and the name of Jesus Christ. As a result, many men and women were baptized. 13Then
Simon himself believed and was baptized. He began following Philip wherever he went, and
he was amazed by the signs and great miracles Philip performed.
14When the apostles in Jerusalem heard that the people of Samaria had accepted God's
message, they sent Peter and John there. 15As soon as they arrived, they prayed for these new
believers to receive the Holy Spirit. 16The Holy Spirit had not yet come upon any of them,
for they had only been baptized in the name of the Lord Jesus. 17Then Peter and John laid
their hands upon these believers, and they received the Holy Spirit.
18When Simon saw that the Spirit was given when the apostles laid their hands on people, he
offered them money to buy this power. 19"Let me have this power, too," he exclaimed, "so that
when I lay my hands on people, they will receive the Holy Spirit!"
20But Peter replied, "May your money be destroyed with you for thinking God's gift can
be bought! 21You can have no part in this, for your heart is not right with God. 22Repent of
your wickedness and pray to the Lord. Perhaps he will forgive your evil thoughts, 23for I can
see that you are full of bitter jealousy and are held captive by sin."
24"Pray to the Lord for me," Simon exclaimed, "that these terrible things you've said won't
happen to me!"
25After testifying and preaching the word of the Lord in Samaria, Peter and John returned
to Jerusalem. And they stopped in many Samaritan villages along the way to preach the Good
News.

Which difficulties in your life has God used to help you grow spiritually? Persecution forced the believers out of their homes in Jerusalem, but with them went the gospel. Often we have to become uncomfortable before we'll move. The next time you are tempted to complain about uncomfortable circumstances, realize that God may be preparing you for a special task.

OCTOBER 19

Unexpected Appointment

ACTS 8:26-40

26As for Philip, an angel of the Lord said to him, "Go south down the desert road that runs
from Jerusalem to Gaza." 27So he started out, and he met the treasurer of Ethiopia, a eunuch
of great authority under the Kandake, the queen of Ethiopia. The eunuch had gone to
Jerusalem to worship, 28and he was now returning. Seated in his carriage, he was reading
aloud from the book of the prophet Isaiah.

29The Holy Spirit said to Philip, "Go over and walk along beside the carriage."

30Philip ran over and heard the man reading from the prophet Isaiah. Philip asked, "Do
you understand what you are reading?"

31The man replied, "How can I, unless someone instructs me?" And he urged Philip to
come up into the carriage and sit with him.

32The passage of Scripture he had been reading was this:

"He was led like a sheep to the slaughter.
And as a lamb is silent before the shearers,
he did not open his mouth.
33He was humiliated and received no justice.
Who can speak of his descendants?
For his life was taken from the earth."

34The eunuch asked Philip, "Tell me, was the prophet talking about himself or someone
else?" 35So beginning with this same Scripture, Philip told him the Good News about Jesus.

36As they rode along, they came to some water, and the eunuch said, "Look! There's some
water! Why can't I be baptized?" 38He ordered the carriage to stop, and they went down into
the water, and Philip baptized him.

39When they came up out of the water, the Spirit of the Lord snatched Philip away.
The eunuch never saw him again but went on his way rejoicing. 40Meanwhile, Philip found
himself farther north at the town of Azotus. He preached the Good News there and in every
town along the way until he came to Caesarea.

Where might you have an open door to share the gospel with others? Philip found the Ethiopian man reading Scripture. Taking advantage of this opportunity to explain the gospel, Philip asked the man if he understood what he was reading. Philip followed the Spirit's leading and, beginning the discussion where the man was (immersed in the prophecies of Isaiah), Philip explained how Jesus Christ fulfilled Isaiah's prophecies. When we share the gospel, we should start where the other person's concerns are focused. Then we can bring the gospel to bear on those concerns.

Paul Meets Jesus

OCTOBER 20

ACTS 9:1-19

Meanwhile, Saul was uttering threats with every breath and was eager to kill the Lord's followers. So he went to the high priest. 2He requested letters addressed to the synagogues in Damascus, asking for their cooperation in the arrest of any followers of the Way he found there. He wanted to bring them—both men and women—back to Jerusalem in chains.

3As he was approaching Damascus on this mission, a light from heaven suddenly shone down around him. 4He fell to the ground and heard a voice saying to him, "Saul! Saul! Why are you persecuting me?"

5"Who are you, lord?" Saul asked.

And the voice replied, "I am Jesus, the one you are persecuting! 6Now get up and go into the city, and you will be told what you must do."

7The men with Saul stood speechless, for they heard the sound of someone's voice but saw no one! 8Saul picked himself up off the ground, but when he opened his eyes he was blind. So his companions led him by the hand to Damascus. 9He remained there blind for three days and did not eat or drink.

10Now there was a believer in Damascus named Ananias. The Lord spoke to him in a vision, calling, "Ananias!"

"Yes, Lord!" he replied.

11The Lord said, "Go over to Straight Street, to the house of Judas. When you get there, ask for a man from Tarsus named Saul. He is praying to me right now. 12I have shown him a vision of a man named Ananias coming in and laying hands on him so he can see again."

13"But Lord," exclaimed Ananias, "I've heard many people talk about the terrible things this man has done to the believers in Jerusalem! 14And he is authorized by the leading priests to arrest everyone who calls upon your name."

15But the Lord said, "Go, for Saul is my chosen instrument to take my message to the Gentiles and to kings, as well as to the people of Israel. 16And I will show him how much he must suffer for my name's sake."

17So Ananias went and found Saul. He laid his hands on him and said, "Brother Saul, the Lord Jesus, who appeared to you on the road, has sent me so that you might regain your sight and be filled with the Holy Spirit." 18Instantly something like scales fell from Saul's eyes, and he regained his sight. Then he got up and was baptized. 19Afterward he ate some food and regained his strength.

Saul stayed with the believers in Damascus for a few days.

What unusual events has God used to catch your attention? As Paul traveled to Damascus, pursuing Christians, he was confronted by the risen Christ and brought face-to-face with the truth of the gospel. Sometimes God breaks into a life in a spectacular manner, and sometimes conversion is a quiet experience. Beware of people who insist that you must have a particular type of conversion experience. The right way to come to faith in Jesus is whichever way God brings you.

OCTOBER 21

Paul's New Life

ACTS 9:20-31

[20]And immediately he began preaching about Jesus in the synagogues, saying, "He is indeed the Son of God!"

[21]All who heard him were amazed. "Isn't this the same man who caused such devastation among Jesus' followers in Jerusalem?" they asked. "And didn't he come here to arrest them and take them in chains to the leading priests?"

[22]Saul's preaching became more and more powerful, and the Jews in Damascus couldn't refute his proofs that Jesus was indeed the Messiah. [23]After a while some of the Jews plotted together to kill him. [24]They were watching for him day and night at the city gate so they could murder him, but Saul was told about their plot. [25]So during the night, some of the other believers lowered him in a large basket through an opening in the city wall.

[26]When Saul arrived in Jerusalem, he tried to meet with the believers, but they were all afraid of him. They did not believe he had truly become a believer! [27]Then Barnabas brought him to the apostles and told them how Saul had seen the Lord on the way to Damascus and how the Lord had spoken to Saul. He also told them that Saul had preached boldly in the name of Jesus in Damascus.

[28]So Saul stayed with the apostles and went all around Jerusalem with them, preaching boldly in the name of the Lord. [29]He debated with some Greek-speaking Jews, but they tried to murder him. [30]When the believers heard about this, they took him down to Caesarea and sent him away to Tarsus, his hometown.

[31]The church then had peace throughout Judea, Galilee, and Samaria, and it became stronger as the believers lived in the fear of the Lord. And with the encouragement of the Holy Spirit, it also grew in numbers.

How comfortable did you feel with other Christians when you first came to faith? It is difficult to change your reputation, and Saul had a terrible reputation with the Christians. But Barnabas, a Jewish convert, became the bridge between Saul and the apostles. New Christians (especially those with tarnished reputations) need sponsors, people who will come alongside them, encourage them, teach them, and introduce them to other believers. Find ways that you can become a Barnabas to new believers.

God Uses Peter

OCTOBER 22

ACTS 9:32-42

32 Meanwhile, Peter traveled from place to place, and he came down to visit the believers in
the town of Lydda. 33 There he met a man named Aeneas, who had been paralyzed and bed-
ridden for eight years. 34 Peter said to him, "Aeneas, Jesus Christ heals you! Get up, and roll
up your sleeping mat!" And he was healed instantly. 35 Then the whole population of Lydda
and Sharon saw Aeneas walking around, and they turned to the Lord.

36 There was a believer in Joppa named Tabitha (which in Greek is Dorcas). She was
always doing kind things for others and helping the poor. 37 About this time she became ill
and died. Her body was washed for burial and laid in an upstairs room. 38 But the believers
had heard that Peter was nearby at Lydda, so they sent two men to beg him, "Please come
as soon as possible!"

39 So Peter returned with them; and as soon as he arrived, they took him to the upstairs
room. The room was filled with widows who were weeping and showing him the coats and
other clothes Dorcas had made for them. 40 But Peter asked them all to leave the room; then
he knelt and prayed. Turning to the body he said, "Get up, Tabitha." And she opened her eyes!
When she saw Peter, she sat up! 41 He gave her his hand and helped her up. Then he called in
the widows and all the believers, and he presented her to them alive.

42 The news spread through the whole town, and many believed in the Lord.

This past week, what special ability did you use to meet someone's need? Dorcas made an enormous impact on her community by "always doing kind things for others and helping the poor." When she died, the room was filled with mourners, people she had helped. And when she was brought back to life, the news raced through the town. God uses great preachers like Peter and Paul, but he also uses those who have gifts of kindness like Dorcas. Rather than wishing you had other gifts, make good use of the gifts God has given you.

OCTOBER 23

Peter Sees a Lesson

ACTS 10:1-22

In Caesarea there lived a Roman army officer named Cornelius, who was a captain of the Italian Regiment. 2He was a devout, God-fearing man, as was everyone in his household. He gave generously to the poor and prayed regularly to God. 3One afternoon about three o'clock, he had a vision in which he saw an angel of God coming toward him. "Cornelius!" the angel said.

4Cornelius stared at him in terror. "What is it, sir?" he asked the angel.

And the angel replied, "Your prayers and gifts to the poor have been received by God as an offering! 5Now send some men to Joppa, and summon a man named Simon Peter. 6He is staying with Simon, a tanner who lives near the seashore."

7As soon as the angel was gone, Cornelius called two of his household servants and a devout soldier, one of his personal attendants. 8He told them what had happened and sent them off to Joppa.

9The next day as Cornelius's messengers were nearing the town, Peter went up on the flat roof to pray. It was about noon, 10and he was hungry. But while a meal was being prepared, he fell into a trance. 11He saw the sky open, and something like a large sheet was let down by its four corners. 12In the sheet were all sorts of animals, reptiles, and birds. 13Then a voice said to him, "Get up, Peter; kill and eat them."

14"No, Lord," Peter declared. "I have never eaten anything that our Jewish laws have declared impure and unclean."

15But the voice spoke again: "Do not call something unclean if God has made it clean." 16The same vision was repeated three times. Then the sheet was suddenly pulled up to heaven.

17Peter was very perplexed. What could the vision mean? Just then the men sent by Cornelius found Simon's house. Standing outside the gate, 18they asked if a man named Simon Peter was staying there.

19Meanwhile, as Peter was puzzling over the vision, the Holy Spirit said to him, "Three men have come looking for you. 20Get up, go downstairs, and go with them without hesitation. Don't worry, for I have sent them."

21So Peter went down and said, "I'm the man you are looking for. Why have you come?"

22They said, "We were sent by Cornelius, a Roman officer. He is a devout and God-fearing man, well respected by all the Jews. A holy angel instructed him to summon you to his house so that he can hear your message."

Do you believe God can bring anyone to faith, regardless of a person's background? Cornelius wasn't a Christian, but he was seeking God, and he was a reverent and generous man. Therefore, God sent Peter to tell Cornelius about Jesus. Those who sincerely seek God will find him! God made Cornelius's knowledge complete.

Peter Learns a Lesson

OCTOBER 24

ACTS 10:24-48

24They arrived in Caesarea the following day. Cornelius was waiting for them and had called together his relatives and close friends. 25As Peter entered his home, Cornelius fell at his feet and worshiped him. 26But Peter pulled him up and said, "Stand up! I'm a human being just like you!" 27So they talked together and went inside, where many others were assembled.

28Peter told them, "You know it is against our laws for a Jewish man to enter a Gentile home like this or to associate with you. But God has shown me that I should no longer think of anyone as impure or unclean. 29So I came without objection as soon as I was sent for. Now tell me why you sent for me."

30Cornelius replied, "Four days ago I was praying in my house about this same time, three o'clock in the afternoon. Suddenly, a man in dazzling clothes was standing in front of me. 31He told me, 'Cornelius, your prayer has been heard, and your gifts to the poor have been noticed by God! 32Now send messengers to Joppa, and summon a man named Simon Peter. He is staying in the home of Simon, a tanner who lives near the seashore.' 33So I sent for you at once, and it was good of you to come. Now we are all here, waiting before God to hear the message the Lord has given you."

34Then Peter replied, "I see very clearly that God shows no favoritism. 35In every nation he accepts those who fear him and do what is right. 36This is the message of Good News for the people of Israel—that there is peace with God through Jesus Christ, who is Lord of all. . . .

42"And he ordered us to preach everywhere and to testify that Jesus is the one appointed by God to be the judge of all—the living and the dead. 43He is the one all the prophets testified about, saying that everyone who believes in him will have their sins forgiven through his name."

44Even as Peter was saying these things, the Holy Spirit fell upon all who were listening to the message. 45The Jewish believers who came with Peter were amazed that the gift of the Holy Spirit had been poured out on the Gentiles, too. 46For they heard them speaking in other tongues and praising God.

Then Peter asked, 47"Can anyone object to their being baptized, now that they have received the Holy Spirit just as we did?" 48So he gave orders for them to be baptized in the name of Jesus Christ. Afterward Cornelius asked him to stay with them for several days.

How has God helped you change some attitudes? Perhaps the greatest barrier to the spread of the gospel in the first century was the Jewish-Gentile conflict. Most of the early believers were Jewish, and to them it was scandalous even to think of associating with Gentiles. But God told Peter to take the gospel to a Roman, and Peter obeyed despite his background and personal feelings. God was making it clear that the Good News of Christ is for everyone! We should not allow any barrier—language, culture, prejudice, geography, economic level, or educational level—to keep us from telling others about Christ.

OCTOBER 25

A Welcome to Gentiles

ACTS 11:1-18

Soon the news reached the apostles and other believers in Judea that the Gentiles had received the word of God. 2But when Peter arrived back in Jerusalem, the Jewish believers criticized him. 3"You entered the home of Gentiles and even ate with them!" they said.

4Then Peter told them exactly what had happened. 5"I was in the town of Joppa," he said, "and while I was praying, I went into a trance and saw a vision. Something like a large sheet was let down by its four corners from the sky. And it came right down to me. 6When I looked inside the sheet, I saw all sorts of tame and wild animals, reptiles, and birds. 7And I heard a voice say, 'Get up, Peter; kill and eat them.'

8" 'No, Lord,' I replied. 'I have never eaten anything that our Jewish laws have declared impure or unclean.'

9"But the voice from heaven spoke again: 'Do not call something unclean if God has made it clean.' 10This happened three times before the sheet and all it contained was pulled back up to heaven.

11"Just then three men who had been sent from Caesarea arrived at the house where we were staying. 12The Holy Spirit told me to go with them and not to worry that they were Gentiles. These six brothers here accompanied me, and we soon entered the home of the man who had sent for us. 13He told us how an angel had appeared to him in his home and had told him, 'Send messengers to Joppa, and summon a man named Simon Peter. 14He will tell you how you and everyone in your household can be saved!'

15"As I began to speak," Peter continued, "the Holy Spirit fell on them, just as he fell on us at the beginning. 16Then I thought of the Lord's words when he said, 'John baptized with water, but you will be baptized with the Holy Spirit.' 17And since God gave these Gentiles the same gift he gave us when we believed in the Lord Jesus Christ, who was I to stand in God's way?"

18When the others heard this, they stopped objecting and began praising God. They said, "We can see that God has also given the Gentiles the privilege of repenting of their sins and receiving eternal life."

On which of your prejudices is God still working? When Peter brought the news of Cornelius's conversion back to Jerusalem, the believers were shocked that he had eaten with Gentiles. After they heard the whole story, however, they began praising God. Their reactions teach us how to handle disagreements with other Christians. Before judging the behavior of fellow believers, it is important to hear them out. The Holy Spirit may have something important to teach us through them.

Christians Helping One Another

OCTOBER 26

ACTS 11:19-29

[19]Meanwhile, the believers who had been scattered during the persecution after Stephen's
death traveled as far as Phoenicia, Cyprus, and Antioch of Syria. They preached the word of
God, but only to Jews. [20]However, some of the believers who went to Antioch from Cyprus
and Cyrene began preaching to the Gentiles about the Lord Jesus. [21]The power of the Lord
was with them, and a large number of these Gentiles believed and turned to the Lord.

[22]When the church at Jerusalem heard what had happened, they sent Barnabas to Antioch.
[23]When he arrived and saw this evidence of God's blessing, he was filled with joy, and he
encouraged the believers to stay true to the Lord. [24]Barnabas was a good man, full of the Holy
Spirit and strong in faith. And many people were brought to the Lord.

[25]Then Barnabas went on to Tarsus to look for Saul. [26]When he found him, he brought
him back to Antioch. Both of them stayed there with the church for a full year, teaching large
crowds of people. (It was at Antioch that the believers were first called Christians.)

[27]During this time some prophets traveled from Jerusalem to Antioch. [28]One of them
named Agabus stood up in one of the meetings and predicted by the Spirit that a great
famine was coming upon the entire Roman world. (This was fulfilled during the reign of
Claudius.) [29]So the believers in Antioch decided to send relief to the brothers and sisters in
Judea, everyone giving as much as they could.

What do you do when you hear stories of extreme poverty or hardship among Christians in other parts of the world? There were serious food shortages during the reign of the Roman Emperor Claudius (AD 41–54) because of a drought that had extended across much of the Roman Empire for many years. It is significant that the church in Antioch helped the church in Jerusalem. The daughter church had grown enough to be able to help the established church. The people of Antioch were motivated to give generously because they cared about the needs of others. This is the cheerful giving that the Bible commends (2 Corinthians 9:7). Reluctant giving reflects a lack of concern for people. Focus your concern on the needy, and you will be motivated to give.

OCTOBER 27

Sorrow and Joy

ACTS 12:1-17

About that time King Herod Agrippa began to persecute some believers in the church. 2He
had the apostle James (John's brother) killed with a sword. 3When Herod saw how much
this pleased the Jewish people, he also arrested Peter. (This took place during the Passover
celebration.) 4Then he imprisoned him, placing him under the guard of four squads of four
soldiers each. Herod intended to bring Peter out for public trial after the Passover. 5But while
Peter was in prison, the church prayed very earnestly for him.

6The night before Peter was to be placed on trial, he was asleep, fastened with two chains
between two soldiers. Others stood guard at the prison gate. 7Suddenly, there was a bright
light in the cell, and an angel of the Lord stood before Peter. The angel struck him on the
side to awaken him and said, "Quick! Get up!" And the chains fell off his wrists. 8Then the
angel told him, "Get dressed and put on your sandals." And he did. "Now put on your coat
and follow me," the angel ordered.

9So Peter left the cell, following the angel. But all the time he thought it was a vision.
He didn't realize it was actually happening. 10They passed the first and second guard posts
and came to the iron gate leading to the city, and this opened for them all by itself. So they
passed through and started walking down the street, and then the angel suddenly left him.

11Peter finally came to his senses. "It's really true!" he said. "The Lord has sent his angel
and saved me from Herod and from what the Jewish leaders had planned to do to me!"

12When he realized this, he went to the home of Mary, the mother of John Mark, where
many were gathered for prayer. 13He knocked at the door in the gate, and a servant girl named
Rhoda came to open it. 14When she recognized Peter's voice, she was so overjoyed that, instead
of opening the door, she ran back inside and told everyone, "Peter is standing at the door!"

15"You're out of your mind!" they said. When she insisted, they decided, "It must be his
angel."

16Meanwhile, Peter continued knocking. When they finally opened the door and saw
him, they were amazed. 17He motioned for them to quiet down and told them how the Lord
had led him out of prison. "Tell James and the other brothers what happened," he said. And
then he went to another place.

How do you react when God answers your prayers? Why did God allow James to die and yet miraculously save Peter? Life is full of difficult questions like this. Why is one child physically handicapped and another child athletically gifted? Why do some people die before realizing their potential? These are questions we cannot possibly answer in this life because we do not see all that God sees. God has chosen to allow evil in this world for a time, but we can trust his leading because he has promised to destroy all evil one day. In the meantime, we know that God will help us use our suffering in a way that strengthens us and glorifies him.

Paul and Barnabas Travel and Preach

OCTOBER 28

ACTS 13:1-12

Among the prophets and teachers of the church at Antioch of Syria were Barnabas, Simeon
(called "the black man"), Lucius (from Cyrene), Manaen (the childhood companion of King
Herod Antipas), and Saul. 2One day as these men were worshiping the Lord and fasting, the
Holy Spirit said, "Appoint Barnabas and Saul for the special work to which I have called
them." 3So after more fasting and prayer, the men laid their hands on them and sent them
on their way.

4So Barnabas and Saul were sent out by the Holy Spirit. They went down to the seaport
of Seleucia and then sailed for the island of Cyprus. 5There, in the town of Salamis, they
went to the Jewish synagogues and preached the word of God. John Mark went with them
as their assistant.

6Afterward they traveled from town to town across the entire island until finally they
reached Paphos, where they met a Jewish sorcerer, a false prophet named Bar-Jesus. 7He had
attached himself to the governor, Sergius Paulus, who was an intelligent man. The governor
invited Barnabas and Saul to visit him, for he wanted to hear the word of God. 8But Elymas,
the sorcerer (as his name means in Greek), interfered and urged the governor to pay no
attention to what Barnabas and Saul said. He was trying to keep the governor from believing.

9Saul, also known as Paul, was filled with the Holy Spirit, and he looked the sorcerer in
the eye. 10Then he said, "You son of the devil, full of every sort of deceit and fraud, and enemy
of all that is good! Will you never stop perverting the true ways of the Lord? 11Watch now, for
the Lord has laid his hand of punishment upon you, and you will be struck blind. You will
not see the sunlight for some time." Instantly mist and darkness came over the man's eyes,
and he began groping around begging for someone to take his hand and lead him.

12When the governor saw what had happened, he became a believer, for he was astonished
at the teaching about the Lord.

Which Christians in your life could help you discover more clearly how God wants you to invest your time and abilities? The church set apart Barnabas and Saul for the work God had for them. They were dedicated for a special purpose. We, too, should dedicate our pastors, missionaries, and Christian workers for their tasks. We can also dedicate ourselves to use our time, money, and talents for God's work. Ask God what he wants you to set apart for him.

OCTOBER 29

Response and Reaction

ACTS 14:1-18

The same thing happened in Iconium. Paul and Barnabas went to the Jewish synagogue and
preached with such power that a great number of both Jews and Greeks became believers.
2Some of the Jews, however, spurned God's message and poisoned the minds of the Gentiles
against Paul and Barnabas. 3But the apostles stayed there a long time, preaching boldly about
the grace of the Lord. And the Lord proved their message was true by giving them power to
do miraculous signs and wonders. 4But the people of the town were divided in their opinion
about them. Some sided with the Jews, and some with the apostles.

5Then a mob of Gentiles and Jews, along with their leaders, decided to attack and stone
them. 6When the apostles learned of it, they fled to the region of Lycaonia—to the towns
of Lystra and Derbe and the surrounding area. 7And there they preached the Good News.

8While they were at Lystra, Paul and Barnabas came upon a man with crippled feet. He
had been that way from birth, so he had never walked. He was sitting 9and listening as Paul
preached. Looking straight at him, Paul realized he had faith to be healed. 10So Paul called
to him in a loud voice, "Stand up!" And the man jumped to his feet and started walking.

11When the crowd saw what Paul had done, they shouted in their local dialect, "These
men are gods in human form!" 12They decided that Barnabas was the Greek god Zeus and
that Paul was Hermes, since he was the chief speaker. 13Now the temple of Zeus was located
just outside the town. So the priest of the temple and the crowd brought bulls and wreaths
of flowers to the town gates, and they prepared to offer sacrifices to the apostles.

14But when the apostles Barnabas and Paul heard what was happening, they tore their
clothing in dismay and ran out among the people, shouting, 15"Friends, why are you doing
this? We are merely human beings—just like you! We have come to bring you the Good
News that you should turn from these worthless things and turn to the living God, who
made heaven and earth, the sea, and everything in them. 16In the past he permitted all the
nations to go their own ways, 17but he never left them without evidence of himself and his
goodness. For instance, he sends you rain and good crops and gives you food and joyful
hearts." 18But even with these words, Paul and Barnabas could scarcely restrain the people
from sacrificing to them.

Do you ever wish you could perform a miraculous act that would convince everyone that Jesus is Lord? We see here that even if we could perform miracles, we wouldn't be able to convince everyone. God gave these men power to do great wonders, but people were still divided. Don't spend your time and energy wishing for miracles. Sow your seeds of the Good News on the best ground you can find in the best way you can, and leave the convincing to the Holy Spirit.

A Church Conference

OCTOBER 30

ACTS 15:1-21

While Paul and Barnabas were at Antioch of Syria, some men from Judea arrived and began to teach the believers: "Unless you are circumcised as required by the law of Moses, you cannot be saved." [2]Paul and Barnabas disagreed with them, arguing vehemently. Finally, the church decided to send Paul and Barnabas to Jerusalem, accompanied by some local believers, to talk to the apostles and elders about this question. . . .

[6]So the apostles and elders met together to resolve this issue. [7]At the meeting, after a long discussion, Peter stood and addressed them as follows: "Brothers, you all know that God chose me from among you some time ago to preach to the Gentiles so that they could hear the Good News and believe. [8]God knows people's hearts, and he confirmed that he accepts Gentiles by giving them the Holy Spirit, just as he did to us. [9]He made no distinction between us and them, for he cleansed their hearts through faith. [10]So why are you now challenging God by burdening the Gentile believers with a yoke that neither we nor our ancestors were able to bear? [11]We believe that we are all saved the same way, by the undeserved grace of the Lord Jesus."

[12]Everyone listened quietly as Barnabas and Paul told about the miraculous signs and wonders God had done through them among the Gentiles.

[13]When they had finished, James stood and said, "Brothers, listen to me. [14]Peter has told you about the time God first visited the Gentiles to take from them a people for himself. . . .

[19]"And so my judgment is that we should not make it difficult for the Gentiles who are turning to God. [20]Instead, we should write and tell them to abstain from eating food offered to idols, from sexual immorality, from eating the meat of strangled animals, and from consuming blood. [21]For these laws of Moses have been preached in Jewish synagogues in every city on every Sabbath for many generations."

Whose standards are more important to you—God's or your own? James's judgment was that Gentile believers did not have to be circumcised, but they should stay away from food offered to idols, from sexual immorality (a common part of idol worship), from eating meat of strangled animals, and from consuming blood (reflecting the biblical teaching that the life is in the blood—Leviticus 17:14). If Gentile Christians would abstain from these practices, they would please God and get along better with their Jewish brothers and sisters in Christ. Of course, there were other actions that are inappropriate for believers, but the Jews were especially concerned about these four. This compromise helped the church to grow unhindered by the cultural differences of Jews and Gentiles. When we share our message across cultural and economic boundaries, we must be sure that the requirements for faith we set up are God's, not people's.

OCTOBER 31

Missionary Movements

ACTS 15:22-40

22 Then the apostles and elders together with the whole church in Jerusalem chose delegates,
and they sent them to Antioch of Syria with Paul and Barnabas to report on this decision.
The men chosen were two of the church leaders—Judas (also called Barsabbas) and Silas.
23 This is the letter they took with them:

> "This letter is from the apostles and elders, your brothers in Jerusalem. It is written to
> the Gentile believers in Antioch, Syria, and Cilicia. Greetings!
>
> 24 "We understand that some men from here have troubled you and upset you with
> their teaching, but we did not send them! 25 So we decided, having come to complete
> agreement, to send you official representatives, along with our beloved Barnabas and
> Paul, 26 who have risked their lives for the name of our Lord Jesus Christ. 27 We are send-
> ing Judas and Silas to confirm what we have decided concerning your question.
>
> 28 "For it seemed good to the Holy Spirit and to us to lay no greater burden on you
> than these few requirements: 29 You must abstain from eating food offered to idols,
> from consuming blood or the meat of strangled animals, and from sexual immorality.
> If you do this, you will do well. Farewell."

30 The messengers went at once to Antioch, where they called a general meeting of the
believers and delivered the letter. 31 And there was great joy throughout the church that day
as they read this encouraging message.

32 Then Judas and Silas, both being prophets, spoke at length to the believers, encouraging
and strengthening their faith. 33 They stayed for a while, and then the believers sent them back
to the church in Jerusalem with a blessing of peace. 35 Paul and Barnabas stayed in Antioch.
They and many others taught and preached the word of the Lord there.

36 After some time Paul said to Barnabas, "Let's go back and visit each city where we previously preached the word of the Lord, to see how the new believers are doing." 37 Barnabas
agreed and wanted to take along John Mark. 38 But Paul disagreed strongly, since John Mark
had deserted them in Pamphylia and had not continued with them in their work. 39 Their
disagreement was so sharp that they separated. Barnabas took John Mark with him and
sailed for Cyprus. 40 Paul chose Silas, and as he left, the believers entrusted him to the Lord's
gracious care.

In what ways is God affecting the way you live and plan for the future? Paul and Barnabas disagreed sharply over Mark. Paul didn't want to take him along because he had left them earlier (Acts 13:13). This disagreement caused the two great preachers to form two teams, opening up two missionary endeavors instead of one. God works even through conflict and disagreements. Later, Mark became vital to Paul's ministry (Colossians 4:10). Christians do not always agree, but problems can be solved by agreeing to disagree and letting God work his will.

November

NOVEMBER 1

Paul, Silas, and Timothy

ACTS 16:1-15

Paul went first to Derbe and then to Lystra, where there was a young disciple named Timothy.
His mother was a Jewish believer, but his father was a Greek. 2Timothy was well thought of
by the believers in Lystra and Iconium, 3so Paul wanted him to join them on their journey.
In deference to the Jews of the area, he arranged for Timothy to be circumcised before they
left, for everyone knew that his father was a Greek. 4Then they went from town to town,
instructing the believers to follow the decisions made by the apostles and elders in Jerusalem.
5So the churches were strengthened in their faith and grew larger every day.

6Next Paul and Silas traveled through the area of Phrygia and Galatia, because the Holy
Spirit had prevented them from preaching the word in the province of Asia at that time.
7Then coming to the borders of Mysia, they headed north for the province of Bithynia, but
again the Spirit of Jesus did not allow them to go there. 8So instead, they went on through
Mysia to the seaport of Troas.

9That night Paul had a vision: A man from Macedonia in northern Greece was standing
there, pleading with him, "Come over to Macedonia and help us!" 10So we decided to leave
for Macedonia at once, having concluded that God was calling us to preach the Good News
there.

11We boarded a boat at Troas and sailed straight across to the island of Samothrace, and
the next day we landed at Neapolis. 12From there we reached Philippi, a major city of that
district of Macedonia and a Roman colony. And we stayed there several days.

13On the Sabbath we went a little way outside the city to a riverbank, where we thought
people would be meeting for prayer, and we sat down to speak with some women who had
gathered there. 14One of them was Lydia from Thyatira, a merchant of expensive purple cloth,
who worshiped God. As she listened to us, the Lord opened her heart, and she accepted what
Paul was saying. 15She and her household were baptized, and she asked us to be her guests.
"If you agree that I am a true believer in the Lord," she said, "come and stay at my home."
And she urged us until we agreed.

How do you discern God's will? We don't know how the Holy Spirit told Paul that he and his men were not to go into Asia. It may have been through a prophet, a vision, an inner conviction, or some circumstance. To know God's will does not mean we must hear his voice. He leads in different ways. When seeking God's will: (1) Make sure your plan is in harmony with God's Word. (2) Ask mature Christians for their advice. (3) Check your motives—are you trying to do what you want or what you think God wants? (4) Pray for God to open and close the doors of circumstances.

Adventures in Jail

NOVEMBER 2

ACTS 16:16-34

16One day as we were going down to the place of prayer, we met a slave girl who had a spirit
that enabled her to tell the future. She earned a lot of money for her masters by telling fortunes. 17She followed Paul and the rest of us, shouting, "These men are servants of the Most
High God, and they have come to tell you how to be saved."
18This went on day after day until Paul got so exasperated that he turned and said to the
demon within her, "I command you in the name of Jesus Christ to come out of her." And
instantly it left her.
19Her masters' hopes of wealth were now shattered, so they grabbed Paul and Silas and
dragged them before the authorities at the marketplace. 20"The whole city is in an uproar
because of these Jews!" they shouted to the city officials. 21"They are teaching customs that
are illegal for us Romans to practice."
22A mob quickly formed against Paul and Silas, and the city officials ordered them stripped
and beaten with wooden rods. 23They were severely beaten, and then they were thrown into
prison. The jailer was ordered to make sure they didn't escape. 24So the jailer put them into
the inner dungeon and clamped their feet in the stocks.
25Around midnight Paul and Silas were praying and singing hymns to God, and the
other prisoners were listening. 26Suddenly, there was a massive earthquake, and the prison
was shaken to its foundations. All the doors immediately flew open, and the chains of every
prisoner fell off! 27The jailer woke up to see the prison doors wide open. He assumed the
prisoners had escaped, so he drew his sword to kill himself. 28But Paul shouted to him, "Stop!
Don't kill yourself! We are all here!"
29The jailer called for lights and ran to the dungeon and fell down trembling before Paul
and Silas. 30Then he brought them out and asked, "Sirs, what must I do to be saved?"
31They replied, "Believe in the Lord Jesus and you will be saved, along with everyone in
your household." 32And they shared the word of the Lord with him and with all who lived
in his household. 33Even at that hour of the night, the jailer cared for them and washed their
wounds. Then he and everyone in his household were immediately baptized. 34He brought
them into his house and set a meal before them, and he and his entire household rejoiced
because they all believed in God.

How would you react to God using a difficult situation of yours to help another person discover him? Paul and Silas's reputation in Philippi was well known. When the jailer realized his own true condition and need, he risked everything to find the answer. The good news of salvation is simply expressed: believe on the Lord Jesus, and you will be saved. When we recognize Jesus as Lord and trust in him, salvation is assured to us. If you have never trusted in Jesus to save you, do so quickly. Your life can be filled with joy, just as the jailer's was.

NOVEMBER 3

Different Responses from Two Cities

ACTS 17:1-15

Paul and Silas then traveled through the towns of Amphipolis and Apollonia and came to
Thessalonica, where there was a Jewish synagogue. 2As was Paul's custom, he went to the
synagogue service, and for three Sabbaths in a row he used the Scriptures to reason with the
people. 3He explained the prophecies and proved that the Messiah must suffer and rise from
the dead. He said, "This Jesus I'm telling you about is the Messiah." 4Some of the Jews who
listened were persuaded and joined Paul and Silas, along with many God-fearing Greek men
and quite a few prominent women.

5But some of the Jews were jealous, so they gathered some troublemakers from the marketplace to form a mob and start a riot. They attacked the home of Jason, searching for Paul
and Silas so they could drag them out to the crowd. 6Not finding them there, they dragged
out Jason and some of the other believers instead and took them before the city council.
"Paul and Silas have caused trouble all over the world," they shouted, "and now they are here
disturbing our city, too. 7And Jason has welcomed them into his home. They are all guilty of
treason against Caesar, for they profess allegiance to another king, named Jesus."

8The people of the city, as well as the city council, were thrown into turmoil by these
reports. 9So the officials forced Jason and the other believers to post bond, and then they
released them.

10That very night the believers sent Paul and Silas to Berea. When they arrived there, they
went to the Jewish synagogue. 11And the people of Berea were more open-minded than those
in Thessalonica, and they listened eagerly to Paul's message. They searched the Scriptures day
after day to see if Paul and Silas were teaching the truth. 12As a result, many Jews believed, as
did many of the prominent Greek women and men.

13But when some Jews in Thessalonica learned that Paul was preaching the word of God
in Berea, they went there and stirred up trouble. 14The believers acted at once, sending Paul
on to the coast, while Silas and Timothy remained behind. 15Those escorting Paul went
with him all the way to Athens; then they returned to Berea with instructions for Silas and
Timothy to hurry and join him.

What part does the Bible play in your evaluation of what you hear and read? How do you evaluate sermons and teachings? The people in Berea opened the Scriptures for themselves and searched to verify or disprove the message they heard. Always compare what you hear with what the Bible says. A preacher or teacher who gives God's true message will never contradict or explain away anything in God's Word.

Paul in Athens

NOVEMBER 4

ACTS 17:16-34

16 While Paul was waiting for them in Athens, he was deeply troubled by all the idols he saw
everywhere in the city. . . .
18 He also had a debate with some of the Epicurean and Stoic philosophers. When he told
them about Jesus and his resurrection, they said, "What's this babbler trying to say with these
strange ideas he's picked up?" Others said, "He seems to be preaching about some foreign
gods."
19 Then they took him to the high council of the city. "Come and tell us about this new
teaching," they said. . . .
22 So Paul, standing before the council, addressed them as follows: "Men of Athens, I
notice that you are very religious in every way, 23 for as I was walking along I saw your many
shrines. And one of your altars had this inscription on it: 'To an Unknown God.' This God,
whom you worship without knowing, is the one I'm telling you about.
24 "He is the God who made the world and everything in it. Since he is Lord of heaven and
earth, he doesn't live in man-made temples, 25 and human hands can't serve his needs—for he has
no needs. He himself gives life and breath to everything, and he satisfies every need. 26 From one
man he created all the nations throughout the whole earth. He decided beforehand when they
should rise and fall, and he determined their boundaries.
27 "His purpose was for the nations to seek after God and perhaps feel their way toward him
and find him—though he is not far from any one of us. 28 For in him we live and move and
exist. As some of your own poets have said, 'We are his offspring.' 29 And since this is true, we
shouldn't think of God as an idol designed by craftsmen from gold or silver or stone.
30 "God overlooked people's ignorance about these things in earlier times, but now he
commands everyone everywhere to repent of their sins and turn to him. 31 For he has set a day
for judging the world with justice by the man he has appointed, and he proved to everyone
who this is by raising him from the dead."
32 When they heard Paul speak about the resurrection of the dead, some laughed in contempt, but others said, "We want to hear more about this later." 33 That ended Paul's discussion
with them, 34 but some joined him and became believers.

How can you share the gospel with confidence? Paul was well prepared to speak to these philosophers. He came from Tarsus, an educational center, and had the training and knowledge to present his beliefs clearly and persuasively. He was a rabbi and had spent much of his life thinking and reasoning through the Scriptures. While it is important to share our faith with conviction, we must also be prepared. The more we know about the Bible, the more convincing our words will be. This does not mean that we should avoid presenting the gospel until we feel prepared. We should work with what we know but always seek to know more in order to reach more people and answer their questions more effectively.

NOVEMBER 5

Paul in Ephesus

ACTS 19:1-19

While Apollos was in Corinth, Paul traveled through the interior regions until he reached Ephesus, on the coast, where he found several believers. 2"Did you receive the Holy Spirit when you believed?" he asked them.

"No," they replied, "we haven't even heard that there is a Holy Spirit."

3"Then what baptism did you experience?" he asked.

And they replied, "The baptism of John."

4Paul said, "John's baptism called for repentance from sin. But John himself told the people to believe in the one who would come later, meaning Jesus."

5As soon as they heard this, they were baptized in the name of the Lord Jesus. 6Then when Paul laid his hands on them, the Holy Spirit came on them, and they spoke in other tongues and prophesied. 7There were about twelve men in all.

8Then Paul went to the synagogue and preached boldly for the next three months, arguing persuasively about the Kingdom of God. . . .

11God gave Paul the power to perform unusual miracles. 12When handkerchiefs or aprons that had merely touched his skin were placed on sick people, they were healed of their diseases, and evil spirits were expelled.

13A group of Jews was traveling from town to town casting out evil spirits. They tried to use the name of the Lord Jesus in their incantation, saying, "I command you in the name of Jesus, whom Paul preaches, to come out!" 14Seven sons of Sceva, a leading priest, were doing this. 15But one time when they tried it, the evil spirit replied, "I know Jesus, and I know Paul, but who are you?" 16Then the man with the evil spirit leaped on them, overpowered them, and attacked them with such violence that they fled from the house, naked and battered.

17The story of what happened spread quickly all through Ephesus, to Jews and Greeks alike. A solemn fear descended on the city, and the name of the Lord Jesus was greatly honored. 18Many who became believers confessed their sinful practices. 19A number of them who had been practicing sorcery brought their incantation books and burned them at a public bonfire. The value of the books was several million dollars.

In what situations are you most likely to become discouraged? Ephesus was considered a center for black magic and other occult practices. The people sought spells to give them success in marriage, wealth, and happiness. Superstition and sorcery were commonplace. God clearly forbids such practices (Deuteronomy 18:9-13). You cannot be a believer and practice occult, black magic, or sorcery. Once you begin to dabble in these areas, it is extremely easy to become obsessed by them, because Satan is very powerful. But God's power is even greater. If you are mixed up or even interested in the occult, learn a lesson from the Ephesians and get rid of anything that lures you into such practices.

The Riot

NOVEMBER 6

ACTS 19:23-41

23About that time, serious trouble developed in Ephesus concerning the Way. 24It began with
Demetrius, a silversmith who had a large business manufacturing silver shrines of the Greek
goddess Artemis. He kept many craftsmen busy. 25He called them together, along with others
employed in similar trades, and addressed them as follows:
"Gentlemen, you know that our wealth comes from this business. 26But as you have seen
and heard, this man Paul has persuaded many people that handmade gods aren't really gods
at all. And he's done this not only here in Ephesus but throughout the entire province! 27Of
course, I'm not just talking about the loss of public respect for our business. I'm also concerned that the temple of the great goddess Artemis will lose its influence and that Artemis—
this magnificent goddess worshiped throughout the province of Asia and all around the
world—will be robbed of her great prestige!"
28At this their anger boiled, and they began shouting, "Great is Artemis of the Ephesians!"
29Soon the whole city was filled with confusion. Everyone rushed to the amphitheater, drag-
ging along Gaius and Aristarchus, who were Paul's traveling companions from Macedonia.
. . .35At last the mayor was able to quiet them down enough to speak. "Citizens of
Ephesus," he said. "Everyone knows that Ephesus is the official guardian of the temple of the
great Artemis, whose image fell down to us from heaven. 36Since this is an undeniable fact,
you should stay calm and not do anything rash. 37You have brought these men here, but they
have stolen nothing from the temple and have not spoken against our goddess.
38"If Demetrius and the craftsmen have a case against them, the courts are in session
and the officials can hear the case at once. Let them make formal charges. 39And if there are
complaints about other matters, they can be settled in a legal assembly. 40I am afraid we are
in danger of being charged with rioting by the Roman government, since there is no cause
for all this commotion. And if Rome demands an explanation, we won't know what to say."
41Then he dismissed them, and they dispersed.

When are you most likely to forget that God is in control? When Paul preached in Ephesus, Demetrius and his fellow craftsmen did not quarrel with his doctrine. Their anger boiled because his preaching threatened their profits. They made silver statues of the Ephesian goddess Artemis. The craftsmen knew that if people started believing in God and discarding the idols, their livelihood would suffer. Demetrius's strategy for stirring up a riot was to appeal to his fellow workmen's love of money and then to encourage them to hide their greed behind the mask of patriotism and religious loyalty. The rioters couldn't see the selfish motives for their rioting—instead they saw themselves as heroes for the sake of their land and beliefs. It is amazing the lengths to which people will go even today to silence Christians. We must be always ready to defend our faith, no matter what the consequences.

NOVEMBER 7

Sleeping in Church

ACTS 20:1-12

When the uproar was over, Paul sent for the believers and encouraged them. Then he said
good-bye and left for Macedonia. 2While there, he encouraged the believers in all the towns
he passed through. Then he traveled down to Greece, 3where he stayed for three months.
He was preparing to sail back to Syria when he discovered a plot by some Jews against his
life, so he decided to return through Macedonia.

4Several men were traveling with him. They were Sopater son of Pyrrhus from Berea;
Aristarchus and Secundus from Thessalonica; Gaius from Derbe; Timothy; and Tychicus
and Trophimus from the province of Asia. 5They went on ahead and waited for us at Troas.
6After the Passover ended, we boarded a ship at Philippi in Macedonia and five days later
joined them in Troas, where we stayed a week.

7On the first day of the week, we gathered with the local believers to share in the Lord's
Supper. Paul was preaching to them, and since he was leaving the next day, he kept talking
until midnight. 8The upstairs room where we met was lighted with many flickering lamps.
9As Paul spoke on and on, a young man named Eutychus, sitting on the windowsill, became
very drowsy. Finally, he fell sound asleep and dropped three stories to his death below.
10Paul went down, bent over him, and took him into his arms. "Don't worry," he said, "he's
alive!" 11Then they all went back upstairs, shared in the Lord's Supper, and ate together.
Paul continued talking to them until dawn, and then he left. 12Meanwhile, the young man
was taken home alive and well, and everyone was greatly relieved.

How does God respond to your human weaknesses? The combination of the heat from the candles and the number of people in the upstairs room making the room very warm, and the late hour, no doubt, helped Eutychus fall asleep and then tumble out the window. Notice that Paul showed concern for the young man, not anger at the interruption. How do you deal with others' weaknesses? Are you able to show compassion?

Saying Good-bye to Ephesus

ACTS 20:16-38

16Paul had decided to sail on past Ephesus, for he didn't want to spend any more time in the
province of Asia. He was hurrying to get to Jerusalem, if possible, in time for the Festival of
Pentecost. 17But when we landed at Miletus, he sent a message to the elders of the church at
Ephesus, asking them to come and meet him.

18When they arrived he declared, "You know that from the day I set foot in the province
of Asia until now 19I have done the Lord's work humbly and with many tears. I have endured
the trials that came to me from the plots of the Jews. 20I never shrank back from telling you
what you needed to hear, either publicly or in your homes. 21I have had one message for Jews
and Greeks alike—the necessity of repenting from sin and turning to God, and of having
faith in our Lord Jesus.

22"And now I am bound by the Spirit to go to Jerusalem. I don't know what awaits me,
23except that the Holy Spirit tells me in city after city that jail and suffering lie ahead. 24But
my life is worth nothing to me unless I use it for finishing the work assigned me by the Lord
Jesus—the work of telling others the Good News about the wonderful grace of God.

25"And now I know that none of you to whom I have preached the Kingdom will ever see
me again. 26I declare today that I have been faithful. If anyone suffers eternal death, it's not
my fault, 27for I didn't shrink from declaring all that God wants you to know.

28"So guard yourselves and God's people. Feed and shepherd God's flock—his church,
purchased with his own blood—over which the Holy Spirit has appointed you as leaders. 29I
know that false teachers, like vicious wolves, will come in among you after I leave, not sparing
the flock. 30Even some men from your own group will rise up and distort the truth in order
to draw a following. 31Watch out! Remember the three years I was with you—my constant
watch and care over you night and day, and my many tears for you.

32"And now I entrust you to God and the message of his grace that is able to build you
up and give you an inheritance with all those he has set apart for himself. . . ."

36When he had finished speaking, he knelt and prayed with them. 37They all cried as they
embraced and kissed him good-bye. 38They were sad most of all because he had said that they
would never see him again. Then they escorted him down to the ship.

When have painful good-byes worked for the best in your life? Paul's relationship with these believers is a beautiful example of Christian fellowship. He had cared for them and loved them, even cried over their needs. They responded with love and care for him and sorrow over his leaving. They had prayed together and comforted one another. Like Paul, you can build strong relationships with other Christians by sharing, caring, sorrowing, rejoicing, and praying with them. You will gather others around you only by giving yourself away to them.

NOVEMBER 9

Difficult Decision

ACTS 21:1-17

After saying farewell to the Ephesian elders, we sailed straight to the island of Cos. The
next day we reached Rhodes and then went to Patara. 2There we boarded a ship sailing for
Phoenicia. 3We sighted the island of Cyprus, passed it on our left, and landed at the harbor
of Tyre, in Syria, where the ship was to unload its cargo.
4We went ashore, found the local believers, and stayed with them a week. These believers
prophesied through the Holy Spirit that Paul should not go on to Jerusalem. 5When we
returned to the ship at the end of the week, the entire congregation, including women and
children, left the city and came down to the shore with us. There we knelt, prayed, 6and said
our farewells. Then we went aboard, and they returned home.
7The next stop after leaving Tyre was Ptolemais, where we greeted the brothers and sisters
and stayed for one day. 8The next day we went on to Caesarea and stayed at the home of
Philip the Evangelist, one of the seven men who had been chosen to distribute food. 9He had
four unmarried daughters who had the gift of prophecy.
10Several days later a man named Agabus, who also had the gift of prophecy, arrived from
Judea. 11He came over, took Paul's belt, and bound his own feet and hands with it. Then he
said, "The Holy Spirit declares, 'So shall the owner of this belt be bound by the Jewish leaders in Jerusalem and turned over to the Gentiles.'" 12When we heard this, we and the local
believers all begged Paul not to go on to Jerusalem.
13But he said, "Why all this weeping? You are breaking my heart! I am ready not only to
be jailed at Jerusalem but even to die for the sake of the Lord Jesus." 14When it was clear that
we couldn't persuade him, we gave up and said, "The Lord's will be done."
15After this we packed our things and left for Jerusalem. 16Some believers from Caesarea
accompanied us, and they took us to the home of Mnason, a man originally from Cyprus
and one of the early believers. 17When we arrived, the brothers and sisters in Jerusalem welcomed us warmly.

What hard decisions do you have to make? Paul knew that he would be imprisoned in Jerusalem. His friends pleaded with him to not go there because of the suffering he would endure, but Paul knew he had to because God wanted him to. No one wants to face hardship or suffering, but a faithful disciple wants above all else to please God. Our desire to please God should overshadow our desire to avoid hardship and suffering. When we really want to do God's will, we must accept all that comes with it—even the pain. Then we can say with Paul, "The Lord's will be done."

Paul in Jerusalem

NOVEMBER 10

ACTS 21:18-34

[18]The next day Paul went with us to meet with James, and all the elders of the Jerusalem church were present. [19]After greeting them, Paul gave a detailed account of the things God had accomplished among the Gentiles through his ministry.

[20]After hearing this, they praised God. And then they said, "You know, dear brother, how many thousands of Jews have also believed, and they all follow the law of Moses very seriously. [21]But the Jewish believers here in Jerusalem have been told that you are teaching all the Jews who live among the Gentiles to turn their backs on the laws of Moses. They've heard that you teach them not to circumcise their children or follow other Jewish customs. [22]What should we do? They will certainly hear that you have come.

[23]"Here's what we want you to do. We have four men here who have completed their vow. [24]Go with them to the Temple and join them in the purification ceremony, paying for them to have their heads ritually shaved. Then everyone will know that the rumors are all false and that you yourself observe the Jewish laws.

[25]"As for the Gentile believers, they should do what we already told them in a letter." . . .

[26]So Paul went to the Temple the next day with the other men. They had already started the purification ritual, so he publicly announced the date when their vows would end and sacrifices would be offered for each of them.

[27]The seven days were almost ended when some Jews from the province of Asia saw Paul in the Temple and roused a mob against him. They grabbed him, [28]yelling, "Men of Israel, help us! This is the man who preaches against our people everywhere and tells everybody to disobey the Jewish laws. He speaks against the Temple—and even defiles this holy place by bringing in Gentiles." . . .

[31]As they were trying to kill him, word reached the commander of the Roman regiment that all Jerusalem was in an uproar. [32]He immediately called out his soldiers and officers and ran down among the crowd. When the mob saw the commander and the troops coming, they stopped beating Paul.

[33]Then the commander arrested him and ordered him bound with two chains. He asked the crowd who he was and what he had done. [34]Some shouted one thing and some another. Since he couldn't find out the truth in all the uproar and confusion, he ordered that Paul be taken to the fortress.

How important is it to you to respect the consciences of others? The Jerusalem Council (Acts 15) had settled the issue of circumcision of Gentile believers. Evidently there was a rumor that Paul had gone far beyond their decision, even forbidding Jews to circumcise their children. This, of course, was not true, and so Paul willingly submitted to Jewish custom to show that he was not working against the council's decision and that he was still Jewish in his lifestyle. Sometimes we must go the extra mile to avoid offending others, especially when not doing so would hinder God's work.

NOVEMBER 11

Paul Speaks

ACTS 22:1-18

"Brothers and esteemed fathers," Paul said, "listen to me as I offer my defense." 2When they
heard him speaking in their own language, the silence was even greater.

3Then Paul said, "I am a Jew, born in Tarsus, a city in Cilicia, and I was brought up and
educated here in Jerusalem under Gamaliel. As his student, I was carefully trained in our
Jewish laws and customs. I became very zealous to honor God in everything I did, just like all
of you today. 4And I persecuted the followers of the Way, hounding some to death, arresting
both men and women and throwing them in prison. 5The high priest and the whole council
of elders can testify that this is so. For I received letters from them to our Jewish brothers
in Damascus, authorizing me to bring the followers of the Way from there to Jerusalem, in
chains, to be punished.

6"As I was on the road, approaching Damascus about noon, a very bright light from
heaven suddenly shone down around me. 7I fell to the ground and heard a voice saying to
me, 'Saul, Saul, why are you persecuting me?'

8" 'Who are you, lord?' I asked.

"And the voice replied, 'I am Jesus the Nazarene, the one you are persecuting.' 9The
people with me saw the light but didn't understand the voice speaking to me.

10"I asked, 'What should I do, Lord?'

"And the Lord told me, 'Get up and go into Damascus, and there you will be told everything you are to do.'

11"I was blinded by the intense light and had to be led by the hand to Damascus by my
companions. 12A man named Ananias lived there. He was a godly man, deeply devoted to the
law, and well regarded by all the Jews of Damascus. 13He came and stood beside me and said,
'Brother Saul, regain your sight.' And that very moment I could see him!

14"Then he told me, 'The God of our ancestors has chosen you to know his will and to
see the Righteous One and hear him speak. 15For you are to be his witness, telling everyone
what you have seen and heard. 16What are you waiting for? Get up and be baptized. Have
your sins washed away by calling on the name of the Lord.'

17"After I returned to Jerusalem, I was praying in the Temple and fell into a trance. 18I
saw a vision of Jesus saying to me, 'Hurry! Leave Jerusalem, for the people here won't accept
your testimony about me.'"

How can you relate what Paul is saying to what God has done in your life? After gaining a hearing and establishing common ground with his audience, Paul gave his testimony. He shared how he had come to faith in Christ. Sound reasoning is good, but it is also important to simply share what Christ has done in our lives. But no matter how we present the message, not everyone will accept it, as Paul knew. We must faithfully and responsibly present the gospel and leave the results to God.

A Plan to Kill Paul

NOVEMBER 12

ACTS 22:30; 23:6-21

[30]The next day the commander ordered the leading priests into session with the Jewish high council. He wanted to find out what the trouble was all about, so he released Paul to have him stand before them.

[23:6]Paul realized that some members of the high council were Sadducees and some were Pharisees, so he shouted, "Brothers, I am a Pharisee, as were my ancestors! And I am on trial because my hope is in the resurrection of the dead!"

[7]This divided the council—the Pharisees against the Sadducees—[8]for the Sadducees say there is no resurrection or angels or spirits, but the Pharisees believe in all of these. [9]So there was a great uproar. Some of the teachers of religious law who were Pharisees jumped up and began to argue forcefully. "We see nothing wrong with him," they shouted. "Perhaps a spirit or an angel spoke to him." [10]As the conflict grew more violent, the commander was afraid they would tear Paul apart. So he ordered his soldiers to go and rescue him by force and take him back to the fortress.

[11]That night the Lord appeared to Paul and said, "Be encouraged, Paul. Just as you have been a witness to me here in Jerusalem, you must preach the Good News in Rome as well."

[12]The next morning a group of Jews got together and bound themselves with an oath not to eat or drink until they had killed Paul. [13]There were more than forty of them in the conspiracy. [14]They went to the leading priests and elders and told them, "We have bound ourselves with an oath to eat nothing until we have killed Paul. [15]So you and the high council should ask the commander to bring Paul back to the council again. Pretend you want to examine his case more fully. We will kill him on the way."

[16]But Paul's nephew—his sister's son—heard of their plan and went to the fortress and told Paul. [17]Paul called for one of the Roman officers and said, "Take this young man to the commander. He has something important to tell him."

[18]So the officer did, explaining, "Paul, the prisoner, called me over and asked me to bring this young man to you because he has something to tell you."

[19]The commander took his hand, led him aside, and asked, "What is it you want to tell me?"

[20]Paul's nephew told him, "Some Jews are going to ask you to bring Paul before the high council tomorrow, pretending they want to get some more information. [21]But don't do it! There are more than forty men hiding along the way ready to ambush him."

How well do you know your rights and fulfill your responsibilities as a citizen of your country? It is easy to overlook young people, assuming that they aren't old enough to do much for the Lord. But this young man played an important role in protecting Paul's life. God can use anyone of any age who is willing to yield to him. Give children and young people the importance that God gives them.

NOVEMBER 13

Paul in Prison

ACTS 23:23–24:27

23Then the commander called two of his officers and ordered, "Get 200 soldiers ready to
leave for Caesarea at nine o'clock tonight. Also take 200 spearmen and 70 mounted troops.
24Provide horses for Paul to ride, and get him safely to Governor Felix." 25Then he wrote this
letter to the governor:

> 26"From Claudius Lysias, to his Excellency, Governor Felix: Greetings!
> 27"This man was seized by some Jews, and they were about to kill him when I
> arrived with the troops. When I learned that he was a Roman citizen, I removed
> him to safety. 28Then I took him to their high council to try to learn the basis of the
> accusations against him. 29I soon discovered the charge was something regarding their
> religious law—certainly nothing worthy of imprisonment or death. 30But when I was
> informed of a plot to kill him, I immediately sent him on to you. I have told his accus-
> ers to bring their charges before you."

31So that night, as ordered, the soldiers took Paul as far as Antipatris. 32They returned to
the fortress the next morning, while the mounted troops took him on to Caesarea. 33When
they arrived in Caesarea, they presented Paul and the letter to Governor Felix. 34He read it
and then asked Paul what province he was from. "Cilicia," Paul answered.
35"I will hear your case myself when your accusers arrive," the governor told him. Then
the governor ordered him kept in the prison at Herod's headquarters.

24:1Five days later Ananias, the high priest, arrived with some of the Jewish elders and the
lawyer Tertullus, to present their case against Paul to the governor. . . .
24A few days later Felix came back with his wife, Drusilla, who was Jewish. Sending for
Paul, they listened as he told them about faith in Christ Jesus. 25As he reasoned with them
about righteousness and self-control and the coming day of judgment, Felix became frightened. "Go away for now," he replied. "When it is more convenient, I'll call for you again."
26He also hoped that Paul would bribe him, so he sent for him quite often and talked with
him.
27After two years went by in this way, Felix was succeeded by Porcius Festus. And because
Felix wanted to gain favor with the Jewish people, he left Paul in prison.

Which would be more difficult for you to handle, the pressure or the prison? The Roman commander ordered Paul sent to Caesarea. Jerusalem was the seat of Jewish government, but Caesarea was the Roman headquarters for the area. God works in amazing and amusing ways. There were many ways that God could have used to get Paul to Caesarea, but he chose to use the Roman army to deliver Paul from his enemies. God's ways are not ours—we are limited, he is not. Don't limit God by asking him to respond your way. When God intervenes, anything can happen, and his ways are much more and much better than you could ever anticipate.

Paul Speaks to Festus

NOVEMBER 14

ACTS 25:1-23

Three days after Festus arrived in Caesarea to take over his new responsibilities, he left for Jerusalem, 2where the leading priests and other Jewish leaders met with him and made their accusations against Paul. 3They asked Festus as a favor to transfer Paul to Jerusalem (planning to ambush and kill him on the way). 4But Festus replied that Paul was at Caesarea and he himself would be returning there soon. 5So he said, "Those of you in authority can return with me. If Paul has done anything wrong, you can make your accusations."

6About eight or ten days later Festus returned to Caesarea, and on the following day he took his seat in court and ordered that Paul be brought in. 7When Paul arrived, the Jewish leaders from Jerusalem gathered around and made many serious accusations they couldn't prove.

8Paul denied the charges. "I am not guilty of any crime against the Jewish laws or the Temple or the Roman government," he said.

9Then Festus, wanting to please the Jews, asked him, "Are you willing to go to Jerusalem and stand trial before me there?"

10But Paul replied, "No! This is the official Roman court, so I ought to be tried right here. You know very well I am not guilty of harming the Jews. 11If I have done something worthy of death, I don't refuse to die. But if I am innocent, no one has a right to turn me over to these men to kill me. I appeal to Caesar!"

12Festus conferred with his advisers and then replied, "Very well! You have appealed to Caesar, and to Caesar you will go!"

13A few days later King Agrippa arrived with his sister, Bernice, to pay their respects to Festus. 14During their stay of several days, Festus discussed Paul's case with the king. "There is a prisoner here," he told him, "whose case was left for me by Felix. 15When I was in Jerusalem, the leading priests and Jewish elders pressed charges against him and asked me to condemn him. 16I pointed out to them that Roman law does not convict people without a trial. They must be given an opportunity to confront their accusers and defend themselves. . . ."

22"I'd like to hear the man myself," Agrippa said.

And Festus replied, "You will—tomorrow!"

23So the next day Agrippa and Bernice arrived at the auditorium with great pomp, accompanied by military officers and prominent men of the city. Festus ordered that Paul be brought in.

If Christianity were outlawed, what evidence could be brought against you to prove you are a Christian? Paul was in prison, but that didn't stop him from making the most of his situation. Military officers and prominent city leaders met in the palace room with Agrippa to hear this case. Paul saw this new audience as yet another opportunity to present the gospel. Rather than complain about your present situation, look for ways to use every opportunity to serve God and share him with others. Your problems may be opportunities in disguise.

NOVEMBER 15

Paul Speaks to Agrippa

ACTS 26:1-32

Then Agrippa said to Paul, "You may speak in your defense."

So Paul, gesturing with his hand, started his defense: 2"I am fortunate, King Agrippa, that you are the one hearing my defense today against all these accusations made by the Jewish leaders, 3for I know you are an expert on all Jewish customs and controversies. Now please listen to me patiently!

4"As the Jewish leaders are well aware, I was given a thorough Jewish training from my earliest childhood among my own people and in Jerusalem. 5If they would admit it, they know that I have been a member of the Pharisees, the strictest sect of our religion. 6Now I am on trial because of my hope in the fulfillment of God's promise made to our ancestors. . . . 8Why does it seem incredible to any of you that God can raise the dead? . . .

20"I preached first to those in Damascus, then in Jerusalem and throughout all Judea, and also to the Gentiles, that all must repent of their sins and turn to God—and prove they have changed by the good things they do. . . . 22I teach nothing except what the prophets and Moses said would happen—23that the Messiah would suffer and be the first to rise from the dead, and in this way announce God's light to Jews and Gentiles alike."

24Suddenly, Festus shouted, "Paul, you are insane. Too much study has made you crazy!"

25But Paul replied, "I am not insane, Most Excellent Festus. What I am saying is the sober truth. 26And King Agrippa knows about these things. I speak boldly, for I am sure these events are all familiar to him, for they were not done in a corner! 27King Agrippa, do you believe the prophets? I know you do—"

28Agrippa interrupted him. "Do you think you can persuade me to become a Christian so quickly?"

29Paul replied, "Whether quickly or not, I pray to God that both you and everyone here in this audience might become the same as I am, except for these chains."

30Then the king, the governor, Bernice, and all the others stood and left. 31As they went out, they talked it over and agreed, "This man hasn't done anything to deserve death or imprisonment."

32And Agrippa said to Festus, "He could have been set free if he hadn't appealed to Caesar."

How comfortable are you with explaining your faith? Paul set forth the facts: Jesus fulfilled the Old Testament prophecies, and his message was turning the world upside down. The history of Jesus' life and the early church are facts that are still there for us to examine. We still have eyewitness accounts of Jesus' life in the Bible as well as historical and archaeological records of the early church to study. Examine the events and facts as verified by many witnesses. Reconfirm your faith with the truth of these accounts.

The Storm at Sea

NOVEMBER 16

ACTS 27:1-26

When the time came, we set sail for Italy. Paul and several other prisoners were placed in the custody of a Roman officer named Julius, a captain of the Imperial Regiment. . . .

[3]The next day when we docked at Sidon, Julius was very kind to Paul and let him go ashore to visit with friends so they could provide for his needs. . . .

[7]We had several days of slow sailing, and after great difficulty we finally neared Cnidus. But the wind was against us, so we sailed across to Crete and along the sheltered coast of the island, past the cape of Salmone. [8]We struggled along the coast with great difficulty and finally arrived at Fair Havens, near the town of Lasea. [9]We had lost a lot of time. The weather was becoming dangerous for sea travel because it was so late in the fall, and Paul spoke to the ship's officers about it.

[10]"Men," he said, "I believe there is trouble ahead if we go on—shipwreck, loss of cargo, and danger to our lives as well." [11]But the officer in charge of the prisoners listened more to the ship's captain and the owner than to Paul. [12]And since Fair Havens was an exposed harbor—a poor place to spend the winter—most of the crew wanted to go on to Phoenix, farther up the coast of Crete, and spend the winter there. Phoenix was a good harbor with only a southwest and northwest exposure.

[13]When a light wind began blowing from the south, the sailors thought they could make it. . . .

[18]The next day, as gale-force winds continued to batter the ship, the crew began throwing the cargo overboard. [19]The following day they even took some of the ship's gear and threw it overboard. [20]The terrible storm raged for many days, blotting out the sun and the stars, until at last all hope was gone.

[21]No one had eaten for a long time. Finally, Paul called the crew together and said, "Men, you should have listened to me in the first place and not left Crete. You would have avoided all this damage and loss. [22]But take courage! None of you will lose your lives, even though the ship will go down. [23]For last night an angel of the God to whom I belong and whom I serve stood beside me, [24]and he said, 'Don't be afraid, Paul, for you will surely stand trial before Caesar! What's more, God in his goodness has granted safety to everyone sailing with you.' [25]So take courage! For I believe God. It will be just as he said. [26]But we will be shipwrecked on an island."

How would your character look, up close and personal? Julius, a hardened Roman centurion, was assigned to guard Paul. Obviously, he had to remain close to Paul at all times. Through this contact, Julius developed a respect for Paul. He gave Paul a certain amount of freedom and later spared his life.

NOVEMBER 17

Shipwreck!

ACTS 27:27-44

27About midnight on the fourteenth night of the storm, as we were being driven across the
Sea of Adria, the sailors sensed land was near. 28They dropped a weighted line and found
that the water was 120 feet deep. But a little later they measured again and found it was only
90 feet deep. 29At this rate they were afraid we would soon be driven against the rocks along
the shore, so they threw out four anchors from the back of the ship and prayed for daylight.
30Then the sailors tried to abandon the ship; they lowered the lifeboat as though they
were going to put out anchors from the front of the ship. 31But Paul said to the commanding
officer and the soldiers, "You will all die unless the sailors stay aboard." 32So the soldiers cut
the ropes to the lifeboat and let it drift away.
33Just as day was dawning, Paul urged everyone to eat. "You have been so worried that
you haven't touched food for two weeks," he said. 34"Please eat something now for your own
good. For not a hair of your heads will perish." 35Then he took some bread, gave thanks to
God before them all, and broke off a piece and ate it. 36Then everyone was encouraged and
began to eat—37all 276 of us who were on board. 38After eating, the crew lightened the ship
further by throwing the cargo of wheat overboard.
39When morning dawned, they didn't recognize the coastline, but they saw a bay with a
beach and wondered if they could get to shore by running the ship aground. 40So they cut
off the anchors and left them in the sea. Then they lowered the rudders, raised the foresail,
and headed toward shore. 41But they hit a shoal and ran the ship aground too soon. The bow
of the ship stuck fast, while the stern was repeatedly smashed by the force of the waves and
began to break apart.
42The soldiers wanted to kill the prisoners to make sure they didn't swim ashore and
escape. 43But the commanding officer wanted to spare Paul, so he didn't let them carry out
their plan. Then he ordered all who could swim to jump overboard first and make for land.
44The others held on to planks or debris from the broken ship. So everyone escaped safely
to shore.

Has God used disasters in your life to teach you? The soldiers would pay with their own lives if any of their prisoners escaped. Their instinctive reaction was to kill the prisoners so they wouldn't get away. Julius, the centurion, was impressed with Paul and wanted to save his life. Julius was the highest-ranking official and therefore could make the decision to spare him. This act preserved Paul for his later ministry in Rome and fulfilled Paul's prediction that all the people on the ship would be saved.

The Winter on Malta

NOVEMBER 18

ACTS 28:1-14

Once we were safe on shore, we learned that we were on the island of Malta. 2The people of the island were very kind to us. It was cold and rainy, so they built a fire on the shore to welcome us.

3As Paul gathered an armful of sticks and was laying them on the fire, a poisonous snake, driven out by the heat, bit him on the hand. 4The people of the island saw it hanging from his hand and said to each other, "A murderer, no doubt! Though he escaped the sea, justice will not permit him to live." 5But Paul shook off the snake into the fire and was unharmed. 6The people waited for him to swell up or suddenly drop dead. But when they had waited a long time and saw that he wasn't harmed, they changed their minds and decided he was a god.

7Near the shore where we landed was an estate belonging to Publius, the chief official of the island. He welcomed us and treated us kindly for three days. 8As it happened, Publius's father was ill with fever and dysentery. Paul went in and prayed for him, and laying his hands on him, he healed him. 9Then all the other sick people on the island came and were healed. 10As a result we were showered with honors, and when the time came to sail, people supplied us with everything we would need for the trip.

11It was three months after the shipwreck that we set sail on another ship that had wintered at the island—an Alexandrian ship with the twin gods as its figurehead. 12Our first stop was Syracuse, where we stayed three days. 13From there we sailed across to Rhegium. A day later a south wind began blowing, so the following day we sailed up the coast to Puteoli. 14There we found some believers, who invited us to spend a week with them. And so we came to Rome.

Do you trust that God knows what will happen all the days of your life? God had promised safe passage to Paul (Acts 27:23-25), and he would let nothing stop his servant. The poisonous snake that bit Paul was unable to harm him. Our lives are in God's hands, to continue on or to come to an end in his good timing. God still had work for Paul to do.

NOVEMBER 19

Paul in Rome

ACTS 28:16-31

16When we arrived in Rome, Paul was permitted to have his own private lodging, though he
was guarded by a soldier.

17Three days after Paul's arrival, he called together the local Jewish leaders. He said to
them, "Brothers, I was arrested in Jerusalem and handed over to the Roman government,
even though I had done nothing against our people or the customs of our ancestors. 18The
Romans tried me and wanted to release me, because they found no cause for the death sentence. 19But when the Jewish leaders protested the decision, I felt it necessary to appeal to
Caesar, even though I had no desire to press charges against my own people. 20I asked you to
come here today so we could get acquainted and so I could explain to you that I am bound
with this chain because I believe that the hope of Israel—the Messiah—has already come."

21They replied, "We have had no letters from Judea or reports against you from anyone
who has come here. 22But we want to hear what you believe, for the only thing we know
about this movement is that it is denounced everywhere."

23So a time was set, and on that day a large number of people came to Paul's lodging. He
explained and testified about the Kingdom of God and tried to persuade them about Jesus
from the Scriptures. Using the law of Moses and the books of the prophets, he spoke to them
from morning until evening. 24Some were persuaded by the things he said, but others did
not believe. 25And after they had argued back and forth among themselves, they left with this
final word from Paul: "The Holy Spirit was right when he said to your ancestors through
Isaiah the prophet,

26'Go and say to this people:
When you hear what I say,
    you will not understand.
When you see what I do,
    you will not comprehend. . . .'

28So I want you to know that this salvation from God has also been offered to the Gentiles,
and they will accept it."

30For the next two years, Paul lived in Rome at his own expense. He welcomed all who
visited him, 31boldly proclaiming the Kingdom of God and teaching about the Lord Jesus
Christ. And no one tried to stop him.

What do you want to do for God? Paul wanted to preach the gospel in Rome, and he eventually got there—in chains, through shipwreck, and after many trials. Paul may have wished for an easier passage, but he knew that God had blessed him in allowing him to preach the message to both Jews and Gentiles in the capital of the empire. God worked all things for good for Paul, and you can trust him to do the same for you. God does not promise you comfort or security, but he will provide the opportunity and means to do his work.

Faith Brings Joy

NOVEMBER 20

ROMANS 5:1-11

Therefore, since we have been made right in God's sight by faith, we have peace with God
because of what Jesus Christ our Lord has done for us. [2]Because of our faith, Christ has
brought us into this place of undeserved privilege where we now stand, and we confidently
and joyfully look forward to sharing God's glory.

[3]We can rejoice, too, when we run into problems and trials, for we know that they help
us develop endurance. [4]And endurance develops strength of character, and character strengthens our confident hope of salvation. [5]And this hope will not lead to disappointment. For
we know how dearly God loves us, because he has given us the Holy Spirit to fill our hearts
with his love.

[6]When we were utterly helpless, Christ came at just the right time and died for us sinners. [7]Now, most people would not be willing to die for an upright person, though someone
might perhaps be willing to die for a person who is especially good. [8]But God showed his
great love for us by sending Christ to die for us while we were still sinners. [9]And since we
have been made right in God's sight by the blood of Christ, he will certainly save us from
God's condemnation. [10]For since our friendship with God was restored by the death of his
Son while we were still his enemies, we will certainly be saved through the life of his Son.
[11]So now we can rejoice in our wonderful new relationship with God because our Lord Jesus
Christ has made us friends of God.

When was the last time you thanked God for all he's done for you? Paul tells us that in the future we will become, but until then we must overcome. This means we will experience difficulties that help us grow. Problems we run into will develop our patience, which in turn will strengthen our character, deepen our trust in God, and give us greater confidence about the future. You probably find your patience tested in some way every day. Thank God for these opportunities to grow, and deal with them in his strength.

NOVEMBER 21

Truly Free from Sin

ROMANS 8:1-16

So now there is no condemnation for those who belong to Christ Jesus. 2And because you belong to him, the power of the life-giving Spirit has freed you from the power of sin that leads to death. 3The law of Moses was unable to save us because of the weakness of our sinful nature. So God did what the law could not do. He sent his own Son in a body like the bodies we sinners have. And in that body God declared an end to sin's control over us by giving his Son as a sacrifice for our sins. 4He did this so that the just requirement of the law would be fully satisfied for us, who no longer follow our sinful nature but instead follow the Spirit.

5Those who are dominated by the sinful nature think about sinful things, but those who are controlled by the Holy Spirit think about things that please the Spirit. 6So letting your sinful nature control your mind leads to death. But letting the Spirit control your mind leads to life and peace. 7For the sinful nature is always hostile to God. It never did obey God's laws, and it never will. 8That's why those who are still under the control of their sinful nature can never please God.

9But you are not controlled by your sinful nature. You are controlled by the Spirit if you have the Spirit of God living in you. (And remember that those who do not have the Spirit of Christ living in them do not belong to him at all.) 10And Christ lives within you, so even though your body will die because of sin, the Spirit gives you life because you have been made right with God. 11The Spirit of God, who raised Jesus from the dead, lives in you. And just as God raised Christ Jesus from the dead, he will give life to your mortal bodies by this same Spirit living within you.

12Therefore, dear brothers and sisters, you have no obligation to do what your sinful nature urges you to do. 13For if you live by its dictates, you will die. But if through the power of the Spirit you put to death the deeds of your sinful nature, you will live. 14For all who are led by the Spirit of God are children of God.

15So you have not received a spirit that makes you fearful slaves. Instead, you received God's Spirit when he adopted you as his own children. Now we call him, "Abba, Father." 16For his Spirit joins with our spirit to affirm that we are God's children.

In what areas are you still struggling with your sinful nature? Paul divides people into two categories—those who let themselves be controlled by their sinful nature and those who follow after the Holy Spirit. All of us would be in the first category if Jesus hadn't offered us a way out. Once we have said yes to Jesus, we will want to continue following him because his way brings life and peace. Every day we must consciously choose to center our lives on God. Use the Bible to discover God's guidelines, and then follow them. Ask yourself in every perplexing situation, What would Jesus want me to do? When the Holy Spirit points out what is right, do it eagerly.

How God Loves

NOVEMBER 22

ROMANS 8:23-39

We, too, wait with eager hope for the day when God will give us our full rights as his adopted children, including the new bodies he has promised us. 24We were given this hope when we were saved. (If we already have something, we don't need to hope for it. 25But if we look forward to something we don't yet have, we must wait patiently and confidently.)

26And the Holy Spirit helps us in our weakness. For example, we don't know what God wants us to pray for. But the Holy Spirit prays for us with groanings that cannot be expressed in words. 27And the Father who knows all hearts knows what the Spirit is saying, for the Spirit pleads for us believers in harmony with God's own will. 28And we know that God causes everything to work together for the good of those who love God and are called according to his purpose for them. 29For God knew his people in advance, and he chose them to become like his Son, so that his Son would be the firstborn among many brothers and sisters. 30And having chosen them, he called them to come to him. And having called them, he gave them right standing with himself. And having given them right standing, he gave them his glory.

31What shall we say about such wonderful things as these? If God is for us, who can ever be against us? 32Since he did not spare even his own Son but gave him up for us all, won't he also give us everything else? 33Who dares accuse us whom God has chosen for his own? No one—for God himself has given us right standing with himself. 34Who then will condemn us? No one—for Christ Jesus died for us and was raised to life for us, and he is sitting in the place of honor at God's right hand, pleading for us.

35Can anything ever separate us from Christ's love? Does it mean he no longer loves us if we have trouble or calamity, or are persecuted, or hungry, or destitute, or in danger, or threatened with death? 36(As the Scriptures say, "For your sake we are killed every day; we are being slaughtered like sheep.") 37No, despite all these things, overwhelming victory is ours through Christ, who loved us.

38And I am convinced that nothing can ever separate us from God's love. Neither death nor life, neither angels nor demons, neither our fears for today nor our worries about tomorrow—not even the powers of hell can separate us from God's love. 39No power in the sky above or in the earth below—indeed, nothing in all creation will ever be able to separate us from the love of God that is revealed in Christ Jesus our Lord.

What things do you feel might be able to separate you from the love of Christ? Believers have always had to face hardships in many forms. These hardships can cause us to fear that we have been abandoned by Christ. But Paul exclaims that it is impossible to be separated from Christ. His death for us is proof of his unconquerable love. Nothing can stop his constant presence with us. God tells us how great his love is so that we will feel totally secure in him. If we believe these wonderful promises, we will not be afraid.

NOVEMBER 23

Living Sacrifice

ROMANS 12:1-21

And so, dear brothers and sisters, I plead with you to give your bodies to God because of all
he has done for you. Let them be a living and holy sacrifice—the kind he will find acceptable.
This is truly the way to worship him. 2Don't copy the behavior and customs of this world,
but let God transform you into a new person by changing the way you think. Then you will
learn to know God's will for you, which is good and pleasing and perfect. . . .

9Don't just pretend to love others. Really love them. Hate what is wrong. Hold tightly
to what is good. 10Love each other with genuine affection, and take delight in honoring each
other. 11Never be lazy, but work hard and serve the Lord enthusiastically. 12Rejoice in our
confident hope. Be patient in trouble, and keep on praying. 13When God's people are in need,
be ready to help them. Always be eager to practice hospitality.

14Bless those who persecute you. Don't curse them; pray that God will bless them. 15Be
happy with those who are happy, and weep with those who weep. 16Live in harmony with
each other. Don't be too proud to enjoy the company of ordinary people. And don't think
you know it all!

17Never pay back evil with more evil. Do things in such a way that everyone can see you
are honorable. 18Do all that you can to live in peace with everyone.

19Dear friends, never take revenge. Leave that to the righteous anger of God. For the
Scriptures say,

"I will take revenge;
I will pay them back,"
says the LORD.

20Instead,

"If your enemies are hungry, feed them.
If they are thirsty, give them something to drink.
In doing this, you will heap
burning coals of shame on their heads."

21Don't let evil conquer you, but conquer evil by doing good.

When you are wronged by someone, are you quick to seek revenge or quick to extend forgiveness? In this day of constant lawsuits and incessant demands for legal rights, Paul's command sounds almost impossible. When people hurt you deeply, instead of giving them what they deserve, Paul says to befriend them. Why does Paul tell us to forgive our enemies? (1) Forgiveness may break a cycle of retaliation and lead to mutual reconciliation. (2) It may make the enemy feel ashamed and change his or her ways. (3) Returning evil for evil hurts you just as much as it hurts your enemy. Even if your enemy never repents, forgiving him or her will free you of a heavy load of bitterness.

Real Love

NOVEMBER 24

1 CORINTHIANS 13:1-13

If I could speak all the languages of earth and of angels, but didn't love others, I would only
be a noisy gong or a clanging cymbal. 2If I had the gift of prophecy, and if I understood all
of God's secret plans and possessed all knowledge, and if I had such faith that I could move
mountains, but didn't love others, I would be nothing. 3If I gave everything I have to the
poor and even sacrificed my body, I could boast about it; but if I didn't love others, I would
have gained nothing.

4Love is patient and kind. Love is not jealous or boastful or proud 5or rude. It does not
demand its own way. It is not irritable, and it keeps no record of being wronged. 6It does not
rejoice about injustice but rejoices whenever the truth wins out. 7Love never gives up, never
loses faith, is always hopeful, and endures through every circumstance.

8Prophecy and speaking in unknown languages and special knowledge will become useless. But love will last forever! 9Now our knowledge is partial and incomplete, and even the
gift of prophecy reveals only part of the whole picture! 10But when the time of perfection
comes, these partial things will become useless.

11When I was a child, I spoke and thought and reasoned as a child. But when I grew
up, I put away childish things. 12Now we see things imperfectly, like puzzling reflections in
a mirror, but then we will see everything with perfect clarity. All that I know now is partial
and incomplete, but then I will know everything completely, just as God now knows me
completely.

13Three things will last forever—faith, hope, and love—and the greatest of these is love.

Which quality of real love do you most need to ask God to increase in your life? Our society confuses love and lust. Unlike lust, God's kind of love is directed outward toward others, not inward toward ourselves. It is utterly unselfish. This kind of love goes against our natural inclinations. It involves unselfish service to others and shows that we care. Faith is the foundation and content of God's message; hope is the attitude and focus; love is the action. When faith and hope are in line, we are free to love completely, because we understand how God loves. It is only as God helps us set aside our own desires and instincts that we can give this love while expecting nothing in return. Thus, the more we become like Christ, the more love we will show to others.

NOVEMBER 25

The Basic Gospel

1 CORINTHIANS 15:1-20

Let me now remind you, dear brothers and sisters, of the Good News I preached to you before. You welcomed it then, and you still stand firm in it. 2It is this Good News that saves you if you continue to believe the message I told you—unless, of course, you believed something that was never true in the first place.

3I passed on to you what was most important and what had also been passed on to me. Christ died for our sins, just as the Scriptures said. 4He was buried, and he was raised from the dead on the third day, just as the Scriptures said. 5He was seen by Peter and then by the Twelve. 6After that, he was seen by more than 500 of his followers at one time, most of whom are still alive, though some have died. 7Then he was seen by James and later by all the apostles. 8Last of all, as though I had been born at the wrong time, I also saw him. 9For I am the least of all the apostles. In fact, I'm not even worthy to be called an apostle after the way I persecuted God's church.

10But whatever I am now, it is all because God poured out his special favor on me—and not without results. For I have worked harder than any of the other apostles; yet it was not I but God who was working through me by his grace. 11So it makes no difference whether I preach or they preach, for we all preach the same message you have already believed.

12But tell me this—since we preach that Christ rose from the dead, why are some of you saying there will be no resurrection of the dead? 13For if there is no resurrection of the dead, then Christ has not been raised either. 14And if Christ has not been raised, then all our preaching is useless, and your faith is useless. 15And we apostles would all be lying about God—for we have said that God raised Christ from the grave. But that can't be true if there is no resurrection of the dead. 16And if there is no resurrection of the dead, then Christ has not been raised. 17And if Christ has not been raised, then your faith is useless and you are still guilty of your sins. 18In that case, all who have died believing in Christ are lost! 19And if our hope in Christ is only for this life, we are more to be pitied than anyone in the world.

20But in fact, Christ has been raised from the dead. He is the first of a great harvest of all who have died.

What parts of the gospel are especially helpful to you in times of doubt or stress? There will always be people who will say that Jesus didn't rise from the dead. Paul assures us that many people saw Jesus after his resurrection, including more than five hundred believers. The Resurrection is a historical fact. Don't be discouraged by doubters who deny it. The resurrection of Christ is the focus of our Christian faith. Because Christ rose from the dead as he promised, we know that what he said is true—he is God. Because he rose, we have certainty that our sins are forgiven. Because he rose, he lives and represents us to God. Because he rose and defeated death, we know we will also be raised.

Victory in Jesus

NOVEMBER 26

1 CORINTHIANS 15:42-58

42It is the same way with the resurrection of the dead. Our earthly bodies are planted in the
ground when we die, but they will be raised to live forever. 43Our bodies are buried in bro-
kenness, but they will be raised in glory. They are buried in weakness, but they will be raised
in strength. 44They are buried as natural human bodies, but they will be raised as spiritual
bodies. For just as there are natural bodies, there are also spiritual bodies.

45The Scriptures tell us, "The first man, Adam, became a living person." But the last
Adam—that is, Christ—is a life-giving Spirit. 46What comes first is the natural body, then
the spiritual body comes later. 47Adam, the first man, was made from the dust of the earth,
while Christ, the second man, came from heaven. 48Earthly people are like the earthly man,
and heavenly people are like the heavenly man. 49Just as we are now like the earthly man, we
will someday be like the heavenly man.

50What I am saying, dear brothers and sisters, is that our physical bodies cannot inherit
the Kingdom of God. These dying bodies cannot inherit what will last forever.

51But let me reveal to you a wonderful secret. We will not all die, but we will all be transformed! 52It will happen in a moment, in the blink of an eye, when the last trumpet is blown.
For when the trumpet sounds, those who have died will be raised to live forever. And we who
are living will also be transformed. 53For our dying bodies must be transformed into bodies
that will never die; our mortal bodies must be transformed into immortal bodies.

54Then, when our dying bodies have been transformed into bodies that will never die,
this Scripture will be fulfilled:

"Death is swallowed up in victory.
55O death, where is your victory?
O death, where is your sting?"

56For sin is the sting that results in death, and the law gives sin its power. 57But thank God!
He gives us victory over sin and death through our Lord Jesus Christ.

58So, my dear brothers and sisters, be strong and immovable. Always work enthusiastically
for the Lord, for you know that nothing you do for the Lord is ever useless.

Do you sometimes feel like your good work for Christ is wasted or overlooked? Paul said that because of the Resurrection, nothing we do is wasted. Sometimes we hesitate to do good because we don't see any results. In order to see the good resulting from our efforts, we need to maintain a heavenly perspective. Truly believing that Christ has won the ultimate victory will affect the way we live right now. Don't let discouragement over an apparent lack of results keep you from working for Christ. Do the good that you have opportunity to do, knowing that your work will have eternal results.

NOVEMBER 27

Weak Containers, Strong Contents

2 CORINTHIANS 4:3-18

3If the Good News we preach is hidden behind a veil, it is hidden only from people who are perishing. 4Satan, who is the god of this world, has blinded the minds of those who don't believe. They are unable to see the glorious light of the Good News. They don't understand this message about the glory of Christ, who is the exact likeness of God.

5You see, we don't go around preaching about ourselves. We preach that Jesus Christ is Lord, and we ourselves are your servants for Jesus' sake. 6For God, who said, "Let there be light in the darkness," has made this light shine in our hearts so we could know the glory of God that is seen in the face of Jesus Christ.

7We now have this light shining in our hearts, but we ourselves are like fragile clay jars containing this great treasure. This makes it clear that our great power is from God, not from ourselves.

8We are pressed on every side by troubles, but we are not crushed. We are perplexed, but not driven to despair. 9We are hunted down, but never abandoned by God. We get knocked down, but we are not destroyed. 10Through suffering, our bodies continue to share in the death of Jesus so that the life of Jesus may also be seen in our bodies.

11Yes, we live under constant danger of death because we serve Jesus, so that the life of Jesus will be evident in our dying bodies. 12So we live in the face of death, but this has resulted in eternal life for you.

13But we continue to preach because we have the same kind of faith the psalmist had when he said, "I believed in God, so I spoke." 14We know that God, who raised the Lord Jesus, will also raise us with Jesus and present us to himself together with you. 15All of this is for your benefit. And as God's grace reaches more and more people, there will be great thanksgiving, and God will receive more and more glory.

16That is why we never give up. Though our bodies are dying, our spirits are being renewed every day. 17For our present troubles are small and won't last very long. Yet they produce for us a glory that vastly outweighs them and will last forever! 18So we don't look at the troubles we can see now; rather, we fix our gaze on things that cannot be seen. For the things we see now will soon be gone, but the things we cannot see will last forever.

To what extent do you see your troubles as opportunities for God to work in your life? Our troubles should not diminish our faith or disillusion us. Instead, we should realize that there is a purpose in our suffering. Problems and human limitations have several benefits: (1) They help us remember Christ's suffering for us. (2) They help keep us from pride. (3) They help us look beyond this brief life. (4) They prove our faith to others. (5) They give God the opportunity to demonstrate his great power. Don't resent your troubles—see them as opportunities!

Two Radically Different Lives

NOVEMBER 28

GALATIANS 5:13-26

13For you have been called to live in freedom, my brothers and sisters. But don't use your
freedom to satisfy your sinful nature. Instead, use your freedom to serve one another in
love. 14For the whole law can be summed up in this one command: "Love your neighbor as
yourself." 15But if you are always biting and devouring one another, watch out! Beware of
destroying one another.

16So I say, let the Holy Spirit guide your lives. Then you won't be doing what your sinful
nature craves. 17The sinful nature wants to do evil, which is just the opposite of what the
Spirit wants. And the Spirit gives us desires that are the opposite of what the sinful nature
desires. These two forces are constantly fighting each other, so you are not free to carry out
your good intentions. 18But when you are directed by the Spirit, you are not under obligation
to the law of Moses.

19When you follow the desires of your sinful nature, the results are very clear: sexual
immorality, impurity, lustful pleasures, 20idolatry, sorcery, hostility, quarreling, jealousy, out-
bursts of anger, selfish ambition, dissension, division, 21envy, drunkenness, wild parties, and
other sins like these. Let me tell you again, as I have before, that anyone living that sort of
life will not inherit the Kingdom of God.

22But the Holy Spirit produces this kind of fruit in our lives: love, joy, peace, patience,
kindness, goodness, faithfulness, 23gentleness, and self-control. There is no law against these
things!

24Those who belong to Christ Jesus have nailed the passions and desires of their sinful
nature to his cross and crucified them there. 25Since we are living by the Spirit, let us follow
the Spirit's leading in every part of our lives. 26Let us not become conceited, or provoke one
another, or be jealous of one another.

Who comes to mind as someone you need to love as you love yourself? When we are not motivated by love, we become critical of others. We stop looking for good in them and see only their faults. Soon the unity of believers becomes broken. Have you talked behind someone's back? Have you focused on others' shortcomings instead of their strengths? Remind yourself of Jesus' command to love others as we love ourselves. When you begin to feel critical of someone, make a list of that person's positive qualities. Don't say anything behind someone's back that you wouldn't say to that person's face.

NOVEMBER 29

God's Action

EPHESIANS 1:3-18

[3]All praise to God, the Father of our Lord Jesus Christ, who has blessed us with every spiritual blessing in the heavenly realms because we are united with Christ. [4]Even before he made the world, God loved us and chose us in Christ to be holy and without fault in his eyes. [5]God decided in advance to adopt us into his own family by bringing us to himself through Jesus Christ. This is what he wanted to do, and it gave him great pleasure. [6]So we praise God for the glorious grace he has poured out on us who belong to his dear Son. [7]He is so rich in kindness and grace that he purchased our freedom with the blood of his Son and forgave our sins. [8]He has showered his kindness on us, along with all wisdom and understanding.

[9]God has now revealed to us his mysterious will regarding Christ—which is to fulfill his own good plan. [10]And this is the plan: At the right time he will bring everything together under the authority of Christ—everything in heaven and on earth. [11]Furthermore, because we are united with Christ, we have received an inheritance from God, for he chose us in advance, and he makes everything work out according to his plan.

[12]God's purpose was that we Jews who were the first to trust in Christ would bring praise and glory to God. [13]And now you Gentiles have also heard the truth, the Good News that God saves you. And when you believed in Christ, he identified you as his own by giving you the Holy Spirit, whom he promised long ago. [14]The Spirit is God's guarantee that he will give us the inheritance he promised and that he has purchased us to be his own people. He did this so we would praise and glorify him.

[15]Ever since I first heard of your strong faith in the Lord Jesus and your love for God's people everywhere, [16]I have not stopped thanking God for you. I pray for you constantly, [17]asking God, the glorious Father of our Lord Jesus Christ, to give you spiritual wisdom and insight so that you might grow in your knowledge of God. [18]I pray that your hearts will be flooded with light so that you can understand the confident hope he has given to those he called—his holy people who are his rich and glorious inheritance.

In what ways has God marked your life? Paul said that God "chose us" in order to emphasize that salvation depends totally on God. We are not saved because we deserve salvation but because God is gracious and freely gives it. We did not influence God's decision to save us; he did it according to his plan. Thus, there is no way to take credit for our salvation or to find room for pride. The mystery of salvation originated in the timeless mind of God long before we existed. It is hard to understand how God could accept us, but because of Christ, we are holy and blameless in his eyes. God chose you, and when you belong to him through Jesus Christ, he looks at you as if you had never sinned.

God's Plan

NOVEMBER 30

EPHESIANS 2:1-22

Once you were dead because of your disobedience and your many sins. [2]You used to live in sin, just like the rest of the world, obeying the devil—the commander of the powers in the unseen world. He is the spirit at work in the hearts of those who refuse to obey God. [3]All of us used to live that way, following the passionate desires and inclinations of our sinful nature. By our very nature we were subject to God's anger, just like everyone else.

[4]But God is so rich in mercy, and he loved us so much, [5]that even though we were dead because of our sins, he gave us life when he raised Christ from the dead. (It is only by God's grace that you have been saved!) [6]For he raised us from the dead along with Christ and seated us with him in the heavenly realms because we are united with Christ Jesus. [7]So God can point to us in all future ages as examples of the incredible wealth of his grace and kindness toward us, as shown in all he has done for us who are united with Christ Jesus.

[8]God saved you by his grace when you believed. And you can't take credit for this; it is a gift from God. [9]Salvation is not a reward for the good things we have done, so none of us can boast about it. [10]For we are God's masterpiece. He has created us anew in Christ Jesus, so we can do the good things he planned for us long ago.

[11]Don't forget that you Gentiles used to be outsiders. You were called "uncircumcised heathens" by the Jews, who were proud of their circumcision, even though it affected only their bodies and not their hearts. [12]In those days you were living apart from Christ. You were excluded from citizenship among the people of Israel, and you did not know the covenant promises God had made to them. You lived in this world without God and without hope. [13]But now you have been united with Christ Jesus. Once you were far away from God, but now you have been brought near to him through the blood of Christ. . . .

[19]So now you Gentiles are no longer strangers and foreigners. You are citizens along with all of God's holy people. You are members of God's family. [20]Together, we are his house, built on the foundation of the apostles and the prophets. And the cornerstone is Christ Jesus himself. [21]We are carefully joined together in him, becoming a holy temple for the Lord. [22]Through him you Gentiles are also being made part of this dwelling where God lives by his Spirit.

When was the last time you reminded yourself and God that you want your life to be used for his purposes? We become Christians through God's unmerited grace, not as the result of any effort, ability, intelligent choice, or act of service on our part. However, out of gratitude for this free gift, we will seek to help and serve others with kindness, love, and gentleness, and not merely to please ourselves. While no action or work we do can help us obtain salvation, God's intention is that our salvation will result in acts of service. We are saved not merely for our own benefit but to serve Christ and build up the church.

December

DECEMBER 1

Picture of the Church

EPHESIANS 4:1-16

Therefore I, a prisoner for serving the Lord, beg you to lead a life worthy of your calling,
for you have been called by God. 2Always be humble and gentle. Be patient with each other,
making allowance for each other's faults because of your love. 3Make every effort to keep
yourselves united in the Spirit, binding yourselves together with peace. 4For there is one body
and one Spirit, just as you have been called to one glorious hope for the future.

5There is one Lord, one faith, one baptism,
6one God and Father of all,
who is over all, in all, and living through all.

7However, he has given each one of us a special gift through the generosity of Christ.
8That is why the Scriptures say,

"When he ascended to the heights,
he led a crowd of captives
and gave gifts to his people."

9Notice that it says "he ascended." This clearly means that Christ also descended to our
lowly world. 10And the same one who descended is the one who ascended higher than all the
heavens, so that he might fill the entire universe with himself.

11Now these are the gifts Christ gave to the church: the apostles, the prophets, the evangelists, and the pastors and teachers. 12Their responsibility is to equip God's people to do his
work and build up the church, the body of Christ. 13This will continue until we all come
to such unity in our faith and knowledge of God's Son that we will be mature in the Lord,
measuring up to the full and complete standard of Christ.

14Then we will no longer be immature like children. We won't be tossed and blown about
by every wind of new teaching. We will not be influenced when people try to trick us with
lies so clever they sound like the truth. 15Instead, we will speak the truth in love, growing in
every way more and more like Christ, who is the head of his body, the church. 16He makes the
whole body fit together perfectly. As each part does its own special work, it helps the other
parts grow, so that the whole body is healthy and growing and full of love.

What is your role in Christ's body? Our oneness in Christ does not destroy our individuality. The Holy Spirit has given each Christian special abilities for building up the church. Now that we have these gifts, it is crucial that we use them. Are you spiritually mature, exercising the gifts God has given you? If you know what your gifts are, look for opportunities to serve. If you don't know, ask God to show you, or ask for the help of your minister or Christian friends in identifying your gifts. Then, as you begin to recognize your special abilities, use them to strengthen and encourage the church.

Armor of God

EPHESIANS 6:10-20

[10]A final word: Be strong in the Lord and in his mighty power. [11]Put on all of God's armor so
that you will be able to stand firm against all strategies of the devil. [12]For we are not fighting
against flesh-and-blood enemies, but against evil rulers and authorities of the unseen world,
against mighty powers in this dark world, and against evil spirits in the heavenly places.

[13]Therefore, put on every piece of God's armor so you will be able to resist the enemy in
the time of evil. Then after the battle you will still be standing firm. [14]Stand your ground,
putting on the belt of truth and the body armor of God's righteousness. [15]For shoes, put on
the peace that comes from the Good News so that you will be fully prepared. [16]In addition to
all of these, hold up the shield of faith to stop the fiery arrows of the devil. [17]Put on salvation
as your helmet, and take the sword of the Spirit, which is the word of God.

[18]Pray in the Spirit at all times and on every occasion. Stay alert and be persistent in your
prayers for all believers everywhere.

[19]And pray for me, too. Ask God to give me the right words so I can boldly explain God's
mysterious plan that the Good News is for Jews and Gentiles alike. [20]I am in chains now,
still preaching this message as God's ambassador. So pray that I will keep on speaking boldly
for him, as I should.

Which of these pieces of armor do you need to learn to use more effectively? Those who are not "flesh-and-blood enemies" are demons over whom Satan has control. They are not mere fantasies—they are very real. We face a powerful army whose goal is to defeat Christ's church. When we believe in Christ, these beings become our enemies, and they try every device to turn us away from him and back to sin. Although we are assured of victory, we must engage in the struggle until Christ returns. Because Satan is constantly battling against all who are on the Lord's side, we need supernatural power to defeat him. God provides this by giving us his Holy Spirit within us and his armor surrounding us. If you feel discouraged, remember that Jesus promises to fight the battle for you as you trust in him.

DECEMBER 3

The Mind of Jesus

PHILIPPIANS 2:1-15

Is there any encouragement from belonging to Christ? Any comfort from his love? Any fellowship together in the Spirit? Are your hearts tender and compassionate? 2Then make me truly happy by agreeing wholeheartedly with each other, loving one another, and working together with one mind and purpose.

3Don't be selfish; don't try to impress others. Be humble, thinking of others as better than yourselves. 4Don't look out only for your own interests, but take an interest in others, too.

5You must have the same attitude that Christ Jesus had.

6Though he was God,
he did not think of equality with God
as something to cling to.
7Instead, he gave up his divine privileges;
he took the humble position of a slave
and was born as a human being.
When he appeared in human form,
8he humbled himself in obedience to God
and died a criminal's death on a cross.

9Therefore, God elevated him to the place of highest honor
and gave him the name above all other names,
10that at the name of Jesus every knee should bow,
in heaven and on earth and under the earth,
11and every tongue declare that Jesus Christ is Lord,
to the glory of God the Father.

12Dear friends, you always followed my instructions when I was with you. And now that I am away, it is even more important. Work hard to show the results of your salvation, obeying God with deep reverence and fear. 13For God is working in you, giving you the desire and the power to do what pleases him.

14Do everything without complaining and arguing, 15so that no one can criticize you. Live clean, innocent lives as children of God, shining like bright lights in a world full of crooked and perverse people.

In what ways would having Christ's mind or attitude help you face this day differently? Often people excuse selfishness, pride, or evil by claiming their "rights." They say, "I can cheat on this test; after all, I deserve to pass this class," or "I can spend all this money on myself—I worked for it," or "I can get an abortion—it's my body." But as believers, we should have a different attitude, an attitude that enables us to give up our rights for the good of others. If we say we follow Christ, we must also want to live as he lived. We should develop his attitude of humble service, even when we are not likely to get recognition for our efforts. Are you selfishly clinging to your rights, or are you willing to serve?

Learning Joy

DECEMBER 4

FROM PHILIPPIANS 3:1-21

Whatever happens, my dear brothers and sisters, rejoice in the Lord. I never get tired of telling
you these things, and I do it to safeguard your faith. . . .
5 I was circumcised when I was eight days old. I am a pure-blooded citizen of Israel and
a member of the tribe of Benjamin—a real Hebrew if there ever was one! I was a member of
the Pharisees, who demand the strictest obedience to the Jewish law. 6 I was so zealous that
I harshly persecuted the church. And as for righteousness, I obeyed the law without fault.
7 I once thought these things were valuable, but now I consider them worthless because of
what Christ has done. 8 Yes, everything else is worthless when compared with the infinite value
of knowing Christ Jesus my Lord. For his sake I have discarded everything else, counting it
all as garbage, so that I could gain Christ 9 and become one with him. I no longer count on
my own righteousness through obeying the law; rather, I become righteous through faith in
Christ. For God's way of making us right with himself depends on faith. . . .
12 I don't mean to say that I have already achieved these things or that I have already
reached perfection. But I press on to possess that perfection for which Christ Jesus first
possessed me. 13 No, dear brothers and sisters, I have not achieved it, but I focus on this one
thing: Forgetting the past and looking forward to what lies ahead, 14 I press on to reach the end
of the race and receive the heavenly prize for which God, through Christ Jesus, is calling us.
15 Let all who are spiritually mature agree on these things. If you disagree on some point, I
believe God will make it plain to you. 16 But we must hold on to the progress we have already
made.
17 Dear brothers and sisters, pattern your lives after mine, and learn from those who follow
our example. 18 For I have told you often before, and I say it again with tears in my eyes, that
there are many whose conduct shows they are really enemies of the cross of Christ. 19 They
are headed for destruction. Their god is their appetite, they brag about shameful things, and
they think only about this life here on earth. 20 But we are citizens of heaven, where the Lord
Jesus Christ lives. And we are eagerly waiting for him to return as our Savior. 21 He will take
our weak mortal bodies and change them into glorious bodies like his own, using the same
power with which he will bring everything under his control.

What kind of follower would a new Christian become if he or she imitated you? Paul challenged the Philippians to pursue Christlikeness by following Paul's own example. This did not mean that they should copy everything he did, for he said that he was not perfect. But as he focused his life on being like Christ, so should they. The Gospels may not yet have been in circulation, so Paul could not tell them to read the Bible to see what Christ was like. Therefore he urged them to follow his example. That Paul could say this is a testimony to his character. Could you do the same?

DECEMBER 5

What We Have in Christ

COLOSSIANS 2:1-15

I want you to know how much I have agonized for you and for the church at Laodicea, and for many other believers who have never met me personally. 2I want them to be encouraged and knit together by strong ties of love. I want them to have complete confidence that they understand God's mysterious plan, which is Christ himself. 3In him lie hidden all the treasures of wisdom and knowledge.

4I am telling you this so no one will deceive you with well-crafted arguments. 5For though I am far away from you, my heart is with you. And I rejoice that you are living as you should and that your faith in Christ is strong.

6And now, just as you accepted Christ Jesus as your Lord, you must continue to follow him. 7Let your roots grow down into him, and let your lives be built on him. Then your faith will grow strong in the truth you were taught, and you will overflow with thankfulness.

8Don't let anyone capture you with empty philosophies and high-sounding nonsense that come from human thinking and from the spiritual powers of this world, rather than from Christ. 9For in Christ lives all the fullness of God in a human body. 10So you also are complete through your union with Christ, who is the head over every ruler and authority.

11When you came to Christ, you were "circumcised," but not by a physical procedure. Christ performed a spiritual circumcision—the cutting away of your sinful nature. 12For you were buried with Christ when you were baptized. And with him you were raised to new life because you trusted the mighty power of God, who raised Christ from the dead.

13You were dead because of your sins and because your sinful nature was not yet cut away. Then God made you alive with Christ, for he forgave all our sins. 14He canceled the record of the charges against us and took it away by nailing it to the cross. 15In this way, he disarmed the spiritual rulers and authorities. He shamed them publicly by his victory over them on the cross.

Is there a dangerous philosophy present in your environment that could affect your relationship with Christ? Paul writes against any philosophy of life based only on human ideas and experiences. Paul himself was a gifted philosopher, so he is not condemning philosophy. He is condemning teaching that credits humanity, not Christ, with being the answer to life's problems. That approach becomes a false religion. There are many man-made approaches to life's problems that totally disregard God. To resist heresy, you must use your mind, keep your eyes on Christ, and study God's Word. When we know Jesus Christ, we don't need to seek God by means of other religions, cults, or worldly philosophies as the Colossians were doing. Christ alone holds the answers to the true meaning of life, because he *is* life. Christ is the unique source of knowledge and power for the Christian life. No Christian needs anything in addition to what Christ has provided to be saved. We are complete in him.

Christian Relationships

DECEMBER 6

COLOSSIANS 3:1-17

Since you have been raised to new life with Christ, set your sights on the realities of heaven,
where Christ sits in the place of honor at God's right hand. [2]Think about the things of
heaven, not the things of earth. [3]For you died to this life, and your real life is hidden with
Christ in God. [4]And when Christ, who is your life, is revealed to the whole world, you will
share in all his glory.

[5]So put to death the sinful, earthly things lurking within you. Have nothing to do with
sexual immorality, impurity, lust, and evil desires. Don't be greedy, for a greedy person is an
idolater, worshiping the things of this world. [6]Because of these sins, the anger of God is coming. [7]You used to do these things when your life was still part of this world. [8]But now is the
time to get rid of anger, rage, malicious behavior, slander, and dirty language. [9]Don't lie to
each other, for you have stripped off your old sinful nature and all its wicked deeds. [10]Put on
your new nature, and be renewed as you learn to know your Creator and become like him.
[11]In this new life, it doesn't matter if you are a Jew or a Gentile, circumcised or uncircumcised,
barbaric, uncivilized, slave, or free. Christ is all that matters, and he lives in all of us.

[12]Since God chose you to be the holy people he loves, you must clothe yourselves with
tenderhearted mercy, kindness, humility, gentleness, and patience. [13]Make allowance for each
other's faults, and forgive anyone who offends you. Remember, the Lord forgave you, so
you must forgive others. [14]Above all, clothe yourselves with love, which binds us all together
in perfect harmony. [15]And let the peace that comes from Christ rule in your hearts. For as
members of one body you are called to live in peace. And always be thankful.

[16]Let the message about Christ, in all its richness, fill your lives. Teach and counsel each
other with all the wisdom he gives. Sing psalms and hymns and spiritual songs to God with
thankful hearts. [17]And whatever you do or say, do it as a representative of the Lord Jesus,
giving thanks through him to God the Father.

What do you envision when you think about heaven? Paul writes that we should have as little desire for this world as a dead person would have. The Christian's real home is where Christ lives. This truth gives us a different perspective on our lives here on earth. To "set your sights on the realities of heaven" means to look at life from God's perspective and seek what he desires. This is the antidote to materialism; we gain the proper perspective on material goods when we take God's view of them. The more we regard the world around us as God does, the more we will live in harmony with him. We must not become too attached to what is only temporary.

DECEMBER 7

Spiritual Reputation

1 THESSALONIANS 1:1-10

This letter is from Paul, Silas, and Timothy.

We are writing to the church in Thessalonica, to you who belong to God the Father and the Lord Jesus Christ.

May God give you grace and peace.

2We always thank God for all of you and pray for you constantly. 3As we pray to our God and Father about you, we think of your faithful work, your loving deeds, and the enduring hope you have because of our Lord Jesus Christ.

4We know, dear brothers and sisters, that God loves you and has chosen you to be his own people. 5For when we brought you the Good News, it was not only with words but also with power, for the Holy Spirit gave you full assurance that what we said was true. And you know of our concern for you from the way we lived when we were with you. 6So you received the message with joy from the Holy Spirit in spite of the severe suffering it brought you. In this way, you imitated both us and the Lord. 7As a result, you have become an example to all the believers in Greece—throughout both Macedonia and Achaia.

8And now the word of the Lord is ringing out from you to people everywhere, even beyond Macedonia and Achaia, for wherever we go we find people telling us about your faith in God. We don't need to tell them about it, 9for they keep talking about the wonderful welcome you gave us and how you turned away from idols to serve the living and true God. 10And they speak of how you are looking forward to the coming of God's Son from heaven—Jesus, whom God raised from the dead. He is the one who has rescued us from the terrors of the coming judgment.

How do you think others would evaluate your spiritual life? We should all respond to the Good News as the Thessalonians did: by turning to God, serving him joyfully, and waiting for his Son, Jesus Christ, to return from heaven. We should turn from sin to God because Christ is coming to judge the earth. We should be fervent in our service because we have little time before Christ returns. We should be prepared for Christ to return because we don't know when he will come.

Living for God

DECEMBER 8

1 THESSALONIANS 4:1-18

Finally, dear brothers and sisters, we urge you in the name of the Lord Jesus to live in a way that pleases God, as we have taught you. You live this way already, and we encourage you to do so even more. [2]For you remember what we taught you by the authority of the Lord Jesus.

[3]God's will is for you to be holy, so stay away from all sexual sin. [4]Then each of you will control his own body and live in holiness and honor—[5]not in lustful passion like the pagans who do not know God and his ways. [6]Never harm or cheat a fellow believer in this matter by violating his wife, for the Lord avenges all such sins, as we have solemnly warned you before. [7]God has called us to live holy lives, not impure lives. [8]Therefore, anyone who refuses to live by these rules is not disobeying human teaching but is rejecting God, who gives his Holy Spirit to you.

[9]But we don't need to write to you about the importance of loving each other, for God himself has taught you to love one another. [10]Indeed, you already show your love for all the believers throughout Macedonia. Even so, dear brothers and sisters, we urge you to love them even more.

[11]Make it your goal to live a quiet life, minding your own business and working with your hands, just as we instructed you before. [12]Then people who are not believers will respect the way you live, and you will not need to depend on others.

[13]And now, dear brothers and sisters, we want you to know what will happen to the believers who have died so you will not grieve like people who have no hope. [14]For since we believe that Jesus died and was raised to life again, we also believe that when Jesus returns, God will bring back with him the believers who have died.

[15]We tell you this directly from the Lord: We who are still living when the Lord returns will not meet him ahead of those who have died. [16]For the Lord himself will come down from heaven with a commanding shout, with the voice of the archangel, and with the trumpet call of God. First, the believers who have died will rise from their graves. [17]Then, together with them, we who are still alive and remain on the earth will be caught up in the clouds to meet the Lord in the air. Then we will be with the Lord forever. [18]So encourage each other with these words.

When a loved one dies, do you respond with devastation or confidence? Because Jesus Christ came back to life, so will all believers. All Christians, including those living when Christ returns, will live with Christ forever. Therefore, we need not despair when loved ones die or world events take a tragic turn. God will turn our tragedies into triumphs, our poverty into riches, our pain into glory, and our defeat into victory. All believers throughout history will stand in God's presence, safe and secure. As Paul comforted the Thessalonians with the promise of the resurrection, so we should comfort and reassure one another with this great hope.

DECEMBER 9

Encouragement

2 THESSALONIANS 1:1-12

This letter is from Paul, Silas, and Timothy.

We are writing to the church in Thessalonica, to you who belong to God our Father and the Lord Jesus Christ.

2May God our Father and the Lord Jesus Christ give you grace and peace.

3Dear brothers and sisters, we can't help but thank God for you, because your faith is flourishing and your love for one another is growing. 4We proudly tell God's other churches about your endurance and faithfulness in all the persecutions and hardships you are suffering. 5And God will use this persecution to show his justice and to make you worthy of his Kingdom, for which you are suffering. 6In his justice he will pay back those who persecute you.

7And God will provide rest for you who are being persecuted and also for us when the Lord Jesus appears from heaven. He will come with his mighty angels, 8in flaming fire, bringing judgment on those who don't know God and on those who refuse to obey the Good News of our Lord Jesus. 9They will be punished with eternal destruction, forever separated from the Lord and from his glorious power. 10When he comes on that day, he will receive glory from his holy people—praise from all who believe. And this includes you, for you believed what we told you about him.

11So we keep on praying for you, asking our God to enable you to live a life worthy of his call. May he give you the power to accomplish all the good things your faith prompts you to do. 12Then the name of our Lord Jesus will be honored because of the way you live, and you will be honored along with him. This is all made possible because of the grace of our God and Lord, Jesus Christ.

If you're currently experiencing hardship, which Christians in your life could encourage you today? As we live for Christ, we will experience troubles and hardships. Some say that troubles are a result of sin or lack of faith, but Paul teaches that they may be a part of God's plan for believers. Our problems help us to look upward and forward, not inward; they help build strong character; and they help us to be sensitive to others who also must struggle. In addition, problems are unavoidable because we are trying to be godly people in an ungodly world. Our troubles may well be a sign of effective Christian living.

Final Requests

DECEMBER 10

2 THESSALONIANS 3:1-18

Finally, dear brothers and sisters, we ask you to pray for us. Pray that the Lord's message will spread rapidly and be honored wherever it goes, just as when it came to you. 2Pray, too, that we will be rescued from wicked and evil people, for not everyone is a believer. 3But the Lord is faithful; he will strengthen you and guard you from the evil one. 4And we are confident in the Lord that you are doing and will continue to do the things we commanded you. 5May the Lord lead your hearts into a full understanding and expression of the love of God and the patient endurance that comes from Christ.

6And now, dear brothers and sisters, we give you this command in the name of our Lord Jesus Christ: Stay away from all believers who live idle lives and don't follow the tradition they received from us. 7For you know that you ought to imitate us. We were not idle when we were with you. 8We never accepted food from anyone without paying for it. We worked hard day and night so we would not be a burden to any of you. 9We certainly had the right to ask you to feed us, but we wanted to give you an example to follow. 10Even while we were with you, we gave you this command: "Those unwilling to work will not get to eat."

11Yet we hear that some of you are living idle lives, refusing to work and meddling in other people's business. 12We command such people and urge them in the name of the Lord Jesus Christ to settle down and work to earn their own living. 13As for the rest of you, dear brothers and sisters, never get tired of doing good.

14Take note of those who refuse to obey what we say in this letter. Stay away from them so they will be ashamed. 15Don't think of them as enemies, but warn them as you would a brother or sister.

16Now may the Lord of peace himself give you his peace at all times and in every situation. The Lord be with you all.

17Here is my greeting in my own handwriting—Paul. I do this in all my letters to prove they are from me.

18May the grace of our Lord Jesus Christ be with you all.

How aware and involved are you in the worldwide spread of the gospel? Some people in the Thessalonian church were falsely teaching that because Christ would return any day, people should set aside their responsibilities, quit work, do no future planning, and just wait for the Lord. But their lack of activity only led them into sin. They became a burden to the church, which was supporting them, and they wasted time that could have been used for helping others. These church members may have thought that they were being more spiritual by not working, but Paul tells them to be responsible and get back to work. Being ready for Christ means obeying him in every area of our lives. Because we know that Christ is coming, we must live in such a way that our faith and lives will please him when he arrives.

DECEMBER 11

Always Going Forward

1 TIMOTHY 4:1-16

Now the Holy Spirit tells us clearly that in the last times some will turn away from the true
faith; they will follow deceptive spirits and teachings that come from demons. 2These people
are hypocrites and liars, and their consciences are dead.

3They will say it is wrong to be married and wrong to eat certain foods. But God created
those foods to be eaten with thanks by faithful people who know the truth. 4Since everything
God created is good, we should not reject any of it but receive it with thanks. 5For we know
it is made acceptable by the word of God and prayer.

6If you explain these things to the brothers and sisters, Timothy, you will be a worthy
servant of Christ Jesus, one who is nourished by the message of faith and the good teaching
you have followed. 7Do not waste time arguing over godless ideas and old wives' tales. Instead,
train yourself to be godly. 8"Physical training is good, but training for godliness is much
better, promising benefits in this life and in the life to come." 9This is a trustworthy saying,
and everyone should accept it. 10This is why we work hard and continue to struggle, for our
hope is in the living God, who is the Savior of all people and particularly of all believers.

11Teach these things and insist that everyone learn them. 12Don't let anyone think less of
you because you are young. Be an example to all believers in what you say, in the way you live,
in your love, your faith, and your purity. 13Until I get there, focus on reading the Scriptures
to the church, encouraging the believers, and teaching them.

14Do not neglect the spiritual gift you received through the prophecy spoken over you
when the elders of the church laid their hands on you. 15Give your complete attention to
these matters. Throw yourself into your tasks so that everyone will see your progress. 16Keep
a close watch on how you live and on your teaching. Stay true to what is right for the sake
of your own salvation and the salvation of those who hear you.

Which of these instructions need to be given a higher priority in your life? Are you in shape both physically and spiritually? In our society much emphasis is placed on physical fitness, but spiritual health (godliness) is even more important. Our physical health is susceptible to disease and injury, but faith can sustain us through these tragedies. To train ourselves to be godly, we must develop our faith by using our God-given abilities in the service of the church. Are you developing your spiritual muscles?

A Friend's Final Words

DECEMBER 12

1 TIMOTHY 6:6-19

6Yet true godliness with contentment is itself great wealth. 7After all, we brought nothing with us when we came into the world, and we can't take anything with us when we leave it. 8So if we have enough food and clothing, let us be content.

9But people who long to be rich fall into temptation and are trapped by many foolish and harmful desires that plunge them into ruin and destruction. 10For the love of money is the root of all kinds of evil. And some people, craving money, have wandered from the true faith and pierced themselves with many sorrows.

11But you, Timothy, are a man of God; so run from all these evil things. Pursue righteousness and a godly life, along with faith, love, perseverance, and gentleness. 12Fight the good fight for the true faith. Hold tightly to the eternal life to which God has called you, which you have declared so well before many witnesses. 13And I charge you before God, who gives life to all, and before Christ Jesus, who gave a good testimony before Pontius Pilate, 14that you obey this command without wavering. Then no one can find fault with you from now until our Lord Jesus Christ comes again. 15For, At just the right time Christ will be revealed from heaven by the blessed and only almighty God, the King of all kings and Lord of all lords. 16He alone can never die, and he lives in light so brilliant that no human can approach him. No human eye has ever seen him, nor ever will. All honor and power to him forever! Amen.

17Teach those who are rich in this world not to be proud and not to trust in their money, which is so unreliable. Their trust should be in God, who richly gives us all we need for our enjoyment. 18Tell them to use their money to do good. They should be rich in good works and generous to those in need, always being ready to share with others. 19By doing this they will be storing up their treasure as a good foundation for the future so that they may experience true life.

Does your attitude toward money match Paul's advice? Despite overwhelming evidence to the contrary, most people still believe that money brings happiness. Rich people craving greater riches can be caught in an endless cycle that ends only in ruin and destruction. How can you keep yourself from the love of money? Paul gives us some guidelines: (1) Realize that one day worldly riches will be gone (verses 7, 17). (2) Be content with what you have (verse 8). (3) Monitor what you are willing to do to get more money (verses 9-10). (4) Love people more than money (verses 10-11). (5) Love God's work more than you love money (verses 10-11). (6) Freely share what you have with others (verse 18).

DECEMBER 13 The Importance of Examples

2 TIMOTHY 1:1-14

This letter is from Paul, chosen by the will of God to be an apostle of Christ Jesus. I have been
sent out to tell others about the life he has promised through faith in Christ Jesus.

2I am writing to Timothy, my dear son.

May God the Father and Christ Jesus our Lord give you grace, mercy, and peace.

3Timothy, I thank God for you—the God I serve with a clear conscience, just as my
ancestors did. Night and day I constantly remember you in my prayers. 4I long to see you
again, for I remember your tears as we parted. And I will be filled with joy when we are
together again.

5I remember your genuine faith, for you share the faith that first filled your grandmother
Lois and your mother, Eunice. And I know that same faith continues strong in you. 6This is
why I remind you to fan into flames the spiritual gift God gave you when I laid my hands
on you. 7For God has not given us a spirit of fear and timidity, but of power, love, and
self-discipline.

8So never be ashamed to tell others about our Lord. And don't be ashamed of me, either,
even though I'm in prison for him. With the strength God gives you, be ready to suffer with
me for the sake of the Good News. 9For God saved us and called us to live a holy life. He did
this, not because we deserved it, but because that was his plan from before the beginning of
time—to show us his grace through Christ Jesus. 10And now he has made all of this plain to us
by the appearing of Christ Jesus, our Savior. He broke the power of death and illuminated the
way to life and immortality through the Good News. 11And God chose me to be a preacher,
an apostle, and a teacher of this Good News.

12That is why I am suffering here in prison. But I am not ashamed of it, for I know the
one in whom I trust, and I am sure that he is able to guard what I have entrusted to him
until the day of his return.

13Hold on to the pattern of wholesome teaching you learned from me—a pattern shaped
by the faith and love that you have in Christ Jesus. 14Through the power of the Holy Spirit
who lives within us, carefully guard the precious truth that has been entrusted to you.

Who has been a good spiritual example for you? How can you thank him or her? Timothy's mother, Eunice, and grandmother Lois, were early Christian converts, possibly through Paul's ministry in their home city of Lystra. They had communicated their strong Christian faith to Timothy, even though his father was probably not a believer. Don't hide your light at home: your family is a fertile field for planting gospel seeds. Let your parents, brothers, and sisters know of your faith in Jesus, and be sure they see Christ's love, helpfulness, and joy in you.

Last Days

DECEMBER 14

2 TIMOTHY 3:1-17

You should know this, Timothy, that in the last days there will be very difficult times. 2For
people will love only themselves and their money. They will be boastful and proud, scoffing at
God, disobedient to their parents, and ungrateful. They will consider nothing sacred. 3They
will be unloving and unforgiving; they will slander others and have no self-control. They
will be cruel and hate what is good. 4They will betray their friends, be reckless, be puffed up
with pride, and love pleasure rather than God. 5They will act religious, but they will reject
the power that could make them godly. Stay away from people like that!

6They are the kind who work their way into people's homes and win the confidence of
vulnerable women who are burdened with the guilt of sin and controlled by various desires.
7(Such women are forever following new teachings, but they are never able to understand
the truth.) 8These teachers oppose the truth just as Jannes and Jambres opposed Moses. They
have depraved minds and a counterfeit faith. 9But they won't get away with this for long.
Someday everyone will recognize what fools they are, just as with Jannes and Jambres.

10But you, Timothy, certainly know what I teach, and how I live, and what my purpose
in life is. You know my faith, my patience, my love, and my endurance. 11You know how
much persecution and suffering I have endured. You know all about how I was persecuted in
Antioch, Iconium, and Lystra—but the Lord rescued me from all of it. 12Yes, and everyone
who wants to live a godly life in Christ Jesus will suffer persecution. 13But evil people and
impostors will flourish. They will deceive others and will themselves be deceived.

14But you must remain faithful to the things you have been taught. You know they are
true, for you know you can trust those who taught you. 15You have been taught the holy
Scriptures from childhood, and they have given you the wisdom to receive the salvation that
comes by trusting in Christ Jesus. 16All Scripture is inspired by God and is useful to teach
us what is true and to make us realize what is wrong in our lives. It corrects us when we are
wrong and teaches us to do what is right. 17God uses it to prepare and equip his people to
do every good work.

How can you tell true teaching from false teaching? The whole Bible is God's inspired Word. Because it is inspired and trustworthy, we should read it and apply it to our lives. The Bible is our standard for testing everything else that claims to be true. It is our safeguard against false teaching and our source of guidance for how we should live. The Bible is our only source of knowledge about how we can be saved. God wants to show you what is true and equip you to live for him. How much time do you spend in God's Word? Read it regularly to discover God's truth and to become confident in your life and faith. Develop a plan for reading the whole Bible so you don't read just the same familiar passages.

DECEMBER 15

Good Counsel

TITUS 3:1-11

Remind the believers to submit to the government and its officers. They should be obedient,
always ready to do what is good. 2They must not slander anyone and must avoid quarreling.
Instead, they should be gentle and show true humility to everyone.

3Once we, too, were foolish and disobedient. We were misled and became slaves to many
lusts and pleasures. Our lives were full of evil and envy, and we hated each other. 4But—

> When God our Savior revealed his kindness and love, 5he saved us, not because of the
> righteous things we had done, but because of his mercy. He washed away our sins, giv-
> ing us a new birth and new life through the Holy Spirit. 6He generously poured out the
> Spirit upon us through Jesus Christ our Savior. 7Because of his grace he made us right
> in his sight and gave us confidence that we will inherit eternal life.

8This is a trustworthy saying, and I want you to insist on these teachings so that all who
trust in God will devote themselves to doing good. These teachings are good and beneficial
for everyone.

9Do not get involved in foolish discussions about spiritual pedigrees or in quarrels and
fights about obedience to Jewish laws. These things are useless and a waste of time. 10If people
are causing divisions among you, give a first and second warning. After that, have nothing
more to do with them. 11For people like that have turned away from the truth, and their own
sins condemn them.

How did your life change when you became a Christian? Paul summarized what Christ does for us when he saves us. We move from a life full of sin to one where we are led by God's Holy Spirit. All our sins, not merely some, are washed away. In becoming Christians, we as believers acknowledge Christ as Lord and recognize Christ's saving work. We gain eternal life with all its treasures. We experience the renewing of our hearts by the Holy Spirit. None of this occurs because we earned or deserved it; it is all God's gift.

The New Life

DECEMBER 16

FROM HEBREWS 10:19-39

19And so, dear brothers and sisters, we can boldly enter heaven's Most Holy Place because of
the blood of Jesus. 20By his death, Jesus opened a new and life-giving way through the curtain
into the Most Holy Place. 21And since we have a great High Priest who rules over God's house,
22let us go right into the presence of God with sincere hearts fully trusting him. For our guilty
consciences have been sprinkled with Christ's blood to make us clean, and our bodies have
been washed with pure water.

23Let us hold tightly without wavering to the hope we affirm, for God can be trusted to
keep his promise. 24Let us think of ways to motivate one another to acts of love and good
works. 25And let us not neglect our meeting together, as some people do, but encourage one
another, especially now that the day of his return is drawing near.

26Dear friends, if we deliberately continue sinning after we have received knowledge of
the truth, there is no longer any sacrifice that will cover these sins. 27There is only the terrible
expectation of God's judgment and the raging fire that will consume his enemies. 28For anyone who refused to obey the law of Moses was put to death without mercy on the testimony
of two or three witnesses. 29Just think how much worse the punishment will be for those who
have trampled on the Son of God, and have treated the blood of the covenant, which made
us holy, as if it were common and unholy, and have insulted and disdained the Holy Spirit
who brings God's mercy to us. . . .

35So do not throw away this confident trust in the Lord. Remember the great reward it
brings you! 36Patient endurance is what you need now, so that you will continue to do God's
will. Then you will receive all that he has promised.

37"For in just a little while,
the Coming One will come and not delay.
38And my righteous ones will live by faith.
But I will take no pleasure in anyone who turns away."

39But we are not like those who turn away from God to their own destruction. We are the
faithful ones, whose souls will be saved.

What do your prayer habits and church-attendance habits say about the real importance of faith in your life? To neglect church meetings is to give up the encouragement and help of other Christians. We gather together to share our faith and to strengthen one another in the Lord. As we get closer to the time of Christ's return, we may face many spiritual struggles, tribulations, and even persecution; anti-Christian forces will grow in strength. Difficulties should never be excuses for missing church services. Rather, as difficulties arise, we should make an even greater effort to be faithful in church attendance.

DECEMBER 17

A Review of Faith

HEBREWS 11:1-13

Faith shows the reality of what we hope for; it is the evidence of things we cannot see. 2Through their faith, the people in days of old earned a good reputation.

3By faith we understand that the entire universe was formed at God's command, that what we now see did not come from anything that can be seen.

4It was by faith that Abel brought a more acceptable offering to God than Cain did. Abel's offering gave evidence that he was a righteous man, and God showed his approval of his gifts. Although Abel is long dead, he still speaks to us by his example of faith.

5It was by faith that Enoch was taken up to heaven without dying—"he disappeared, because God took him." For before he was taken up, he was known as a person who pleased God. 6And it is impossible to please God without faith. Anyone who wants to come to him must believe that God exists and that he rewards those who sincerely seek him.

7It was by faith that Noah built a large boat to save his family from the flood. He obeyed God, who warned him about things that had never happened before. By his faith Noah condemned the rest of the world, and he received the righteousness that comes by faith.

8It was by faith that Abraham obeyed when God called him to leave home and go to another land that God would give him as his inheritance. He went without knowing where he was going. 9And even when he reached the land God promised him, he lived there by faith—for he was like a foreigner, living in tents. And so did Isaac and Jacob, who inherited the same promise. 10Abraham was confidently looking forward to a city with eternal foundations, a city designed and built by God.

11It was by faith that even Sarah was able to have a child, though she was barren and was too old. She believed that God would keep his promise. . . .

13All these people died still believing what God had promised them. They did not receive what was promised, but they saw it all from a distance and welcomed it. They agreed that they were foreigners and nomads here on earth.

How steady is your faith in Christ? Do you remember how you felt when you were little and your birthday approached? You were excited and anxious. You knew you would certainly receive gifts and other special treats. But some things would be a surprise. Birthdays combined assurance and anticipation, and so does faith! Faith is the conviction based on past experience that God's new and fresh surprises will surely be ours. Two words that can describe our faith are *confidence* and *certainty*. These two qualities need a secure beginning and ending point. The beginning point of faith is believing in God's character—he is who he says. The end point is believing in God's promises—he will do what he says. True faith is believing God will fulfill his promises even if we don't see those promises materializing now.

Our Turn

HEBREWS 12:1-13

Therefore, since we are surrounded by such a huge crowd of witnesses to the life of faith, let
us strip off every weight that slows us down, especially the sin that so easily trips us up. And
let us run with endurance the race God has set before us. 2We do this by keeping our eyes on
Jesus, the champion who initiates and perfects our faith. Because of the joy awaiting him, he
endured the cross, disregarding its shame. Now he is seated in the place of honor beside God's
throne. 3Think of all the hostility he endured from sinful people; then you won't become
weary and give up. 4After all, you have not yet given your lives in your struggle against sin.

5And have you forgotten the encouraging words God spoke to you as his children? He
said,

> "My child, don't make light of the LORD's discipline,
> and don't give up when he corrects you.
> 6For the LORD disciplines those he loves,
> and he punishes each one he accepts as his child."

7As you endure this divine discipline, remember that God is treating you as his own children.
Who ever heard of a child who is never disciplined by its father? 8If God doesn't discipline you
as he does all of his children, it means that you are illegitimate and are not really his children
at all. 9Since we respected our earthly fathers who disciplined us, shouldn't we submit even
more to the discipline of the Father of our spirits, and live forever?

10For our earthly fathers disciplined us for a few years, doing the best they knew how. But
God's discipline is always good for us, so that we might share in his holiness. 11No discipline
is enjoyable while it is happening—it's painful! But afterward there will be a peaceful harvest
of right living for those who are trained in this way.

12So take a new grip with your tired hands and strengthen your weak knees. 13Mark out
a straight path for your feet so that those who are weak and lame will not fall but become
strong.

Who loves his child more—the father who allows his child to do as he or she pleases, or the one who corrects, trains, and even punishes his child to help him or her learn what is right? It is never pleasant to be corrected and disciplined by God, but his discipline is a sign of his deep love for us. We may respond to discipline in several ways: (1) We can accept it with resignation. (2) We can accept it with self-pity, thinking we really don't deserve it. (3) We can be angry and resentful toward God. (4) We can accept it gratefully, as the appropriate response to a loving Father.

DECEMBER 19

Tough Times, Happy People

JAMES 1:2-27

[2]Dear brothers and sisters, when troubles of any kind come your way, consider it an opportunity for great joy. [3]For you know that when your faith is tested, your endurance has a chance
to grow. [4]So let it grow, for when your endurance is fully developed, you will be perfect and
complete, needing nothing.

[5]If you need wisdom, ask our generous God, and he will give it to you. He will not rebuke
you for asking. [6]But when you ask him, be sure that your faith is in God alone. Do not waver,
for a person with divided loyalty is as unsettled as a wave of the sea that is blown and tossed
by the wind. [7]Such people should not expect to receive anything from the Lord. [8]Their loyalty is divided between God and the world, and they are unstable in everything they do. . . .

[12]God blesses those who patiently endure testing and temptation. Afterward they will
receive the crown of life that God has promised to those who love him. [13]And remember,
when you are being tempted, do not say, "God is tempting me." God is never tempted to
do wrong, and he never tempts anyone else. [14]Temptation comes from our own desires,
which entice us and drag us away. [15]These desires give birth to sinful actions. And when sin
is allowed to grow, it gives birth to death. . . .

[19]Understand this, my dear brothers and sisters: You must all be quick to listen, slow to
speak, and slow to get angry. [20]Human anger does not produce the righteousness God desires.
[21]So get rid of all the filth and evil in your lives, and humbly accept the word God has planted
in your hearts, for it has the power to save your souls.

[22]But don't just listen to God's word. You must do what it says. Otherwise, you are only
fooling yourselves. [23]For if you listen to the word and don't obey, it is like glancing at your
face in a mirror. [24]You see yourself, walk away, and forget what you look like. [25]But if you look
carefully into the perfect law that sets you free, and if you do what it says and don't forget
what you heard, then God will bless you for doing it.

[26]If you claim to be religious but don't control your tongue, you are fooling yourself, and
your religion is worthless. [27]Pure and genuine religion in the sight of God the Father means
caring for orphans and widows in their distress and refusing to let the world corrupt you.

In what difficulty could you use the "James plan" right now? We can't really know the depth of our character until we see how we react under pressure. It is easy to be kind to others when everything is going well, but can we still be kind when others are treating us unfairly? God wants to make us perfect and complete, not to keep us from all pain. Instead of complaining about our struggles, we should see them as opportunities for growth. Thank God for promising to be with you in rough times. Ask him to help you solve your problems or to give you the strength to endure them. Then be patient. God will not leave you alone with your problems; he will stay close and help you grow.

Valuing Other People

DECEMBER 20

JAMES 2:1-13

My dear brothers and sisters, how can you claim to have faith in our glorious Lord Jesus
Christ if you favor some people over others?
2For example, suppose someone comes into your meeting dressed in fancy clothes and
expensive jewelry, and another comes in who is poor and dressed in dirty clothes. 3If you give
special attention and a good seat to the rich person, but you say to the poor one, "You can
stand over there, or else sit on the floor"—well, 4doesn't this discrimination show that your
judgments are guided by evil motives?
5Listen to me, dear brothers and sisters. Hasn't God chosen the poor in this world to be
rich in faith? Aren't they the ones who will inherit the Kingdom he promised to those who
love him? 6But you dishonor the poor! Isn't it the rich who oppress you and drag you into
court? 7Aren't they the ones who slander Jesus Christ, whose noble name you bear?
8Yes indeed, it is good when you obey the royal law as found in the Scriptures: "Love your
neighbor as yourself." 9But if you favor some people over others, you are committing a sin.
You are guilty of breaking the law.
10For the person who keeps all of the laws except one is as guilty as a person who has
broken all of God's laws. 11For the same God who said, "You must not commit adultery,"
also said, "You must not murder." So if you murder someone but do not commit adultery,
you have still broken the law.
12So whatever you say or whatever you do, remember that you will be judged by the law
that sets you free. 13There will be no mercy for those who have not shown mercy to others.
But if you have been merciful, God will be merciful when he judges you.

Which tendencies do you have to watch out for in how you treat others? Often we treat well-dressed, impressive-looking people better than people who look poor. We do this because we would rather identify with successful people than with people who seem to be failures. We feel better about ourselves when we associate with people we admire. The irony, as James reminds us, is that the supposed winners may have gained their impressive lifestyle at our expense. In addition, the rich find it hard to identify with the Lord Jesus, who came as a humble servant. Are you easily impressed by status, wealth, or fame? Are you partial to the "haves" while ignoring the "have nots"? This prejudice is sin. God views all people as equals, and if he favors anyone, it is the poor and the powerless who cannot help themselves. We should follow his example.

DECEMBER 21

Words as Weapons

JAMES 3:1-12

Dear brothers and sisters, not many of you should become teachers in the church, for we
who teach will be judged more strictly. 2Indeed, we all make many mistakes. For if we could
control our tongues, we would be perfect and could also control ourselves in every other way.
3We can make a large horse go wherever we want by means of a small bit in its mouth.
4And a small rudder makes a huge ship turn wherever the pilot chooses to go, even though
the winds are strong. 5In the same way, the tongue is a small thing that makes grand speeches.
But a tiny spark can set a great forest on fire. 6And among all the parts of the body, the
tongue is a flame of fire. It is a whole world of wickedness, corrupting your entire body. It
can set your whole life on fire, for it is set on fire by hell itself.
7People can tame all kinds of animals, birds, reptiles, and fish, 8but no one can tame
the tongue. It is restless and evil, full of deadly poison. 9Sometimes it praises our Lord and
Father, and sometimes it curses those who have been made in the image of God. 10And so
blessing and cursing come pouring out of the same mouth. Surely, my brothers and sisters,
this is not right! 11Does a spring of water bubble out with both fresh water and bitter water?
12Does a fig tree produce olives, or a grapevine produce figs? No, and you can't draw fresh
water from a salty spring.

How sharp would others consider your tongue? What you say and what you don't say are both important. Proper speech is not only saying the right words at the right time but also controlling your desire to say what you shouldn't. Examples of wrongly using the tongue include gossiping, putting others down, bragging, manipulating, false teaching, exaggerating, complaining, flattering, and lying. Before you speak, ask yourself: Is it true? Is it necessary? Is it kind?

Living Stones

DECEMBER 22

1 PETER 2:1-9

So get rid of all evil behavior. Be done with all deceit, hypocrisy, jealousy, and all unkind
speech. 2Like newborn babies, you must crave pure spiritual milk so that you will grow into
a full experience of salvation. Cry out for this nourishment, 3now that you have had a taste
of the Lord's kindness.

4You are coming to Christ, who is the living cornerstone of God's temple. He was rejected
by people, but he was chosen by God for great honor.

5And you are living stones that God is building into his spiritual temple. What's more,
you are his holy priests. Through the mediation of Jesus Christ, you offer spiritual sacrifices
that please God. 6As the Scriptures say,

"I am placing a cornerstone in Jerusalem,
chosen for great honor,
and anyone who trusts in him
will never be disgraced."

7Yes, you who trust him recognize the honor God has given him. But for those who reject
him,

"The stone that the builders rejected
has now become the cornerstone."

8And,

"He is the stone that makes people stumble,
the rock that makes them fall."

They stumble because they do not obey God's word, and so they meet the fate that was
planned for them.

9But you are not like that, for you are a chosen people. You are royal priests, a holy nation,
God's very own possession. As a result, you can show others the goodness of God, for he
called you out of the darkness into his wonderful light.

How strong is your desire to grow spiritually? One characteristic all children share is that they want to grow up, to be like the big kids or like their parents. When we are born again, we are spiritual babies. If we are healthy, we will want to grow. It's sad when we are satisfied to stay where we are as the months and years roll by. Crying for milk is a natural instinct for a baby, but an adult may have to learn to crave spiritual nourishment. Once we see our needs and begin to find comfort and fulfillment in Christ, however, our spiritual appetites will increase, and we will start to mature. What spiritual food can you take today?

DECEMBER 23

Relationships and Pain

1 PETER 3:8-22

8Finally, all of you should be of one mind. Sympathize with each other. Love each other as
brothers and sisters. Be tenderhearted, and keep a humble attitude. 9Don't repay evil for evil.
Don't retaliate with insults when people insult you. Instead, pay them back with a blessing.
That is what God has called you to do, and he will grant you his blessing. 10For the Scriptures
say,

> "If you want to enjoy life
> and see many happy days,
> keep your tongue from speaking evil
> and your lips from telling lies.
> 11Turn away from evil and do good.
> Search for peace, and work to maintain it.
> 12The eyes of the LORD watch over those who do right,
> and his ears are open to their prayers.
> But the LORD turns his face
> against those who do evil."

13Now, who will want to harm you if you are eager to do good? 14But even if you suffer for
doing what is right, God will reward you for it. So don't worry or be afraid of their threats.
15Instead, you must worship Christ as Lord of your life. And if someone asks about your hope
as a believer, always be ready to explain it. 16But do this in a gentle and respectful way. Keep
your conscience clear. Then if people speak against you, they will be ashamed when they see
what a good life you live because you belong to Christ. 17Remember, it is better to suffer for
doing good, if that is what God wants, than to suffer for doing wrong!

18Christ suffered for our sins once for all time. He never sinned, but he died for sinners
to bring you safely home to God. He suffered physical death, but he was raised to life in the
Spirit. . . .

22Now Christ has gone to heaven. He is seated in the place of honor next to God, and all
the angels and authorities and powers accept his authority.

How willing are you to conduct your relationships God's way, even when there are difficulties? In our sinful world, it is often acceptable to tear people down verbally or get back at them if we feel hurt. Remembering Jesus' teaching to turn the other cheek, Peter encourages his readers to pay back wrongs by praying for the offenders. In God's Kingdom, revenge is unacceptable behavior. So is insulting a person, no matter how indirectly it is done. Rise above getting back at those who hurt you. Instead of reacting angrily to those people, pray for them.

Knowing God

DECEMBER 24

2 PETER 1:2-15

2May God give you more and more grace and peace as you grow in your knowledge of God
and Jesus our Lord.
3By his divine power, God has given us everything we need for living a godly life. We
have received all of this by coming to know him, the one who called us to himself by means
of his marvelous glory and excellence. 4And because of his glory and excellence, he has given
us great and precious promises. These are the promises that enable you to share his divine
nature and escape the world's corruption caused by human desires.
5In view of all this, make every effort to respond to God's promises. Supplement your
faith with a generous provision of moral excellence, and moral excellence with knowledge,
6and knowledge with self-control, and self-control with patient endurance, and patient
endurance with godliness, 7and godliness with brotherly affection, and brotherly affection
with love for everyone.
8The more you grow like this, the more productive and useful you will be in your knowledge of our Lord Jesus Christ. 9But those who fail to develop in this way are shortsighted or
blind, forgetting that they have been cleansed from their old sins.
10So, dear brothers and sisters, work hard to prove that you really are among those God
has called and chosen. Do these things, and you will never fall away. 11Then God will give
you a grand entrance into the eternal Kingdom of our Lord and Savior Jesus Christ.
12Therefore, I will always remind you about these things—even though you already know
them and are standing firm in the truth you have been taught. 13And it is only right that I
should keep on reminding you as long as I live. 14For our Lord Jesus Christ has shown me that
I must soon leave this earthly life, 15so I will work hard to make sure you always remember
these things after I am gone.

How would you answer someone who asked you what it means to know God? Outstanding coaches constantly review the basics of a sport with their teams, and good athletes can execute the fundamentals consistently well. We must not neglect the basics of our faith as we go on to study deeper truths. Just as an athlete needs constant practice, we need constant reminders of the fundamentals of our faith and of how we came to believe in the first place. Don't allow yourself to be bored or impatient with messages on the basics of the Christian life. Instead, take the attitude of an athlete who continues to practice and refine the basics even as he or she learns more advanced skills. Our faith must go beyond what we believe; it must become a dynamic part of all we do, resulting in good fruit and spiritual maturity. Salvation does not depend on good works, but it results in good works. If you claim to be saved while remaining unchanged, you have not understood faith or what God has done for you.

DECEMBER 25

The Way of Forgiveness

1 JOHN 1:1-10

We proclaim to you the one who existed from the beginning, whom we have heard and seen.
We saw him with our own eyes and touched him with our own hands. He is the Word of
life. 2This one who is life itself was revealed to us, and we have seen him. And now we testify
and proclaim to you that he is the one who is eternal life. He was with the Father, and then
he was revealed to us. 3We proclaim to you what we ourselves have actually seen and heard
so that you may have fellowship with us. And our fellowship is with the Father and with his
Son, Jesus Christ. 4We are writing these things so that you may fully share our joy.

5This is the message we heard from Jesus and now declare to you: God is light, and there
is no darkness in him at all. 6So we are lying if we say we have fellowship with God but go on
living in spiritual darkness; we are not practicing the truth. 7But if we are living in the light,
as God is in the light, then we have fellowship with each other, and the blood of Jesus, his
Son, cleanses us from all sin.

8If we claim we have no sin, we are only fooling ourselves and not living in the truth. 9But
if we confess our sins to him, he is faithful and just to forgive us our sins and to cleanse us
from all wickedness. 10If we claim we have not sinned, we are calling God a liar and showing
that his word has no place in our hearts.

Do you understand the true nature and purpose of confession? True confession will free us to enjoy fellowship with Christ. It will ease our conscience and lighten our cares. But some Christians do not understand how confession works. They feel so guilty that they confess the same sins over and over, and then they wonder if they have forgotten something. Other Christians believe that God forgives them for only the sins they confess, but if they died with unconfessed sins, they would be lost forever. These Christians do not understand that God wants to forgive us. He allowed his beloved Son to die just so he could pardon us. When we come to Christ, he forgives all the sins we have committed or will ever commit. We don't need to confess the same sins all over again, and we don't need to be afraid that God will reject us if we don't keep our slate perfectly clear at all times. Of course we want to continue to confess our sins, but not because we think failure to do so will make us lose our salvation. Our hope in Christ is secure. Instead, we should confess so that we can enjoy maximum fellowship and joy with Christ. True confession also involves a commitment not to continue in sin. We are not genuinely confessing our sins before God if we are planning to commit the sin again and just want temporary forgiveness. We must pray for strength to resist the temptation the next time.

God Is Love

DECEMBER 26

1 JOHN 3:1-23

See how very much our Father loves us, for he calls us his children, and that is what we are! But the people who belong to this world don't recognize that we are God's children because they don't know him. 2Dear friends, we are already God's children, but he has not yet shown us what we will be like when Christ appears. But we do know that we will be like him, for we will see him as he really is. 3And all who have this eager expectation will keep themselves pure, just as he is pure.

4Everyone who sins is breaking God's law, for all sin is contrary to the law of God. 5And you know that Jesus came to take away our sins, and there is no sin in him. 6Anyone who continues to live in him will not sin. But anyone who keeps on sinning does not know him or understand who he is.

7Dear children, don't let anyone deceive you about this: When people do what is right, it shows that they are righteous, even as Christ is righteous. 8But when people keep on sinning, it shows that they belong to the devil, who has been sinning since the beginning. But the Son of God came to destroy the works of the devil. 9Those who have been born into God's family do not make a practice of sinning, because God's life is in them. So they can't keep on sinning, because they are children of God. 10So now we can tell who are children of God and who are children of the devil. Anyone who does not live righteously and does not love other believers does not belong to God.

11This is the message you have heard from the beginning: We should love one another. . . .

16We know what real love is because Jesus gave up his life for us. So we also ought to give up our lives for our brothers and sisters. 17If someone has enough money to live well and sees a brother or sister in need but shows no compassion—how can God's love be in that person?

18Dear children, let's not merely say that we love each other; let us show the truth by our actions. 19Our actions will show that we belong to the truth, so we will be confident when we stand before God. 20Even if we feel guilty, God is greater than our feelings, and he knows everything.

21Dear friends, if we don't feel guilty, we can come to God with bold confidence. 22And we will receive from him whatever we ask because we obey him and do the things that please him.

23And this is his commandment: We must believe in the name of his Son, Jesus Christ, and love one another, just as he commanded us.

How can you tell if your love is growing? Real love is an action, not a feeling. It produces selfless, sacrificial giving. The greatest act of love anyone can do is to give himself or herself for others. How can we lay down our lives? Sometimes it is easier to say we will die for others than it is to truly live for them. That involves putting others' desires before ours.

DECEMBER 27

The Life God Gives

1 JOHN 5:1-20

Everyone who believes that Jesus is the Christ has become a child of God. And everyone who loves the Father loves his children, too. [2]We know we love God's children if we love God and obey his commandments. [3]Loving God means keeping his commandments, and his commandments are not burdensome. [4]For every child of God defeats this evil world, and we achieve this victory through our faith. [5]And who can win this battle against the world? Only those who believe that Jesus is the Son of God.

[6]And Jesus Christ was revealed as God's Son by his baptism in water and by shedding his blood on the cross—not by water only, but by water and blood. And the Spirit, who is truth, confirms it with his testimony. [7]So we have these three witnesses—[8]the Spirit, the water, and the blood—and all three agree. [9]Since we believe human testimony, surely we can believe the greater testimony that comes from God. And God has testified about his Son. . . .

[11]And this is what God has testified: He has given us eternal life, and this life is in his Son. [12]Whoever has the Son has life; whoever does not have God's Son does not have life.

[13]I have written this to you who believe in the name of the Son of God, so that you may know you have eternal life. [14]And we are confident that he hears us whenever we ask for anything that pleases him. [15]And since we know he hears us when we make our requests, we also know that he will give us what we ask for.

[16]If you see a fellow believer sinning in a way that does not lead to death, you should pray, and God will give that person life. But there is a sin that leads to death, and I am not saying you should pray for those who commit it. [17]All wicked actions are sin, but not every sin leads to death.

[18]We know that God's children do not make a practice of sinning, for God's Son holds them securely, and the evil one cannot touch them. [19]We know that we are children of God and that the world around us is under the control of the evil one.

[20]And we know that the Son of God has come, and he has given us understanding so that we can know the true God. And now we live in fellowship with the true God because we live in fellowship with his Son, Jesus Christ. He is the only true God, and he is eternal life.

How do you know that you have eternal life? Some people hope they will be given eternal life. John says that we can know we have it. Our certainty is based on God's promise that he has given us eternal life through his Son. This is true whether you feel close to God or distant from him. Eternal life is not based on feelings but on facts. You can know you have eternal life if you believe God's truth. If you lack assurance as to whether you are a Christian, ask yourself if you have honestly committed your life to Christ as your Savior and Lord. If so, you know by faith that you are indeed a child of God.

Family Matters

DECEMBER 28

2 JOHN 4-6; 3 JOHN 5-8; JUDE 17-25

[4]How happy I was to meet some of your children and find them living according to the truth,
just as the Father commanded.

[5]I am writing to remind you, dear friends, that we should love one another. This is not
a new commandment, but one we have had from the beginning. [6]Love means doing what
God has commanded us, and he has commanded us to love one another, just as you heard
from the beginning.

[3JN] [5]Dear friend, you are being faithful to God when you care for the traveling teachers who
pass through, even though they are strangers to you. [6]They have told the church here of
your loving friendship. Please continue providing for such teachers in a manner that pleases
God. [7]For they are traveling for the Lord, and they accept nothing from people who are not
believers. [8]So we ourselves should support them so that we can be their partners as they teach
the truth.

[JUDE] [17]But you, my dear friends, must remember what the apostles of our Lord Jesus Christ
predicted. [18]They told you that in the last times there would be scoffers whose purpose in
life is to satisfy their ungodly desires. [19]These people are the ones who are creating divisions
among you. They follow their natural instincts because they do not have God's Spirit in them.

[20]But you, dear friends, must build each other up in your most holy faith, pray in the
power of the Holy Spirit, [21]and await the mercy of our Lord Jesus Christ, who will bring you
eternal life. In this way, you will keep yourselves safe in God's love.

[22]And you must show mercy to those whose faith is wavering. [23]Rescue others by snatching
them from the flames of judgment. Show mercy to still others, but do so with great caution,
hating the sins that contaminate their lives.

[24]Now all glory to God, who is able to keep you from falling away and will bring you
with great joy into his glorious presence without a single fault. [25]All glory to him who alone
is God, our Savior through Jesus Christ our Lord. All glory, majesty, power, and authority
are his before all time, and in the present, and beyond all time! Amen.

How often do you go out of your way to meet the needs of other Christians? In the church's early days, traveling prophets, evangelists, and teachers were helped on their way by people who housed and fed them. Hospitality is a lost art for many Christians today. We would do well to invite more people into our homes for meals—fellow church members, young people, traveling missionaries, those in need, visitors. This is an active and much-appreciated way to show your love. In fact, it is probably more important today than ever before. Because of our individualistic, self-centered society, there are many lonely people who wonder if anyone cares whether they live or die. If you find such a lonely person, show him or her that you care!

DECEMBER 29

Jesus the King

REVELATION 1:1-18

This is a revelation from Jesus Christ, which God gave him to show his servants the events
that must soon take place. He sent an angel to present this revelation to his servant John,
2who faithfully reported everything he saw. This is his report of the word of God and the
testimony of Jesus Christ.
3God blesses the one who reads the words of this prophecy to the church, and he blesses
all who listen to its message and obey what it says, for the time is near.
4This letter is from John to the seven churches in the province of Asia.
Grace and peace to you from the one who is, who always was, and who is still to come;
from the sevenfold Spirit before his throne; 5and from Jesus Christ. . . .
8"I am the Alpha and the Omega—the beginning and the end," says the Lord God. "I am
the one who is, who always was, and who is still to come—the Almighty One."
9I, John, am your brother and your partner in suffering and in God's Kingdom and in
the patient endurance to which Jesus calls us. I was exiled to the island of Patmos for preaching the word of God and for my testimony about Jesus. 10It was the Lord's Day, and I was
worshiping in the Spirit. Suddenly, I heard behind me a loud voice like a trumpet blast. 11It
said, "Write in a book everything you see, and send it to the seven churches in the cities of
Ephesus, Smyrna, Pergamum, Thyatira, Sardis, Philadelphia, and Laodicea."
12When I turned to see who was speaking to me, I saw seven gold lampstands. 13And
standing in the middle of the lampstands was someone like the Son of Man. He was wearing
a long robe with a gold sash across his chest. 14His head and his hair were white like wool,
as white as snow. And his eyes were like flames of fire. 15His feet were like polished bronze
refined in a furnace, and his voice thundered like mighty ocean waves. 16He held seven stars
in his right hand, and a sharp two-edged sword came from his mouth. And his face was like
the sun in all its brilliance.
17When I saw him, I fell at his feet as if I were dead. But he laid his right hand on me and
said, "Don't be afraid! I am the First and the Last. 18I am the living one. I died, but look—I
am alive forever and ever! And I hold the keys of death and the grave."

What do you think Jesus looks like? John recognized Jesus because he lived with him for three years and had seen him both as the Preacher and as the glorified Son of God at the Transfiguration. Jesus' white hair indicates his wisdom; his blazing eyes symbolize judgment; the golden sash across his chest reveals him as the High Priest who goes into God's presence to obtain forgiveness of sin for those who believe in him. Jesus is not just a humble earthly teacher; he is the glorious God. When you read John's vision, keep in mind that his words are truth from the King of kings. Don't just read his words for their interesting and amazing portrayal of the future. Let the truth about Christ penetrate your life, deepen your faith in him, and strengthen your commitment to follow him no matter what the cost.

Everything Made New

DECEMBER 30

REVELATION 21:1-21

Then I saw a new heaven and a new earth, for the old heaven and the old earth had disappeared. And the sea was also gone. 2And I saw the holy city, the new Jerusalem, coming down
from God out of heaven like a bride beautifully dressed for her husband.

3I heard a loud shout from the throne, saying, "Look, God's home is now among his
people! He will live with them, and they will be his people. God himself will be with them.
4He will wipe every tear from their eyes, and there will be no more death or sorrow or crying
or pain. All these things are gone forever."

5And the one sitting on the throne said, "Look, I am making everything new!" And then
he said to me, "Write this down, for what I tell you is trustworthy and true." 6And he also
said, "It is finished! I am the Alpha and the Omega—the Beginning and the End. To all who
are thirsty I will give freely from the springs of the water of life. 7All who are victorious will
inherit all these blessings, and I will be their God, and they will be my children. . . ."

9Then one of the seven angels who held the seven bowls containing the seven last plagues
came and said to me, "Come with me! I will show you the bride, the wife of the Lamb."

10So he took me in the Spirit to a great, high mountain, and he showed me the holy city,
Jerusalem, descending out of heaven from God. 11It shone with the glory of God and spar-
kled like a precious stone—like jasper as clear as crystal. 12The city wall was broad and high,
with twelve gates guarded by twelve angels. And the names of the twelve tribes of Israel were
written on the gates. 13There were three gates on each side—east, north, south, and west.
14The wall of the city had twelve foundation stones, and on them were written the names of
the twelve apostles of the Lamb. . . .

18The wall was made of jasper, and the city was pure gold, as clear as glass. 19The wall of
the city was built on foundation stones inlaid with twelve precious stones: the first was jasper,
the second sapphire, the third agate, the fourth emerald, 20the fifth onyx, the sixth carnelian,
the seventh chrysolite, the eighth beryl, the ninth topaz, the tenth chrysoprase, the eleventh
jacinth, the twelfth amethyst.

21The twelve gates were made of pearls—each gate from a single pearl! And the main street
was pure gold, as clear as glass.

Have you ever wondered what eternity will be like? The "holy city, the new Jerusalem" is described as the place where God will wipe away all tears. Forevermore, there will be no death, sorrow, tears, or pain. What a wonderful truth! No matter what you are going through, it's not the last word. God has written the final chapter, and it includes eternal joy for those who love him. We do not know as much as we would like, but it is enough to know that eternity with God will be more wonderful than we can imagine.

DECEMBER 31

Life in the New City

REVELATION 22:6-21

[6]Then the angel said to me, "Everything you have heard and seen is trustworthy and true. The Lord God, who inspires his prophets, has sent his angel to tell his servants what will happen soon." . . .

[12]"Look, I am coming soon, bringing my reward with me to repay all people according
to their deeds. [13]I am the Alpha and the Omega, the First and the Last, the Beginning
and the End."

[14]Blessed are those who wash their robes. They will be permitted to enter through the
gates of the city and eat the fruit from the tree of life. [15]Outside the city are the dogs—the sorcerers, the sexually immoral, the murderers, the idol worshipers, and all who love to live a lie.

[16]"I, Jesus, have sent my angel to give you this message for the churches. I am both the source of David and the heir to his throne. I am the bright morning star."

[17]The Spirit and the bride say, "Come." Let anyone who hears this say, "Come." Let anyone who is thirsty come. Let anyone who desires drink freely from the water of life. [18]And I
solemnly declare to everyone who hears the words of prophecy written in this book: If anyone
adds anything to what is written here, God will add to that person the plagues described in
this book. [19]And if anyone removes any of the words from this book of prophecy, God will
remove that person's share in the tree of life and in the holy city that are described in this
book.

[20]He who is the faithful witness to all these things says, "Yes, I am coming soon!"
Amen! Come, Lord Jesus!

[21]May the grace of the Lord Jesus be with God's holy people.

When was the last time you felt truly excited about eternity in heaven? Revelation closes human history as Genesis opened it—in paradise. But there is one distinct difference in Revelation—evil is gone forever. Genesis describes Adam and Eve walking and talking with God; Revelation describes people worshiping him face-to-face. Genesis describes a garden with an evil serpent; Revelation describes a perfect city with no evil. The Garden of Eden was destroyed by sin, but paradise is recreated in the new Jerusalem. The book of Revelation ends with an urgent request: "Come, Lord Jesus!" In a world of problems, persecution, evil, and immorality, Christ calls us to endure in our faith. Our efforts to better our world are important, but their results cannot compare with the transformation that Jesus will bring about when he returns. He alone controls human history and forgives sin, and he will recreate the earth and bring lasting peace. No matter what happens on earth, God is in control. Evil will not last forever, and there will be a wonderful reward waiting for all those who believe in Jesus Christ as Savior and Lord.